YOU'RE READING THE WRONG WAY!

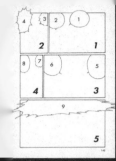

SPY x FAMILY reads from right to left, starting in the upper-right corner. Japanese is read from right to left, meaning that action, sound effects and word-balloon order are completely reversed from English order.

W9-AXZ-226

JoJo's
BIZARRE ADVENTURE

★ PART 4 ★
DIAMOND IS UNBREAKABLE

Story & Art by
HIROHIKO ARAKI

A MULTIGENERATIONAL TALE OF THE HEROIC JOESTAR FAMILY AND THEIR NEVER-ENDING BATTLE AGAINST EVIL.

In April 1999, Jotaro Kujo travels to a town in Japan called Morioh to find a young man named Josuke Higashikata, the secret love child of his grandfather, Joseph Joestar. Upon finding him, Jotaro is surprised to learn that Josuke also possesses a Stand. After their strange meeting, the pair team up to investigate the town's proliferation of unusual Stands!

DEATH NOTE
ALL-IN-ONE EDITION

Story by **Tsugumi Ohba**   Art by **Takeshi Obata**

Light Yagami is an ace student with great prospects—
and he's bored out of his mind. But all that changes
when he finds the Death Note, a notebook dropped by
a rogue Shinigami death god. Any human whose name
is written in the notebook dies, and now Light has
vowed to use the power of the Death Note to rid the
world of evil. But when criminals begin dropping dead,
the authorities send the legendary detective L to track
down the killer. With L hot on his heels, will Light lose
sight of his noble goal...or his life?

*Includes a
NEW epilogue
chapter!*

All 12 volumes in ONE monstrously large edition!

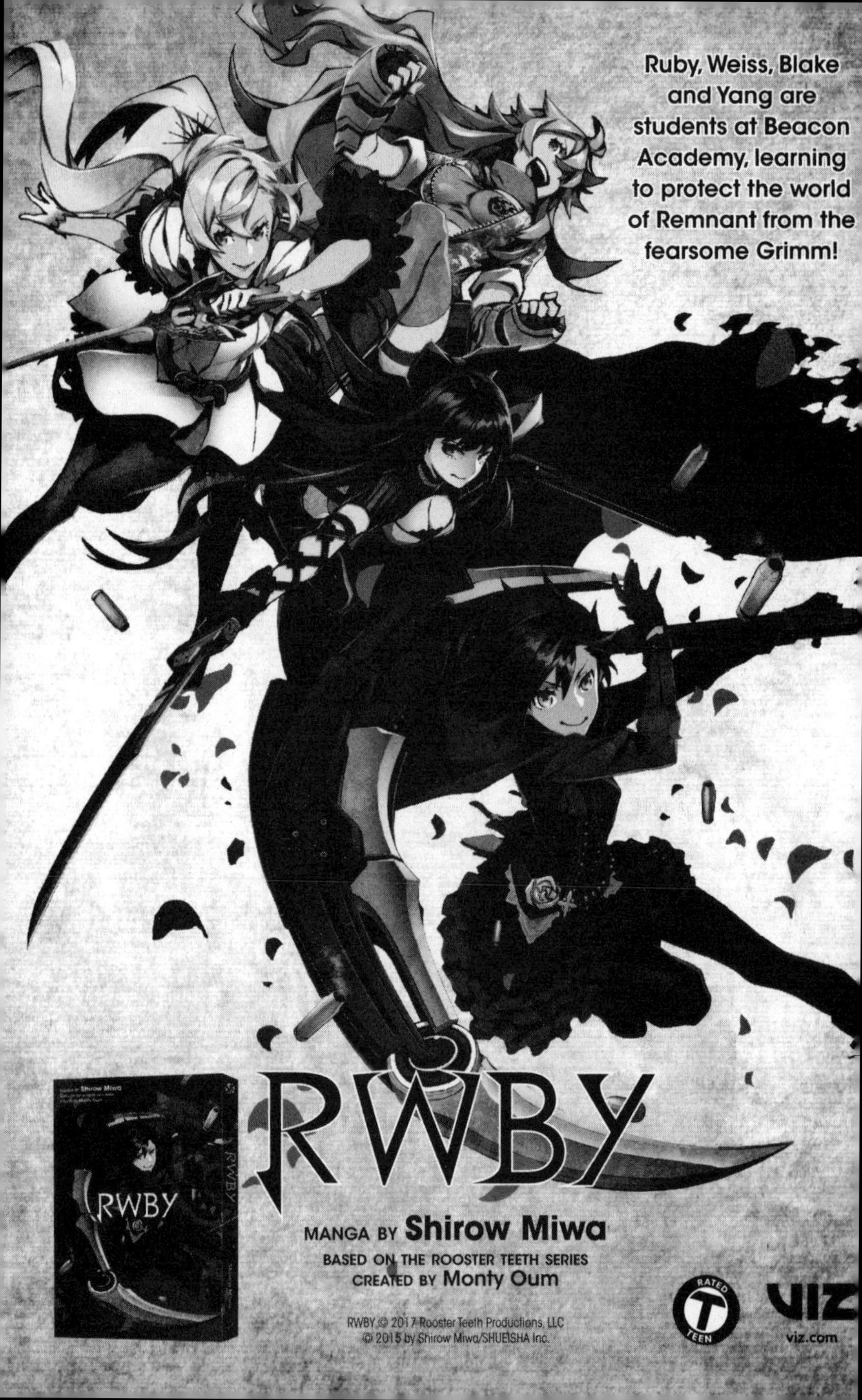
Ruby, Weiss, Blake and Yang are students at Beacon Academy, learning to protect the world of Remnant from the fearsome Grimm!
RWBY
MANGA BY Shirow Miwa
BASED ON THE ROOSTER TEETH SERIES
CREATED BY Monty Oum
RWBY © 2017 Rooster Teeth Productions, LLC
© 2015 by Shirow Miwa/SHUEISHA Inc.
RATED T TEEN
VIZ
viz.com

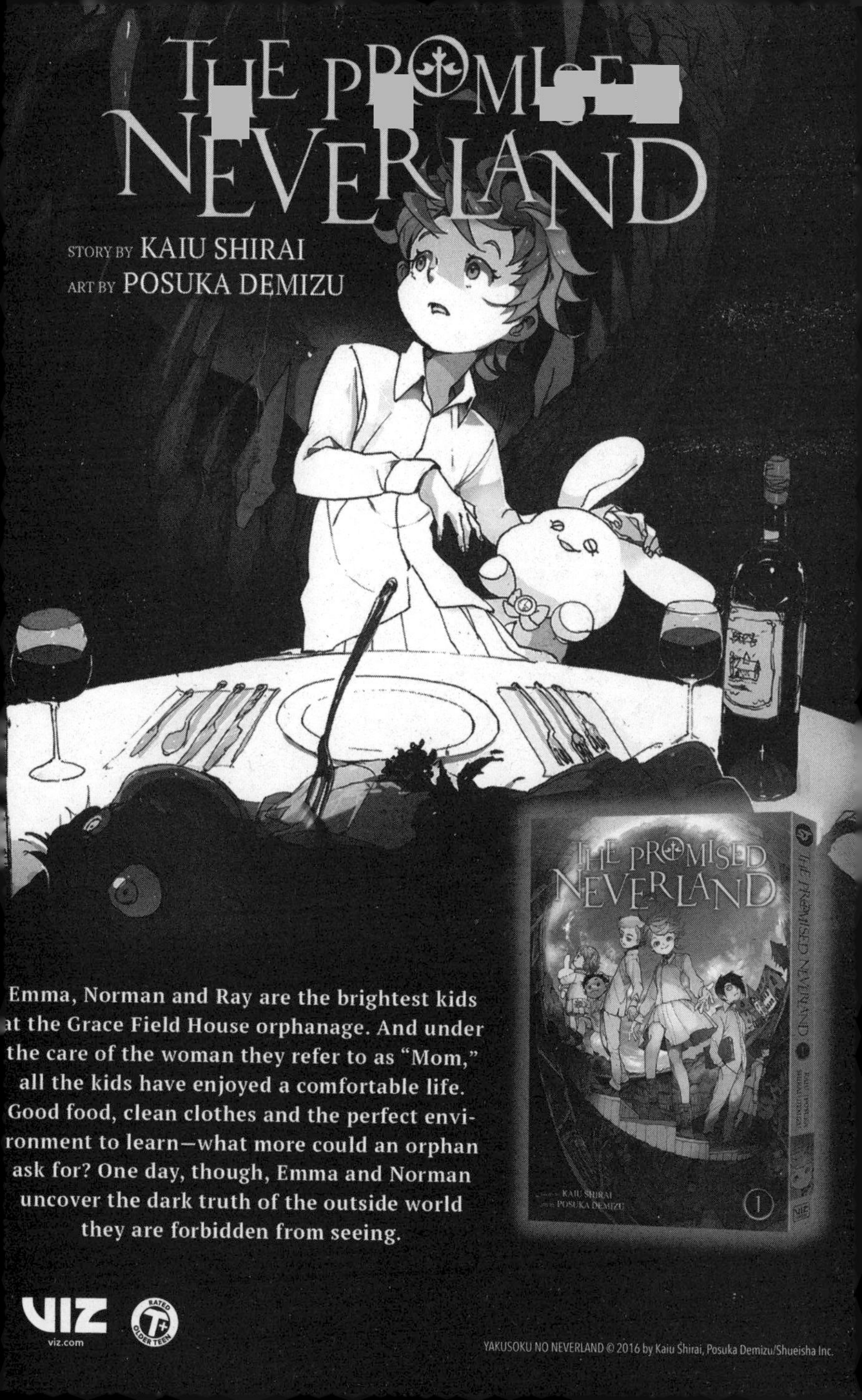
THE PROMISED NEVERLAND
STORY BY KAIU SHIRAI
ART BY POSUKA DEMIZU
THE PROMISED NEVERLAND
KAIU SHIRAI
POSUKA DEMIZU
1
Emma, Norman and Ray are the brightest kids at the Grace Field House orphanage. And under the care of the woman they refer to as "Mom," all the kids have enjoyed a comfortable life. Good food, clean clothes and the perfect environment to learn—what more could an orphan ask for? One day, though, Emma and Norman uncover the dark truth of the outside world they are forbidden from seeing.
VIZ
viz.com
RATED T+ OLDER TEEN
YAKUSOKU NO NEVERLAND © 2016 by Kaiu Shirai, Posuka Demizu/Shueisha Inc.

SPY×FAMILY 1

SHONEN JUMP Edition

STORY AND ART BY **TATSUYA ENDO**

Translation **CASEY LOE**

Touch-Up Art & Lettering **RINA MAPA**

Design **JIMMY PRESLER**

Editor **AMY YU**

First published in Japan in 2019 by SHUEISHA Inc., Tokyo.
English translation rights arranged by SHUEISHA Inc.

Printed in the U.S.A.

Published by VIZ Media, LLC
P.O. Box 77010
San Francisco, CA 94107

10 9 8
First printing, June 2020
Eighth printing, November 2021

RATED T+ OLDER TEEN ratings.viz.com

PARENTAL ADVISORY
SPY x FAMILY is rated T+ for Older Teen and is recommended for ages 16 and up. This volume contains realistic violence.

VIZ MEDIA
viz.com

SHONEN JUMP

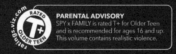

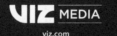

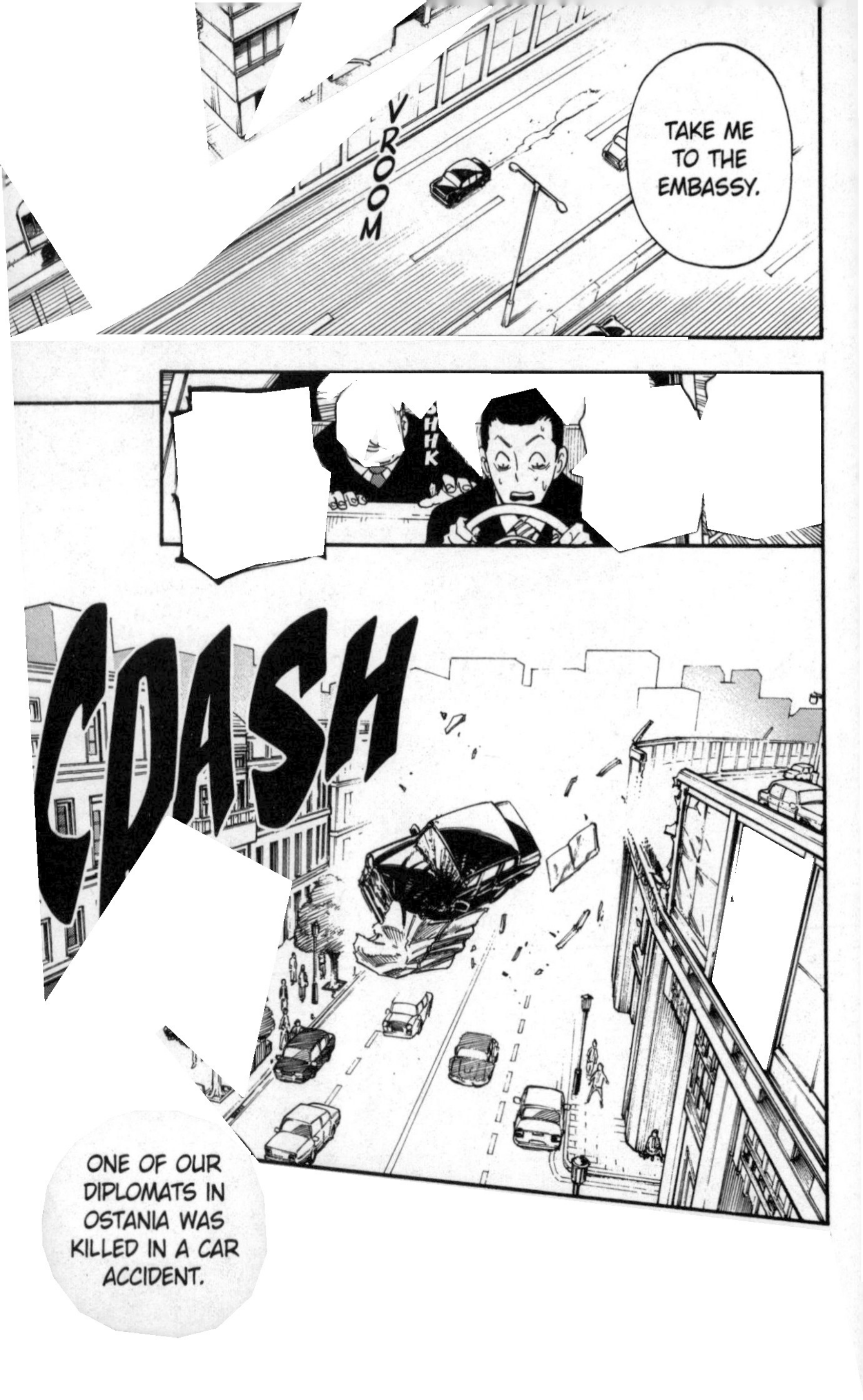
TAKE ME TO THE EMBASSY.
VROOOM
SHHK
CRASH
ONE OF OUR DIPLOMATS IN OSTANIA WAS KILLED IN A CAR ACCIDENT.

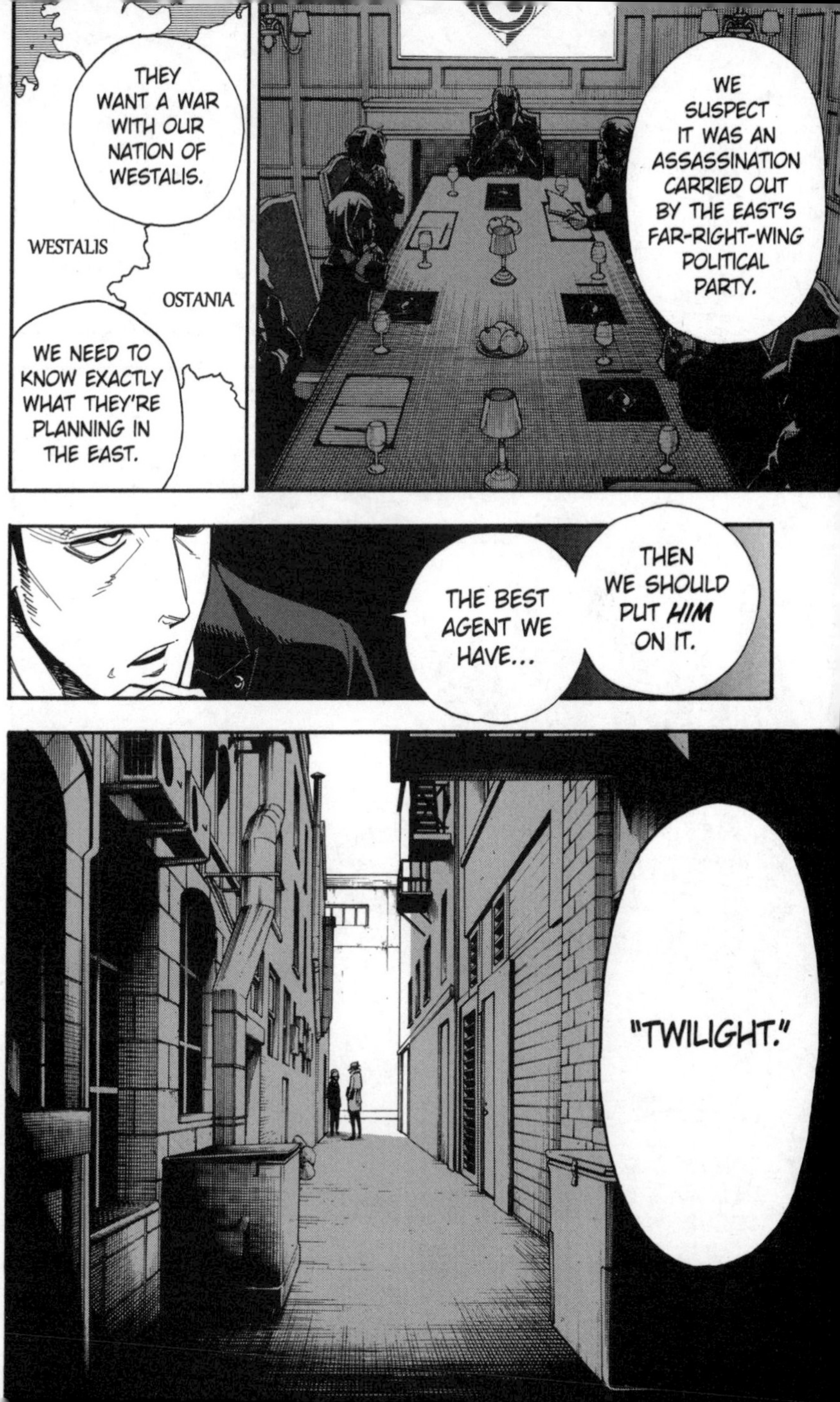
WE SUSPECT IT WAS AN ASSASSINATION CARRIED OUT BY THE EAST'S FAR-RIGHT-WING POLITICAL PARTY.
THEY WANT A WAR WITH OUR NATION OF WESTALIS.
WESTALIS
OSTANIA
WE NEED TO KNOW EXACTLY WHAT THEY'RE PLANNING IN THE EAST.
THEN WE SHOULD PUT *HIM* ON IT.
THE BEST AGENT WE HAVE...
"TWILIGHT."

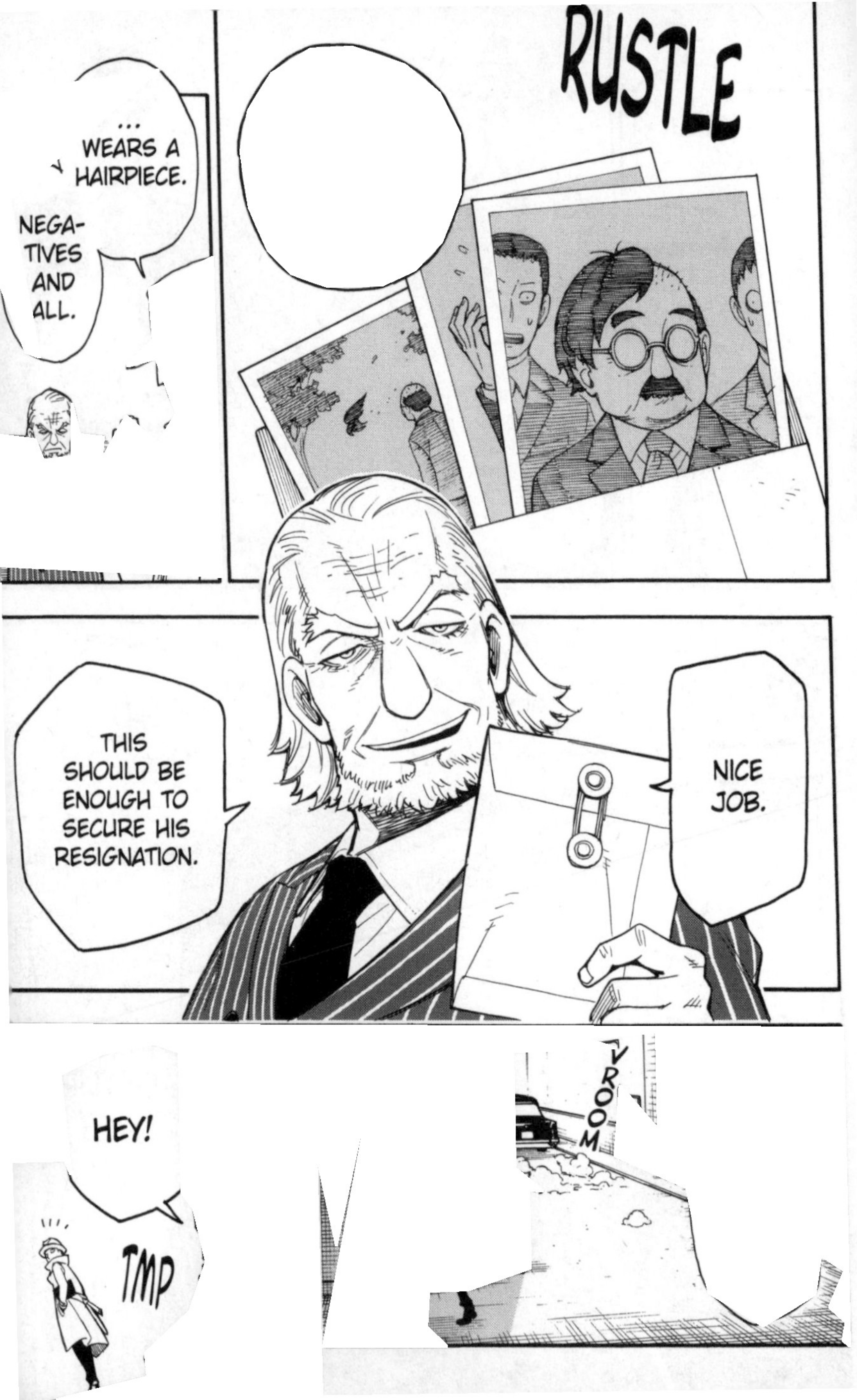
RUSTLE
... WEARS A HAIRPIECE.
NEGATIVES AND ALL.
NICE JOB.
THIS SHOULD BE ENOUGH TO SECURE HIS RESIGNATION.
VROOM
HEY!
TMP

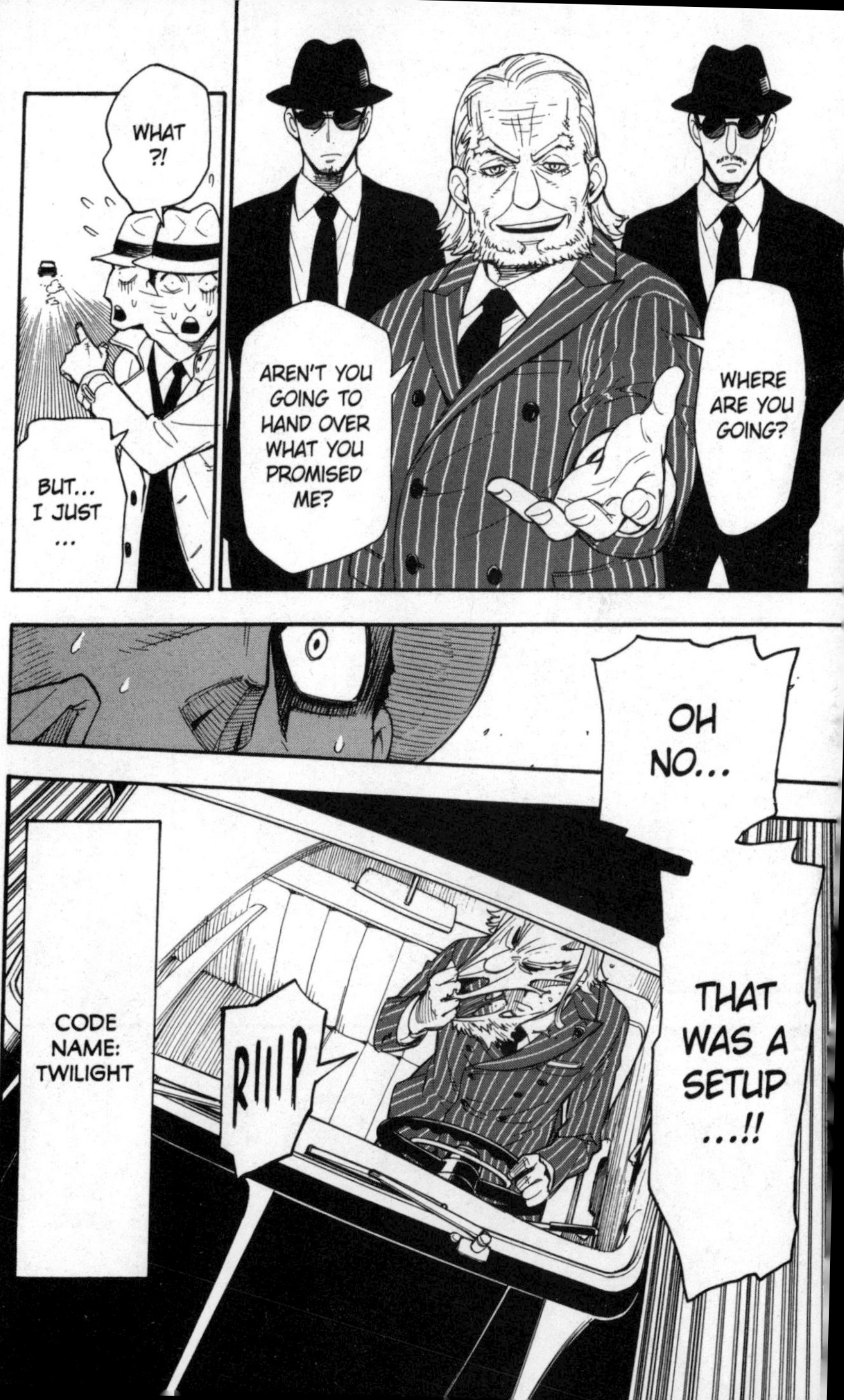
WHERE ARE YOU GOING?
AREN'T YOU GOING TO HAND OVER WHAT YOU PROMISED ME?
WHAT ?!
BUT... I JUST ...
OH NO...
THAT WAS A SETUP ...!!
RIIIP
CODE NAME: TWILIGHT

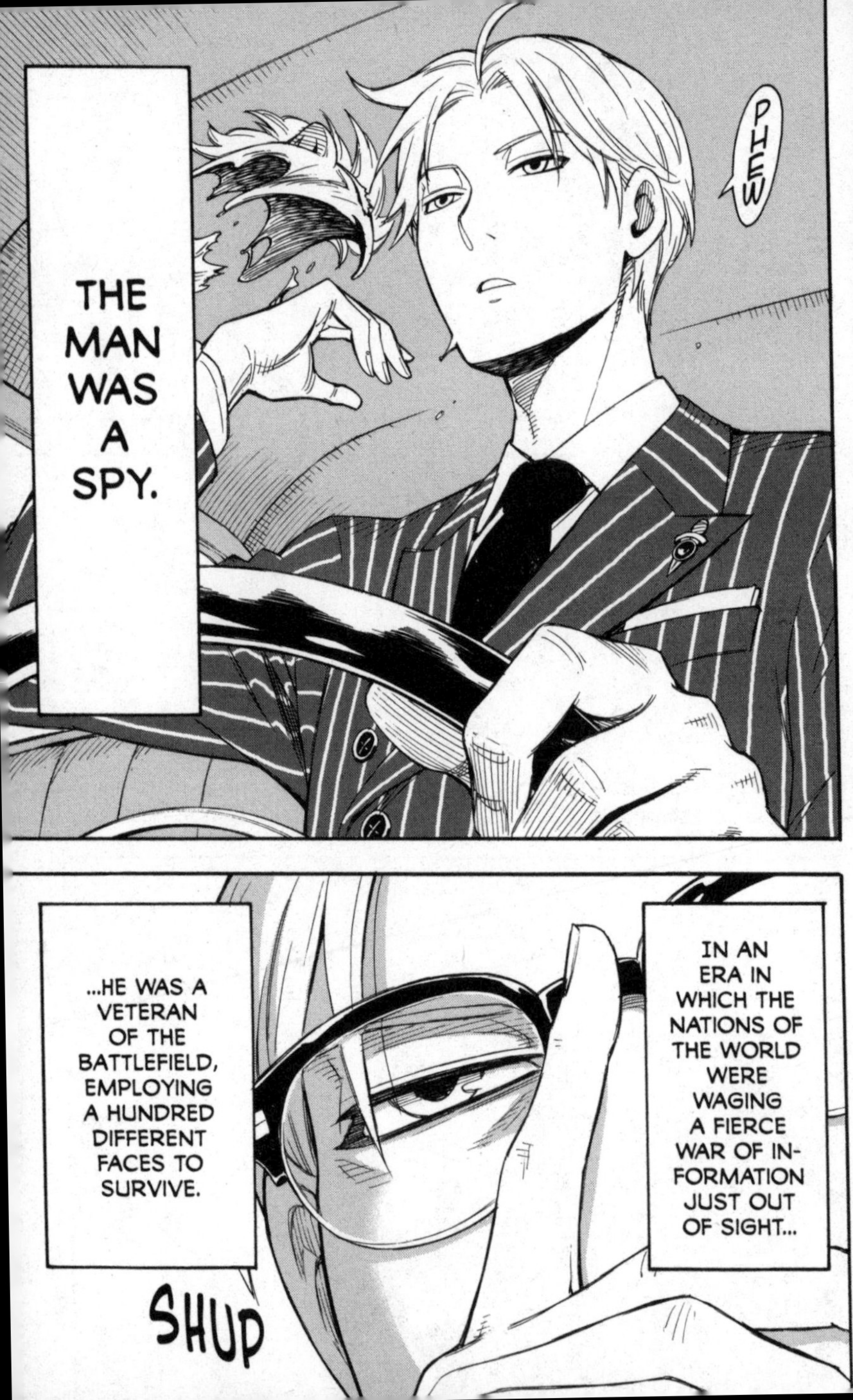
PHEW
THE MAN WAS A SPY.
IN AN ERA IN WHICH THE NATIONS OF THE WORLD WERE WAGING A FIERCE WAR OF IN-FORMATION JUST OUT OF SIGHT...
...HE WAS A VETERAN OF THE BATTLEFIELD, EMPLOYING A HUNDRED DIFFERENT FACES TO SURVIVE.
SHUP

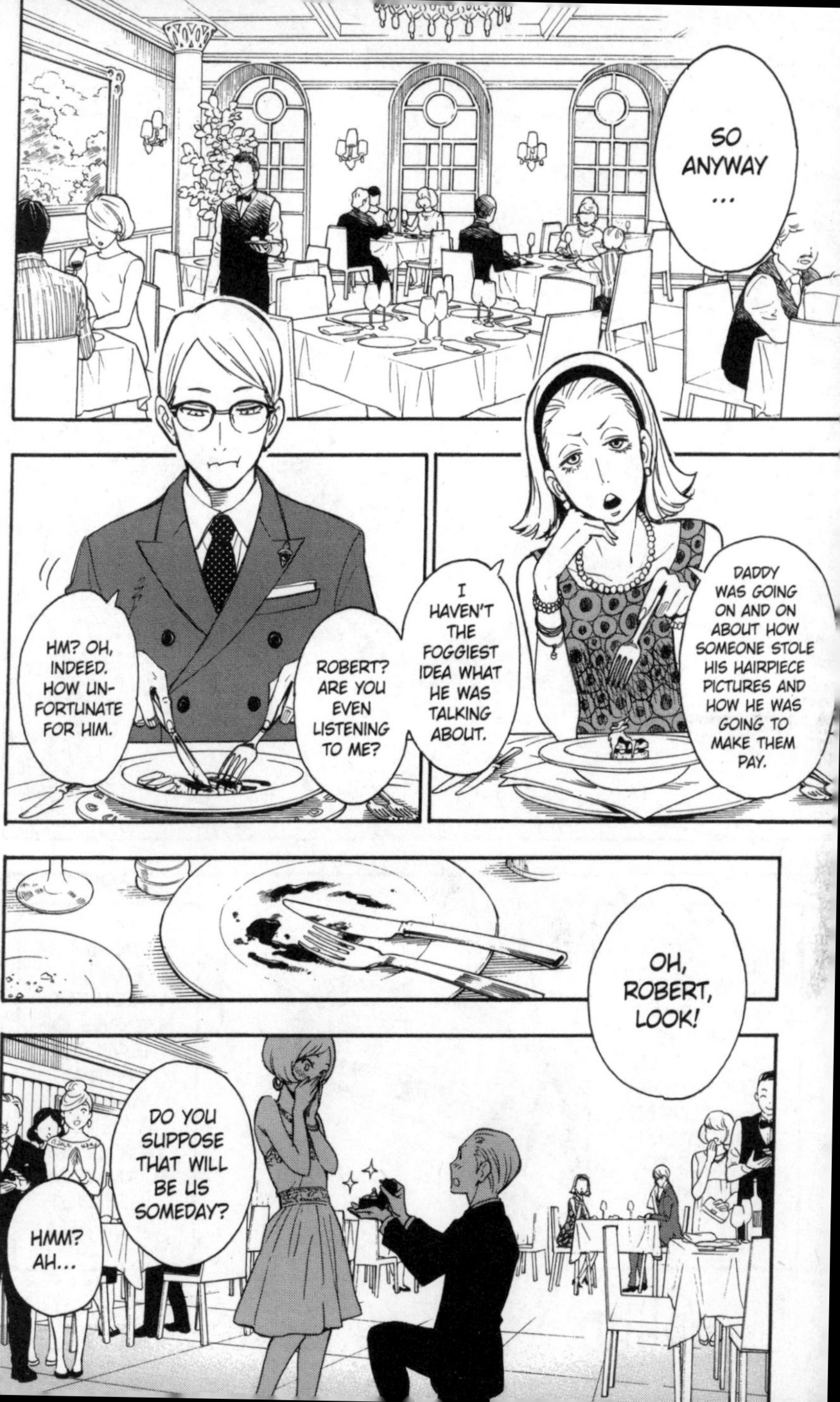
SO ANYWAY ...
DADDY WAS GOING ON AND ON ABOUT HOW SOMEONE STOLE HIS HAIRPIECE PICTURES AND HOW HE WAS GOING TO MAKE THEM PAY.
I HAVEN'T THE FOGGIEST IDEA WHAT HE WAS TALKING ABOUT.
ROBERT? ARE YOU EVEN LISTENING TO ME?
HM? OH, INDEED. HOW UN-FORTUNATE FOR HIM.
OH, ROBERT, LOOK!
DO YOU SUPPOSE THAT WILL BE US SOMEDAY?
HMM? AH...

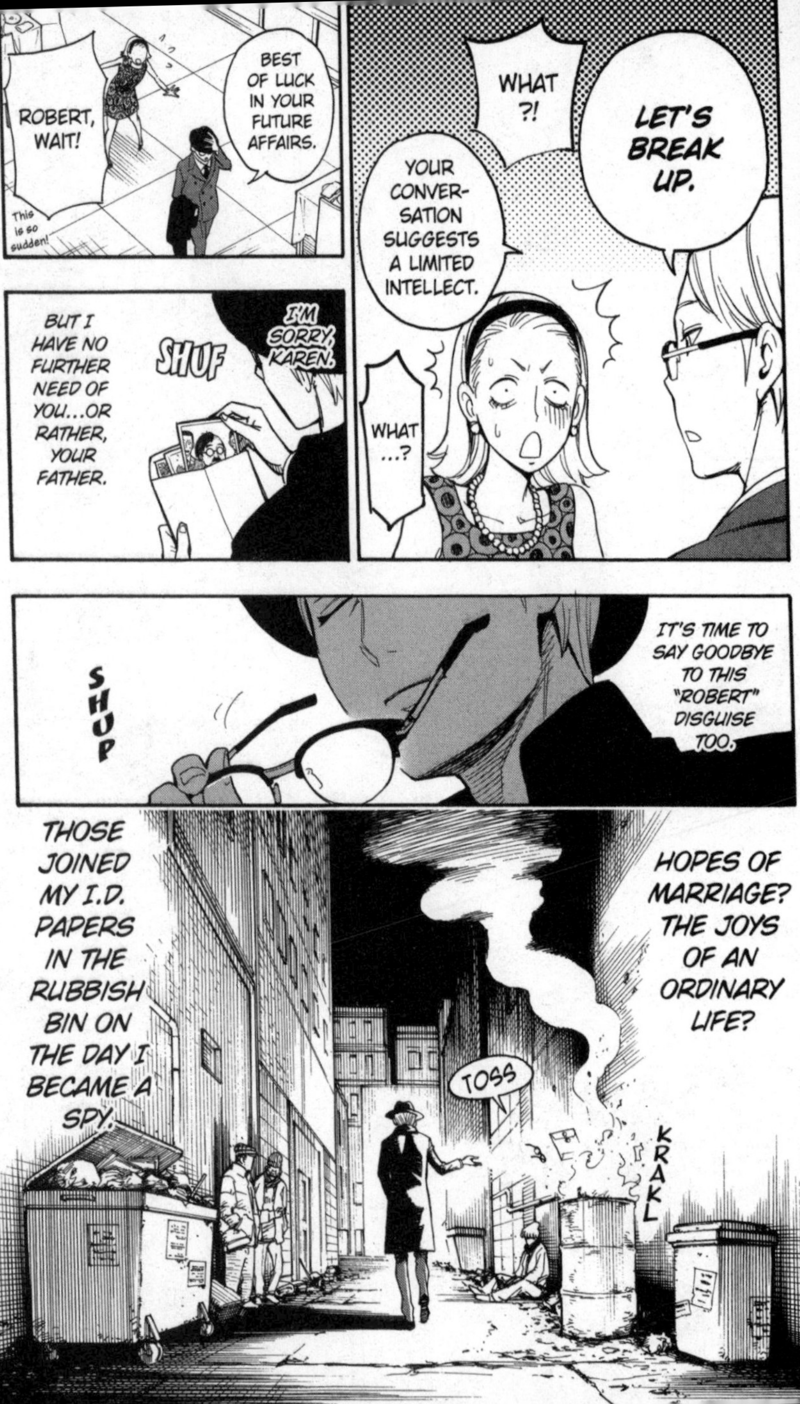
LET'S BREAK UP.
WHAT ?!
YOUR CONVERSATION SUGGESTS A LIMITED INTELLECT.
WHAT ...?
BEST OF LUCK IN YOUR FUTURE AFFAIRS.
ROBERT, WAIT!
This is so sudden!
I'M SORRY, KAREN.
SHUF
BUT I HAVE NO FURTHER NEED OF YOU...OR RATHER, YOUR FATHER.
IT'S TIME TO SAY GOODBYE TO THIS "ROBERT" DISGUISE TOO.
SHUP
HOPES OF MARRIAGE? THE JOYS OF AN ORDINARY LIFE?
TOSS
KRAKL
THOSE JOINED MY I.D. PAPERS IN THE RUBBISH BIN ON THE DAY I BECAME A SPY.

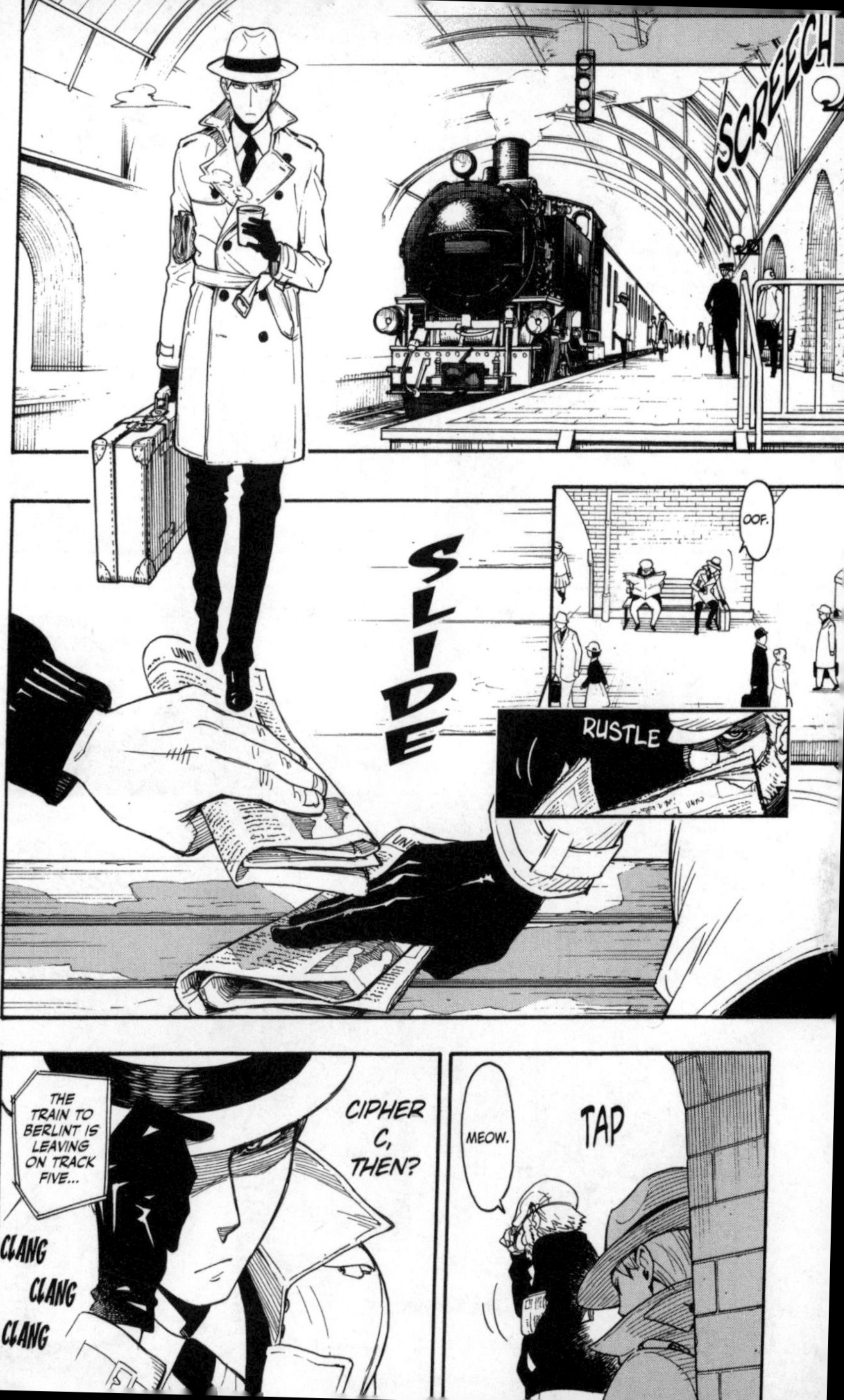
SCREECH
OOF.
RUSTLE
SLIDE
MEOW.
TAP
THE TRAIN TO BERLINT IS LEAVING ON TRACK FIVE...
CIPHER C, THEN?
CLANG
CLANG
CLANG

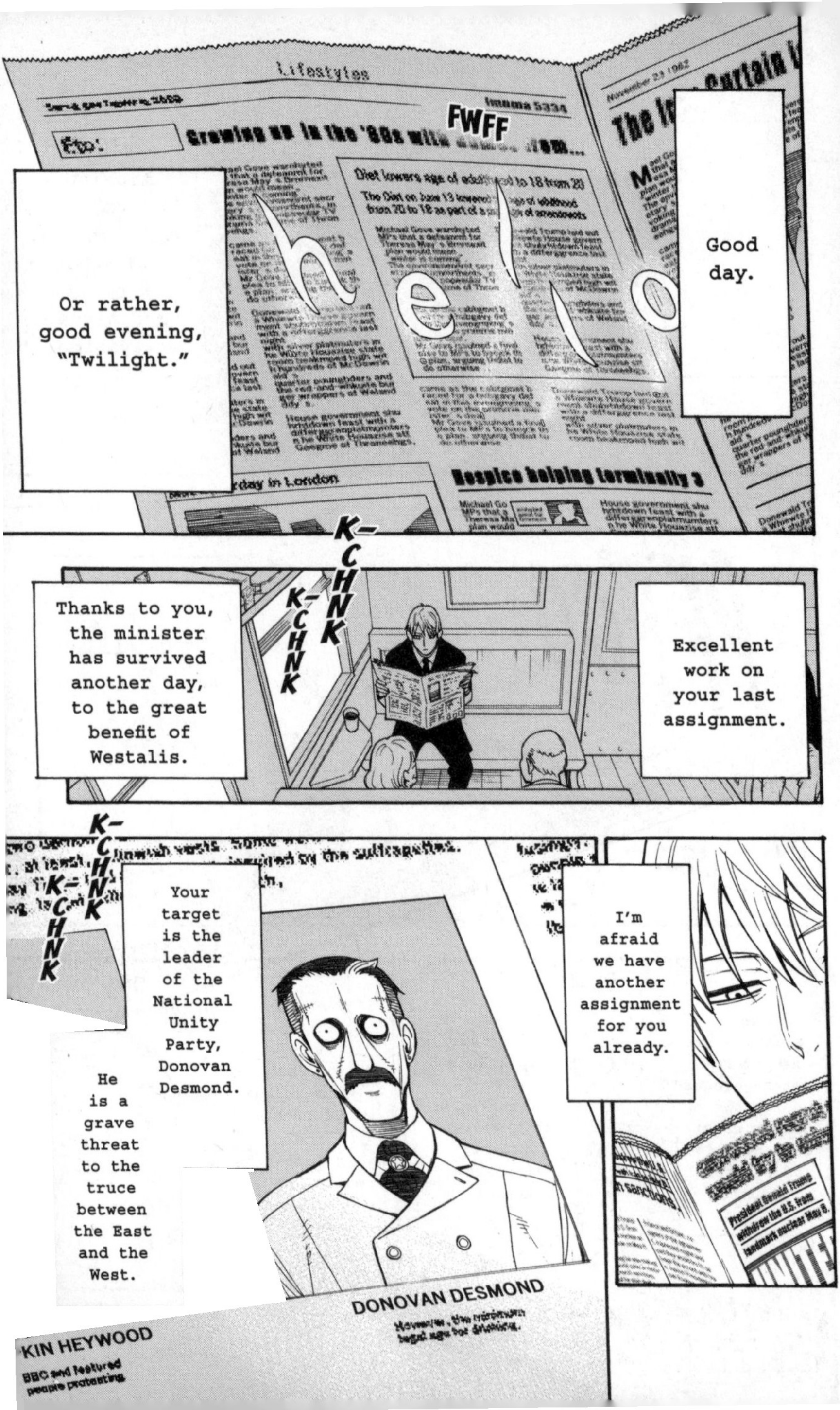
Lifestyles
FWFF
hello
Good day.
Or rather, good evening, "Twilight."
K-CHNK
K-CHNK
Excellent work on your last assignment.
Thanks to you, the minister has survived another day, to the great benefit of Westalis.
I'm afraid we have another assignment for you already.
K-CHNK
K-CHNK
Your target is the leader of the National Unity Party, Donovan Desmond.
He is a grave threat to the truce between the East and the West.
DONOVAN DESMOND
KIN HEYWOOD

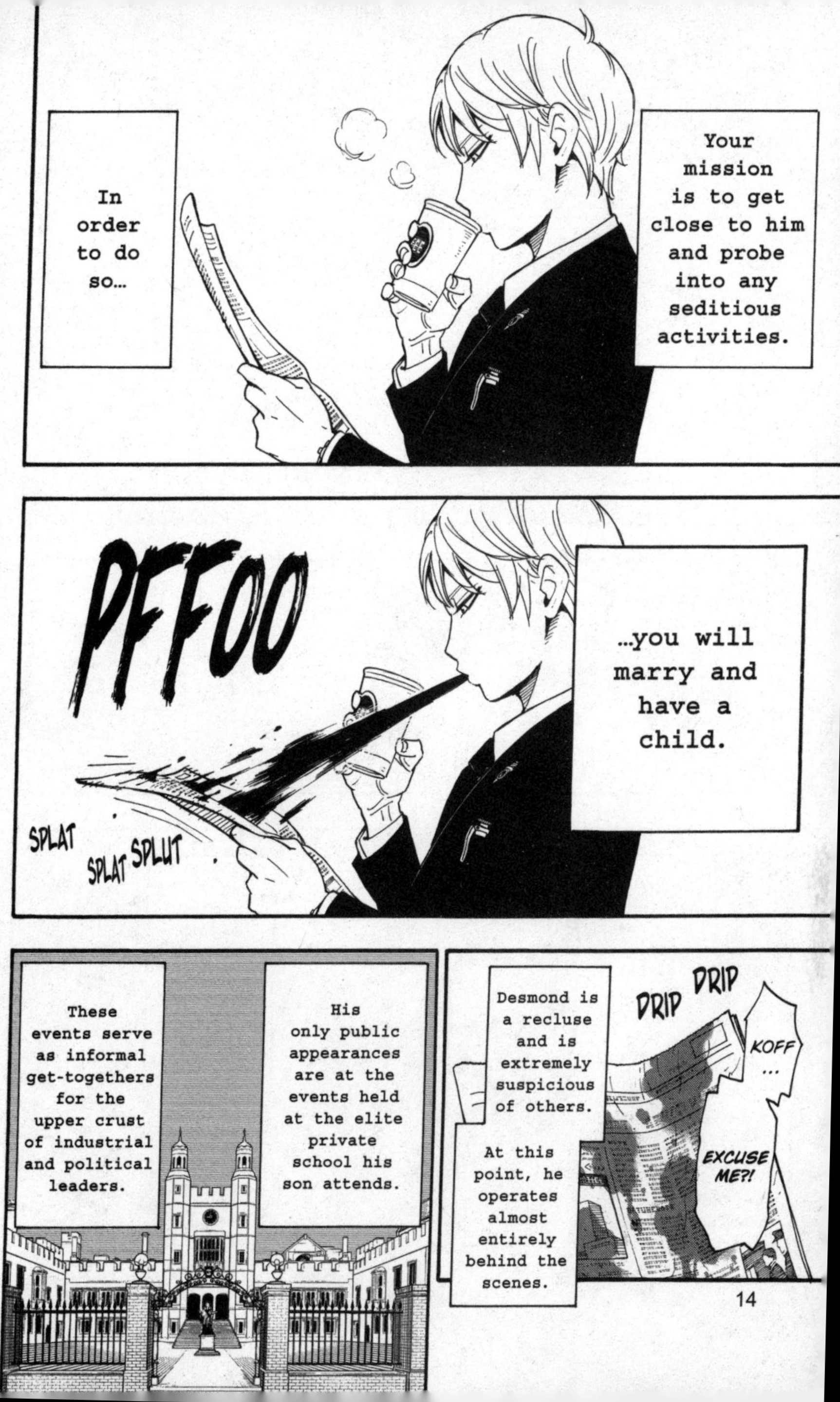
Your mission is to get close to him and probe into any seditious activities.
In order to do so...
...you will marry and have a child.
PFFOO
SPLUT
SPLAT
SPLAT
DRIP
DRIP
KOFF ...
EXCUSE ME?!
Desmond is a recluse and is extremely suspicious of others.
At this point, he operates almost entirely behind the scenes.
His only public appearances are at the events held at the elite private school his son attends.
These events serve as informal get-togethers for the upper crust of industrial and political leaders.

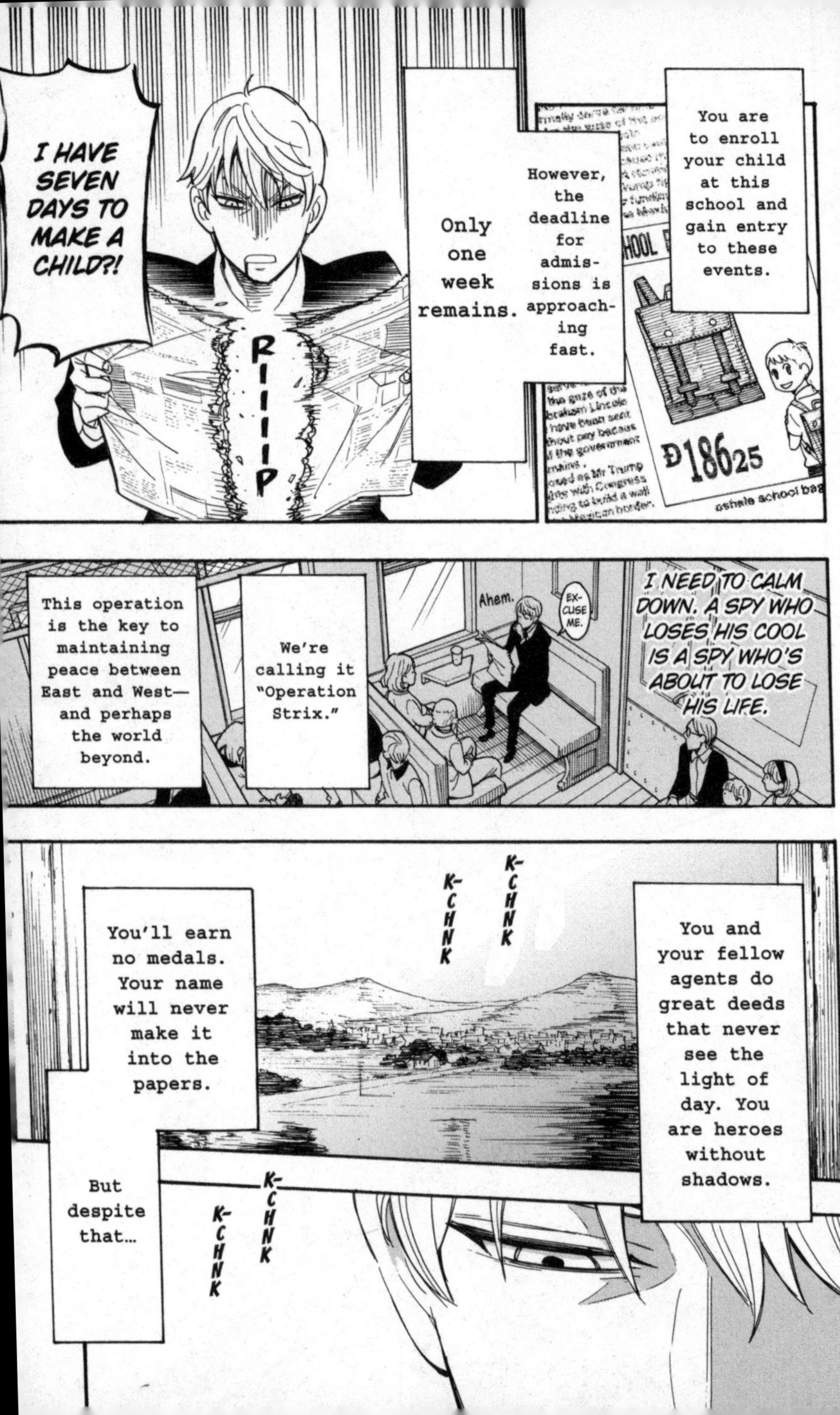

You are to enroll your child at this school and gain entry to these events.
Ð18625
However, the deadline for admissions is approaching fast.
Only one week remains.
RIIIP
I HAVE SEVEN DAYS TO MAKE A CHILD?!
I NEED TO CALM DOWN. A SPY WHO LOSES HIS COOL IS A SPY WHO'S ABOUT TO LOSE HIS LIFE.
EX-CUSE ME.
Ahem.
We're calling it "Operation Strix."
This operation is the key to maintaining peace between East and West—and perhaps the world beyond.
You and your fellow agents do great deeds that never see the light of day. You are heroes without shadows.
K-CHNK
K-CHNK
You'll earn no medals. Your name will never make it into the papers.
K-CHNK
K-CHNK
But despite that...

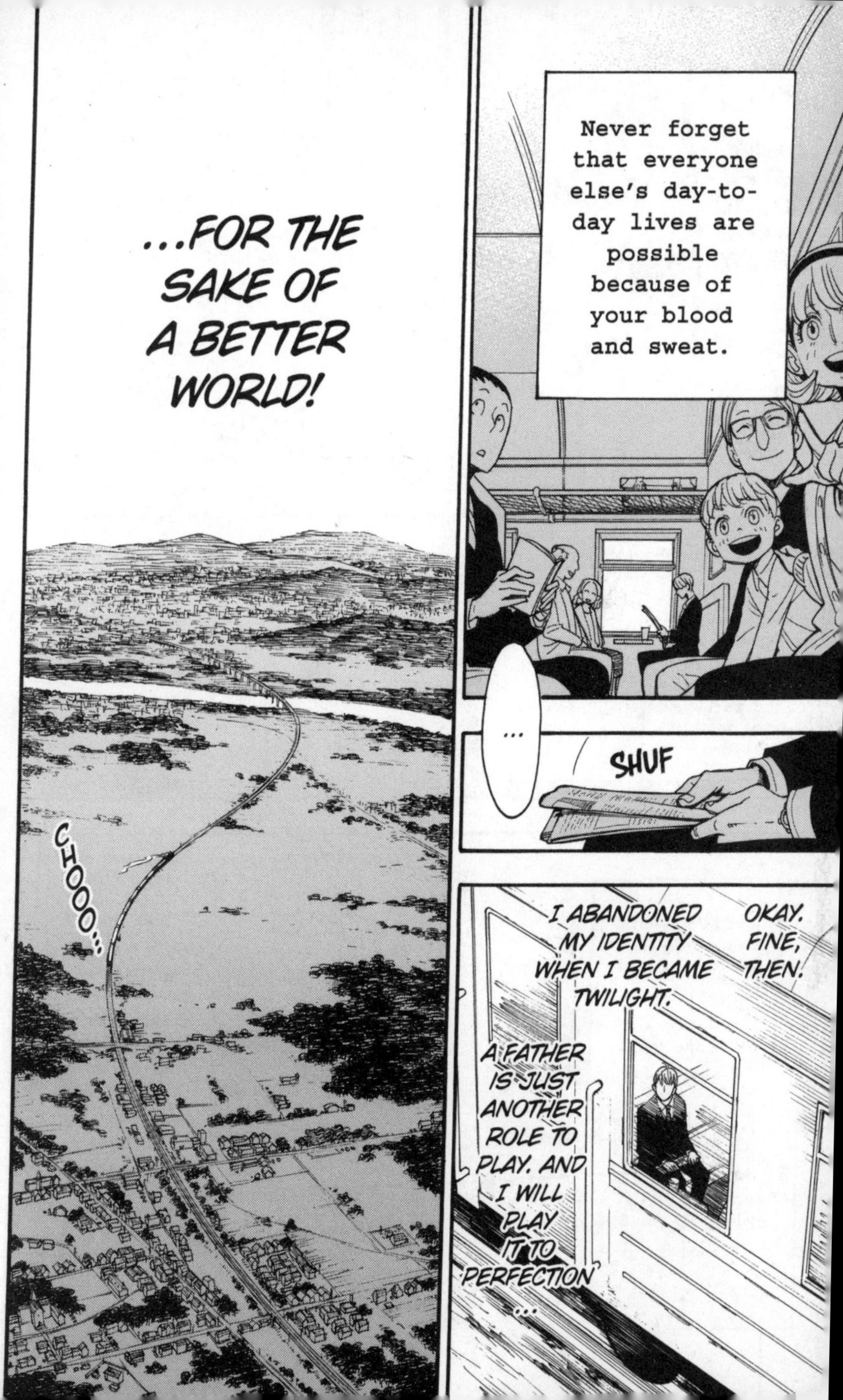
Never forget that everyone else's day-to-day lives are possible because of your blood and sweat.
...
SHUF
OKAY. FINE, THEN.
I ABANDONED MY IDENTITY WHEN I BECAME TWILIGHT.
A FATHER IS JUST ANOTHER ROLE TO PLAY. AND I WILL PLAY IT TO PERFECTION...
...FOR THE SAKE OF A BETTER WORLD!
CHOOO...

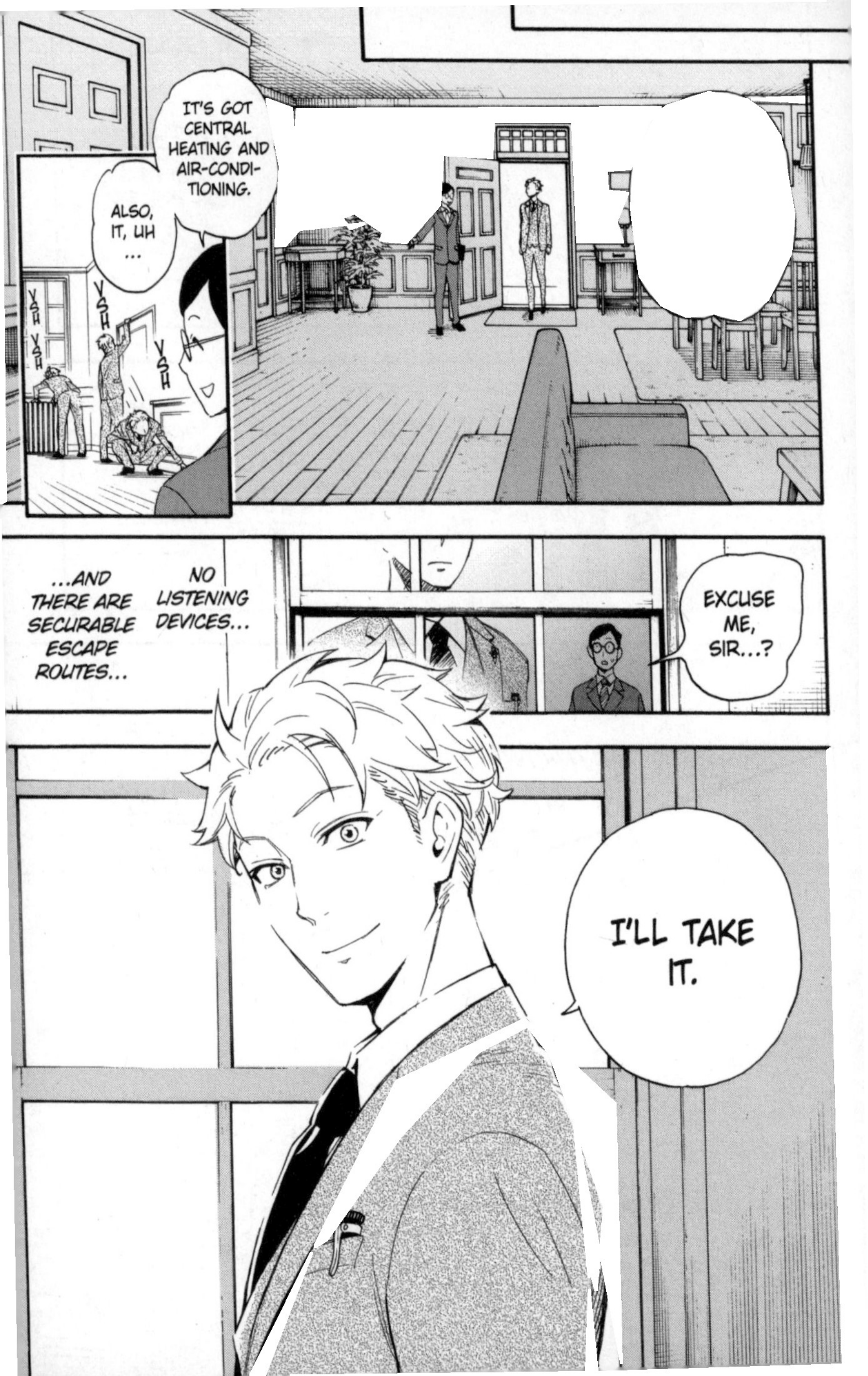
IT'S GOT CENTRAL HEATING AND AIR-CONDITIONING.
ALSO, IT, UH ...
VSH VSH
VSH
VSH
EXCUSE ME, SIR...?
NO LISTENING DEVICES...
...AND THERE ARE SECURABLE ESCAPE ROUTES...
I'LL TAKE IT.

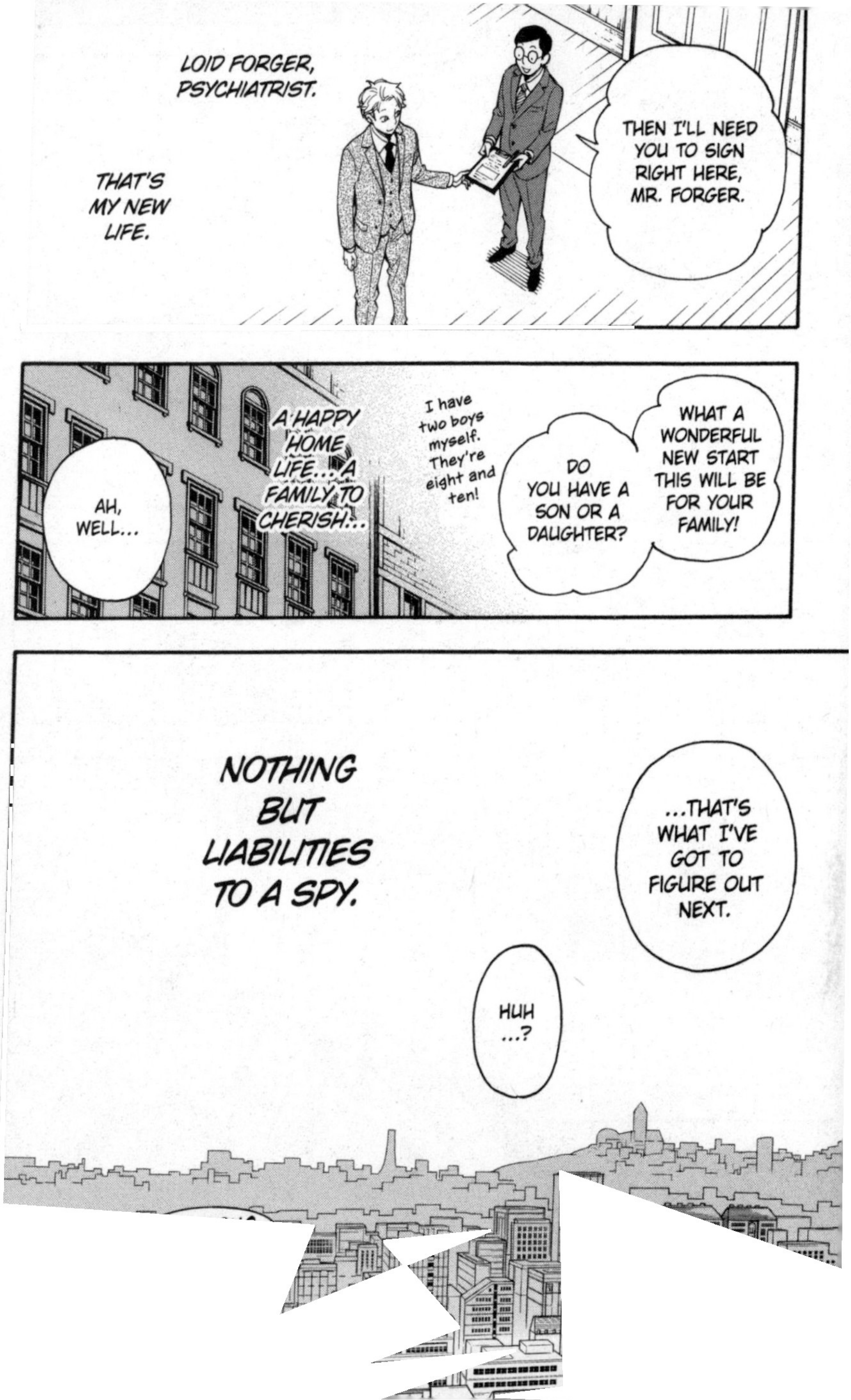
THEN I'LL NEED YOU TO SIGN RIGHT HERE, MR. FORGER.
LOID FORGER, PSYCHIATRIST.
THAT'S MY NEW LIFE.
WHAT A WONDERFUL NEW START THIS WILL BE FOR YOUR FAMILY!
DO YOU HAVE A SON OR A DAUGHTER?
I have two boys myself. They're eight and ten!
A HAPPY HOME LIFE... A FAMILY TO CHERISH...
AH, WELL...
...THAT'S WHAT I'VE GOT TO FIGURE OUT NEXT.
NOTHING BUT LIABILITIES TO A SPY.
HUH ...?

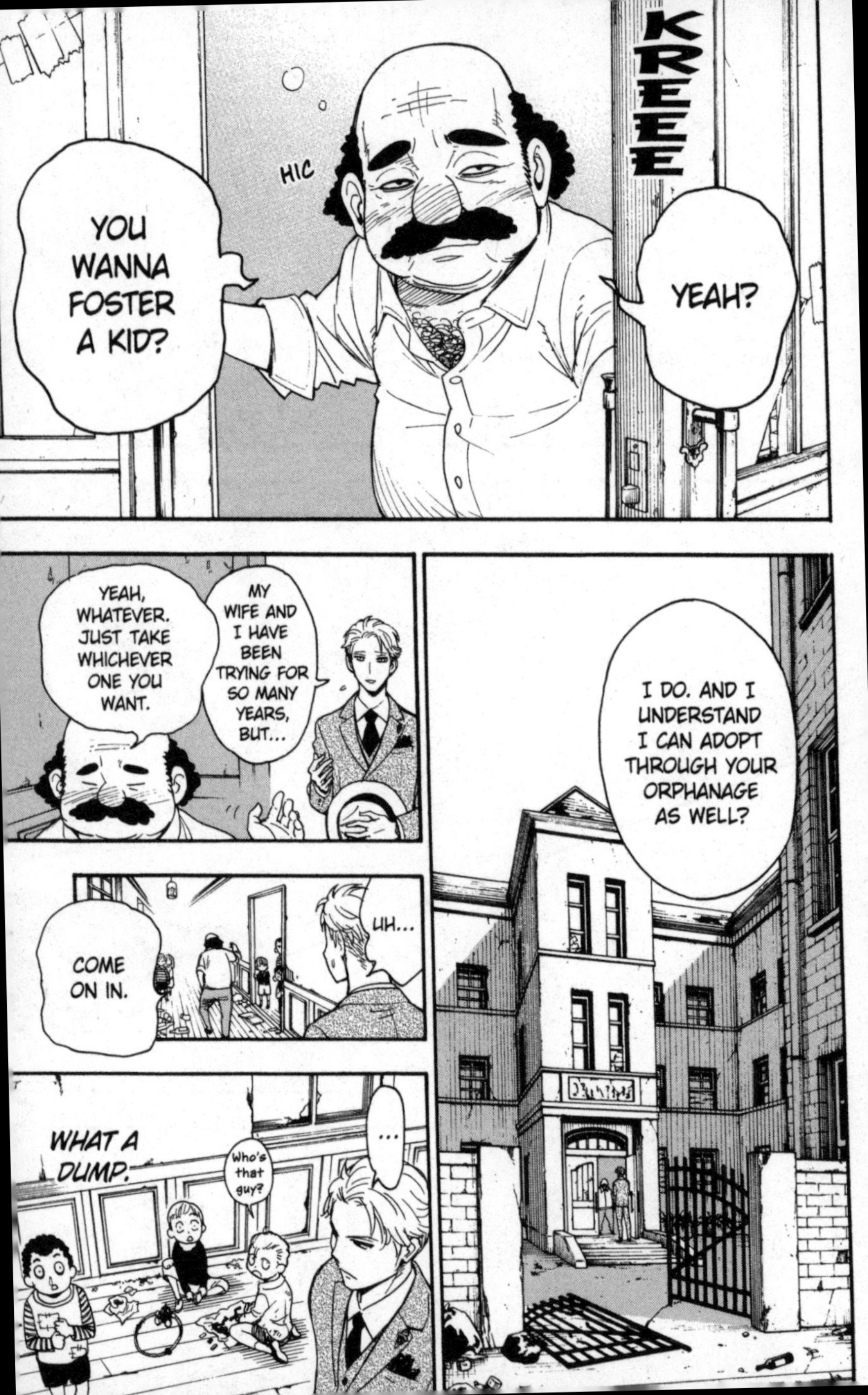
KREEE
YEAH?
HIC
YOU WANNA FOSTER A KID?
I DO. AND I UNDERSTAND I CAN ADOPT THROUGH YOUR ORPHANAGE AS WELL?
MY WIFE AND I HAVE BEEN TRYING FOR SO MANY YEARS, BUT...
YEAH, WHATEVER. JUST TAKE WHICHEVER ONE YOU WANT.
UH...
COME ON IN.
...
Who's that guy?
WHAT A DUMP.

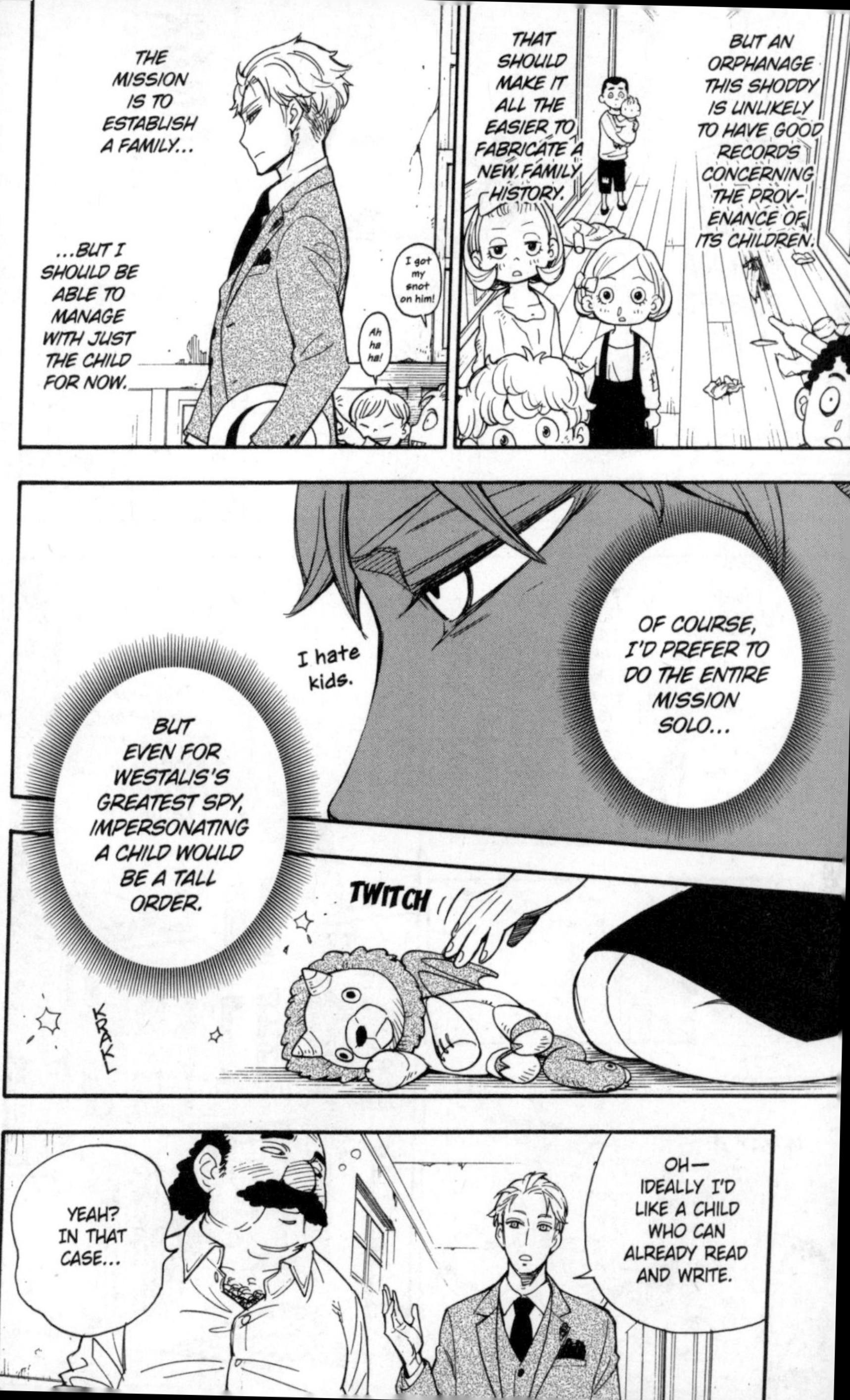
BUT AN ORPHANAGE THIS SHODDY IS UNLIKELY TO HAVE GOOD RECORDS CONCERNING THE PROVENANCE OF ITS CHILDREN.
THAT SHOULD MAKE IT ALL THE EASIER TO FABRICATE A NEW FAMILY HISTORY.
THE MISSION IS TO ESTABLISH A FAMILY...
...BUT I SHOULD BE ABLE TO MANAGE WITH JUST THE CHILD FOR NOW.
I got my snot on him!
Ah ha ha!
OF COURSE, I'D PREFER TO DO THE ENTIRE MISSION SOLO...
I hate kids.
BUT EVEN FOR WESTALIS'S GREATEST SPY, IMPERSONATING A CHILD WOULD BE A TALL ORDER.
TWITCH
KRAKL
OH— IDEALLY I'D LIKE A CHILD WHO CAN ALREADY READ AND WRITE.
YEAH? IN THAT CASE...

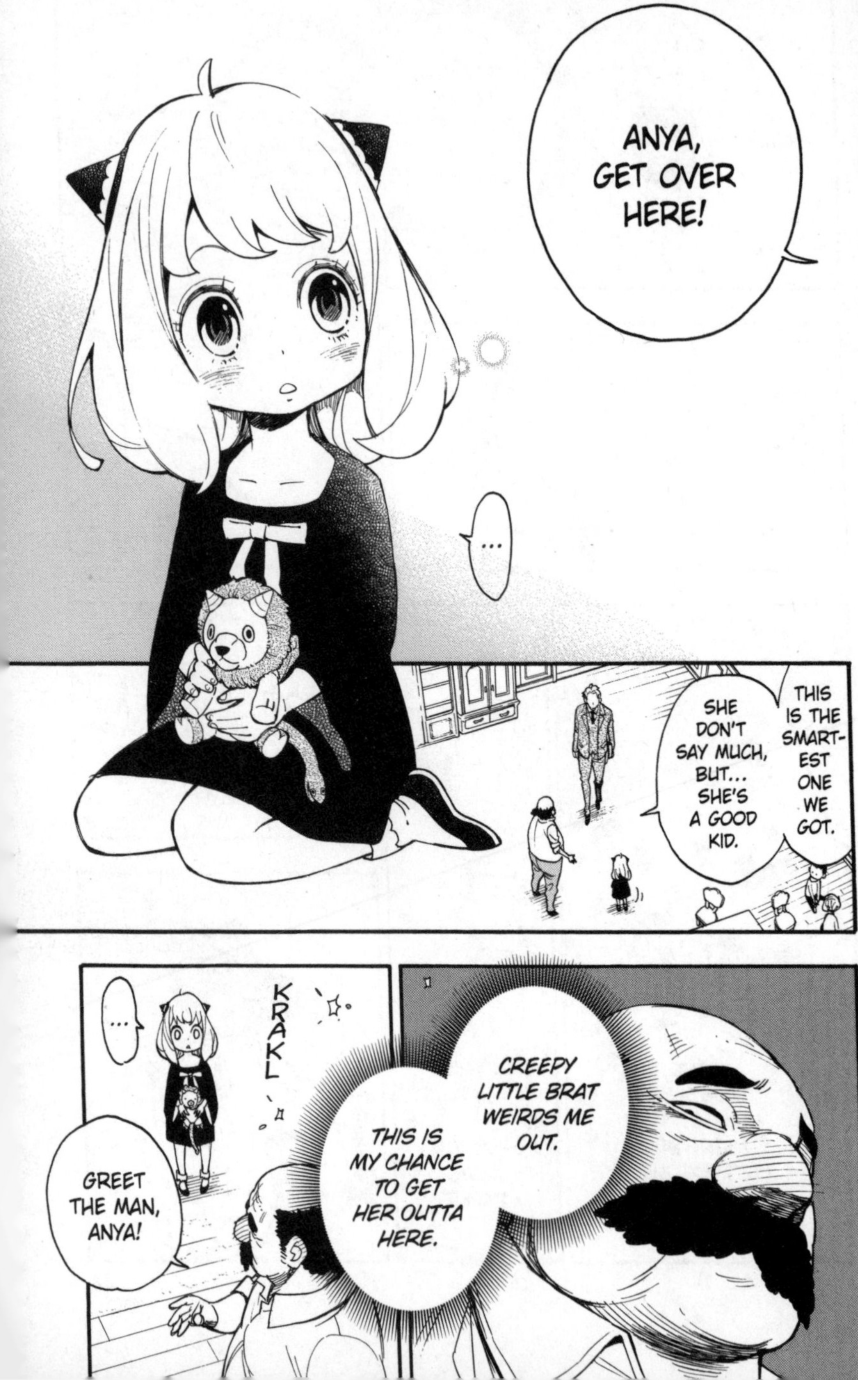
ANYA, GET OVER HERE!
...
THIS IS THE SMART-EST ONE WE GOT.
SHE DON'T SAY MUCH, BUT... SHE'S A GOOD KID.
CREEPY LITTLE BRAT WEIRDS ME OUT.
THIS IS MY CHANCE TO GET HER OUTTA HERE.
...
KRAKL
GREET THE MAN, ANYA!

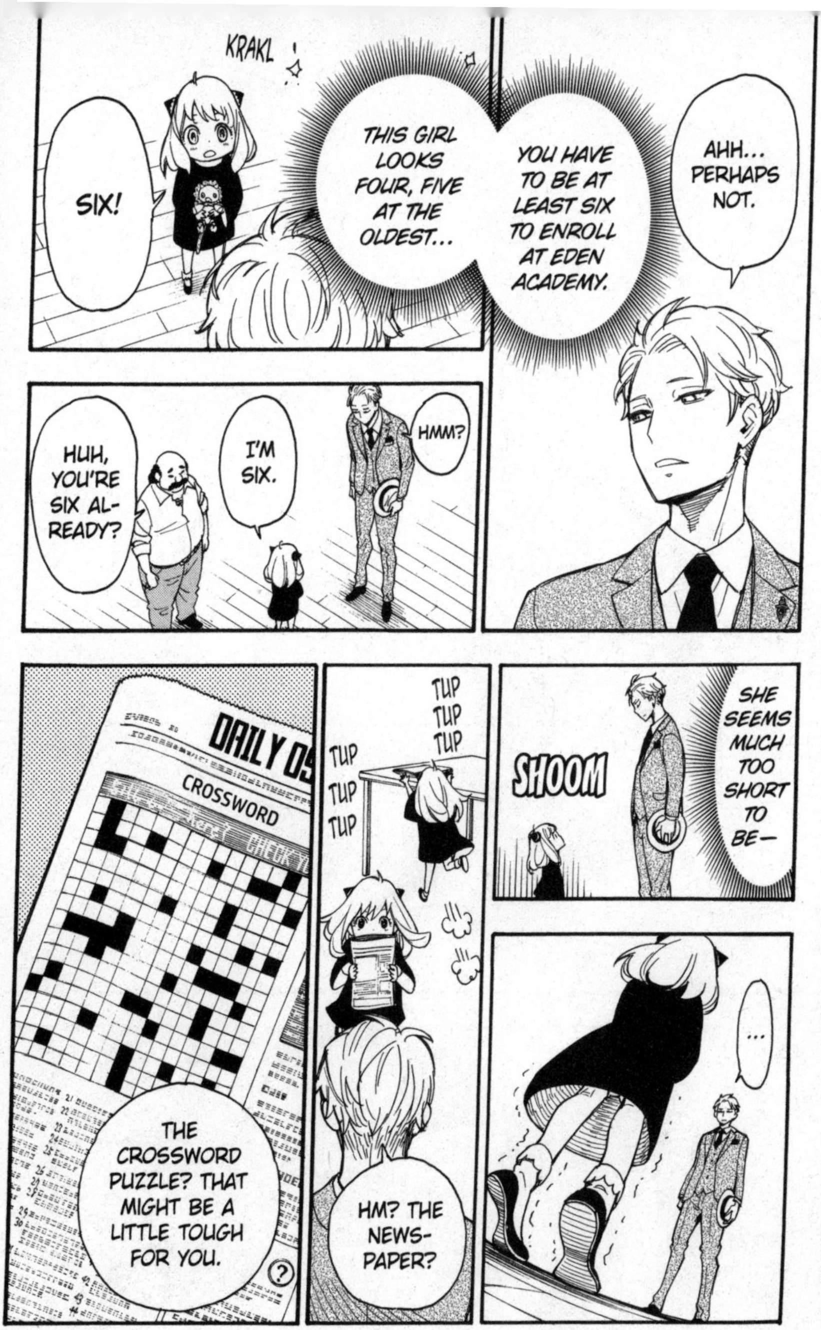
KRAKL
SIX!
THIS GIRL LOOKS FOUR, FIVE AT THE OLDEST...
YOU HAVE TO BE AT LEAST SIX TO ENROLL AT EDEN ACADEMY.
AHH... PERHAPS NOT.
HMM?
I'M SIX.
HUH, YOU'RE SIX AL-READY?
SHE SEEMS MUCH TOO SHORT TO BE—
SHOOM
...
TUP TUP TUP
TUP TUP TUP
HM? THE NEWS-PAPER?
DAILY OS
CROSSWORD
THE CROSSWORD PUZZLE? THAT MIGHT BE A LITTLE TOUGH FOR YOU.

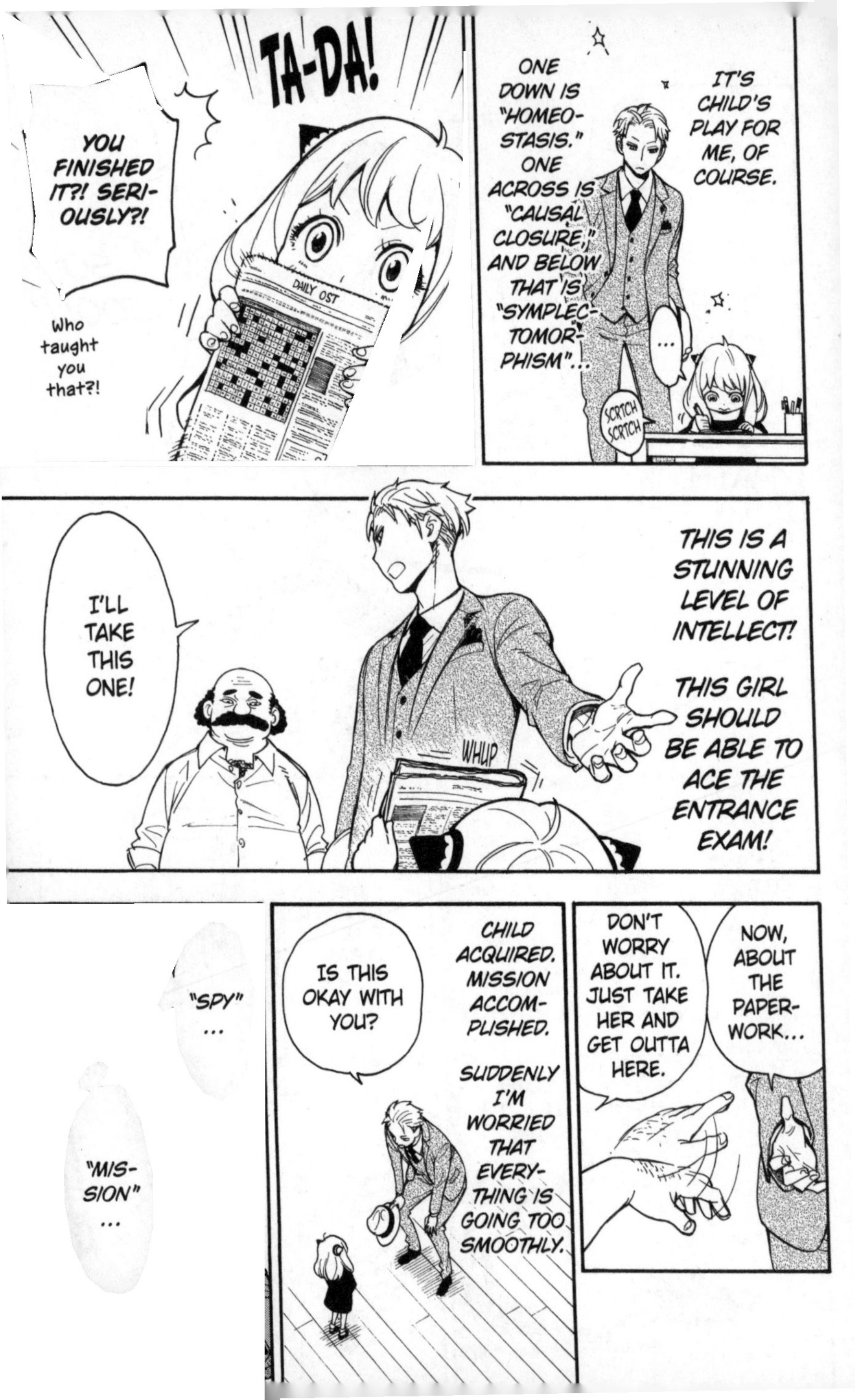
IT'S CHILD'S PLAY FOR ME, OF COURSE.
ONE DOWN IS "HOMEOSTASIS." ONE ACROSS IS "CAUSAL CLOSURE," AND BELOW THAT IS "SYMPLECTOMORPHISM"...
...
SCRTCH SCRTCH
TA-DA!
YOU FINISHED IT?! SERIOUSLY?!
DAILY OST
Who taught you that?!
THIS IS A STUNNING LEVEL OF INTELLECT!
THIS GIRL SHOULD BE ABLE TO ACE THE ENTRANCE EXAM!
WHUP
I'LL TAKE THIS ONE!
NOW, ABOUT THE PAPERWORK...
DON'T WORRY ABOUT IT. JUST TAKE HER AND GET OUTTA HERE.
CHILD ACQUIRED. MISSION ACCOMPLISHED.
SUDDENLY I'M WORRIED THAT EVERYTHING IS GOING TOO SMOOTHLY.
IS THIS OKAY WITH YOU?
"SPY"...
"MISSION"...

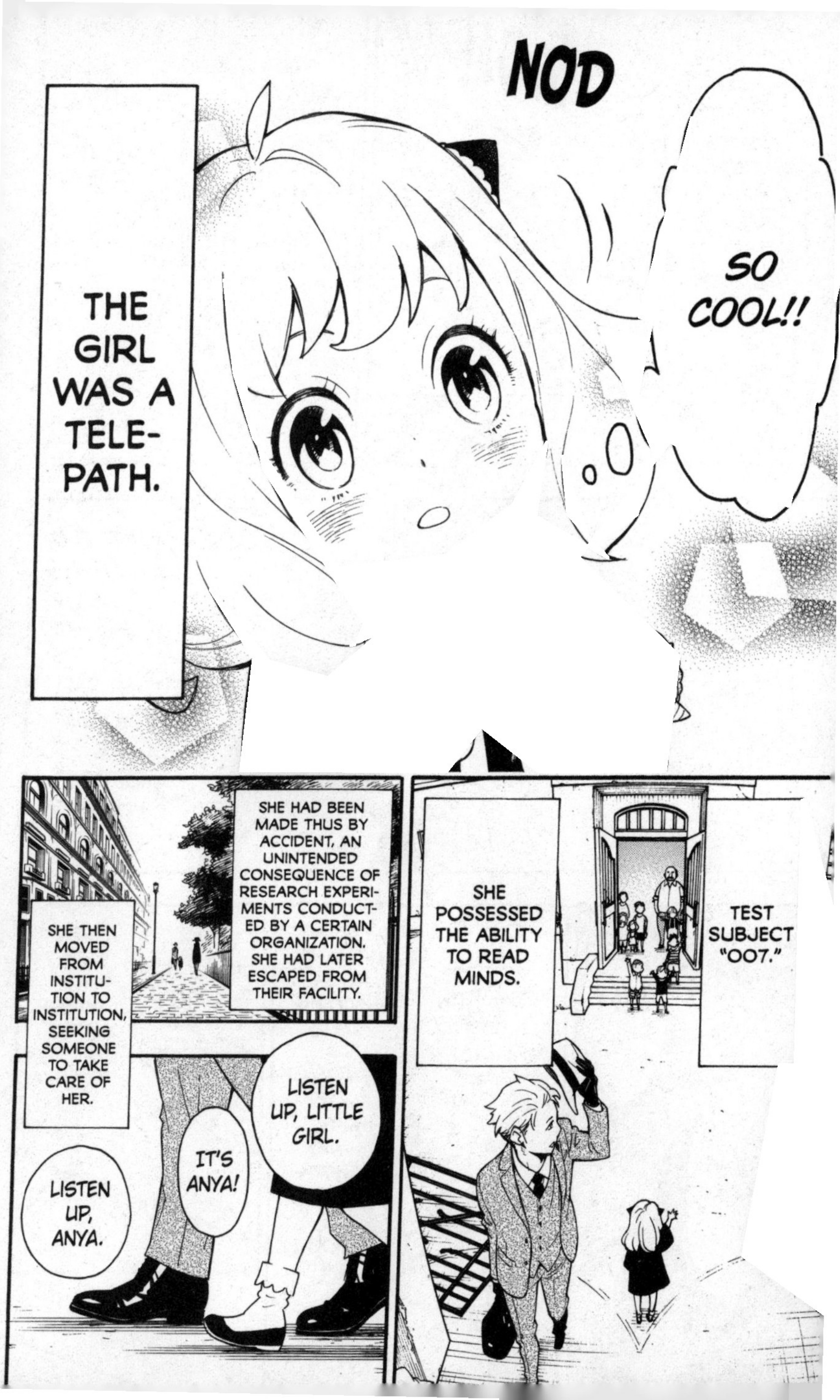
NOD
SO COOL!!
THE GIRL WAS A TELEPATH.
TEST SUBJECT "007."
SHE POSSESSED THE ABILITY TO READ MINDS.
SHE HAD BEEN MADE THUS BY ACCIDENT, AN UNINTENDED CONSEQUENCE OF RESEARCH EXPERIMENTS CONDUCTED BY A CERTAIN ORGANIZATION. SHE HAD LATER ESCAPED FROM THEIR FACILITY.
SHE THEN MOVED FROM INSTITUTION TO INSTITUTION, SEEKING SOMEONE TO TAKE CARE OF HER.
LISTEN UP, LITTLE GIRL.
IT'S ANYA!
LISTEN UP, ANYA.

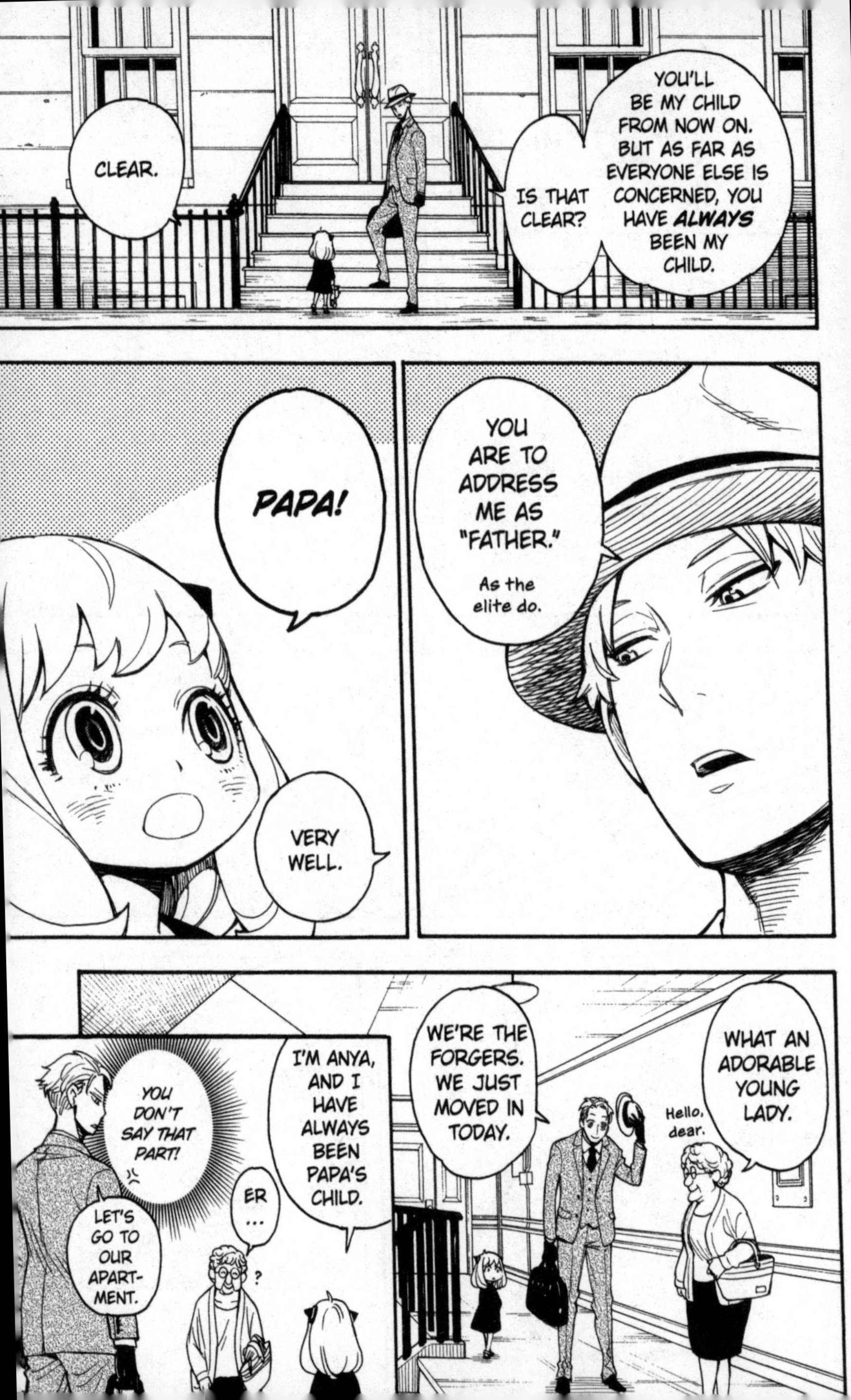
YOU'LL BE MY CHILD FROM NOW ON. BUT AS FAR AS EVERYONE ELSE IS CONCERNED, YOU HAVE *ALWAYS* BEEN MY CHILD.
IS THAT CLEAR?
CLEAR.
YOU ARE TO ADDRESS ME AS "FATHER."
As the elite do.
PAPA!
VERY WELL.
WHAT AN ADORABLE YOUNG LADY.
Hello, dear.
WE'RE THE FORGERS. WE JUST MOVED IN TODAY.
I'M ANYA, AND I HAVE ALWAYS BEEN PAPA'S CHILD.
ER ...
YOU DON'T SAY THAT PART!
?
LET'S GO TO OUR APARTMENT.

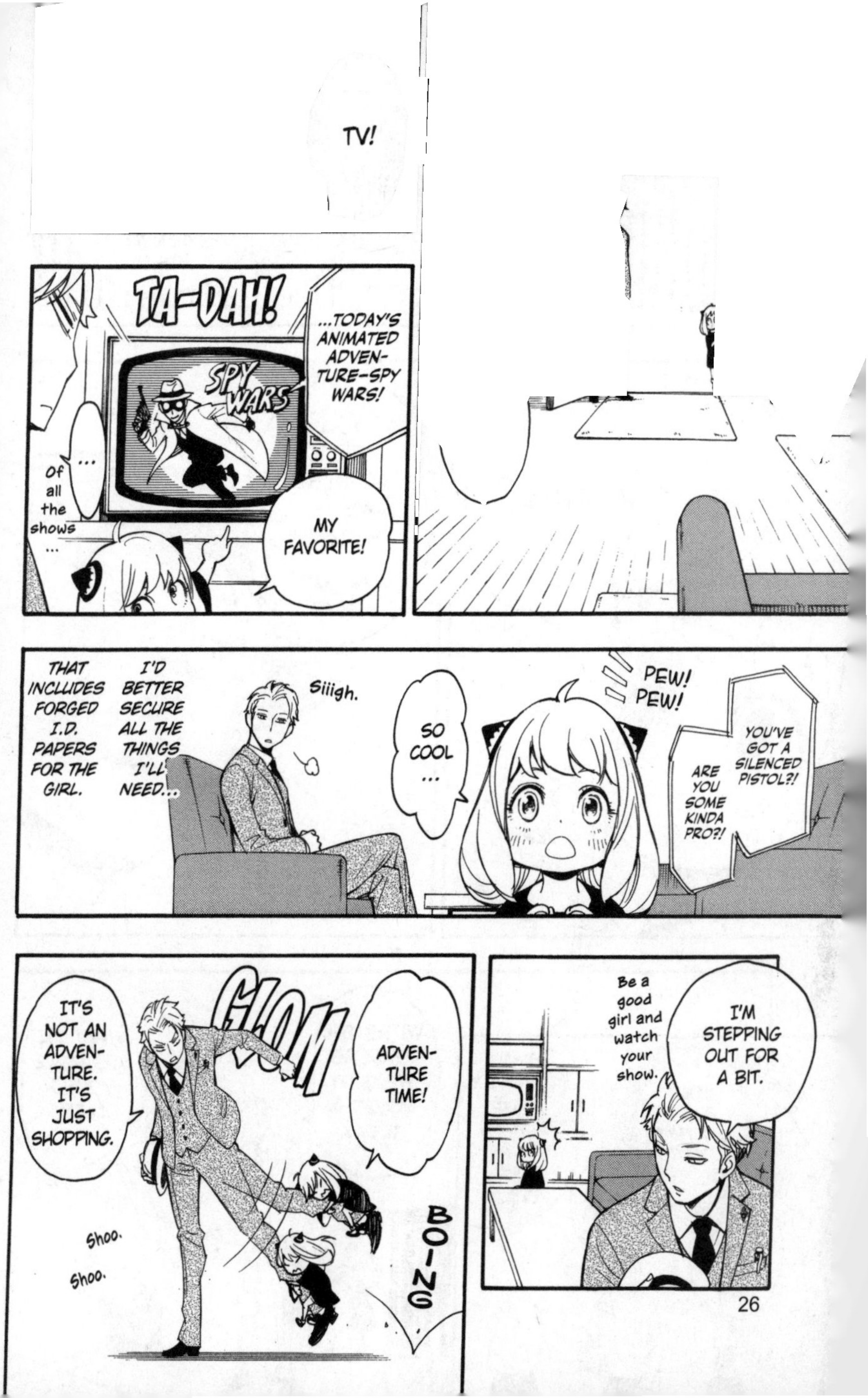
TV!
TA-DAH!
...TODAY'S ANIMATED ADVEN-TURE-SPY WARS!
SPY WARS
MY FAVORITE!
...
Of all the shows ...
YOU'VE GOT A SILENCED PISTOL?!
ARE YOU SOME KINDA PRO?!
PEW! PEW!
SO COOL ...
Siiigh.
I'D BETTER SECURE ALL THE THINGS I'LL NEED...
THAT INCLUDES FORGED I.D. PAPERS FOR THE GIRL.
I'M STEPPING OUT FOR A BIT.
Be a good girl and watch your show.
ADVEN-TURE TIME!
GLOM
IT'S NOT AN ADVEN-TURE. IT'S JUST SHOPPING.
BOING
Shoo.
Shoo.

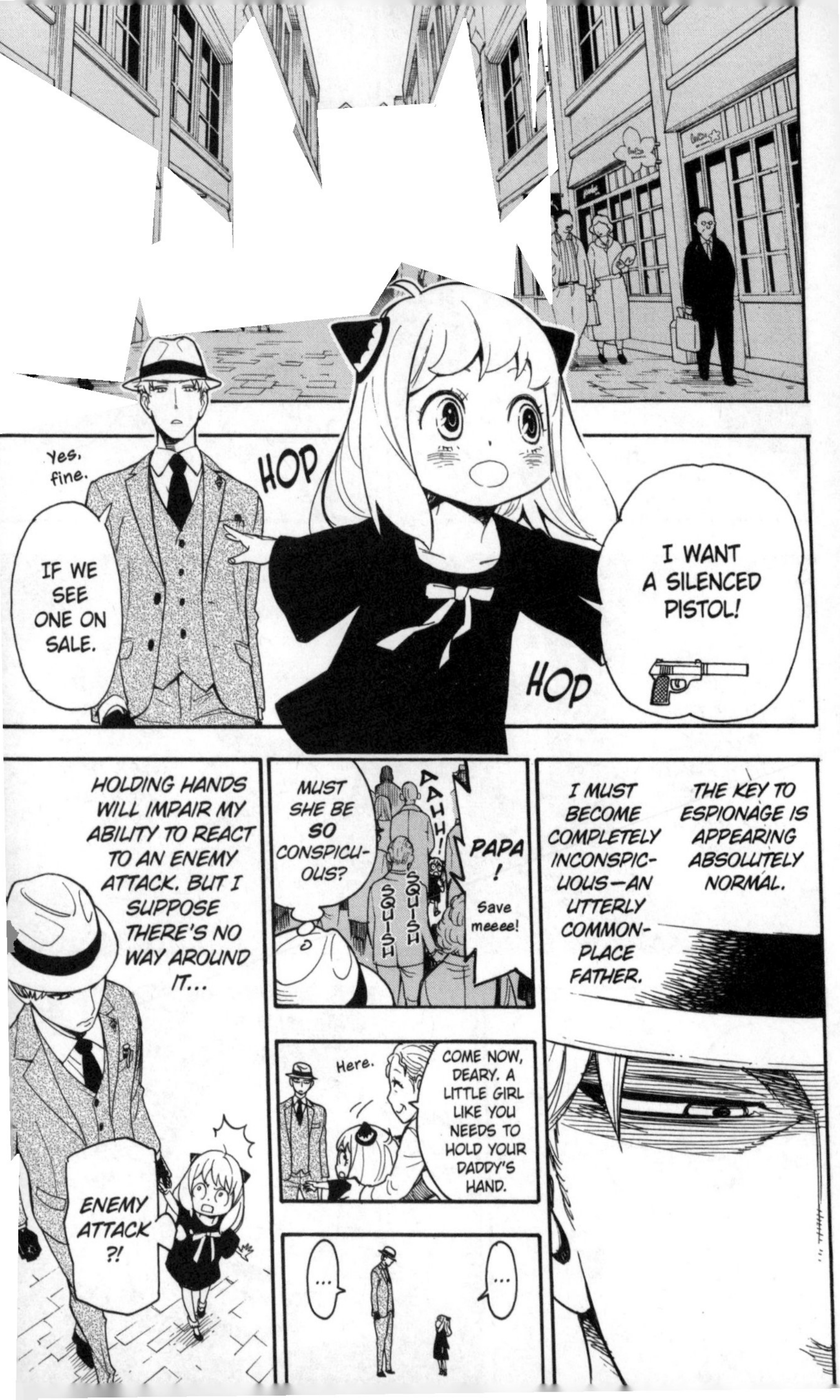
I WANT A SILENCED PISTOL!
HOP
HOP
Yes, fine.
IF WE SEE ONE ON SALE.
THE KEY TO ESPIONAGE IS APPEARING ABSOLUTELY NORMAL.
I MUST BECOME COMPLETELY INCONSPICUOUS—AN UTTERLY COMMONPLACE FATHER.
PAPA!
Save meeee!
AHHH!
SQUISH
SQUISH
MUST SHE BE SO CONSPICUOUS?
COME NOW, DEARY. A LITTLE GIRL LIKE YOU NEEDS TO HOLD YOUR DADDY'S HAND.
Here.
...
...
HOLDING HANDS WILL IMPAIR MY ABILITY TO REACT TO AN ENEMY ATTACK. BUT I SUPPOSE THERE'S NO WAY AROUND IT...
ENEMY ATTACK?!

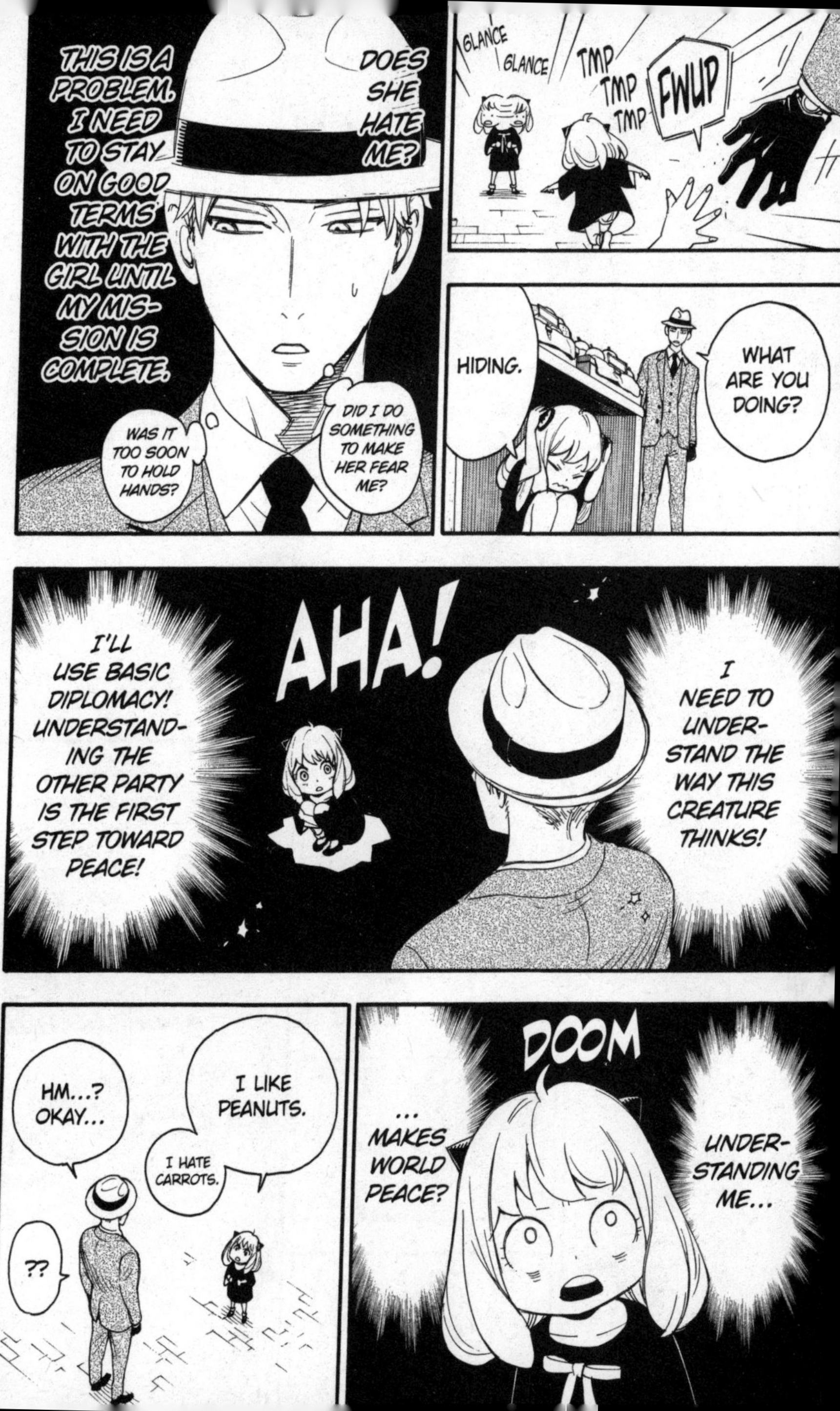
GLANCE
GLANCE
TMP
TMP
TMP
FWUP
WHAT ARE YOU DOING?
HIDING.
DOES SHE HATE ME?
THIS IS A PROBLEM. I NEED TO STAY ON GOOD TERMS WITH THE GIRL UNTIL MY MISSION IS COMPLETE.
DID I DO SOMETHING TO MAKE HER FEAR ME?
WAS IT TOO SOON TO HOLD HANDS?
I NEED TO UNDERSTAND THE WAY THIS CREATURE THINKS!
AHA!
I'LL USE BASIC DIPLOMACY! UNDERSTANDING THE OTHER PARTY IS THE FIRST STEP TOWARD PEACE!
DOOM
UNDERSTANDING ME...
...MAKES WORLD PEACE?
I LIKE PEANUTS.
HM...? OKAY...
I HATE CARROTS.
??

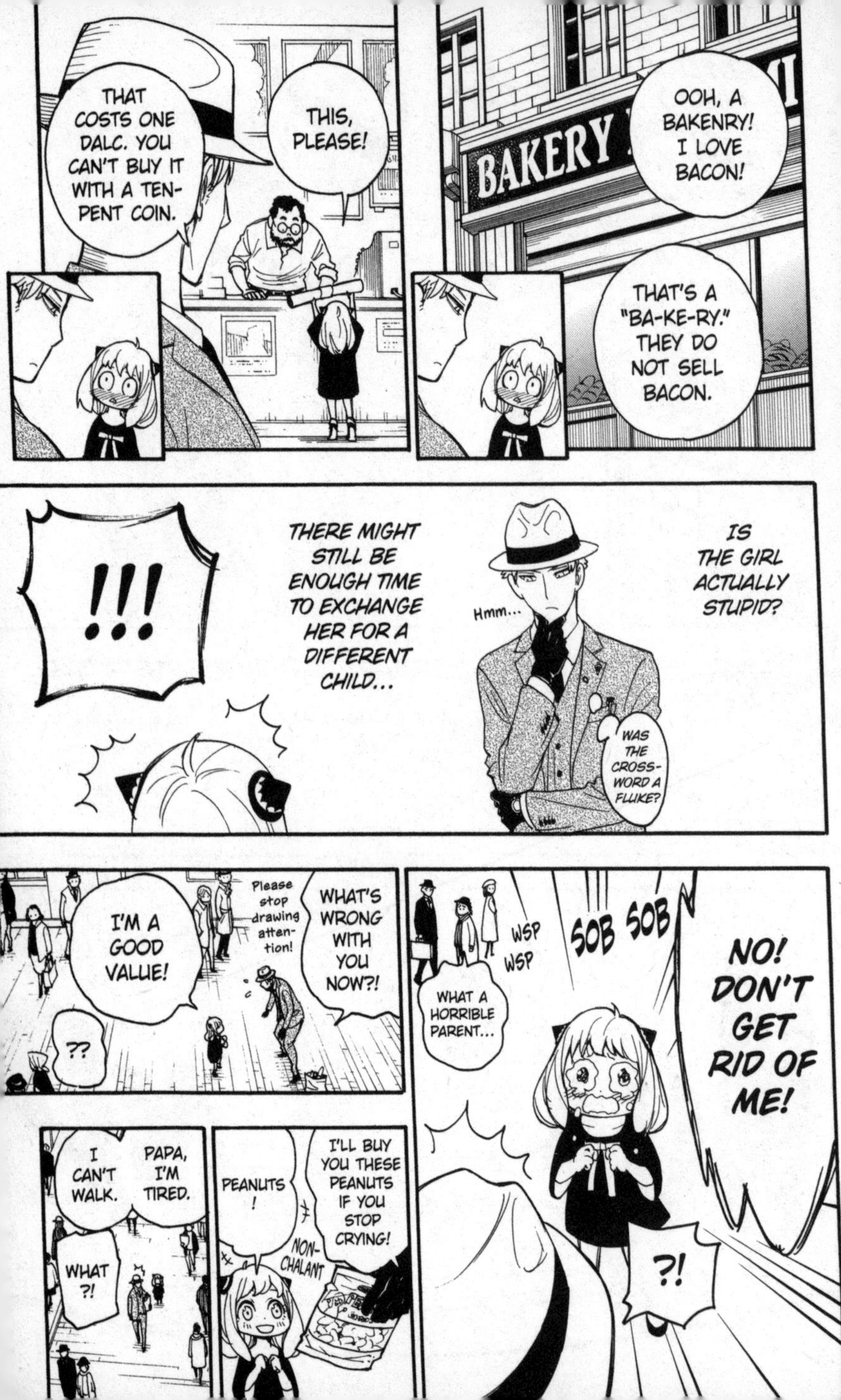

OOH, A BAKENRY! I LOVE BACON!
BAKERY
THAT'S A "BA-KE-RY." THEY DO NOT SELL BACON.
THIS, PLEASE!
THAT COSTS ONE DALC. YOU CAN'T BUY IT WITH A TEN-PENT COIN.
IS THE GIRL ACTUALLY STUPID?
Hmm...
WAS THE CROSS-WORD A FLUKE?
THERE MIGHT STILL BE ENOUGH TIME TO EXCHANGE HER FOR A DIFFERENT CHILD...
!!!
SOB SOB
NO! DON'T GET RID OF ME!
WSP WSP
WHAT A HORRIBLE PARENT...
?!
WHAT'S WRONG WITH YOU NOW?!
Please stop drawing attention!
I'M A GOOD VALUE!
??
I'LL BUY YOU THESE PEANUTS IF YOU STOP CRYING!
PEANUTS!
NON-CHALANT
PAPA, I'M TIRED.
I CAN'T WALK.
WHAT?!

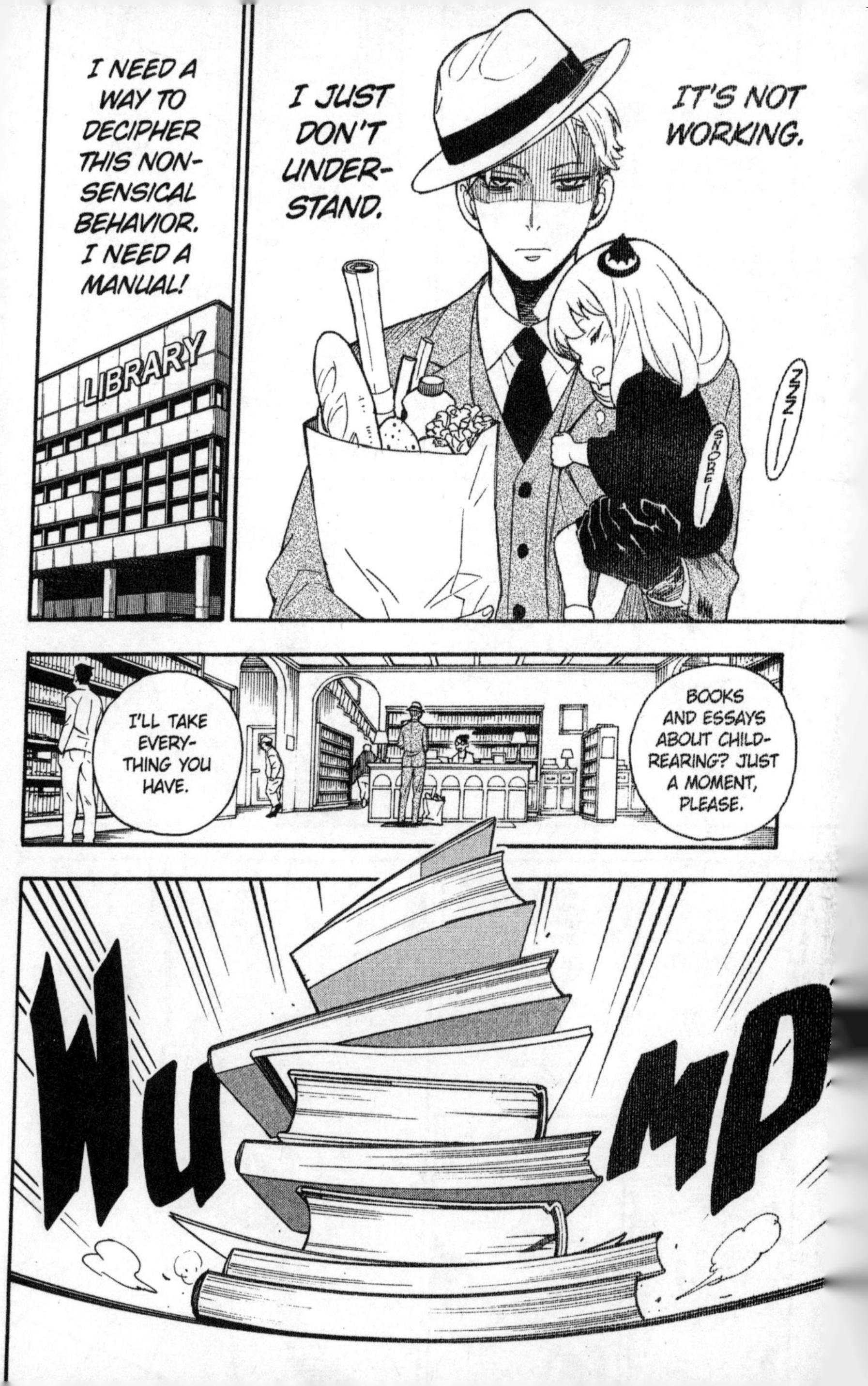
IT'S NOT WORKING.
I JUST DON'T UNDERSTAND.
ZZZ
SNORE
I NEED A WAY TO DECIPHER THIS NON-SENSICAL BEHAVIOR. I NEED A MANUAL!
LIBRARY
BOOKS AND ESSAYS ABOUT CHILD-REARING? JUST A MOMENT, PLEASE.
I'LL TAKE EVERY-THING YOU HAVE.
WUMP

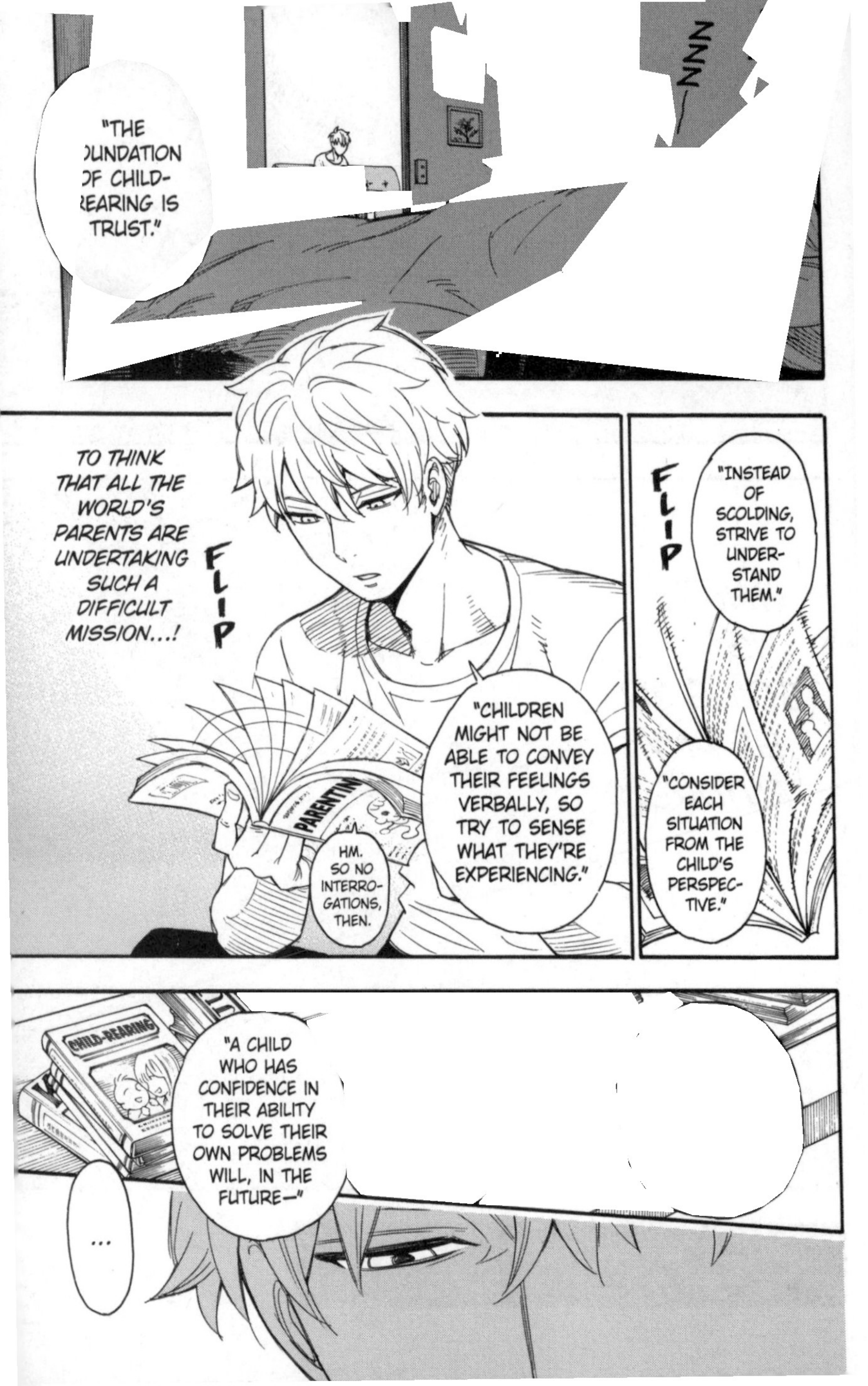
"THE OUNDATION OF CHILD-REARING IS TRUST."
"INSTEAD OF SCOLDING, STRIVE TO UNDER-STAND THEM."
FLIP
"CONSIDER EACH SITUATION FROM THE CHILD'S PERSPEC-TIVE."
TO THINK THAT ALL THE WORLD'S PARENTS ARE UNDERTAKING SUCH A DIFFICULT MISSION...!
FLIP
"CHILDREN MIGHT NOT BE ABLE TO CONVEY THEIR FEELINGS VERBALLY, SO TRY TO SENSE WHAT THEY'RE EXPERIENCING."
PARENTIN
HM. SO NO INTERRO-GATIONS, THEN.
"A CHILD WHO HAS CONFIDENCE IN THEIR ABILITY TO SOLVE THEIR OWN PROBLEMS WILL, IN THE FUTURE—"
CHILD-REARING
...

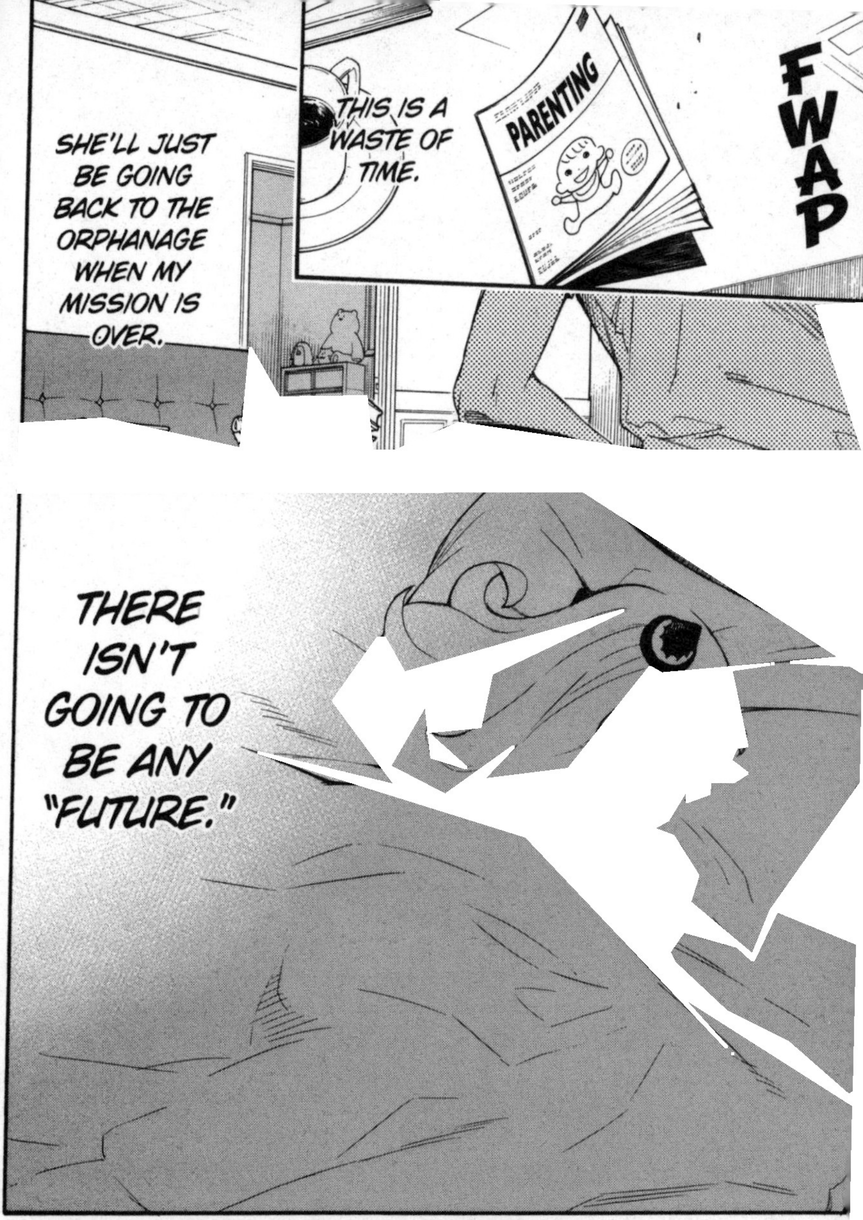
FWAP
PARENTING
THIS IS A WASTE OF TIME.
SHE'LL JUST BE GOING BACK TO THE ORPHANAGE WHEN MY MISSION IS OVER.
THERE ISN'T GOING TO BE ANY "FUTURE."

[redacted]

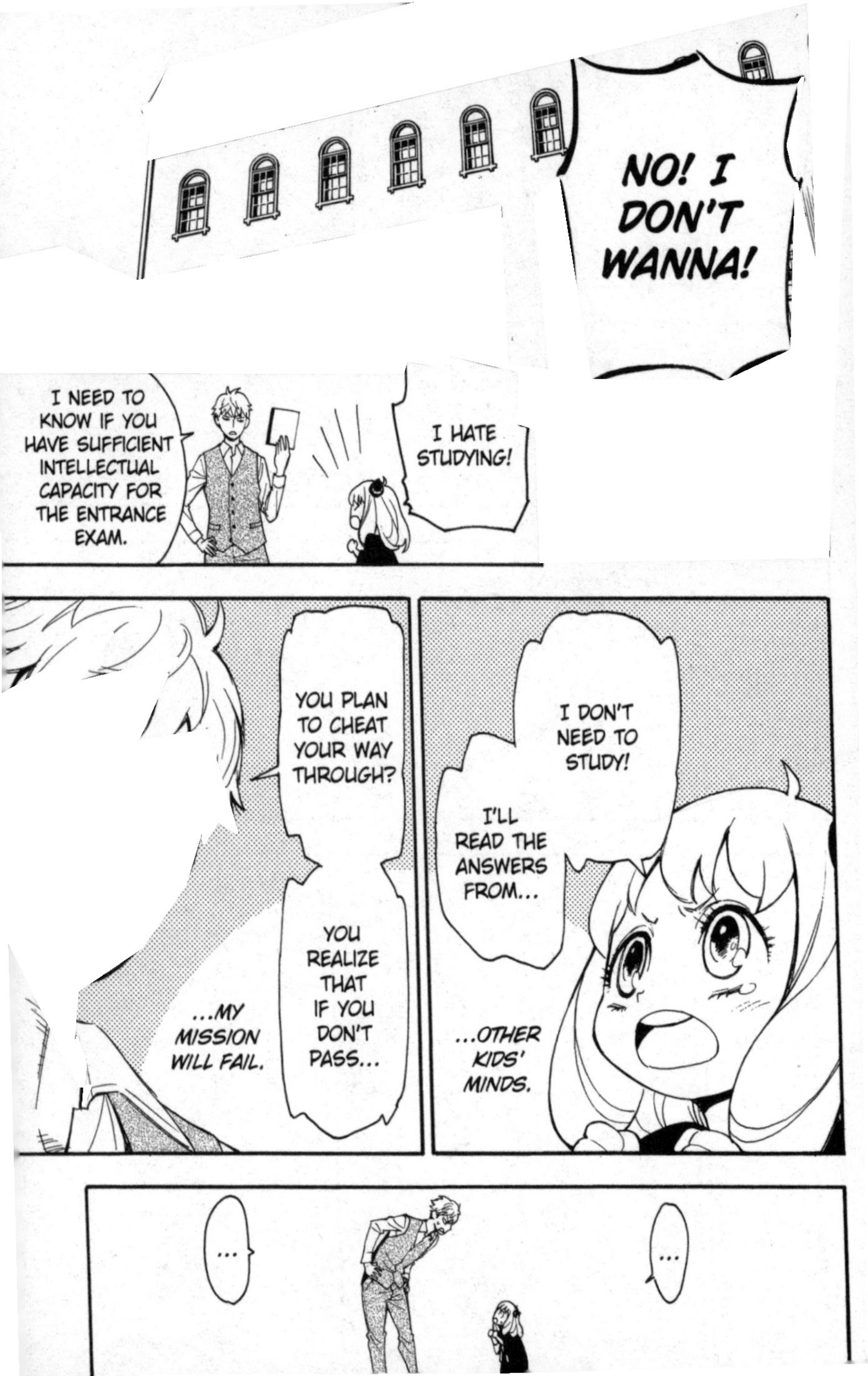
NO! I DON'T WANNA!
I HATE STUDYING!
I NEED TO KNOW IF YOU HAVE SUFFICIENT INTELLECTUAL CAPACITY FOR THE ENTRANCE EXAM.
I DON'T NEED TO STUDY!
I'LL READ THE ANSWERS FROM...
...OTHER KIDS' MINDS.
YOU PLAN TO CHEAT YOUR WAY THROUGH?
YOU REALIZE THAT IF YOU DON'T PASS...
...MY MISSION WILL FAIL.
...
...

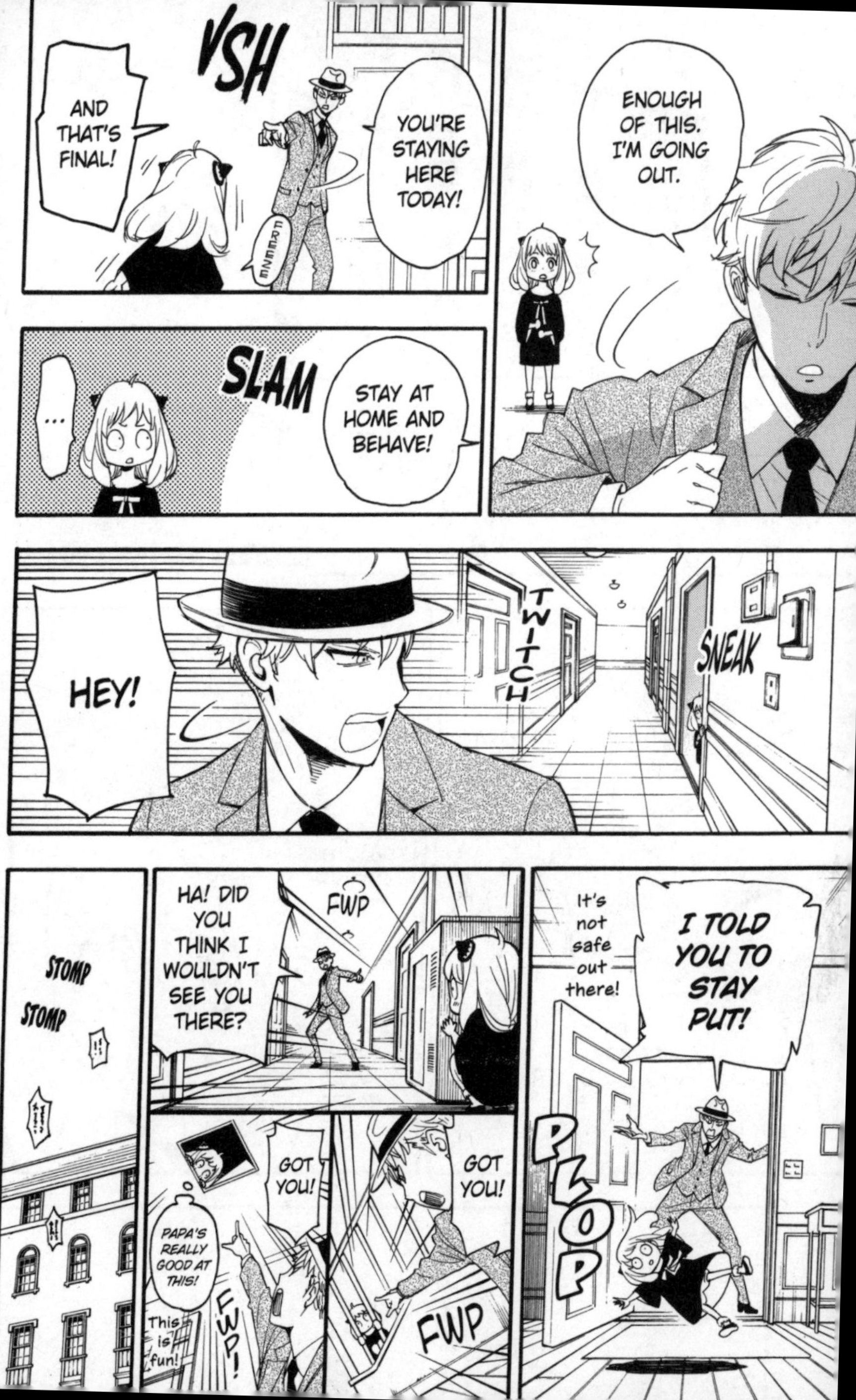
ENOUGH OF THIS. I'M GOING OUT.
YOU'RE STAYING HERE TODAY!
VSH
FREEZE
AND THAT'S FINAL!
STAY AT HOME AND BEHAVE!
SLAM
...
SNEAK
TWITCH
HEY!
I TOLD YOU TO STAY PUT!
It's not safe out there!
PLOP
FWP
HA! DID YOU THINK I WOULDN'T SEE YOU THERE?
GOT YOU!
FWP
GOT YOU!
FWP!
PAPA'S REALLY GOOD AT THIS!
This is fun!
STOMP
STOMP

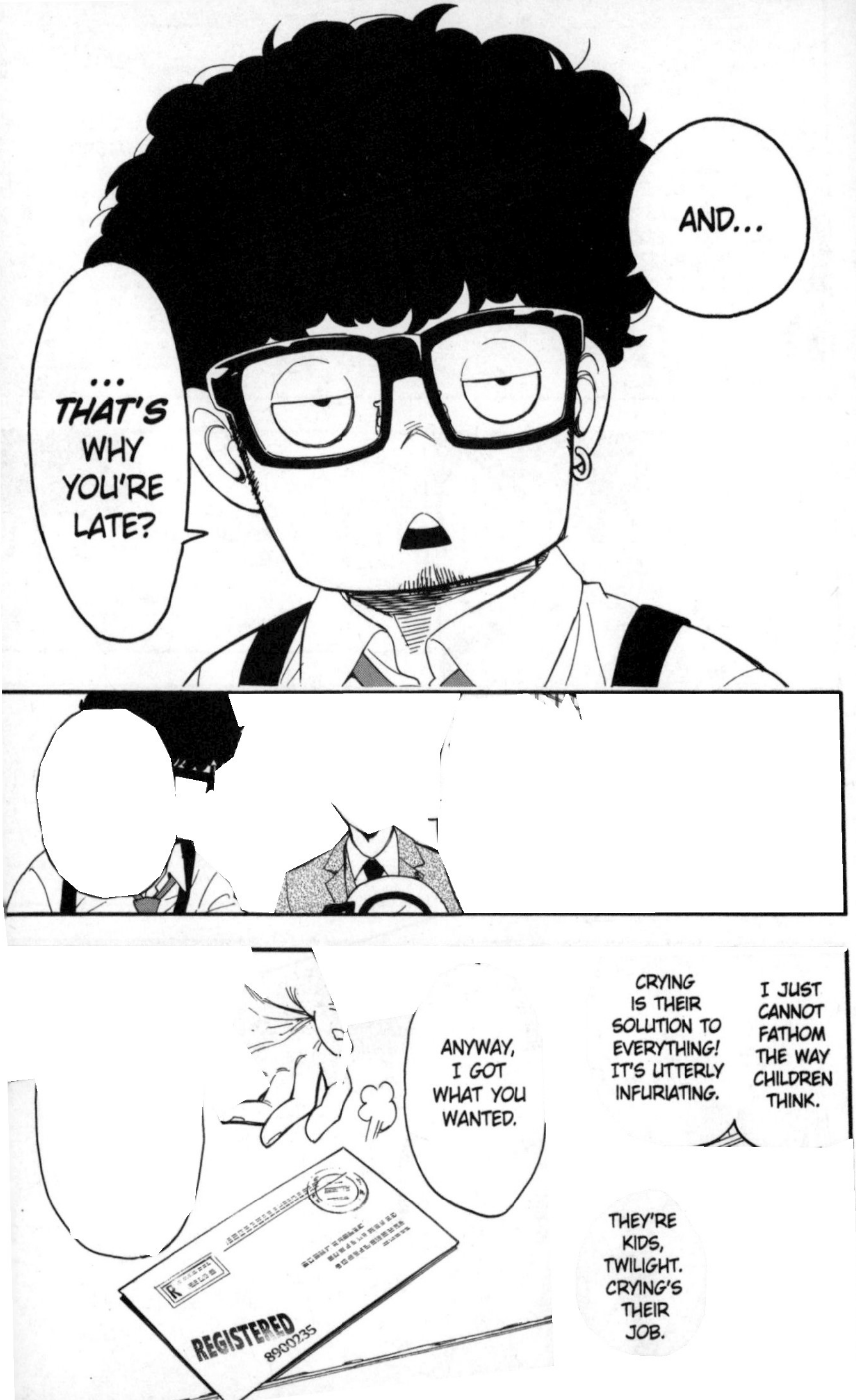
AND...
...THAT'S WHY YOU'RE LATE?
I JUST CANNOT FATHOM THE WAY CHILDREN THINK.
CRYING IS THEIR SOLUTION TO EVERYTHING! IT'S UTTERLY INFURIATING.
THEY'RE KIDS, TWILIGHT. CRYING'S THEIR JOB.
ANYWAY, I GOT WHAT YOU WANTED.
REGISTERED
8900235

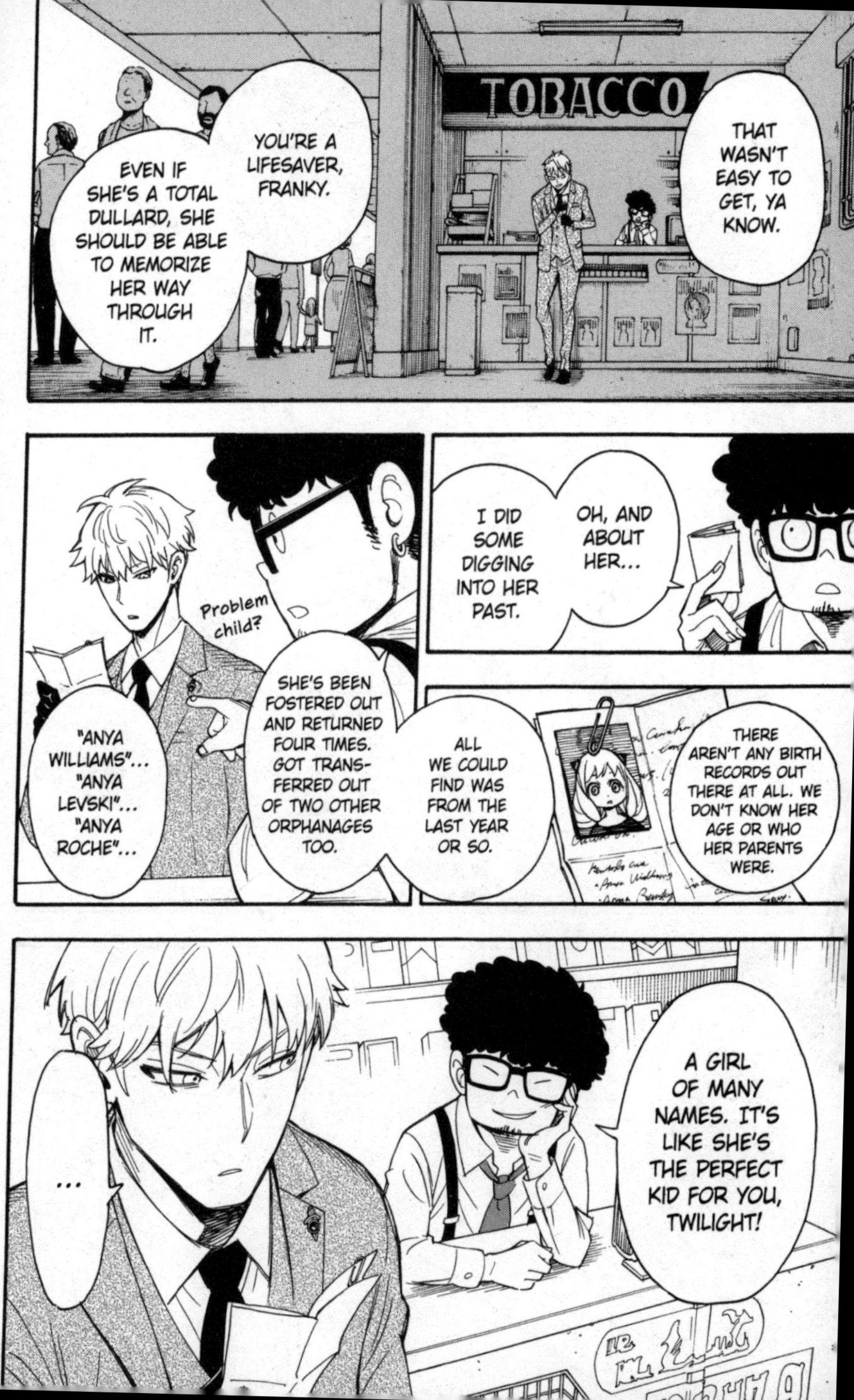
TOBACCO
THAT WASN'T EASY TO GET, YA KNOW.
YOU'RE A LIFESAVER, FRANKY.
EVEN IF SHE'S A TOTAL DULLARD, SHE SHOULD BE ABLE TO MEMORIZE HER WAY THROUGH IT.
OH, AND ABOUT HER...
I DID SOME DIGGING INTO HER PAST.
THERE AREN'T ANY BIRTH RECORDS OUT THERE AT ALL. WE DON'T KNOW HER AGE OR WHO HER PARENTS WERE.
ALL WE COULD FIND WAS FROM THE LAST YEAR OR SO.
Problem child?
SHE'S BEEN FOSTERED OUT AND RETURNED FOUR TIMES. GOT TRANSFERRED OUT OF TWO OTHER ORPHANAGES TOO.
"ANYA WILLIAMS"... "ANYA LEVSKI"... "ANYA ROCHE"...
A GIRL OF MANY NAMES. IT'S LIKE SHE'S THE PERFECT KID FOR YOU, TWILIGHT!
...

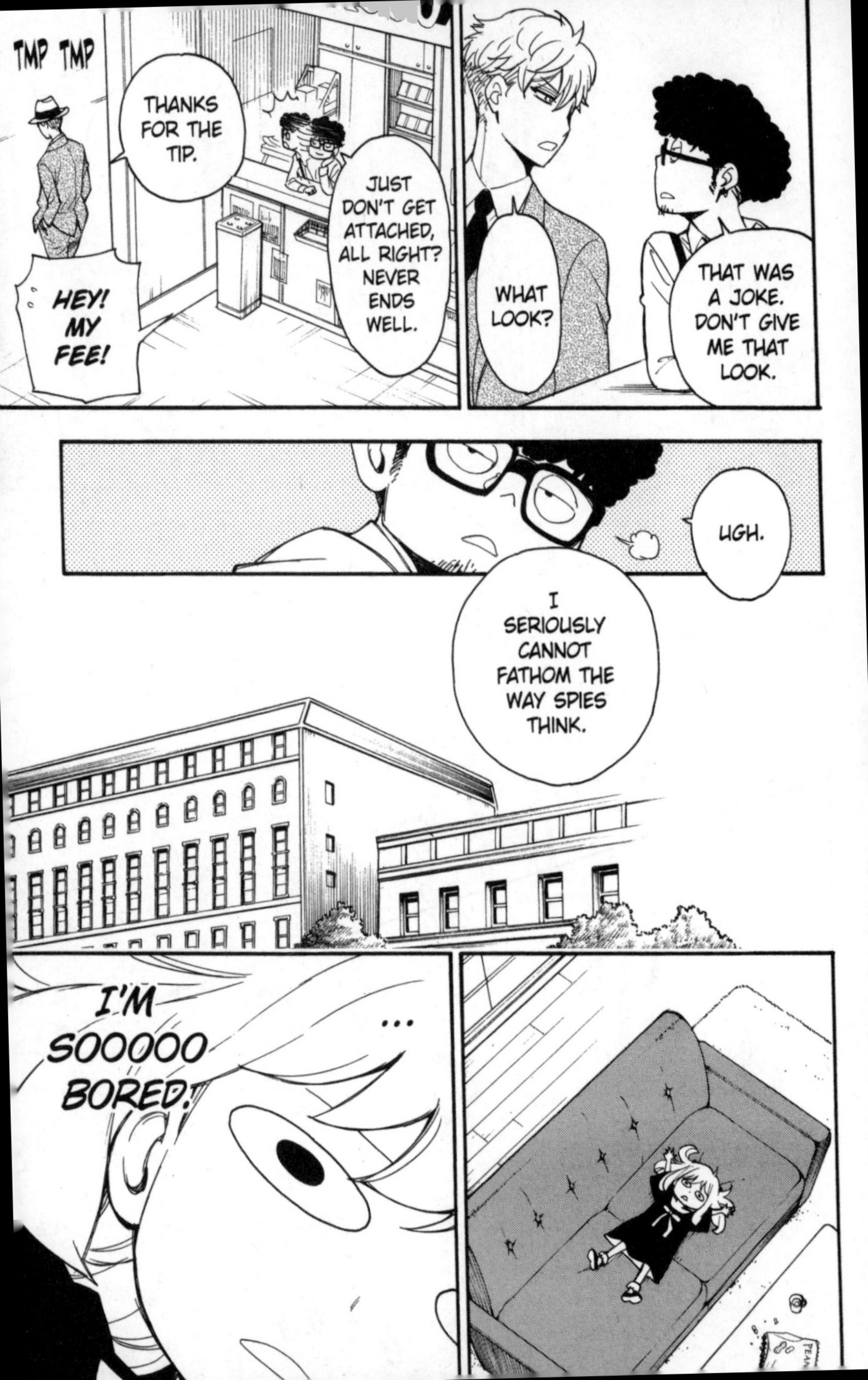
THAT WAS A JOKE. DON'T GIVE ME THAT LOOK.
WHAT LOOK?
JUST DON'T GET ATTACHED, ALL RIGHT? NEVER ENDS WELL.
THANKS FOR THE TIP.
TMP TMP
HEY! MY FEE!
UGH.
I SERIOUSLY CANNOT FATHOM THE WAY SPIES THINK.
...
I'M SOOOOO BORED!

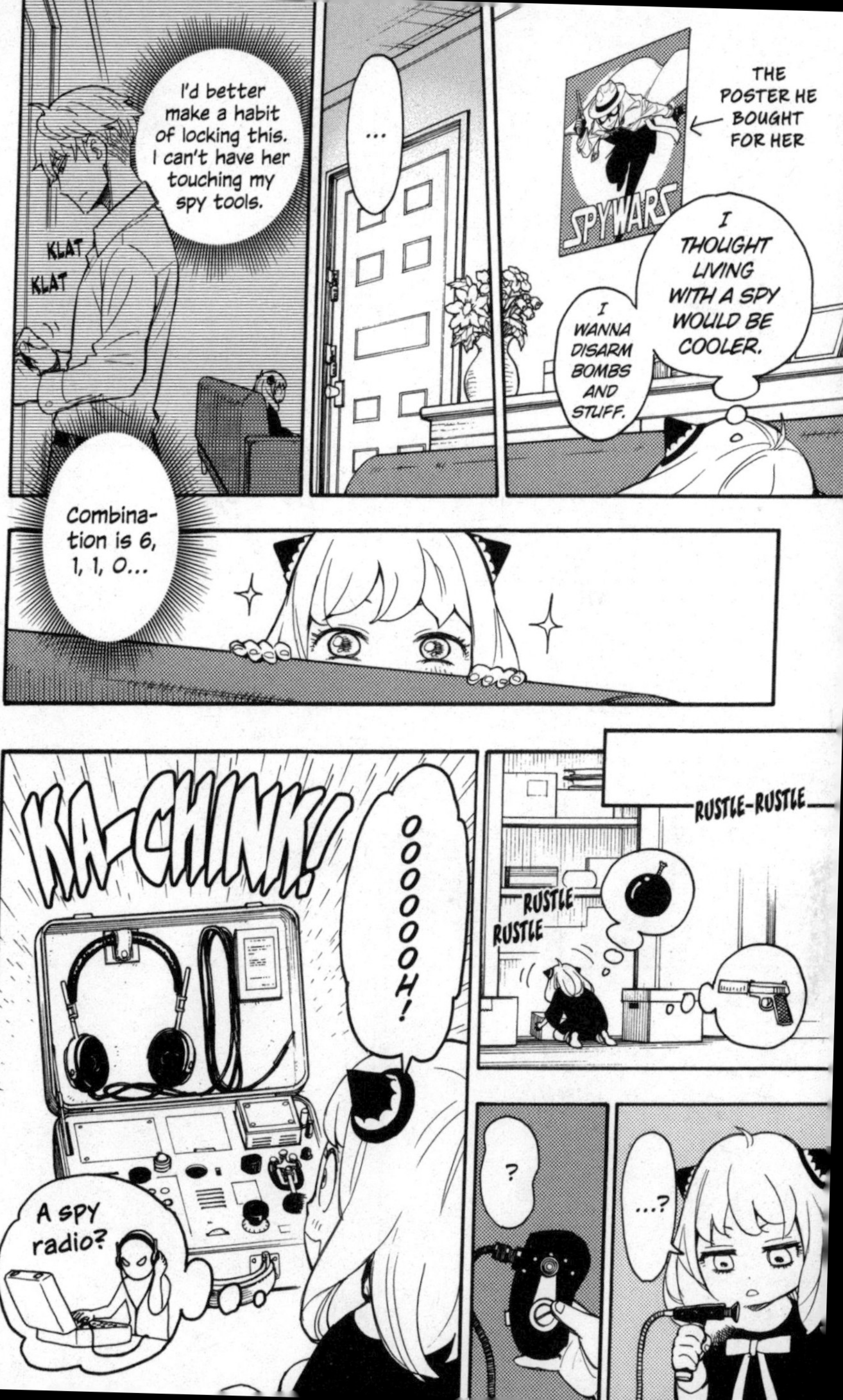
THE POSTER HE BOUGHT FOR HER
SPYWARS
I THOUGHT LIVING WITH A SPY WOULD BE COOLER.
I WANNA DISARM BOMBS AND STUFF.
...
I'd better make a habit of locking this. I can't have her touching my spy tools.
KLAT
KLAT
Combination is 6, 1, 1, 0...
RUSTLE-RUSTLE
RUSTLE
RUSTLE
...?
?
KA-CHINK!
OOOOOOOH!
A spy radio?

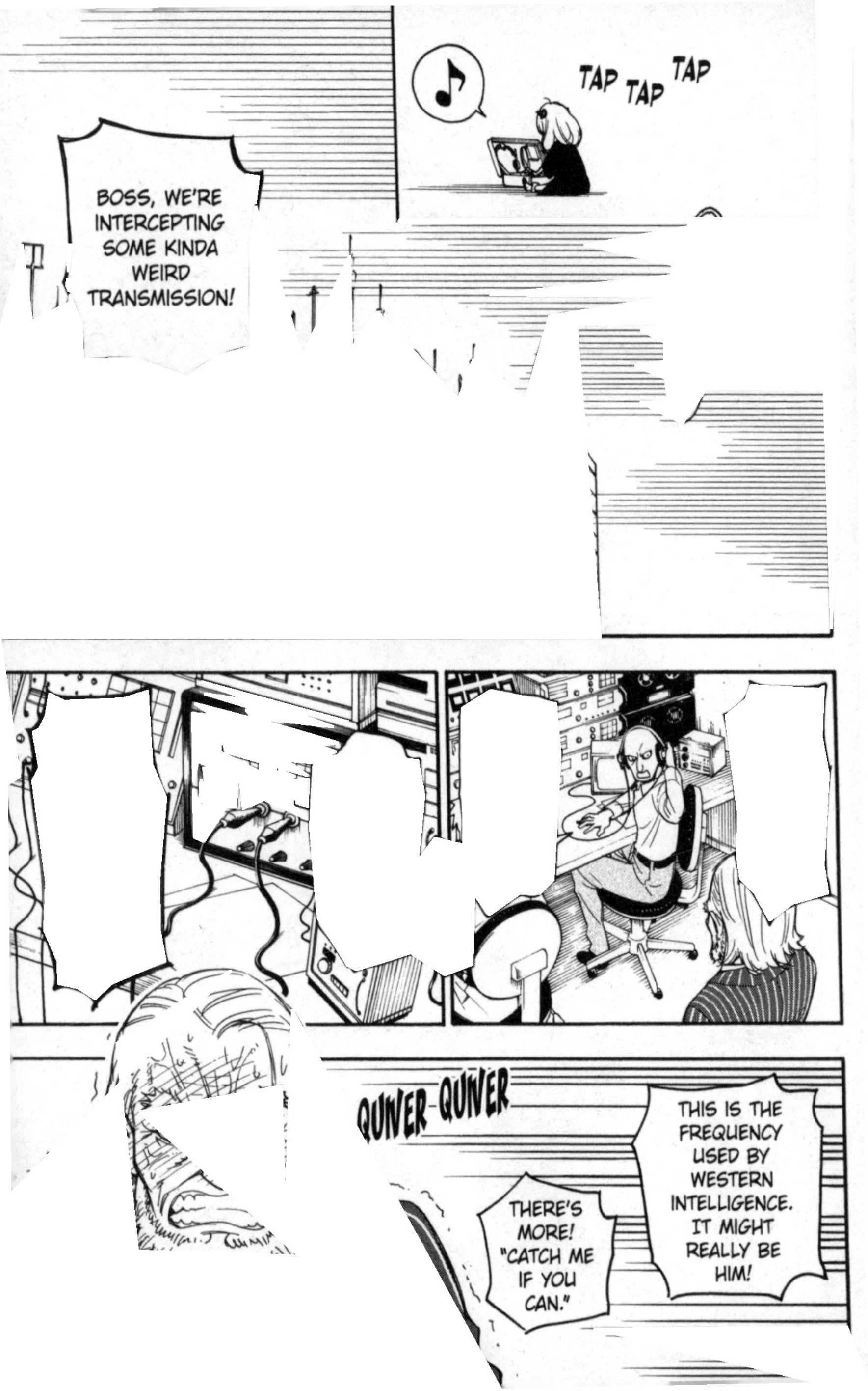
♪
TAP TAP TAP
BOSS, WE'RE INTERCEPTING SOME KINDA WEIRD TRANSMISSION!
THIS IS THE FREQUENCY USED BY WESTERN INTELLIGENCE. IT MIGHT REALLY BE HIM!
THERE'S MORE! "CATCH ME IF YOU CAN."
QUIVER-QUIVER

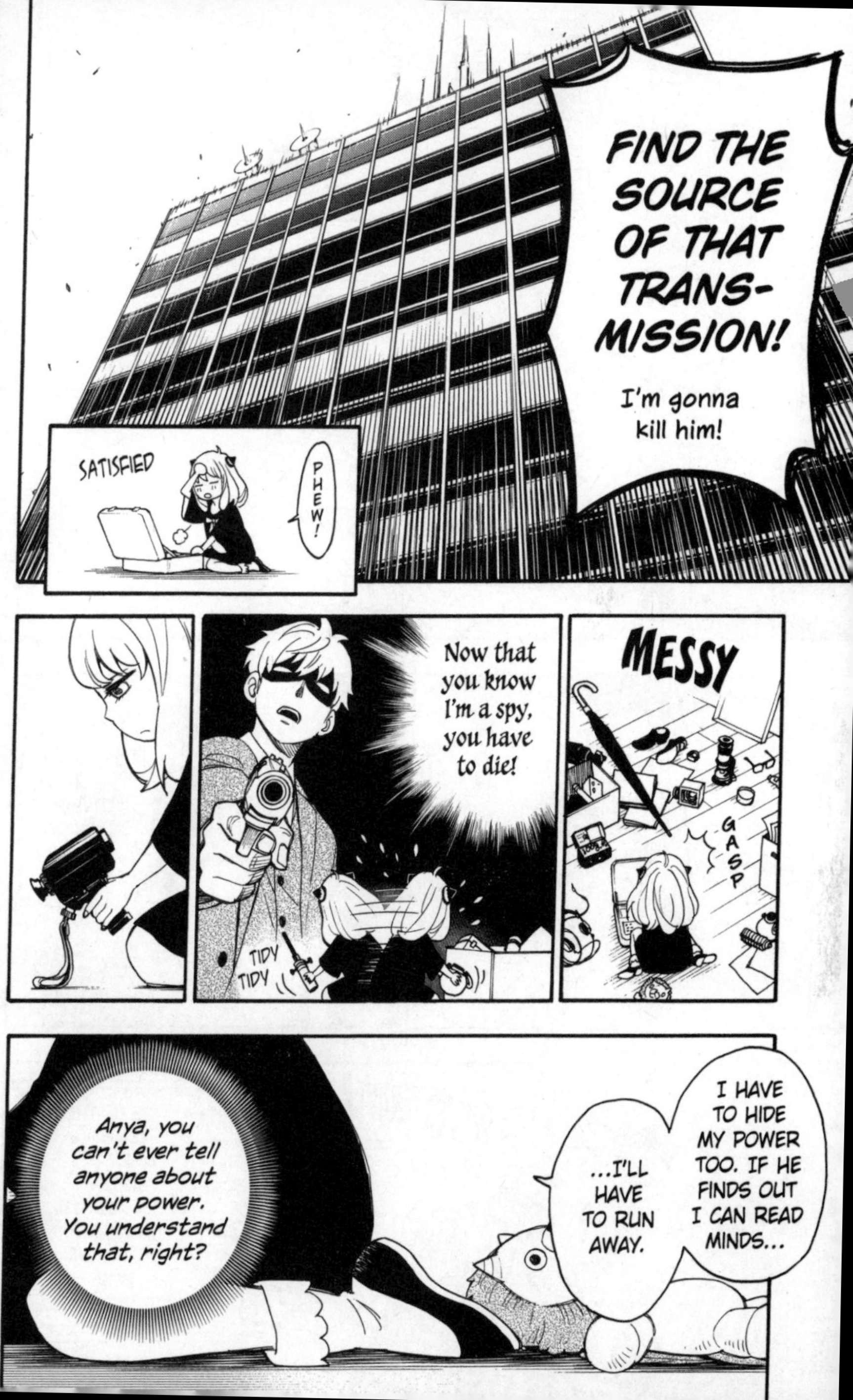
FIND THE SOURCE OF THAT TRANS-MISSION!
I'm gonna kill him!
PHEW!
SATISFIED
MESSY
GASP
Now that you know I'm a spy, you have to die!
TIDY TIDY
I HAVE TO HIDE MY POWER TOO. IF HE FINDS OUT I CAN READ MINDS...
...I'LL HAVE TO RUN AWAY.
Anya, you can't ever tell anyone about your power. You understand that, right?

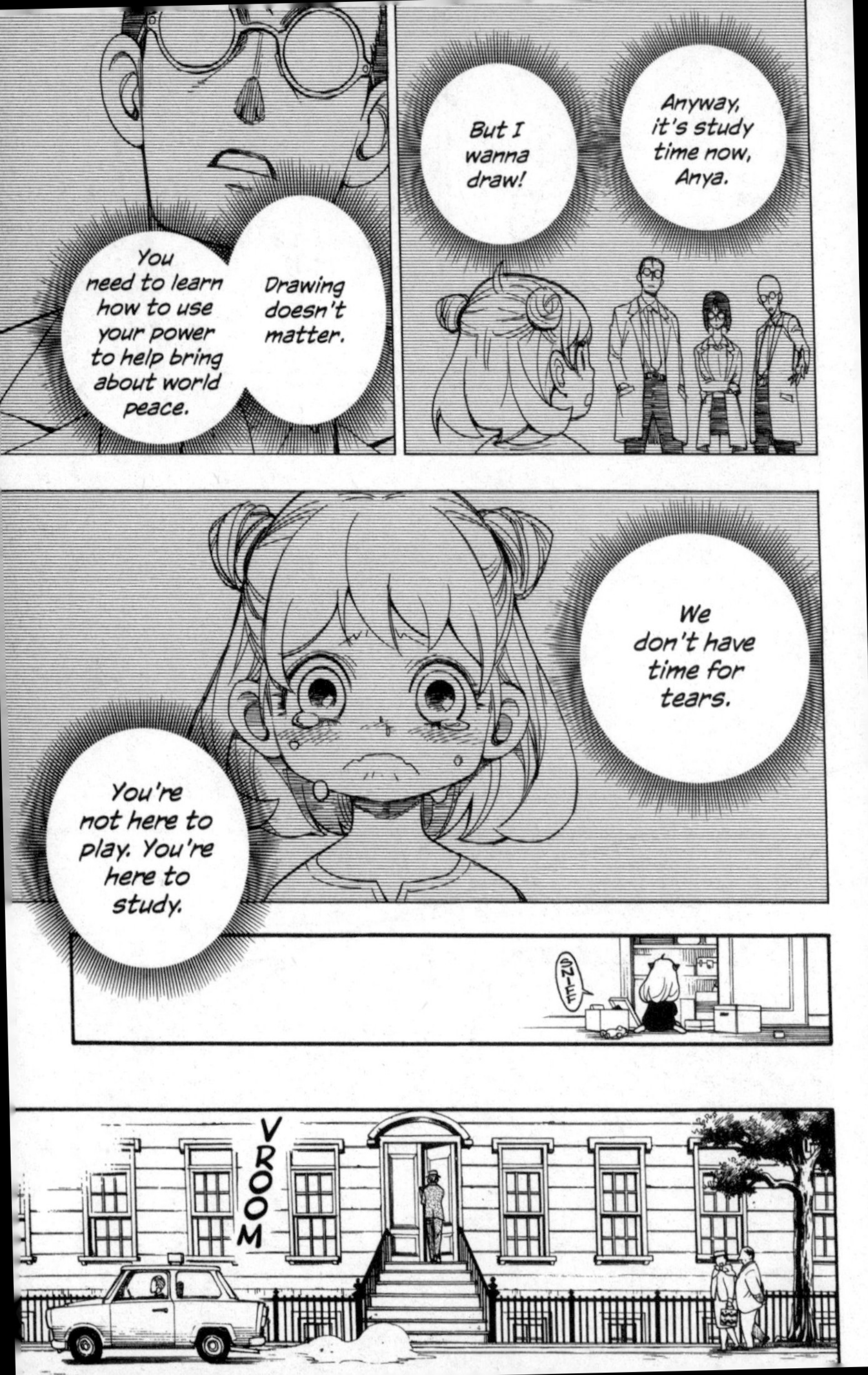
Anyway, it's study time now, Anya.
But I wanna draw!
Drawing doesn't matter.
You need to learn how to use your power to help bring about world peace.
We don't have time for tears.
You're not here to play. You're here to study.
SNIFF
VROOM

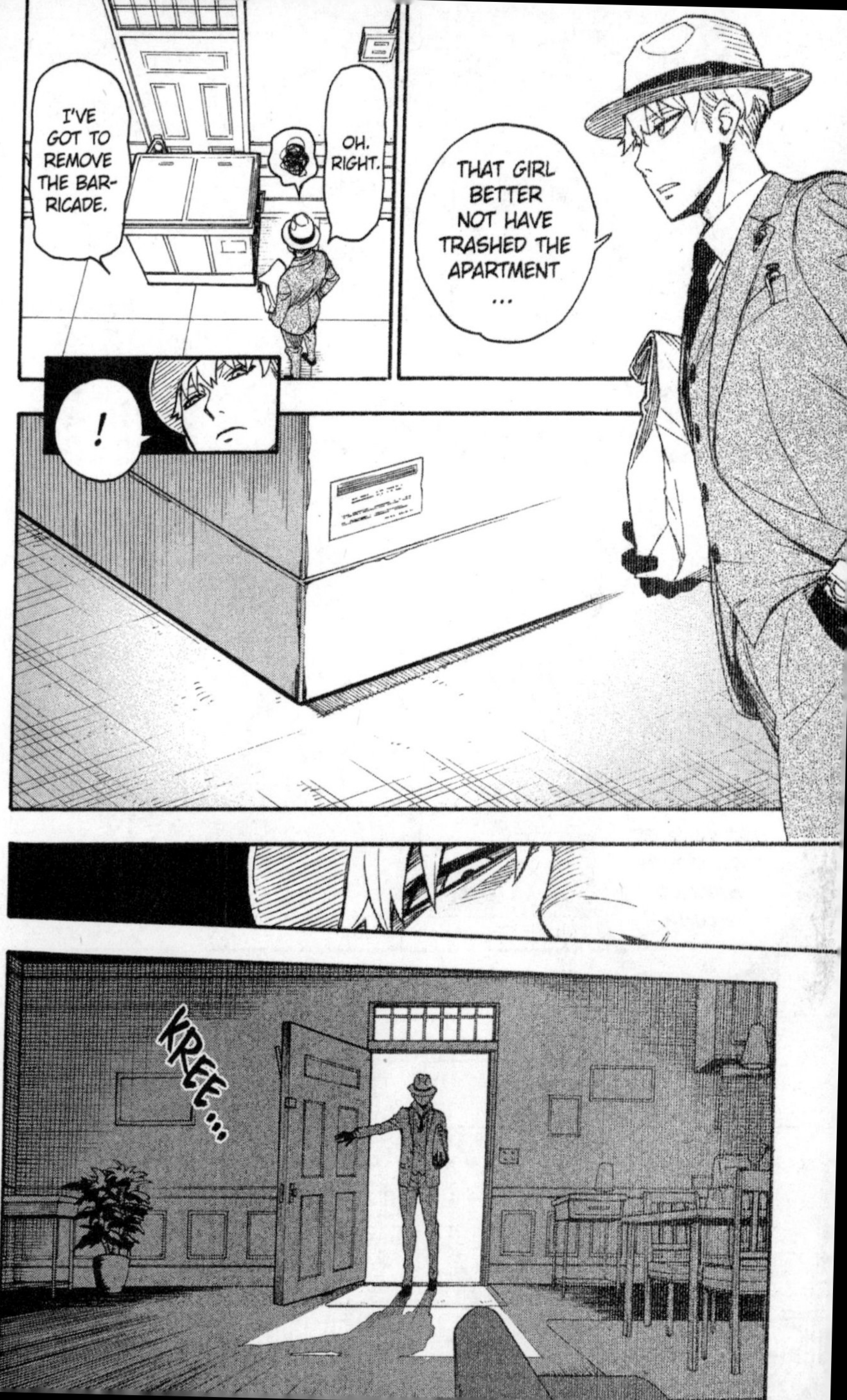
THAT GIRL BETTER NOT HAVE TRASHED THE APARTMENT ...
OH. RIGHT.
I'VE GOT TO REMOVE THE BAR-RICADE.
!
KREE...

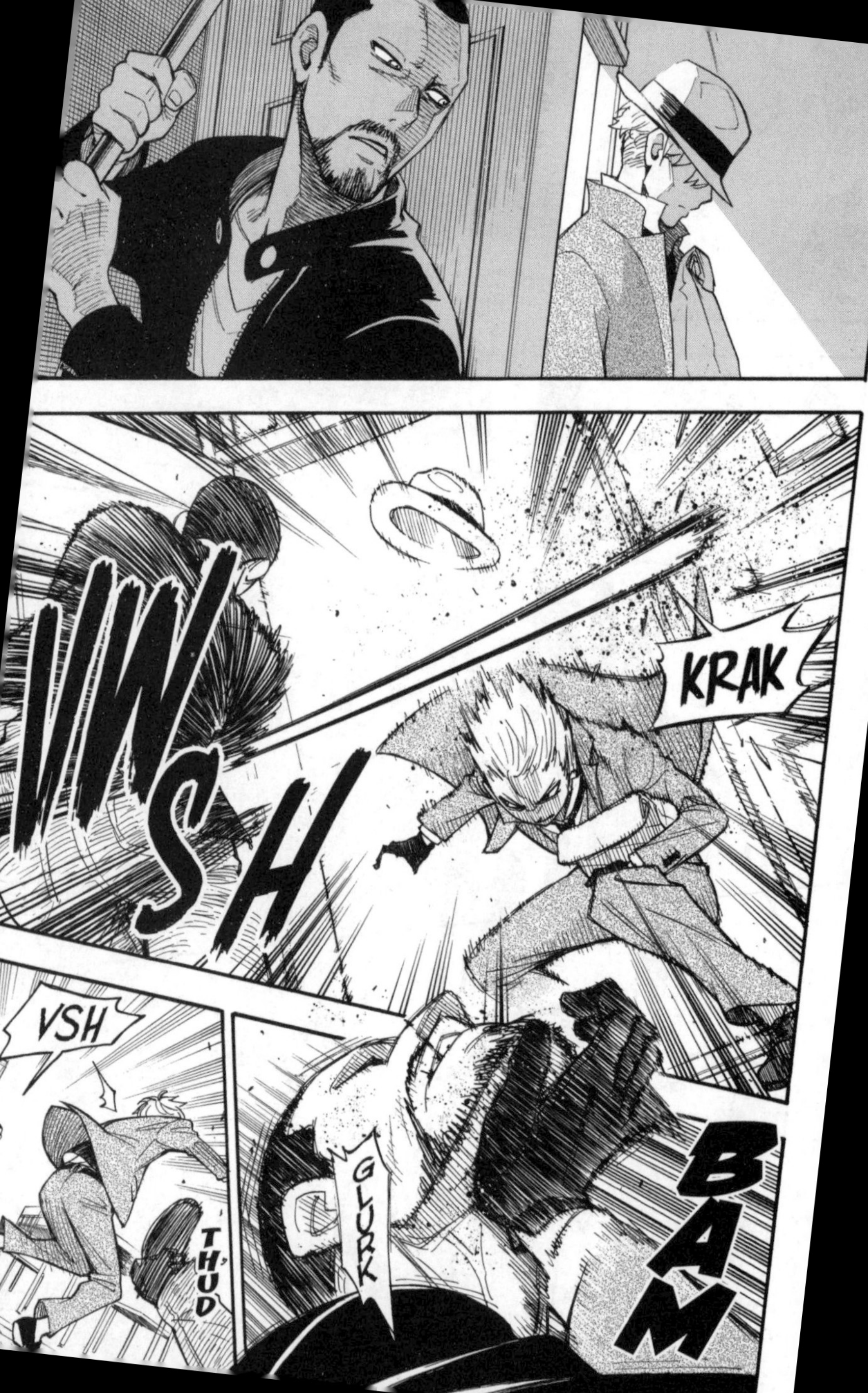
KRAK
WWSH
BAM
GLURK
VSH
THUD

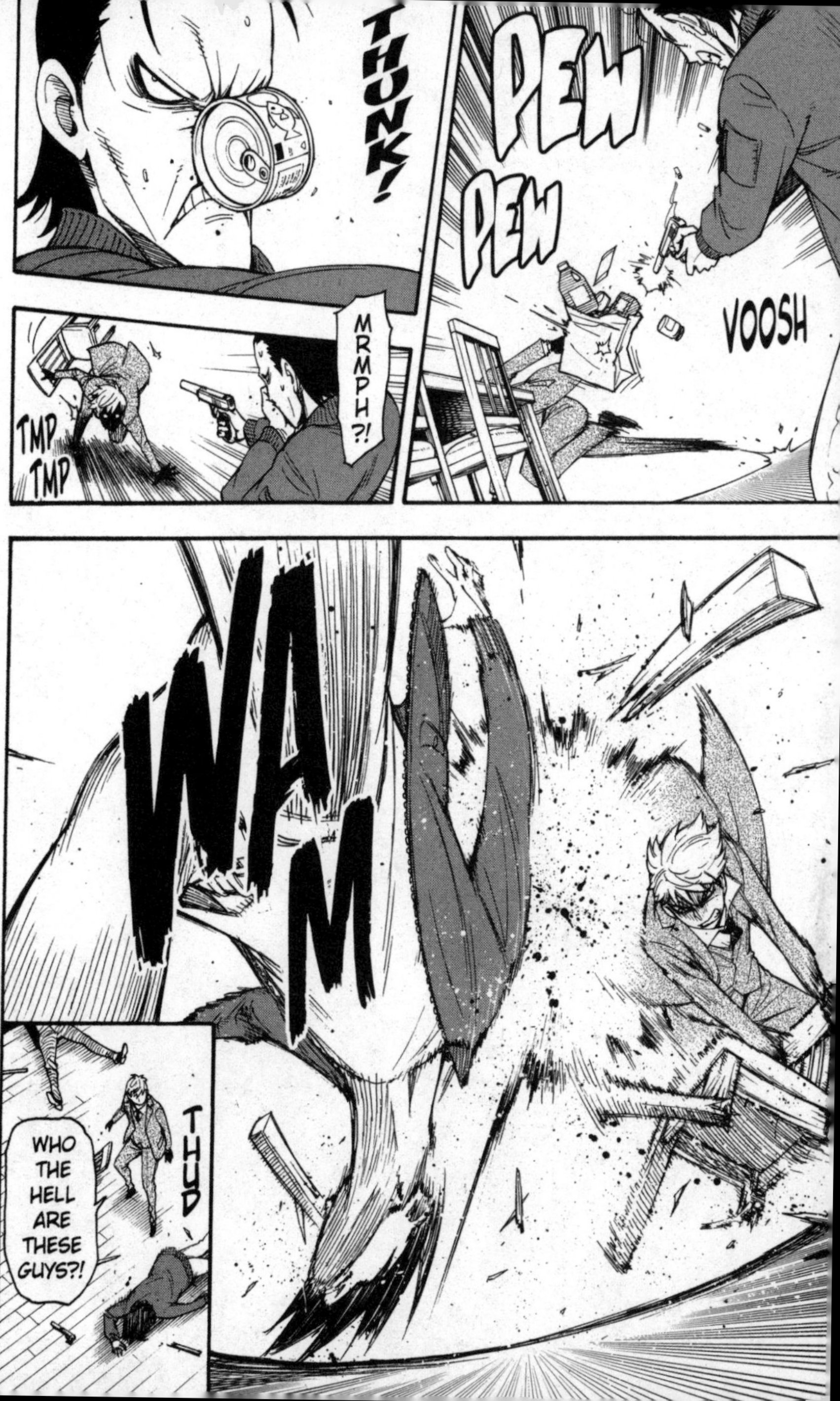
PEW
PEW
VOOSH
THUNK!
MRMPH?!
TMP TMP
WAM
THUD
WHO THE HELL ARE THESE GUYS?!

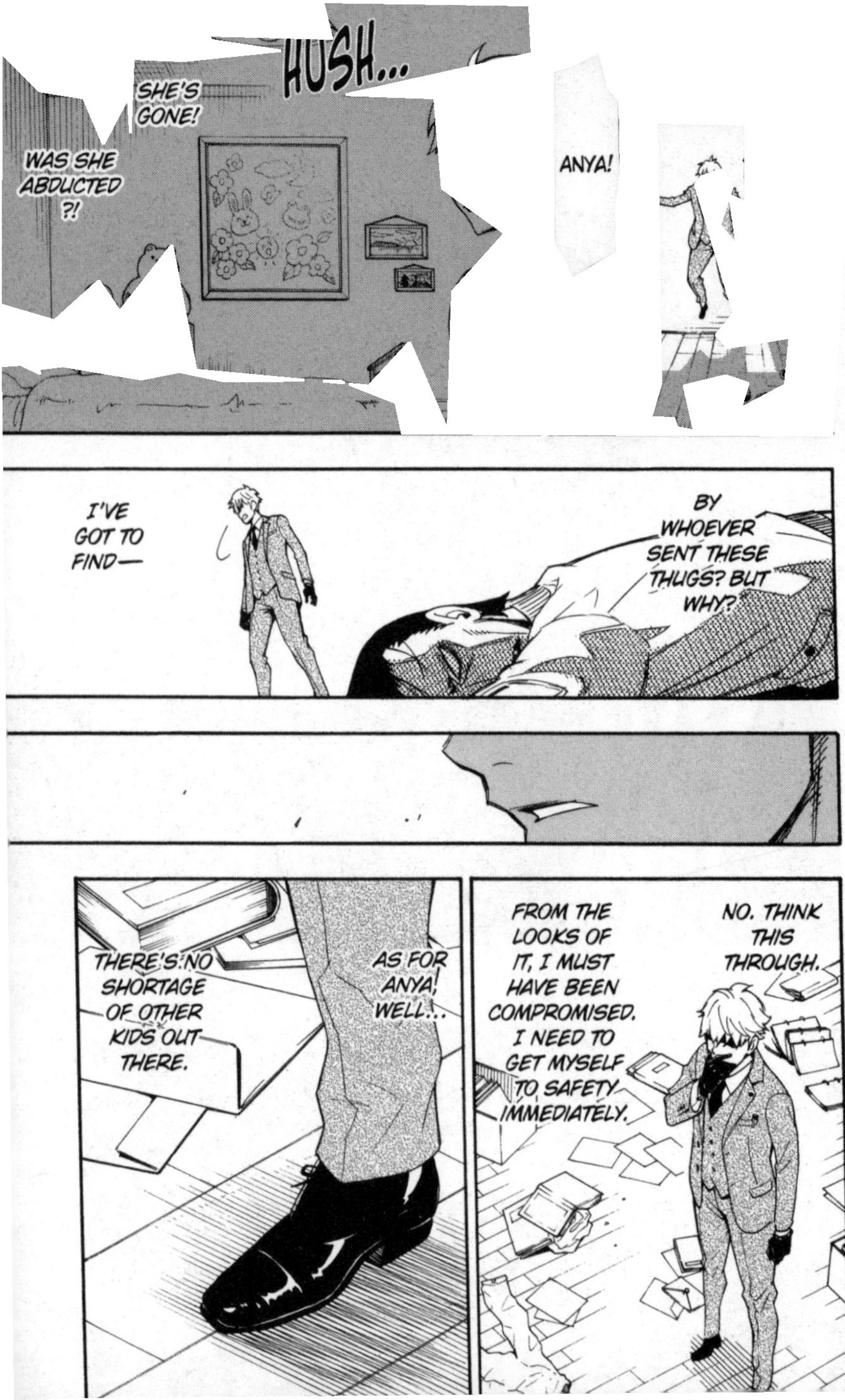
ANYA!
HUSH...
SHE'S GONE!
WAS SHE ABDUCTED ?!
BY WHOEVER SENT THESE THUGS? BUT WHY?
I'VE GOT TO FIND—
NO. THINK THIS THROUGH.
FROM THE LOOKS OF IT, I MUST HAVE BEEN COMPROMISED. I NEED TO GET MYSELF TO SAFETY IMMEDIATELY.
AS FOR ANYA, WELL...
THERE'S NO SHORTAGE OF OTHER KIDS OUT THERE.

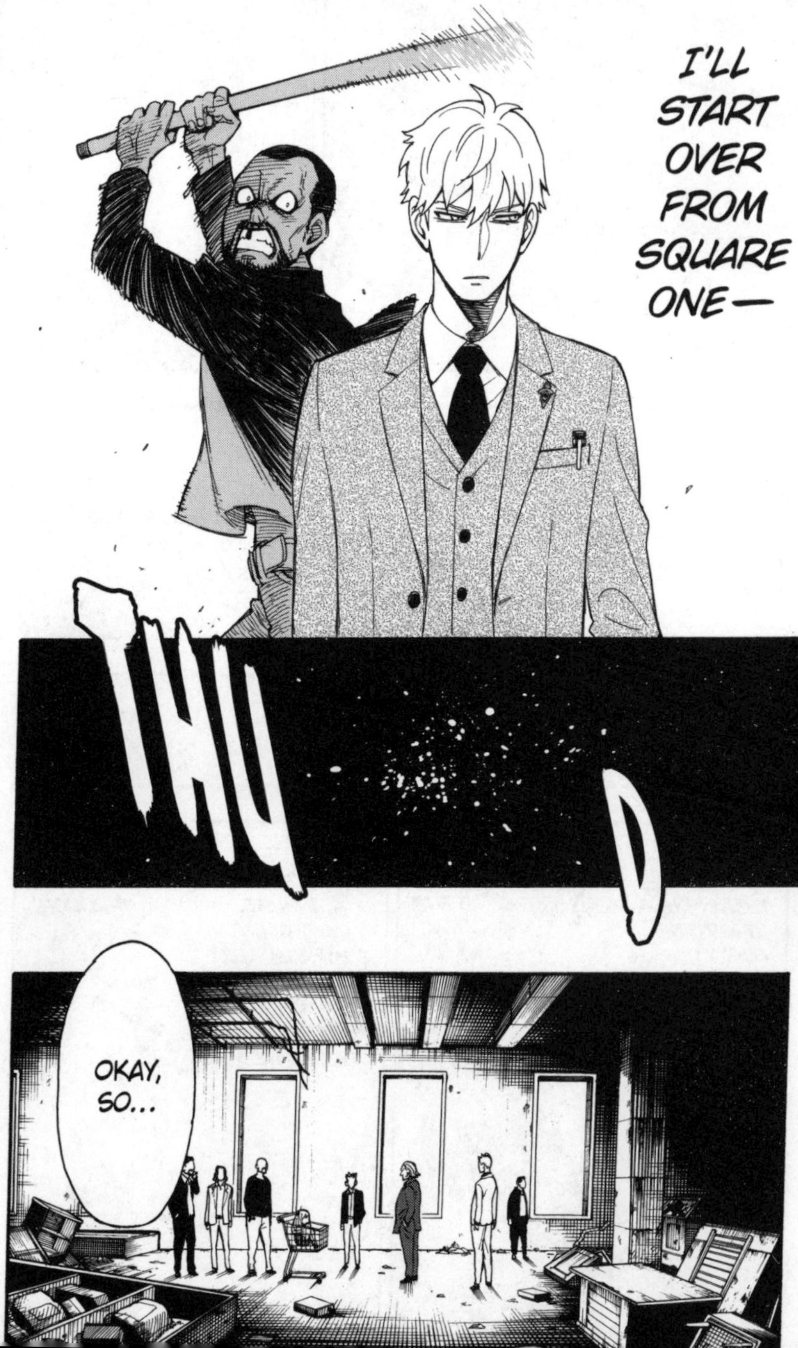
I'LL START OVER FROM SQUARE ONE—
THUD
OKAY, SO...

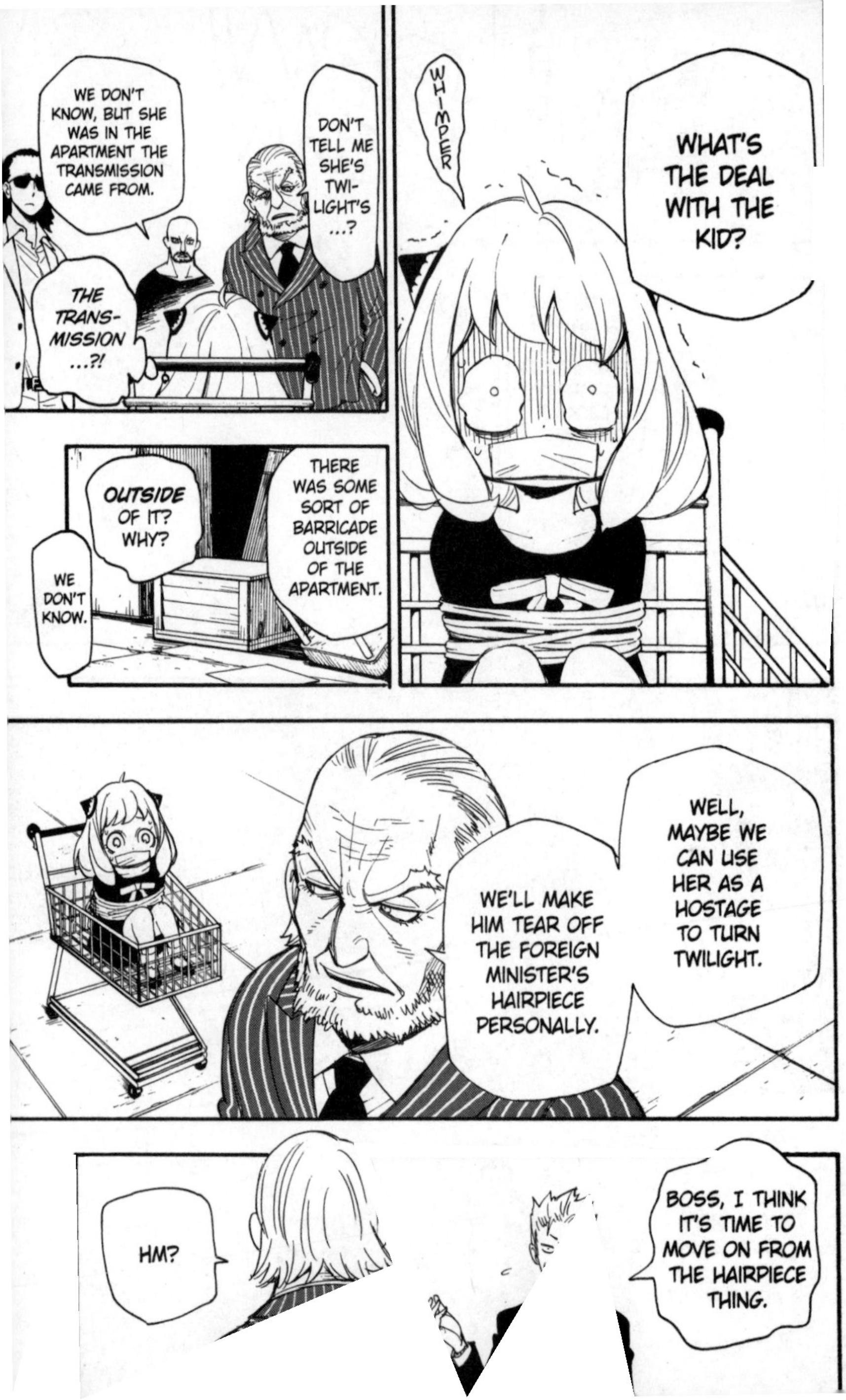
WHIMPER
WHAT'S THE DEAL WITH THE KID?
DON'T TELL ME SHE'S TWI-LIGHT'S ...?
WE DON'T KNOW, BUT SHE WAS IN THE APARTMENT THE TRANSMISSION CAME FROM.
THE TRANS-MISSION ...?!
THERE WAS SOME SORT OF BARRICADE OUTSIDE OF THE APARTMENT.
OUTSIDE OF IT? WHY?
WE DON'T KNOW.
WELL, MAYBE WE CAN USE HER AS A HOSTAGE TO TURN TWILIGHT.
WE'LL MAKE HIM TEAR OFF THE FOREIGN MINISTER'S HAIRPIECE PERSONALLY.
BOSS, I THINK IT'S TIME TO MOVE ON FROM THE HAIRPIECE THING.
HM?

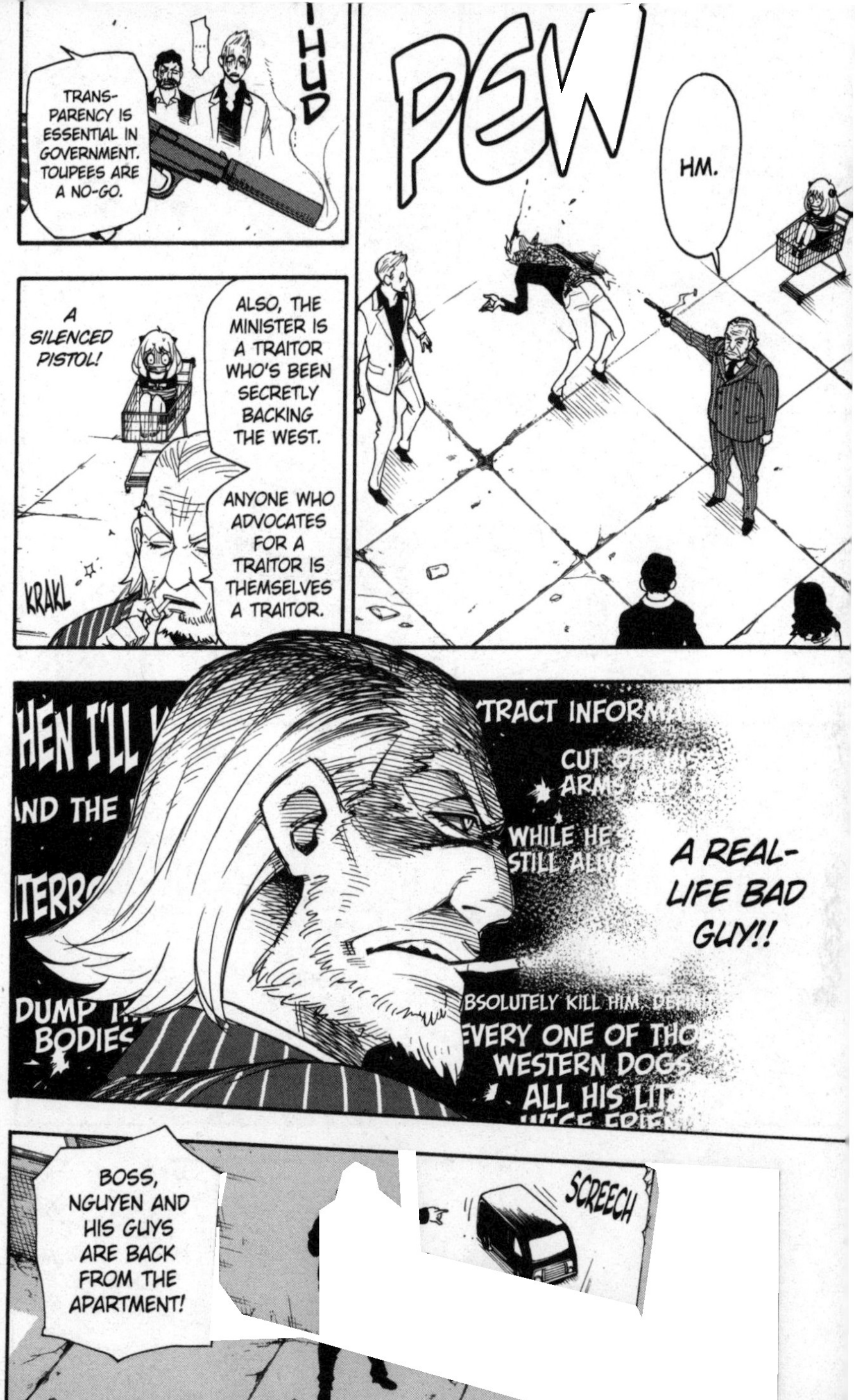
PEW
HM.
THUD
...
TRANSPARENCY IS ESSENTIAL IN GOVERNMENT. TOUPEES ARE A NO-GO.
ALSO, THE MINISTER IS A TRAITOR WHO'S BEEN SECRETLY BACKING THE WEST.
ANYONE WHO ADVOCATES FOR A TRAITOR IS THEMSELVES A TRAITOR.
A SILENCED PISTOL!
KRAKL
A REAL-LIFE BAD GUY!!
SCREECH
BOSS, NGUYEN AND HIS GUYS ARE BACK FROM THE APARTMENT!

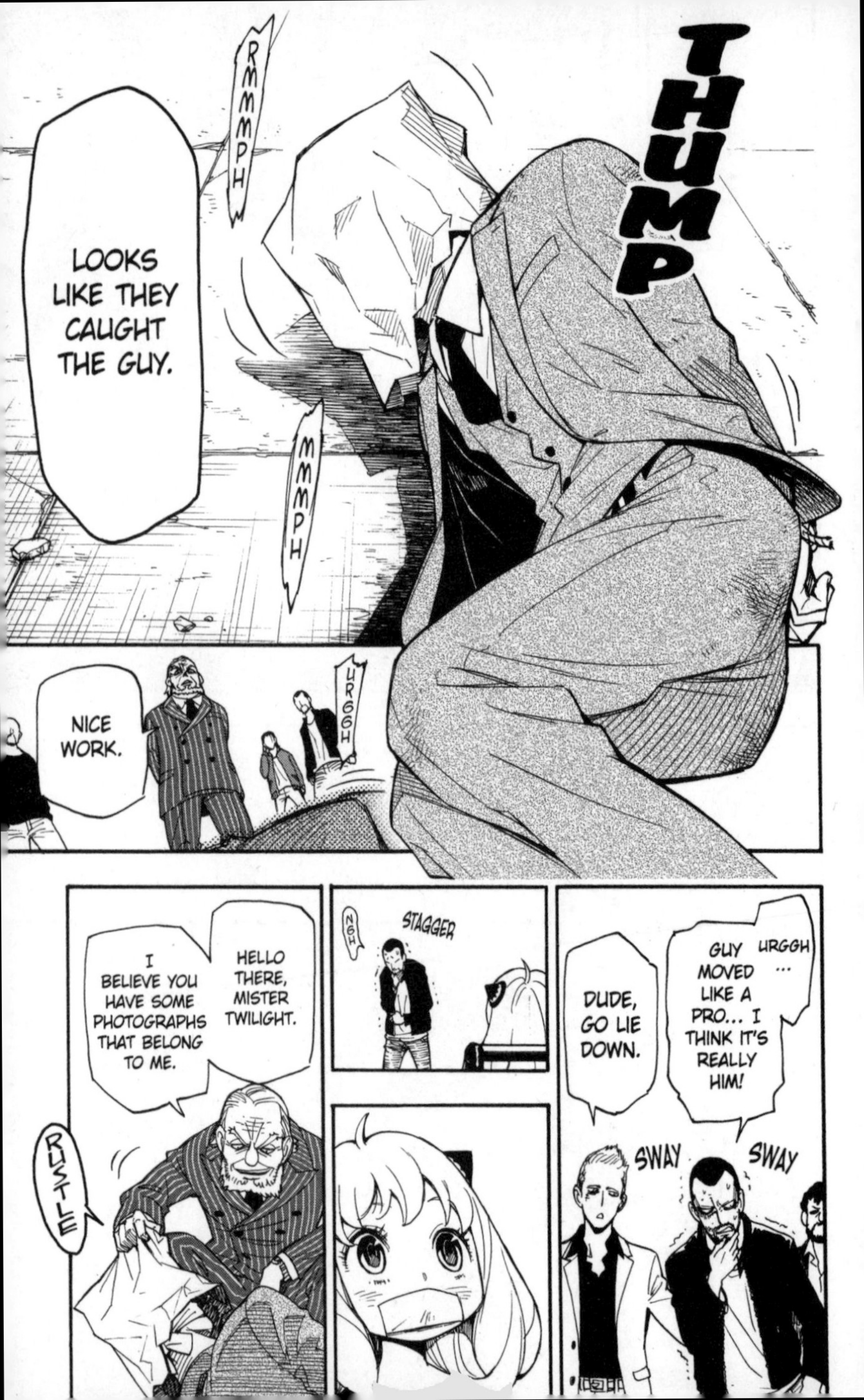
THUMP
RMMMPH
LOOKS LIKE THEY CAUGHT THE GUY.
MMMMPH
URGGH
NICE WORK.
URGGH ...
GUY MOVED LIKE A PRO... I THINK IT'S REALLY HIM!
DUDE, GO LIE DOWN.
SWAY
SWAY
STAGGER
NGH
HELLO THERE, MISTER TWILIGHT.
I BELIEVE YOU HAVE SOME PHOTOGRAPHS THAT BELONG TO ME.
RUSTLE

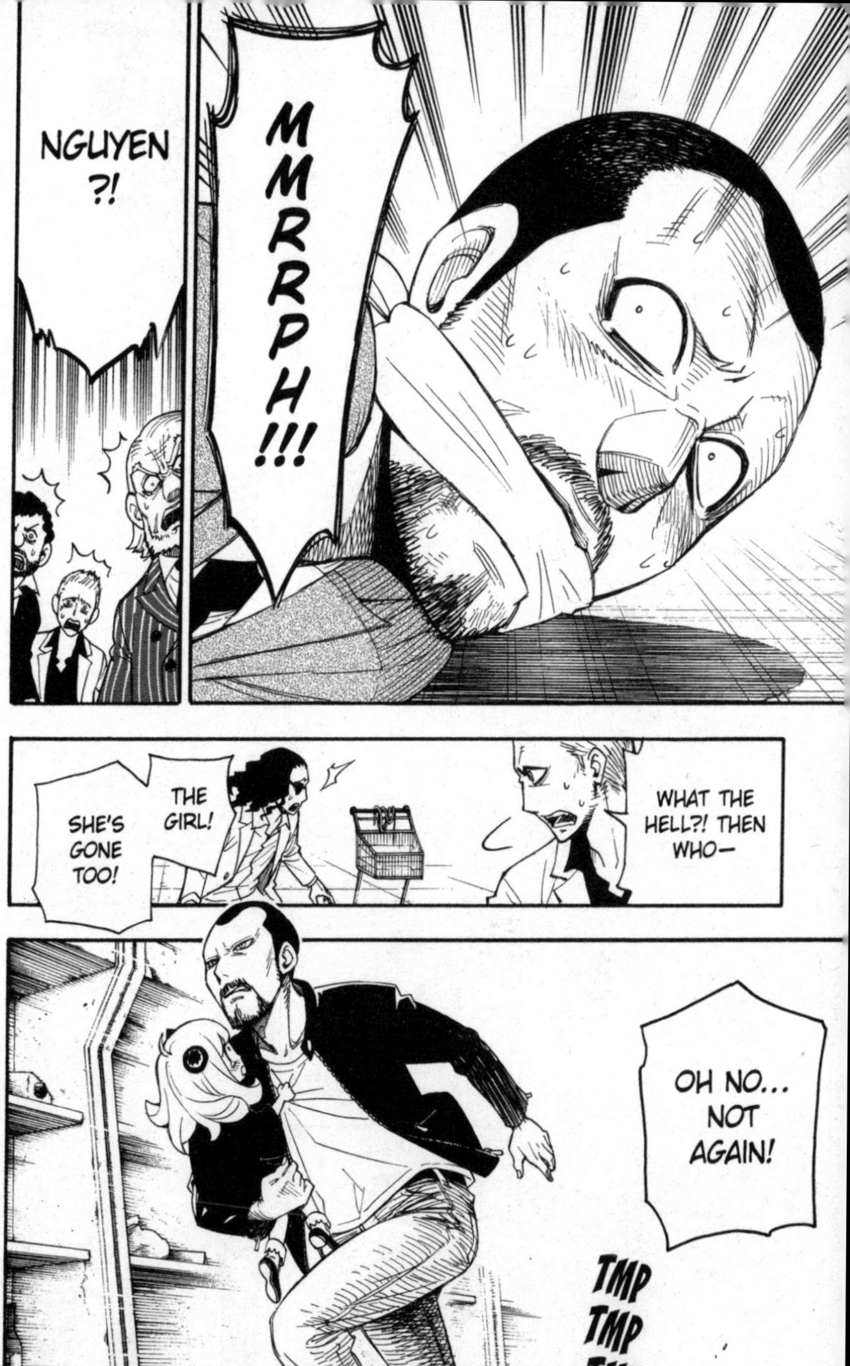
MMRRPH!!!
NGUYEN?!
WHAT THE HELL?! THEN WHO—
THE GIRL!
SHE'S GONE TOO!
OH NO... NOT AGAIN!
TMP TMP TMP

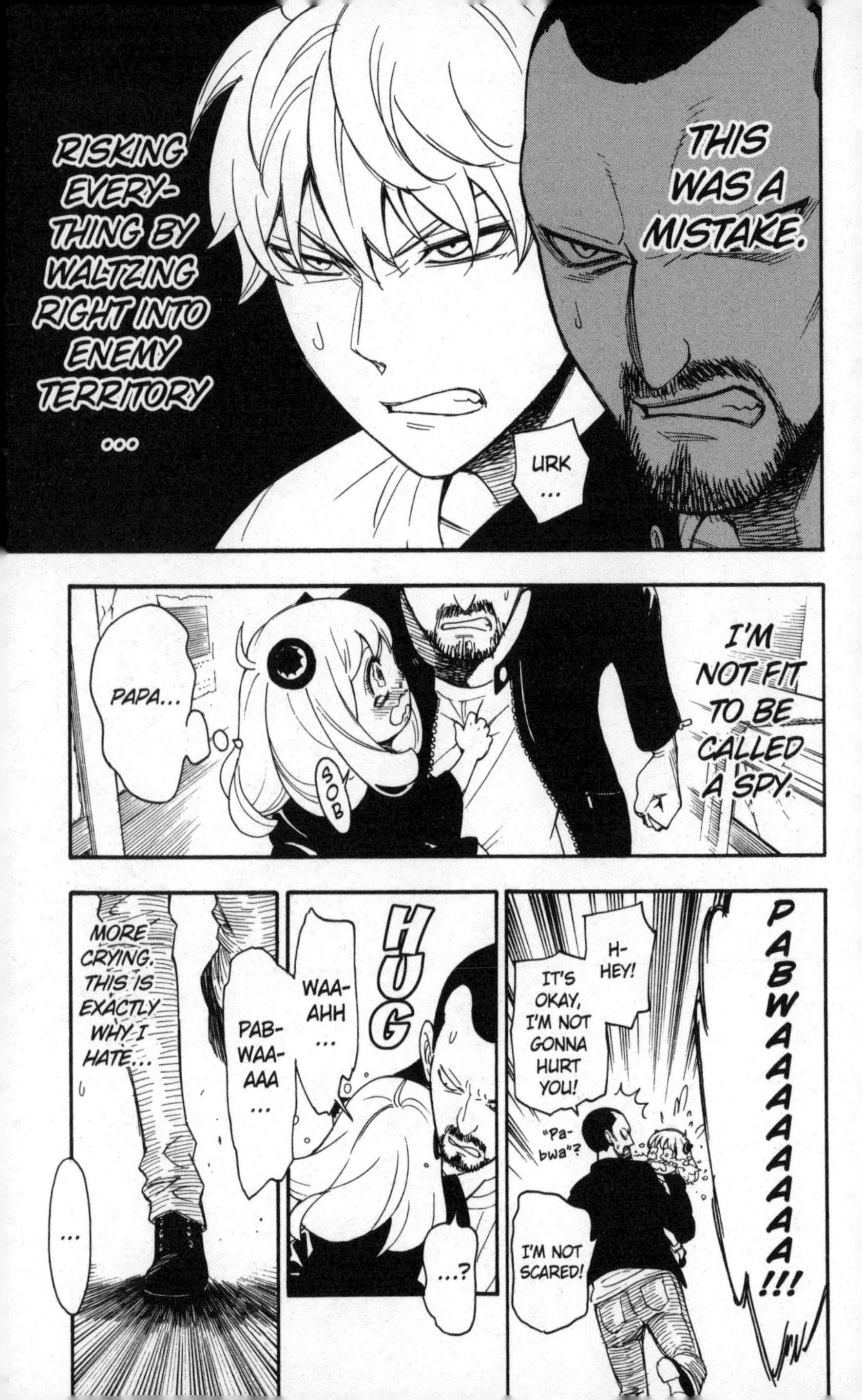
THIS WAS A MISTAKE.
URK ...
RISKING EVERY-THING BY WALTZING RIGHT INTO ENEMY TERRITORY ...
I'M NOT FIT TO BE CALLED A SPY.
SOB
PAPA...
PABWAAAAAAAAAAAA!!!
H-HEY!
IT'S OKAY, I'M NOT GONNA HURT YOU!
"Pa-bwa"?
I'M NOT SCARED!
HUG
WAA-AHH ...
PAB-WAA-AAA ...
...?
MORE CRYING. THIS IS EXACTLY WHY I HATE...
...

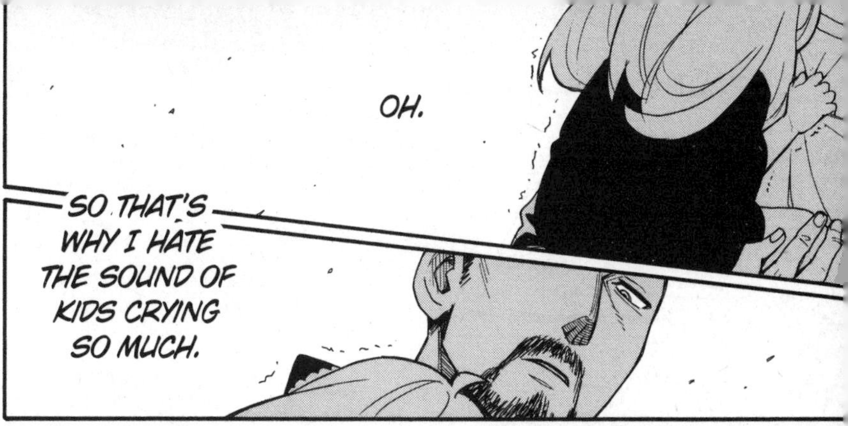
OH.
SO THAT'S WHY I HATE THE SOUND OF KIDS CRYING SO MUCH.

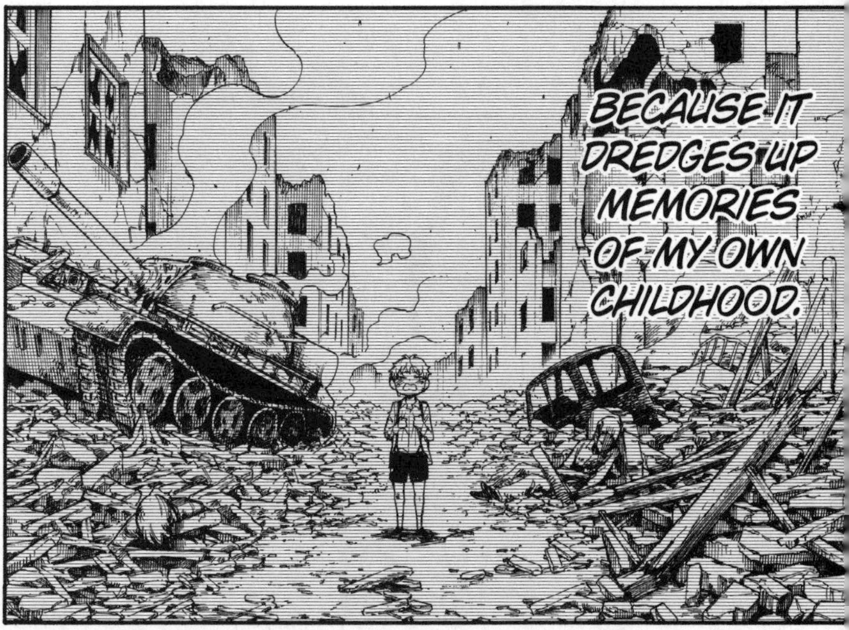
BECAUSE IT DREDGES UP MEMORIES OF MY OWN CHILDHOOD.

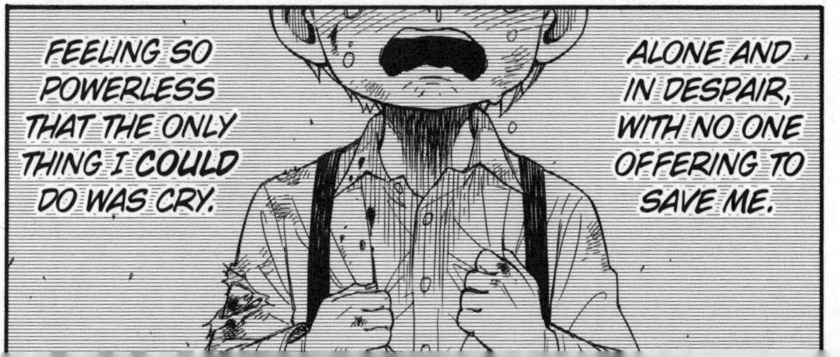
ALONE AND IN DESPAIR, WITH NO ONE OFFERING TO SAVE ME.
FEELING SO POWERLESS THAT THE ONLY THING I COULD DO WAS CRY.

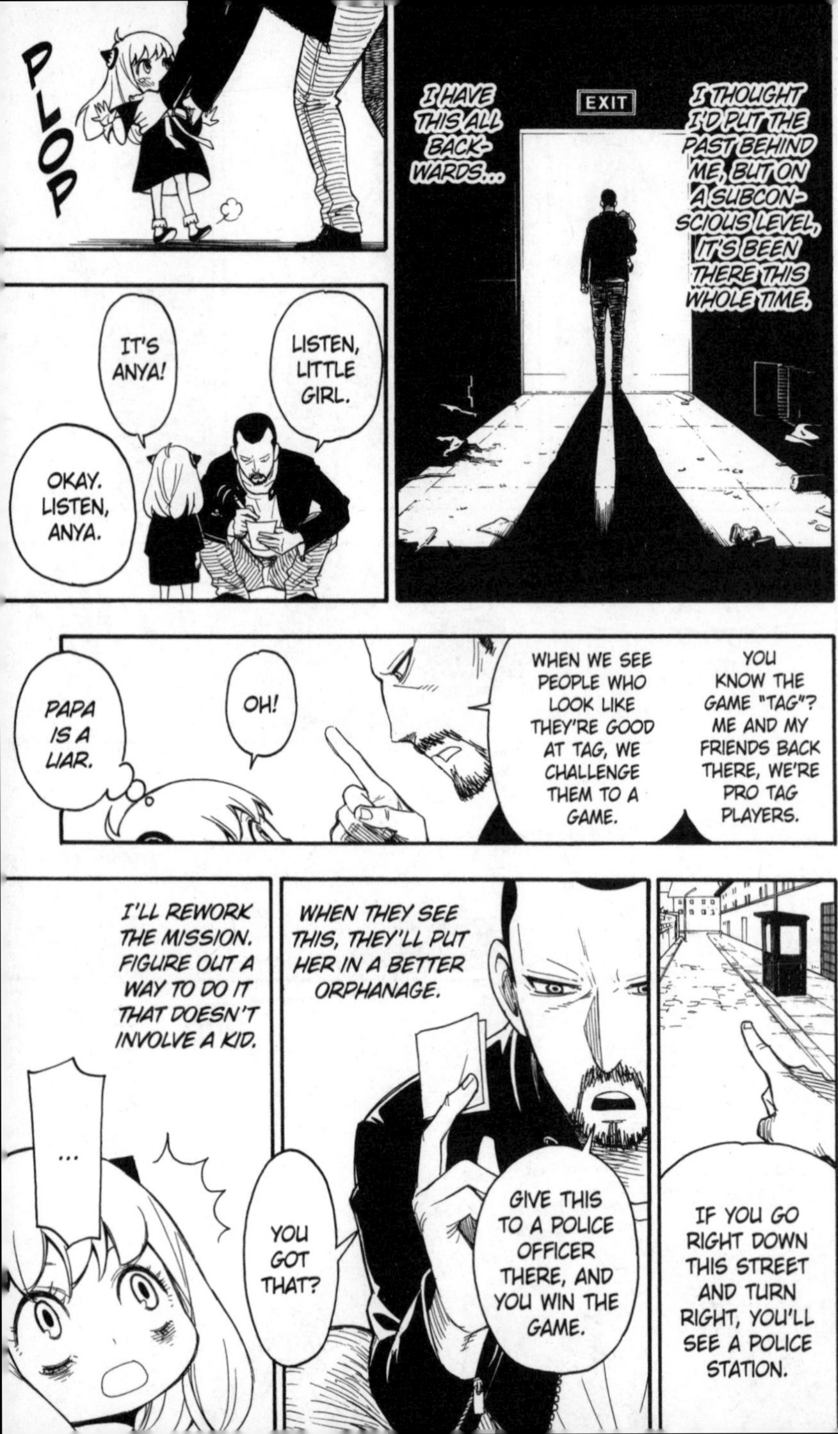
I THOUGHT I'D PUT THE PAST BEHIND ME, BUT ON A SUBCONSCIOUS LEVEL, IT'S BEEN THERE THIS WHOLE TIME.
I HAVE THIS ALL BACKWARDS...
EXIT
PLOP
LISTEN, LITTLE GIRL.
IT'S ANYA!
OKAY. LISTEN, ANYA.
YOU KNOW THE GAME "TAG"? ME AND MY FRIENDS BACK THERE, WE'RE PRO TAG PLAYERS.
WHEN WE SEE PEOPLE WHO LOOK LIKE THEY'RE GOOD AT TAG, WE CHALLENGE THEM TO A GAME.
OH!
PAPA IS A LIAR.
IF YOU GO RIGHT DOWN THIS STREET AND TURN RIGHT, YOU'LL SEE A POLICE STATION.
GIVE THIS TO A POLICE OFFICER THERE, AND YOU WIN THE GAME.
YOU GOT THAT?
WHEN THEY SEE THIS, THEY'LL PUT HER IN A BETTER ORPHANAGE.
I'LL REWORK THE MISSION. FIGURE OUT A WAY TO DO IT THAT DOESN'T INVOLVE A KID.
...

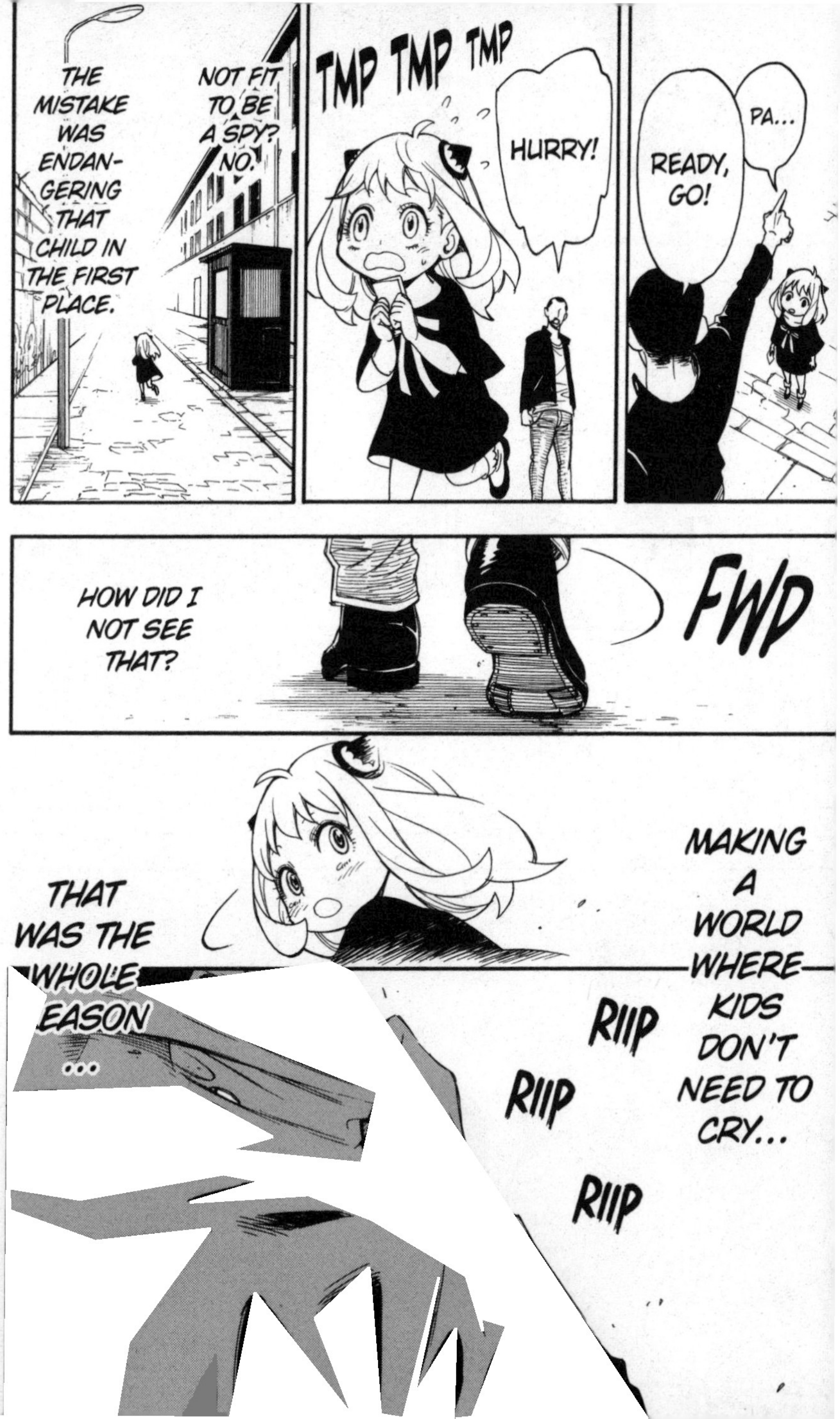
PA...
READY, GO!
TMP TMP TMP
HURRY!
NOT FIT TO BE A SPY? NO.
THE MISTAKE WAS ENDANGERING THAT CHILD IN THE FIRST PLACE.
FWD
HOW DID I NOT SEE THAT?
MAKING A WORLD WHERE KIDS DON'T NEED TO CRY...
THAT WAS THE WHOLE REASON...
RIIP
RIIP
RIIP

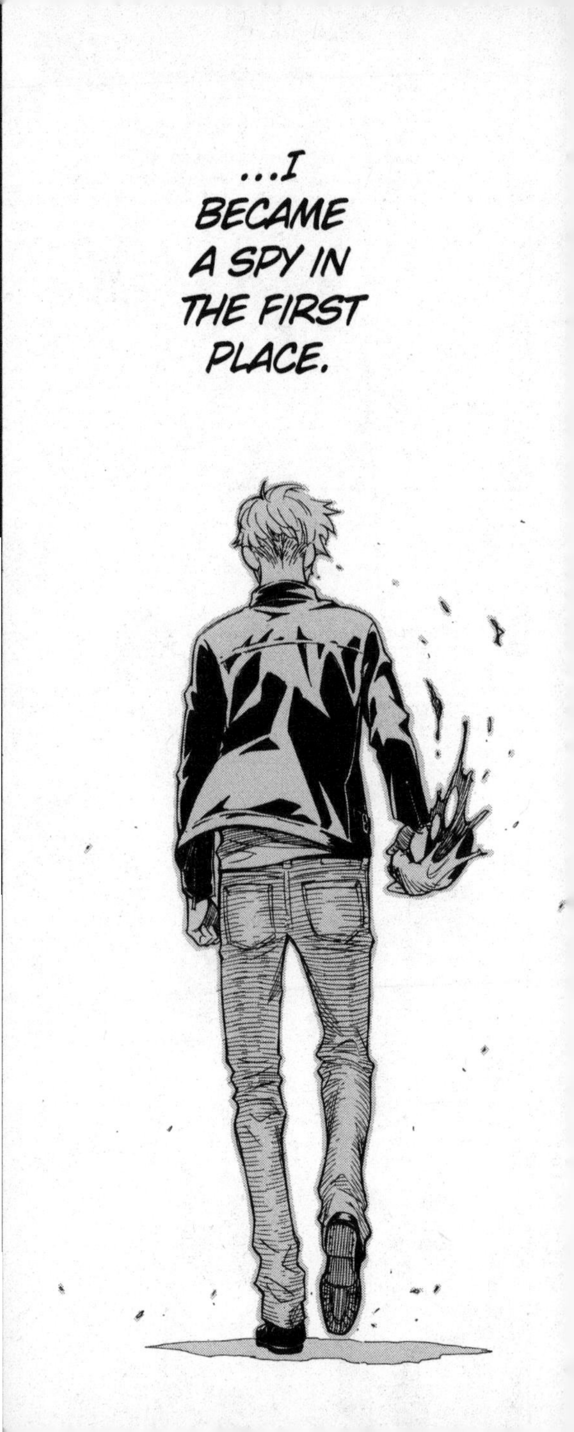
...I BECAME A SPY IN THE FIRST PLACE.
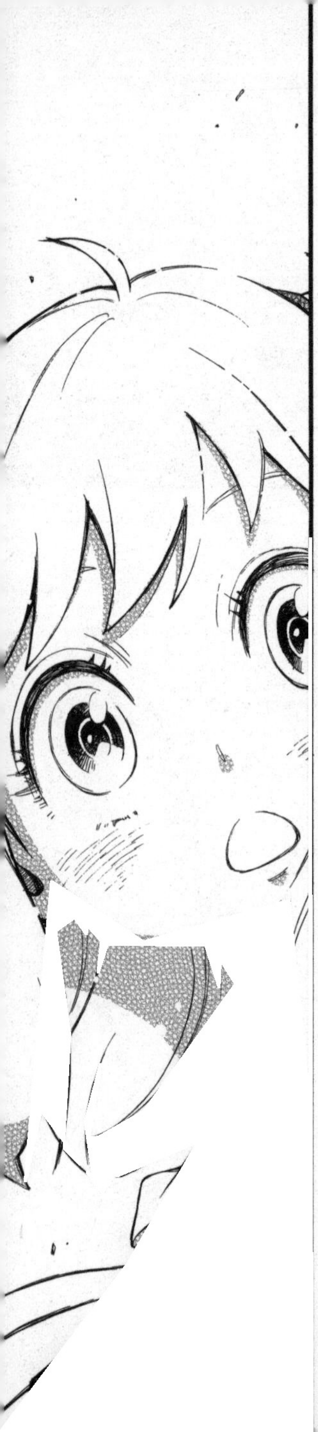

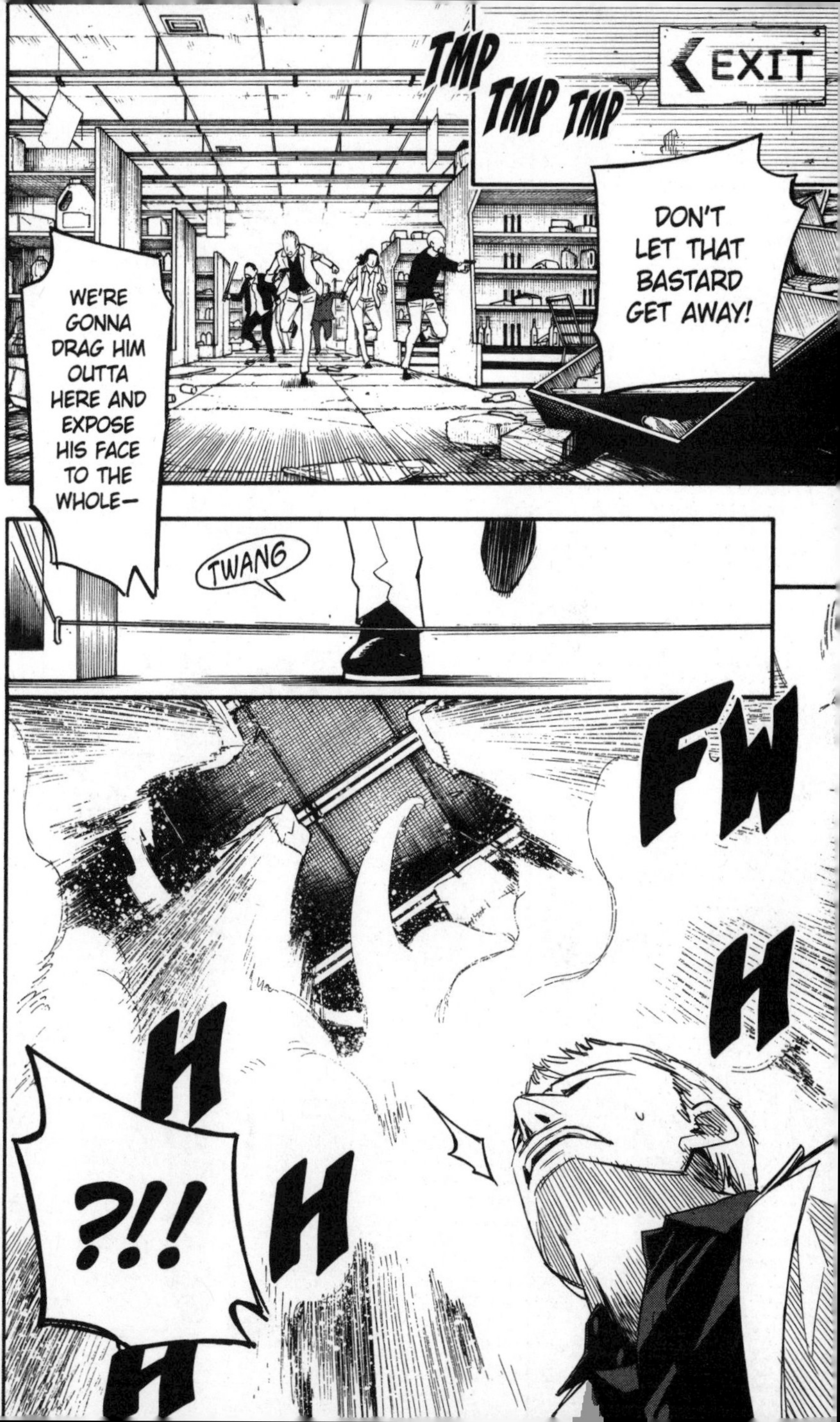
EXIT
TMP TMP TMP
DON'T LET THAT BASTARD GET AWAY!
WE'RE GONNA DRAG HIM OUTTA HERE AND EXPOSE HIS FACE TO THE WHOLE—
TWANG
FWHH
?!!
HHH

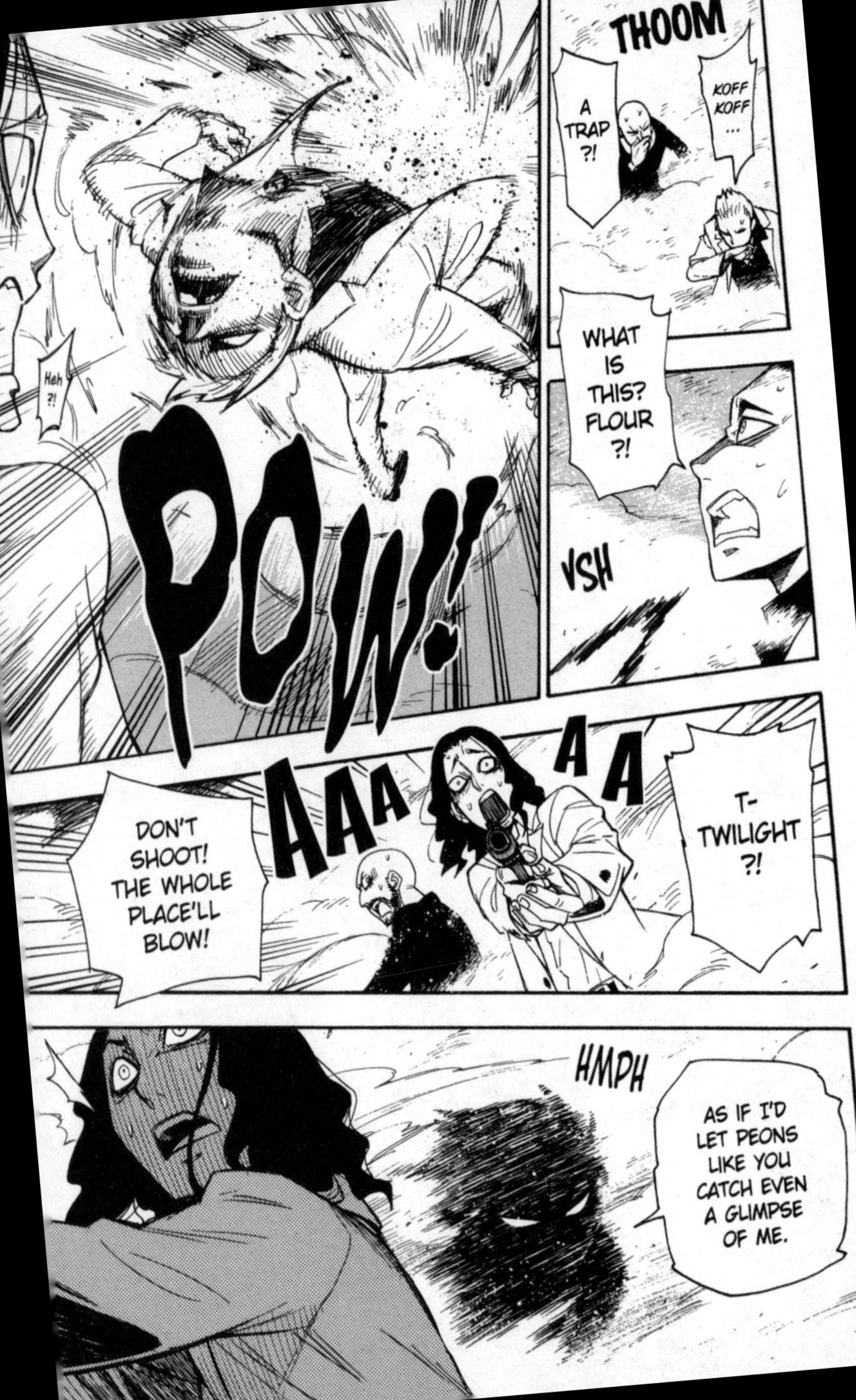
THOOM
KOFF KOFF ...
A TRAP ?!
WHAT IS THIS? FLOUR ?!
VSH
Heh ?!
POW!
T-TWILIGHT ?!
AAAAA
DON'T SHOOT! THE WHOLE PLACE'LL BLOW!
HMPH
AS IF I'D LET PEONS LIKE YOU CATCH EVEN A GLIMPSE OF ME.

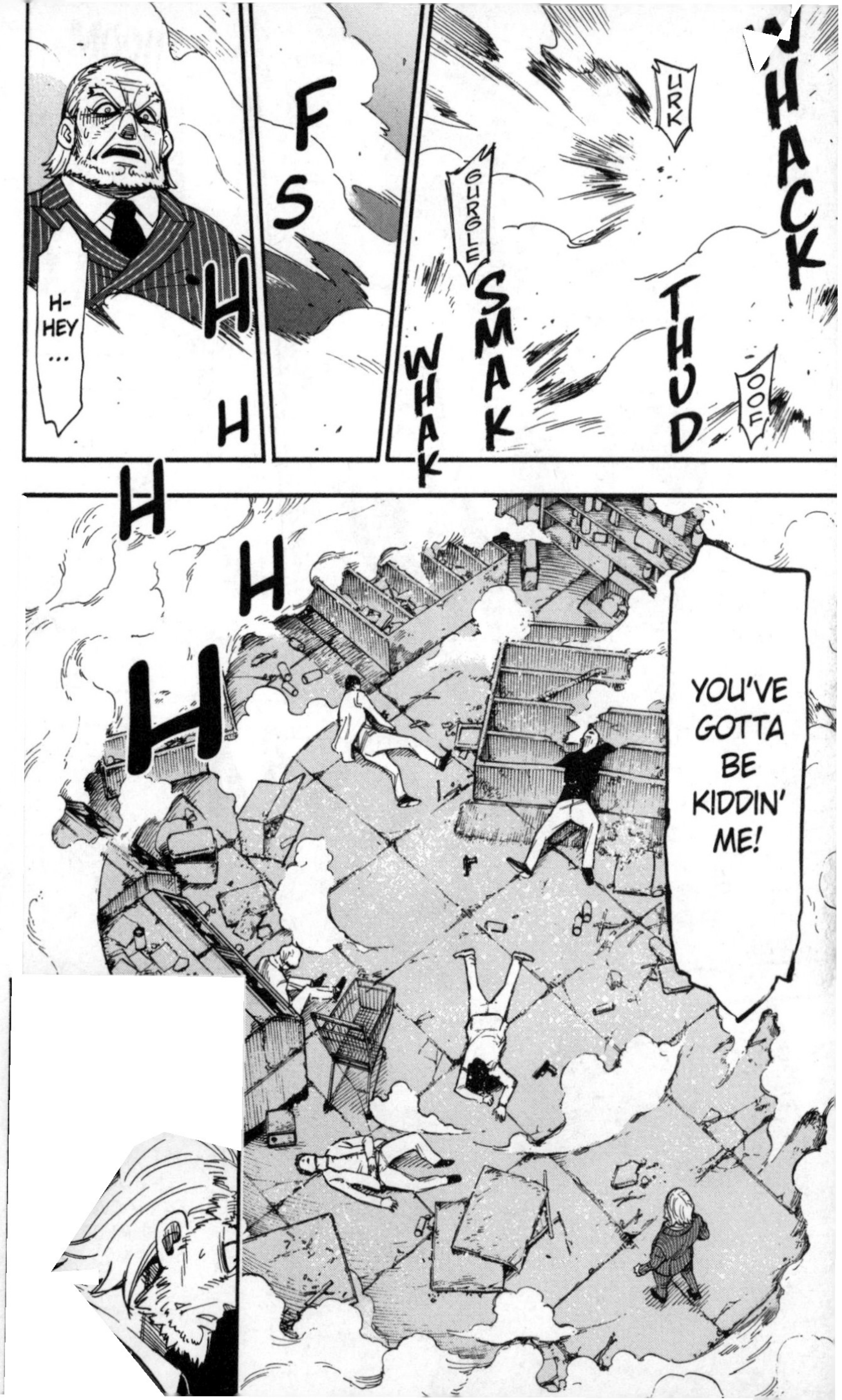

WHACK
URK
THUD
OOF
GURGLE
SMAK
WHAK
FS
H-HEY...
HHHHH
YOU'VE GOTTA BE KIDDIN' ME!

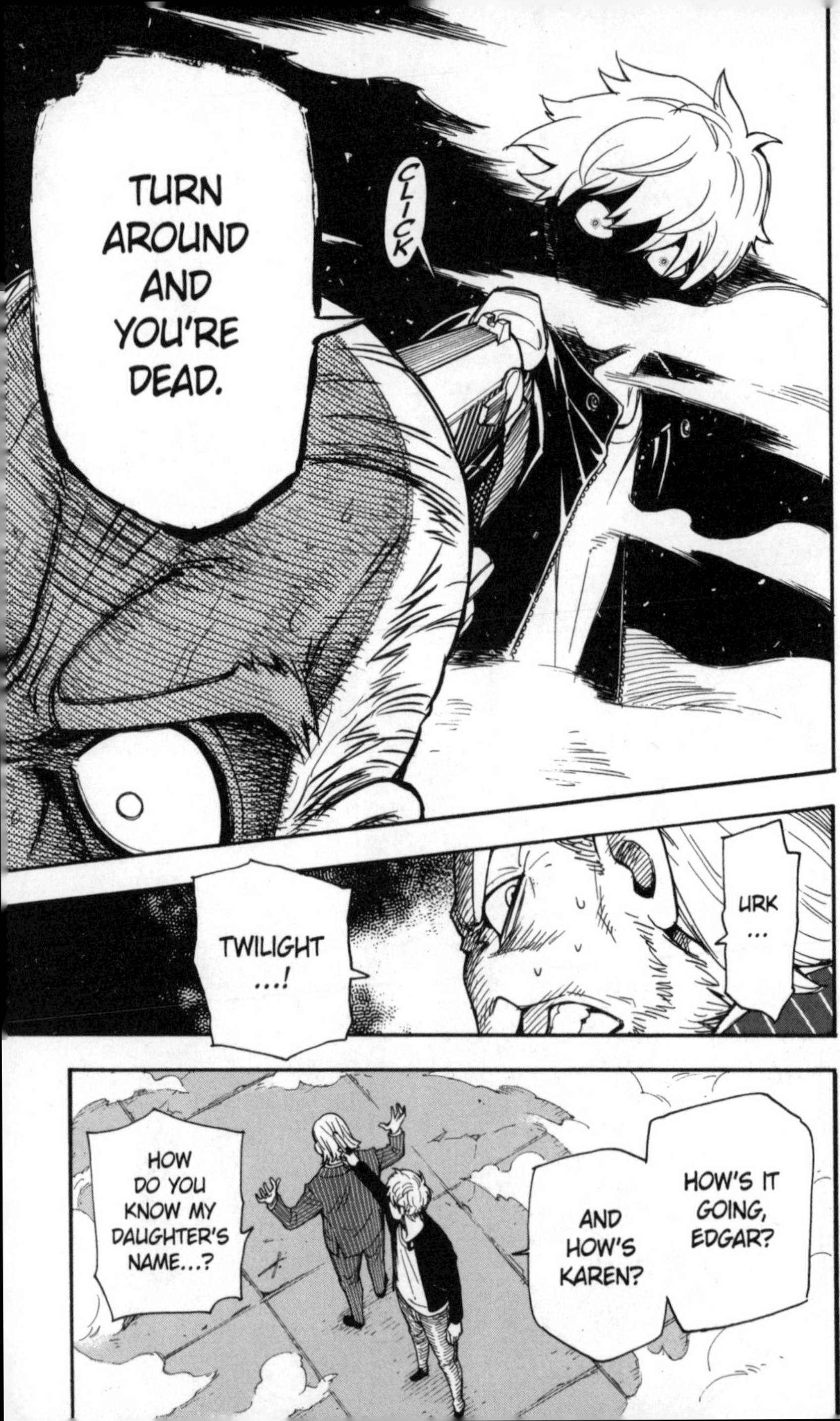
CLICK
TURN AROUND AND YOU'RE DEAD.
URK...
TWILIGHT...!
HOW'S IT GOING, EDGAR?
AND HOW'S KAREN?
HOW DO YOU KNOW MY DAUGHTER'S NAME...?

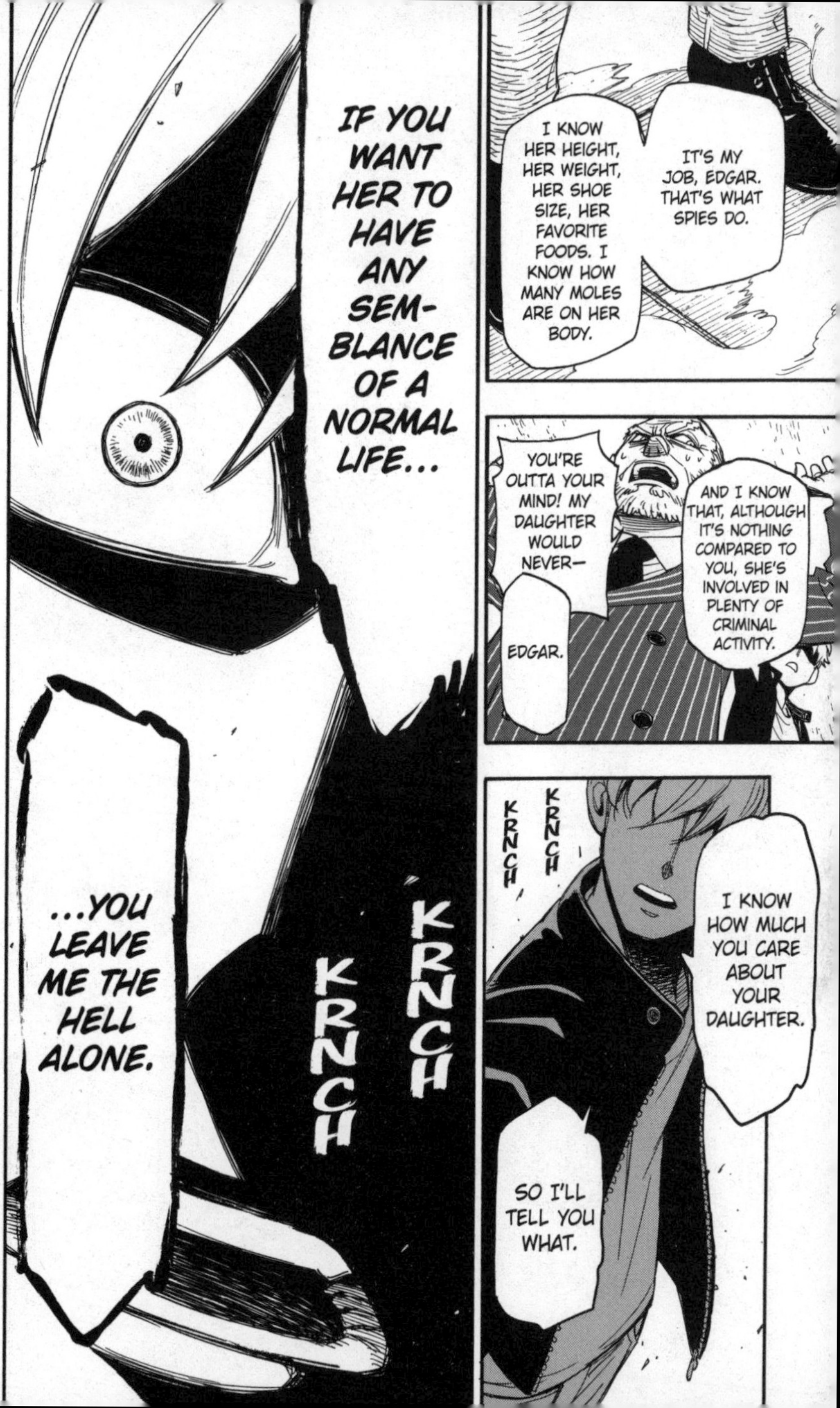
IT'S MY JOB, EDGAR. THAT'S WHAT SPIES DO.
I KNOW HER HEIGHT, HER WEIGHT, HER SHOE SIZE, HER FAVORITE FOODS. I KNOW HOW MANY MOLES ARE ON HER BODY.
AND I KNOW THAT, ALTHOUGH IT'S NOTHING COMPARED TO YOU, SHE'S INVOLVED IN PLENTY OF CRIMINAL ACTIVITY.
YOU'RE OUTTA YOUR MIND! MY DAUGHTER WOULD NEVER—
EDGAR.
KRNCH
KRNCH
I KNOW HOW MUCH YOU CARE ABOUT YOUR DAUGHTER.
SO I'LL TELL YOU WHAT.
IF YOU WANT HER TO HAVE ANY SEM-BLANCE OF A NORMAL LIFE...
KRNCH
KRNCH
...YOU LEAVE ME THE HELL ALONE.

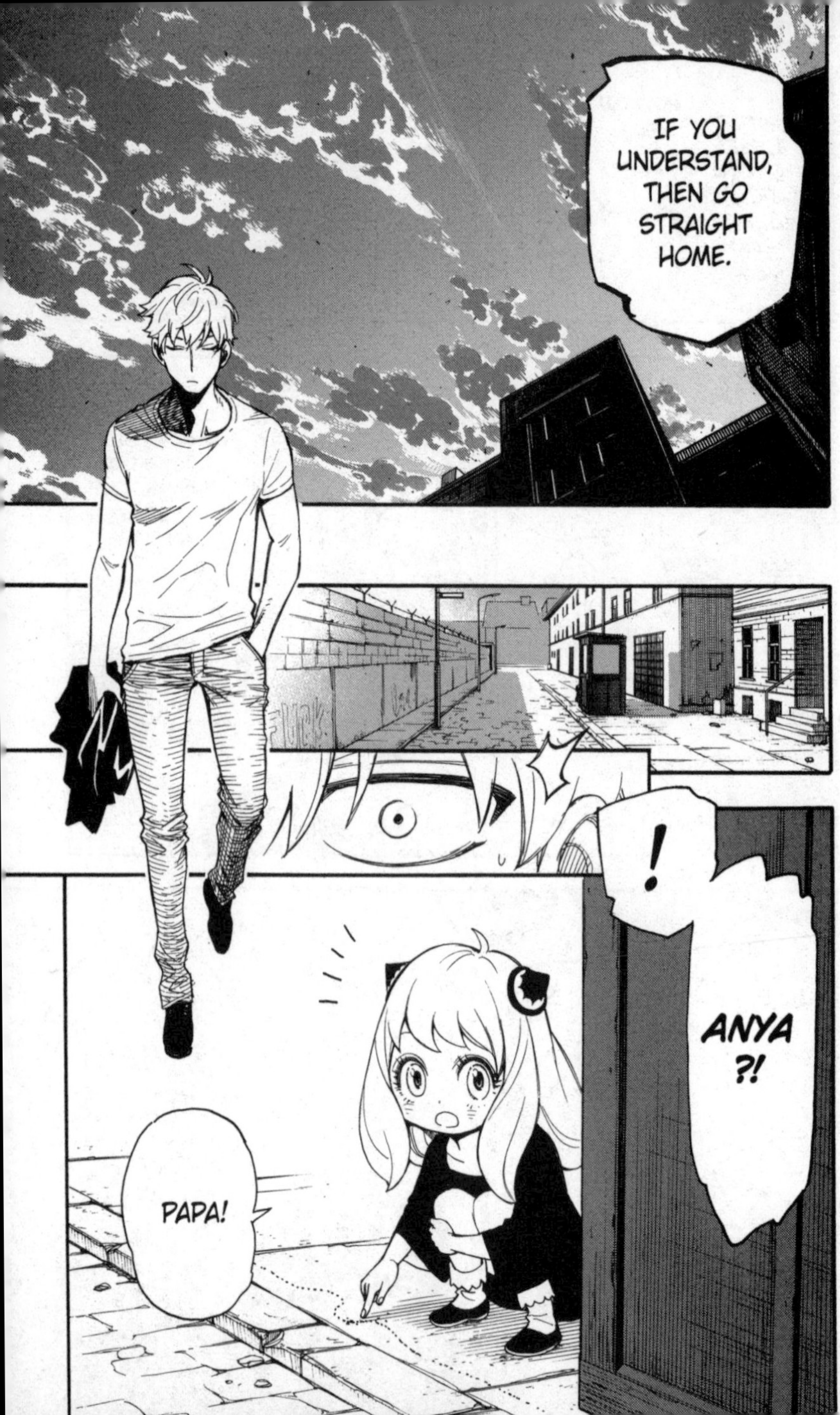
IF YOU UNDERSTAND, THEN GO STRAIGHT HOME.
!
ANYA ?!
PAPA!

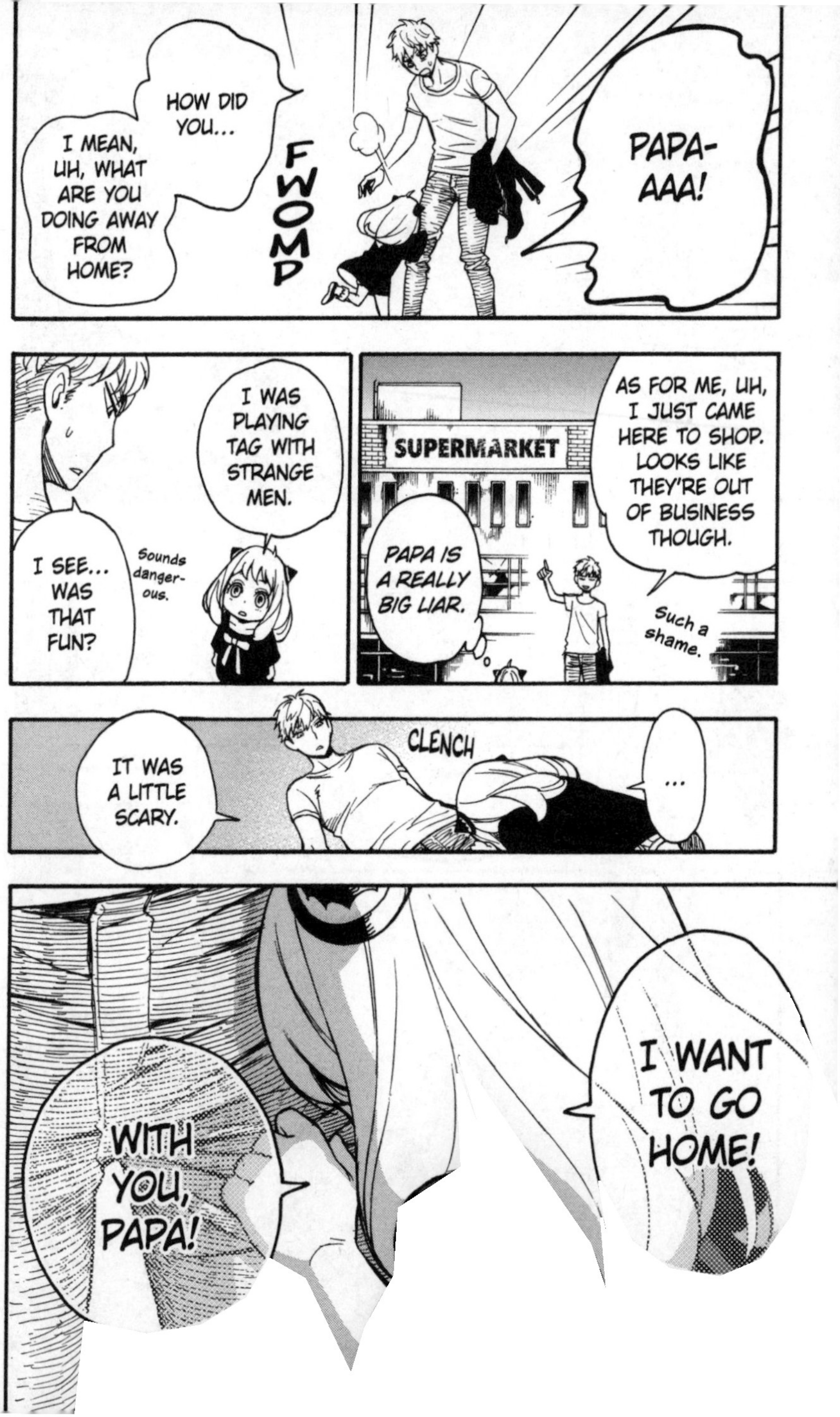
PAPA-AAA!
FWOMP
HOW DID YOU...
I MEAN, UH, WHAT ARE YOU DOING AWAY FROM HOME?
AS FOR ME, UH, I JUST CAME HERE TO SHOP. LOOKS LIKE THEY'RE OUT OF BUSINESS THOUGH.
SUPERMARKET
PAPA IS A REALLY BIG LIAR.
Such a shame.
I WAS PLAYING TAG WITH STRANGE MEN.
Sounds danger-ous.
I SEE... WAS THAT FUN?
...
CLENCH
IT WAS A LITTLE SCARY.
I WANT TO GO HOME!
WITH YOU, PAPA!

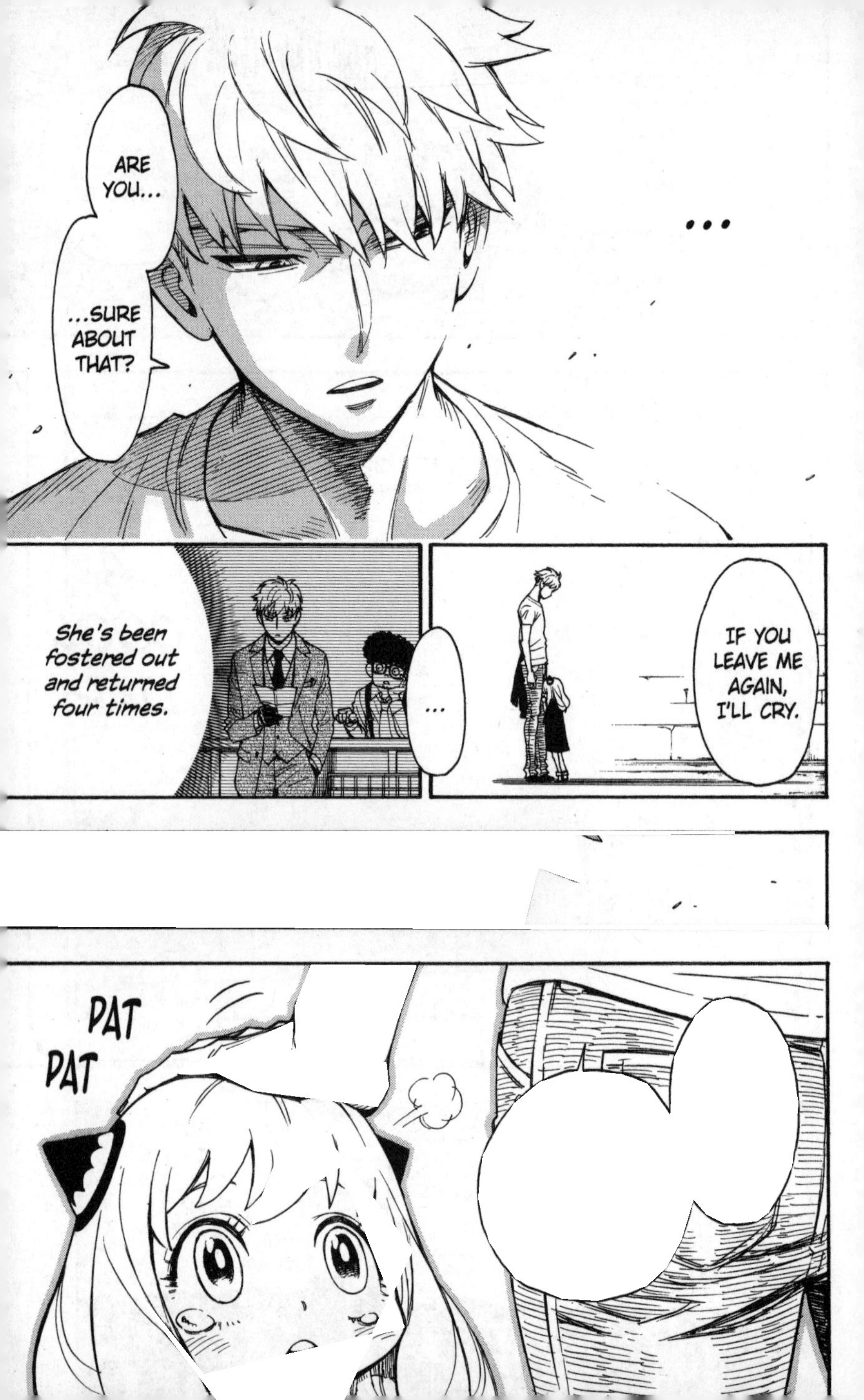
...
ARE YOU...
...SURE ABOUT THAT?
IF YOU LEAVE ME AGAIN, I'LL CRY.
...
She's been fostered out and returned four times.
PAT PAT

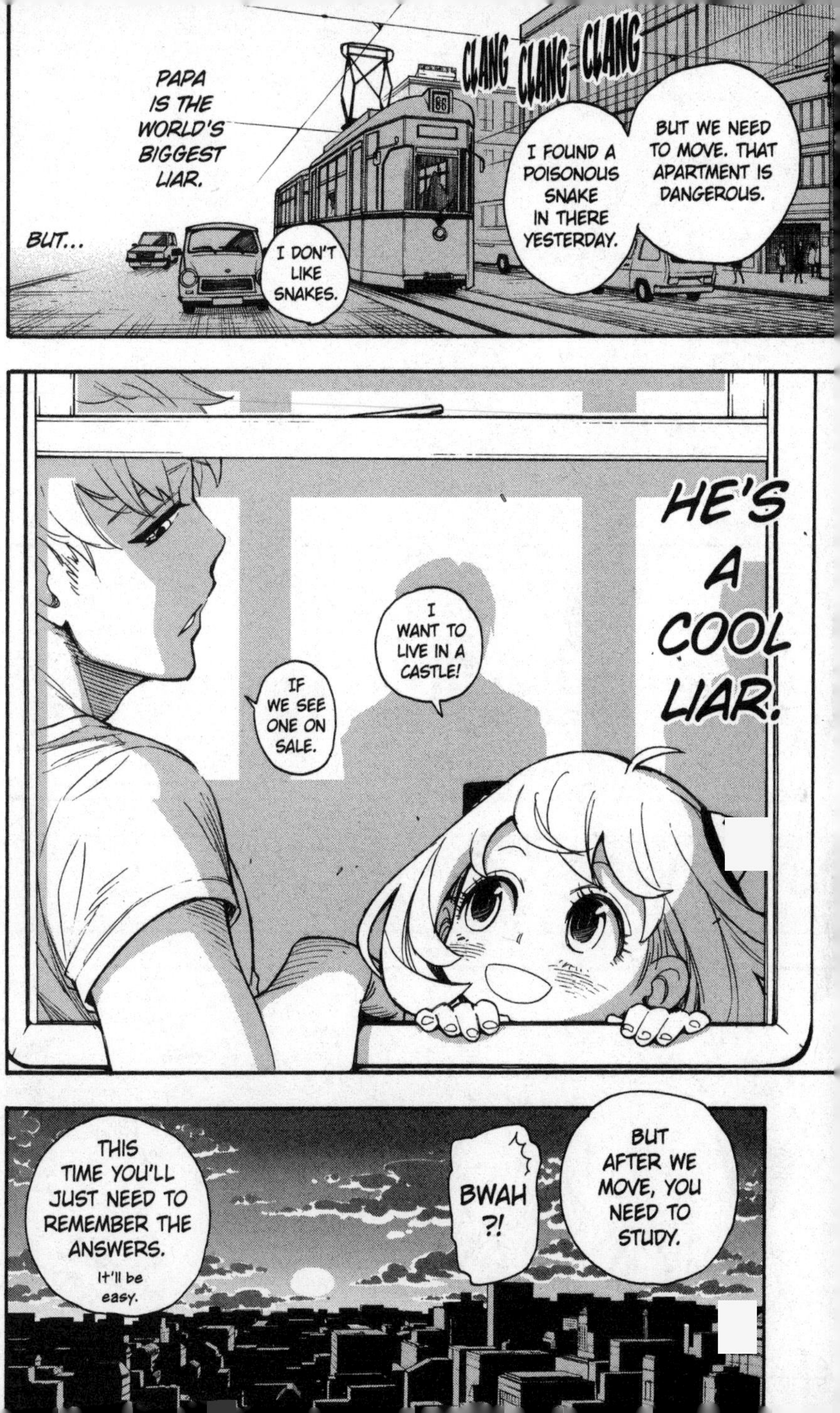
CLANG CLANG CLANG
BUT WE NEED TO MOVE. THAT APARTMENT IS DANGEROUS.
I FOUND A POISONOUS SNAKE IN THERE YESTERDAY.
PAPA IS THE WORLD'S BIGGEST LIAR.
I DON'T LIKE SNAKES.
BUT...
HE'S A COOL LIAR.
I WANT TO LIVE IN A CASTLE!
IF WE SEE ONE ON SALE.
BUT AFTER WE MOVE, YOU NEED TO STUDY.
BWAH ?!
THIS TIME YOU'LL JUST NEED TO REMEMBER THE ANSWERS.
It'll be easy.

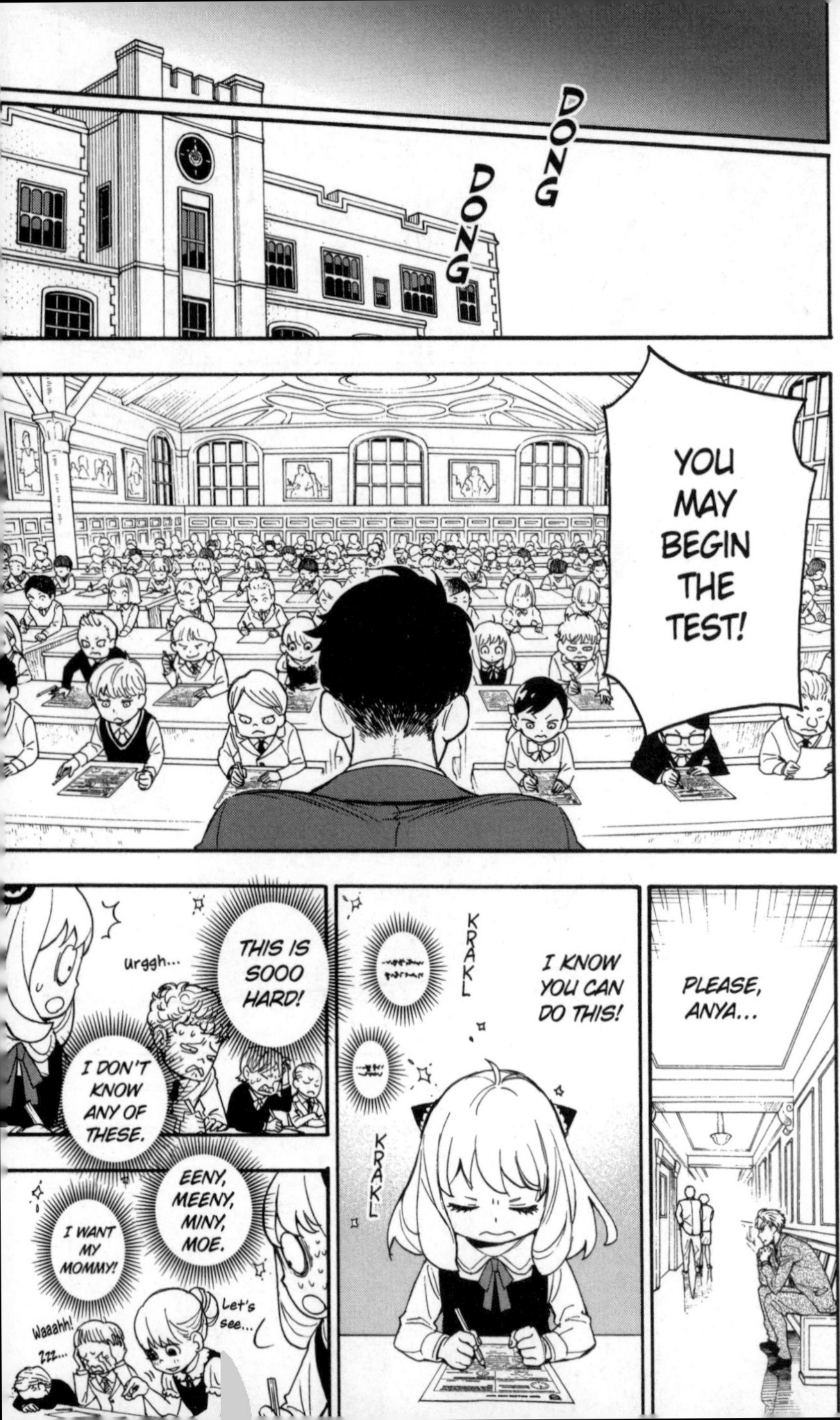

DONG
DONG
YOU MAY BEGIN THE TEST!
PLEASE, ANYA...
I KNOW YOU CAN DO THIS!
KRAKL
KRAKL
THIS IS SOOO HARD!
urggh...
I DON'T KNOW ANY OF THESE.
EENY, MEENY, MINY, MOE.
I WANT MY MOMMY!
Let's see...
Waaahh!
zzz...

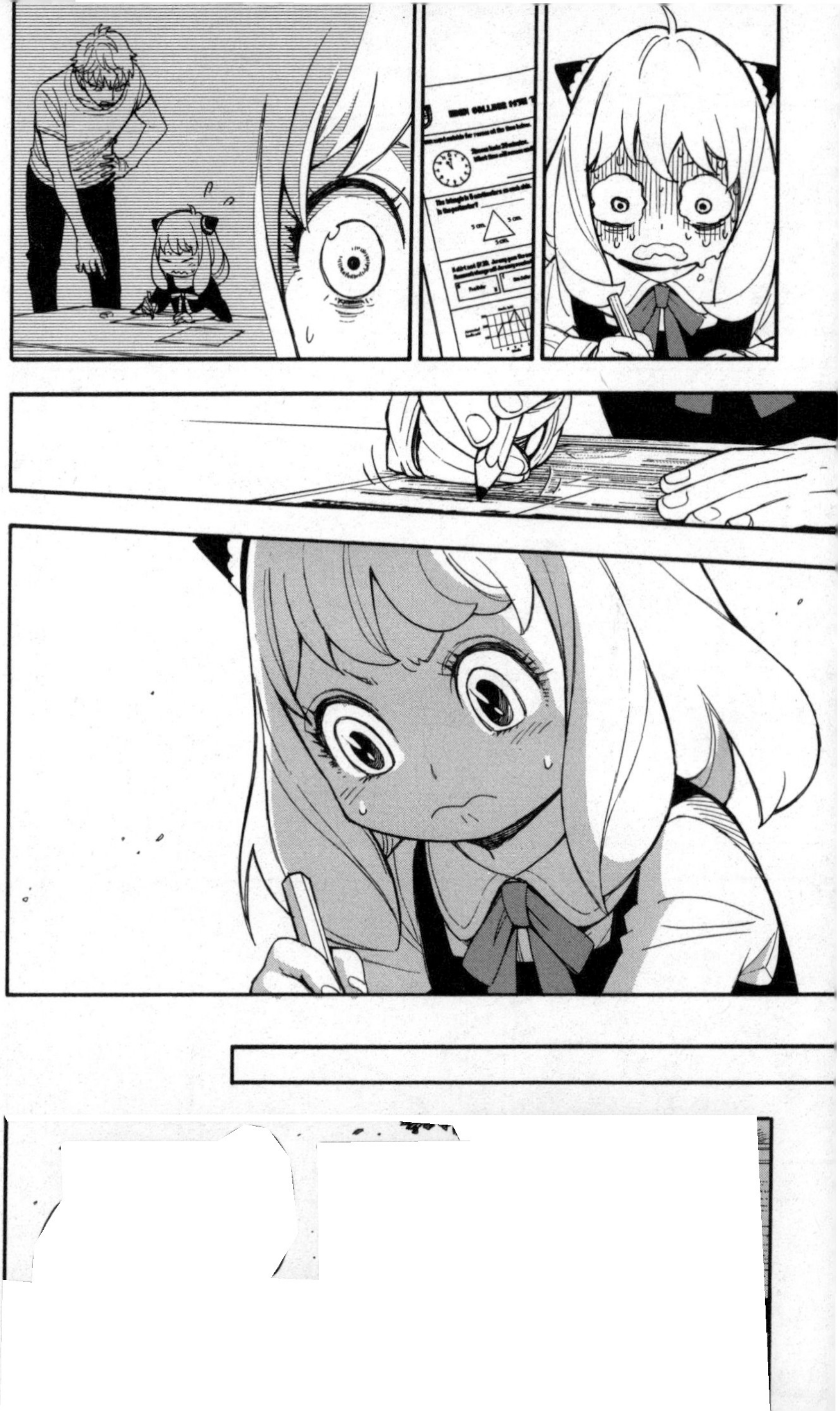

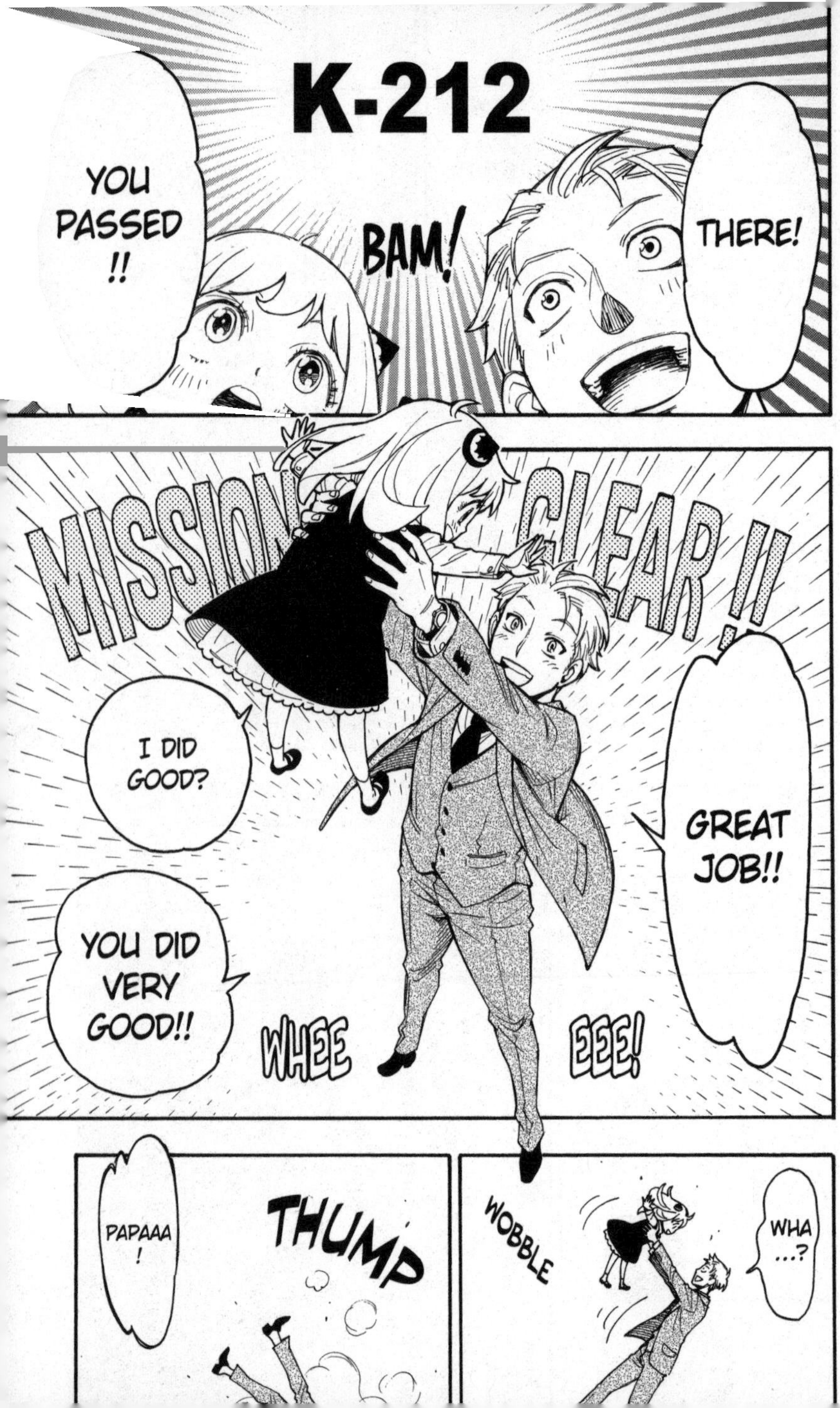
K-212
THERE!
BAM!
YOU PASSED!!
MISSION CLEAR!!
GREAT JOB!!
I DID GOOD?
YOU DID VERY GOOD!!
WHEE EEE!
WHA...?
WOBBLE
THUMP
PAPAAA!

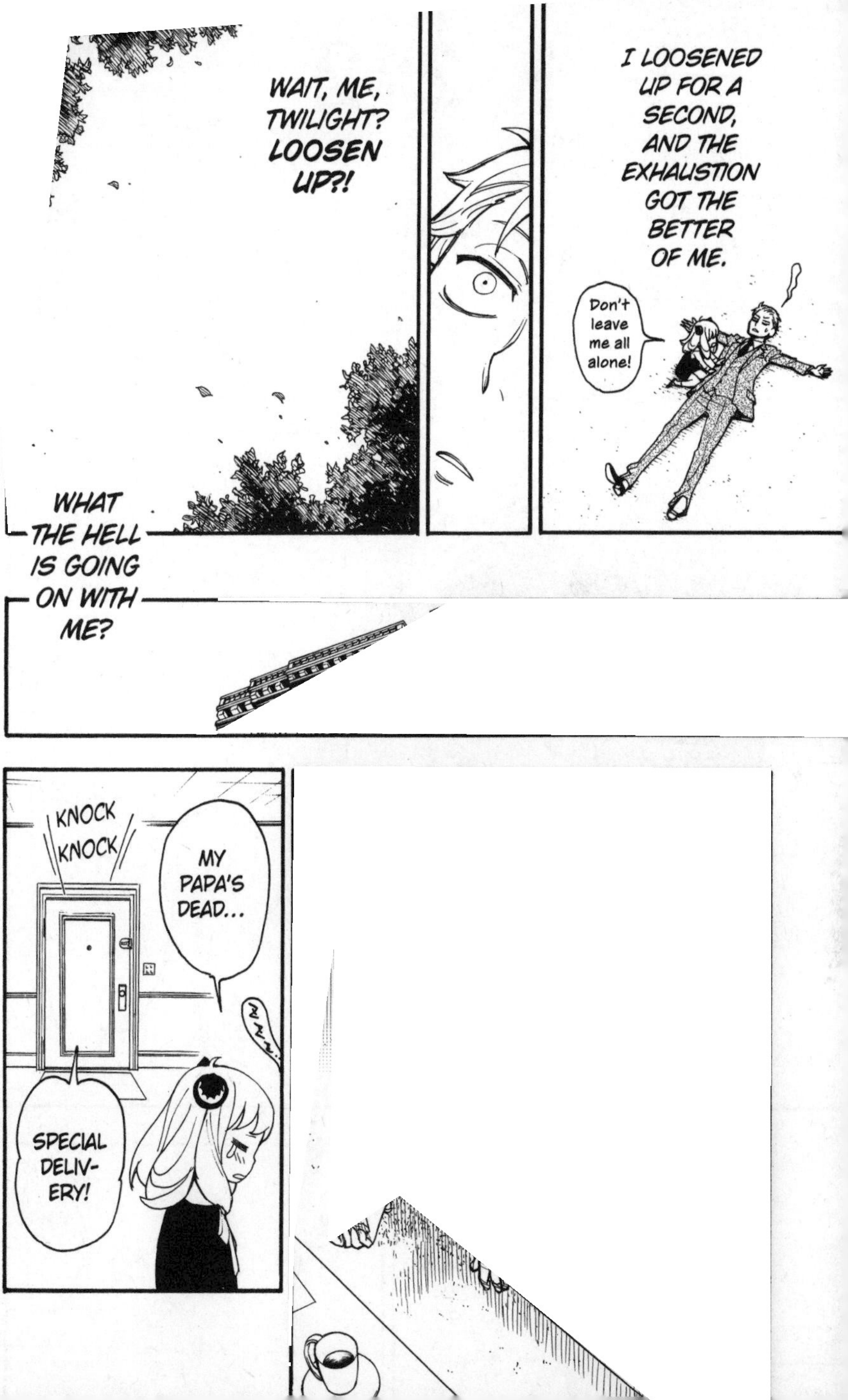
I LOOSENED UP FOR A SECOND, AND THE EXHAUSTION GOT THE BETTER OF ME.
Don't leave me all alone!
WAIT, ME, TWILIGHT? LOOSEN UP?!
WHAT THE HELL IS GOING ON WITH ME?
MY PAPA'S DEAD...
KNOCK KNOCK
ZZZ
SPECIAL DELIV-ERY!

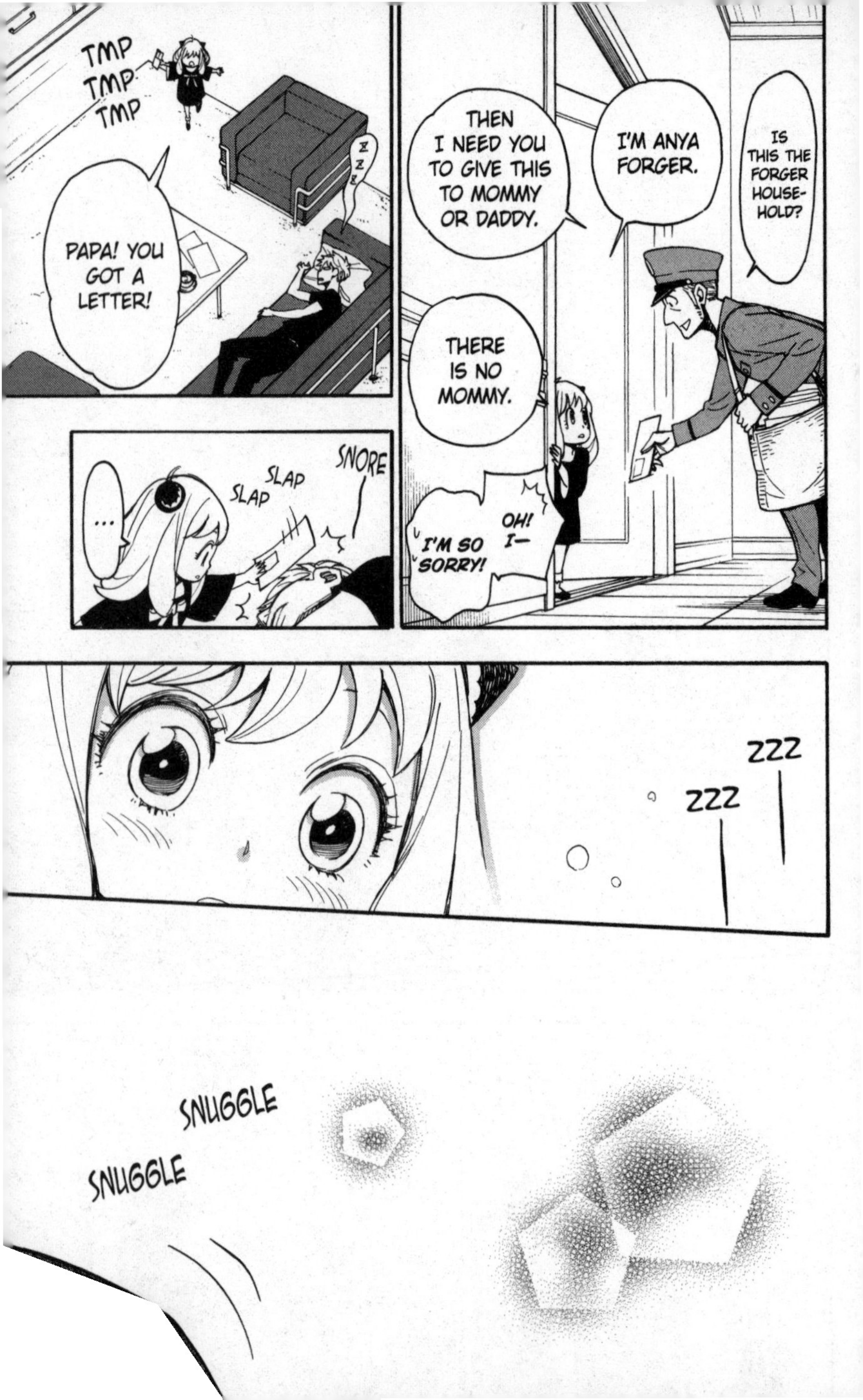
IS THIS THE FORGER HOUSEHOLD?
I'M ANYA FORGER.
THEN I NEED YOU TO GIVE THIS TO MOMMY OR DADDY.
THERE IS NO MOMMY.
OH! I—
I'M SO SORRY!
TMP TMP TMP
Z Z Z
PAPA! YOU GOT A LETTER!
SNORE
SLAP SLAP
...
ZZZ
ZZZ
SNUGGLE
SNUGGLE

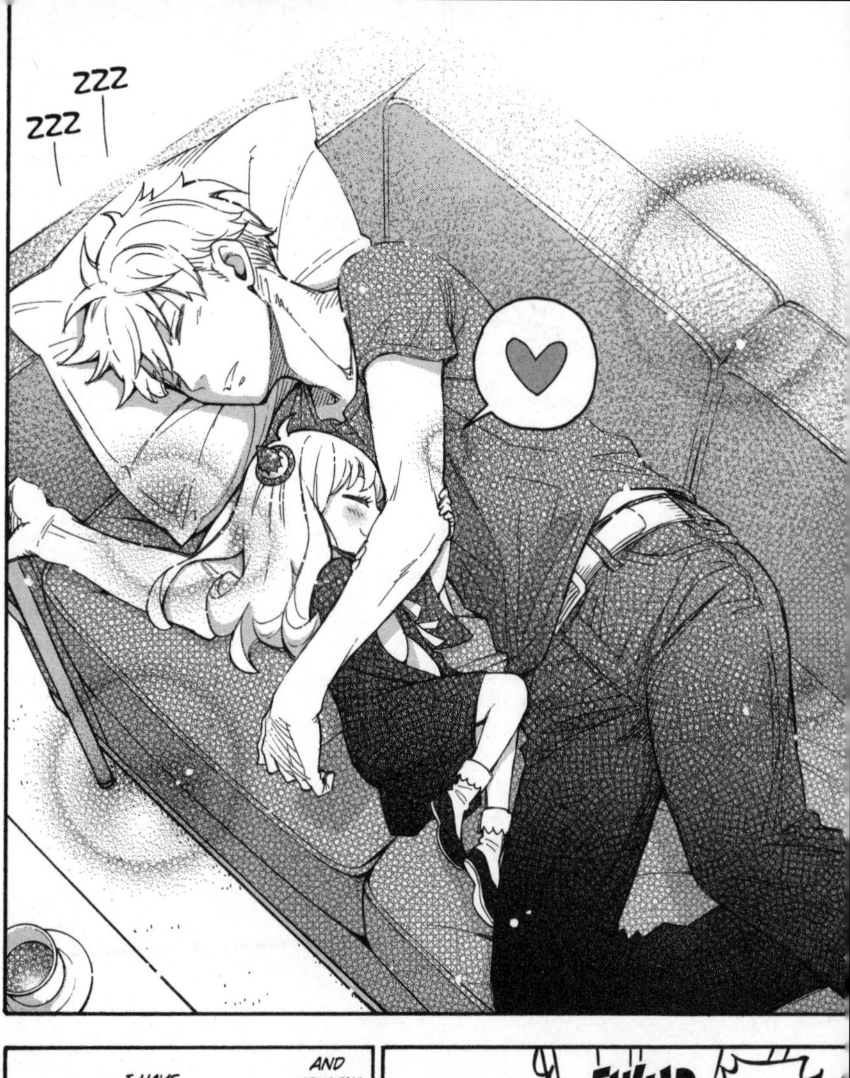
ZZZ
ZZZ

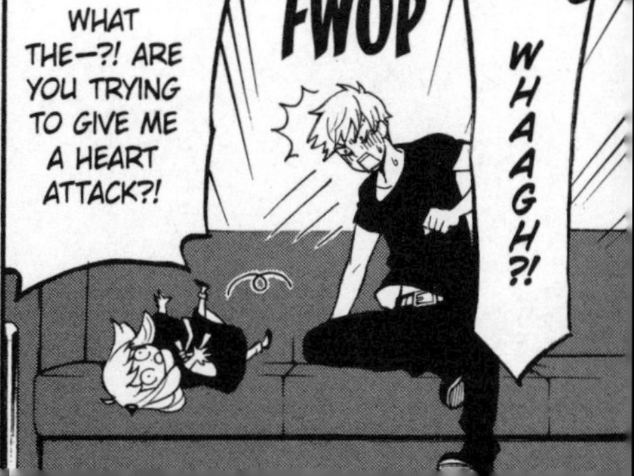
WHAAAGH?!
FWUP
WHAT THE—?! ARE YOU TRYING TO GIVE ME A HEART ATTACK?!

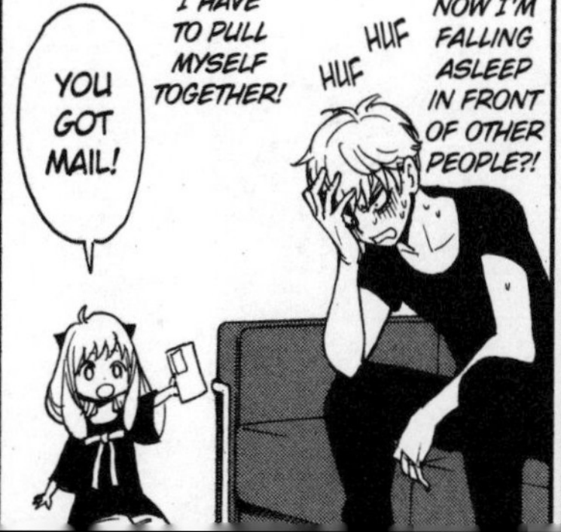
AND NOW I'M FALLING ASLEEP IN FRONT OF OTHER PEOPLE?!
HUF HUF
I HAVE TO PULL MYSELF TOGETHER!
YOU GOT MAIL!

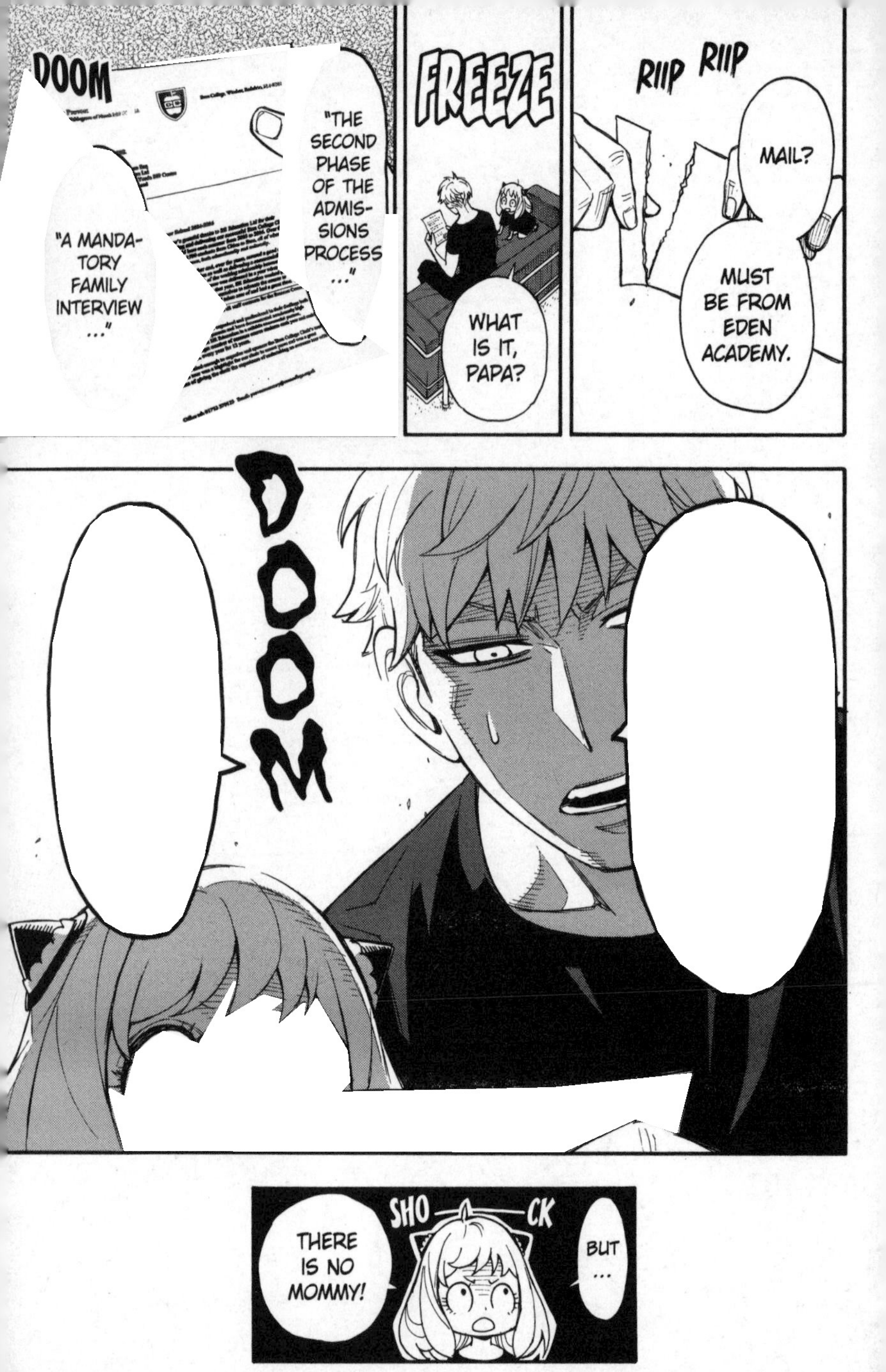
RIIP RIIP
MAIL?
MUST BE FROM EDEN ACADEMY.
FREEZE
WHAT IS IT, PAPA?
DOOM
"THE SECOND PHASE OF THE ADMIS- SIONS PROCESS ..."
"A MANDA- TORY FAMILY INTERVIEW ..."
DOOM
SHO—CK
BUT ...
THERE IS NO MOMMY!

SPY×FAMILY

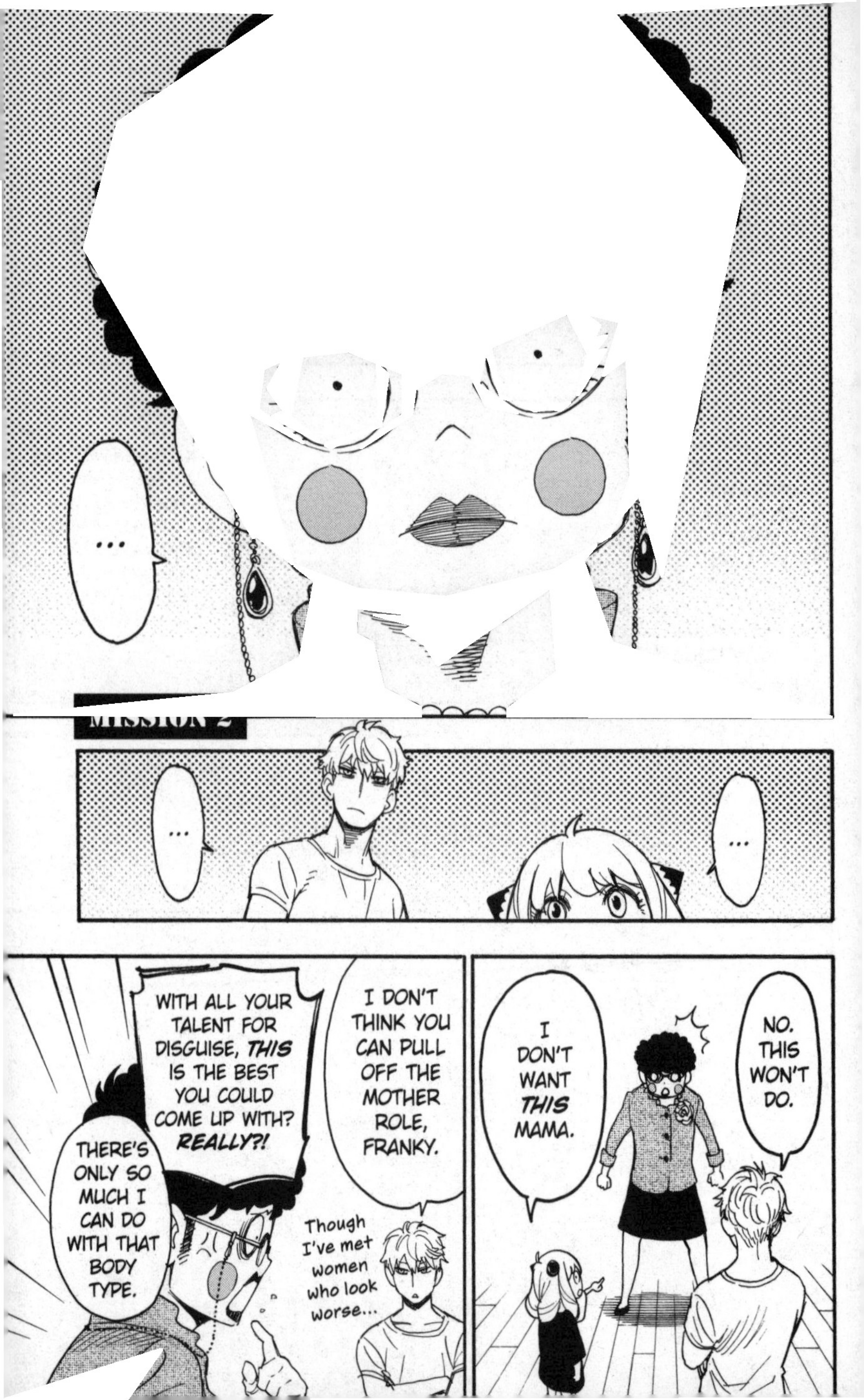
...
MISSION 2
...
...
NO. THIS WON'T DO.
I DON'T WANT *THIS* MAMA.
I DON'T THINK YOU CAN PULL OFF THE MOTHER ROLE, FRANKY.
WITH ALL YOUR TALENT FOR DISGUISE, *THIS* IS THE BEST YOU COULD COME UP WITH? *REALLY?!*
Though I've met women who look worse...
THERE'S ONLY SO MUCH I CAN DO WITH THAT BODY TYPE.

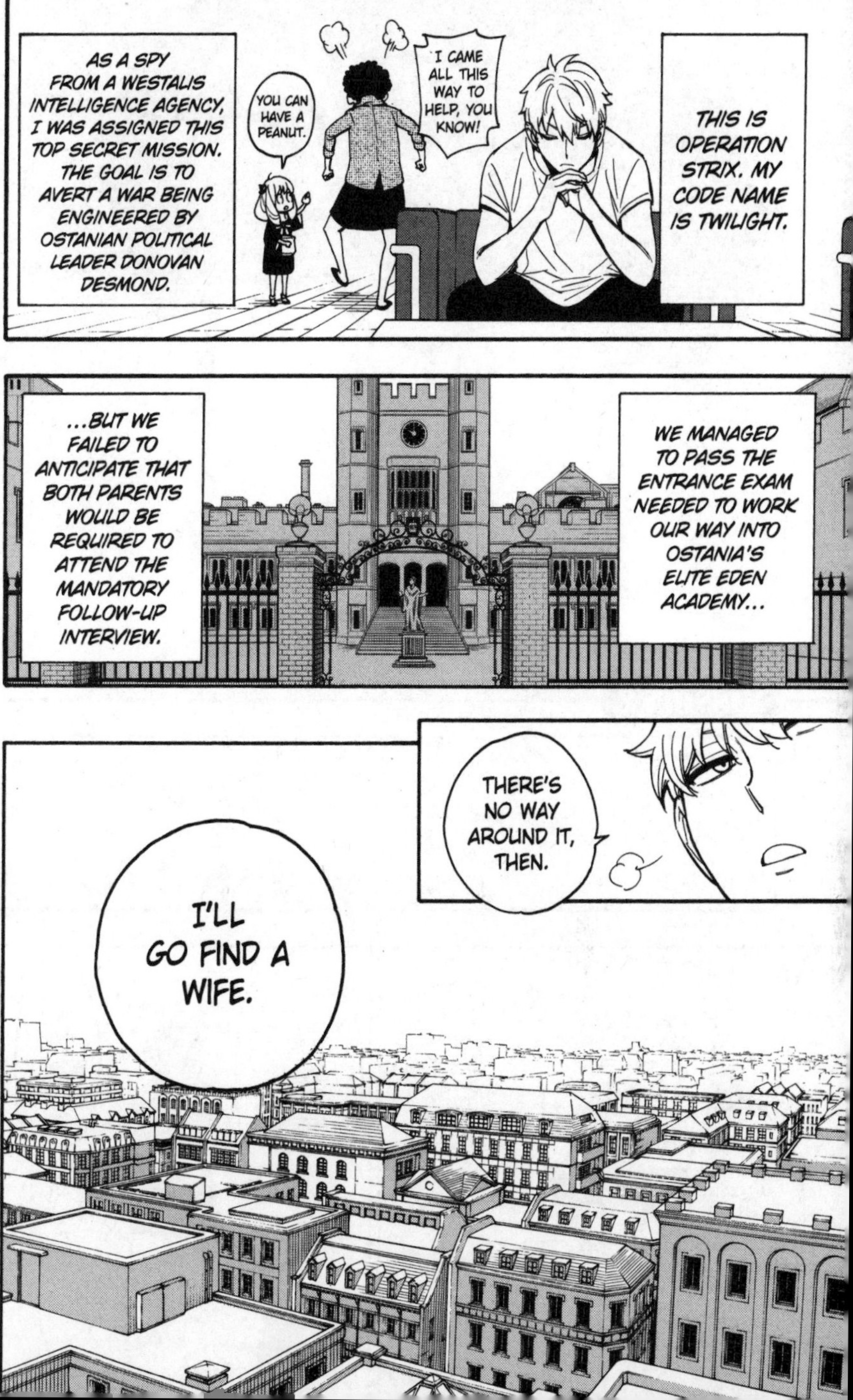
THIS IS OPERATION STRIX. MY CODE NAME IS TWILIGHT.
I CAME ALL THIS WAY TO HELP, YOU KNOW!
YOU CAN HAVE A PEANUT.
AS A SPY FROM A WESTALIS INTELLIGENCE AGENCY, I WAS ASSIGNED THIS TOP SECRET MISSION. THE GOAL IS TO AVERT A WAR BEING ENGINEERED BY OSTANIAN POLITICAL LEADER DONOVAN DESMOND.
WE MANAGED TO PASS THE ENTRANCE EXAM NEEDED TO WORK OUR WAY INTO OSTANIA'S ELITE EDEN ACADEMY...
...BUT WE FAILED TO ANTICIPATE THAT BOTH PARENTS WOULD BE REQUIRED TO ATTEND THE MANDATORY FOLLOW-UP INTERVIEW.
THERE'S NO WAY AROUND IT, THEN.
I'LL GO FIND A WIFE.

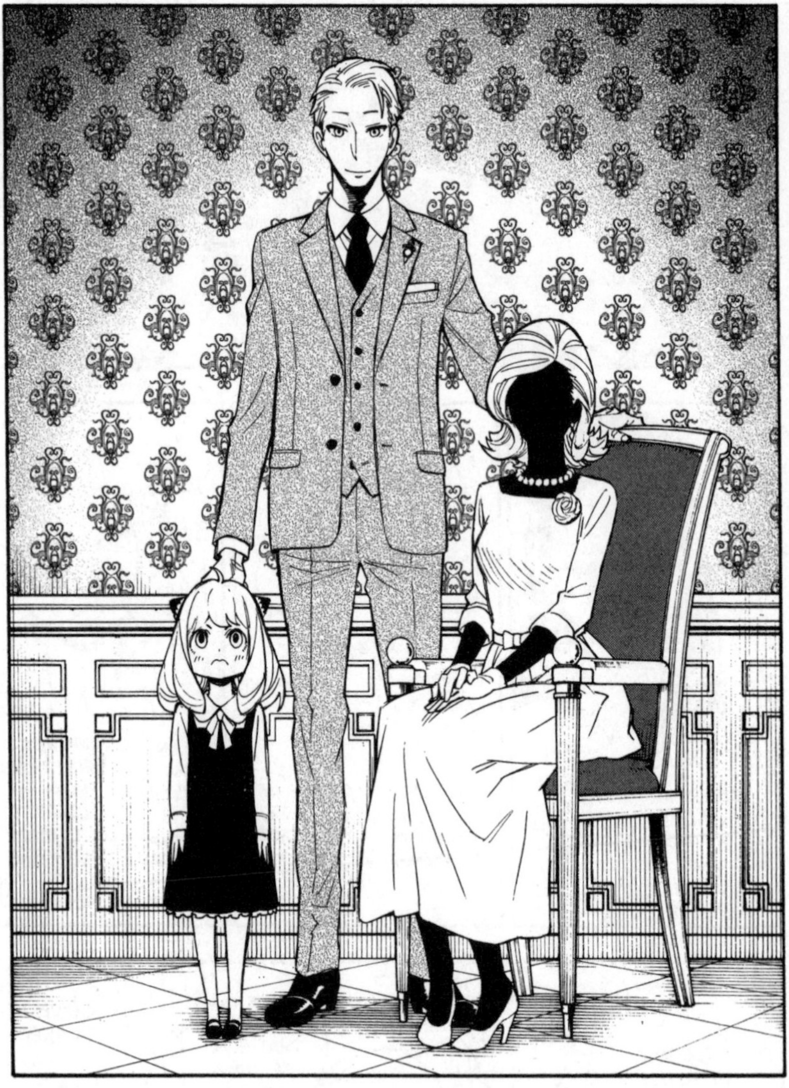

MISSION 2

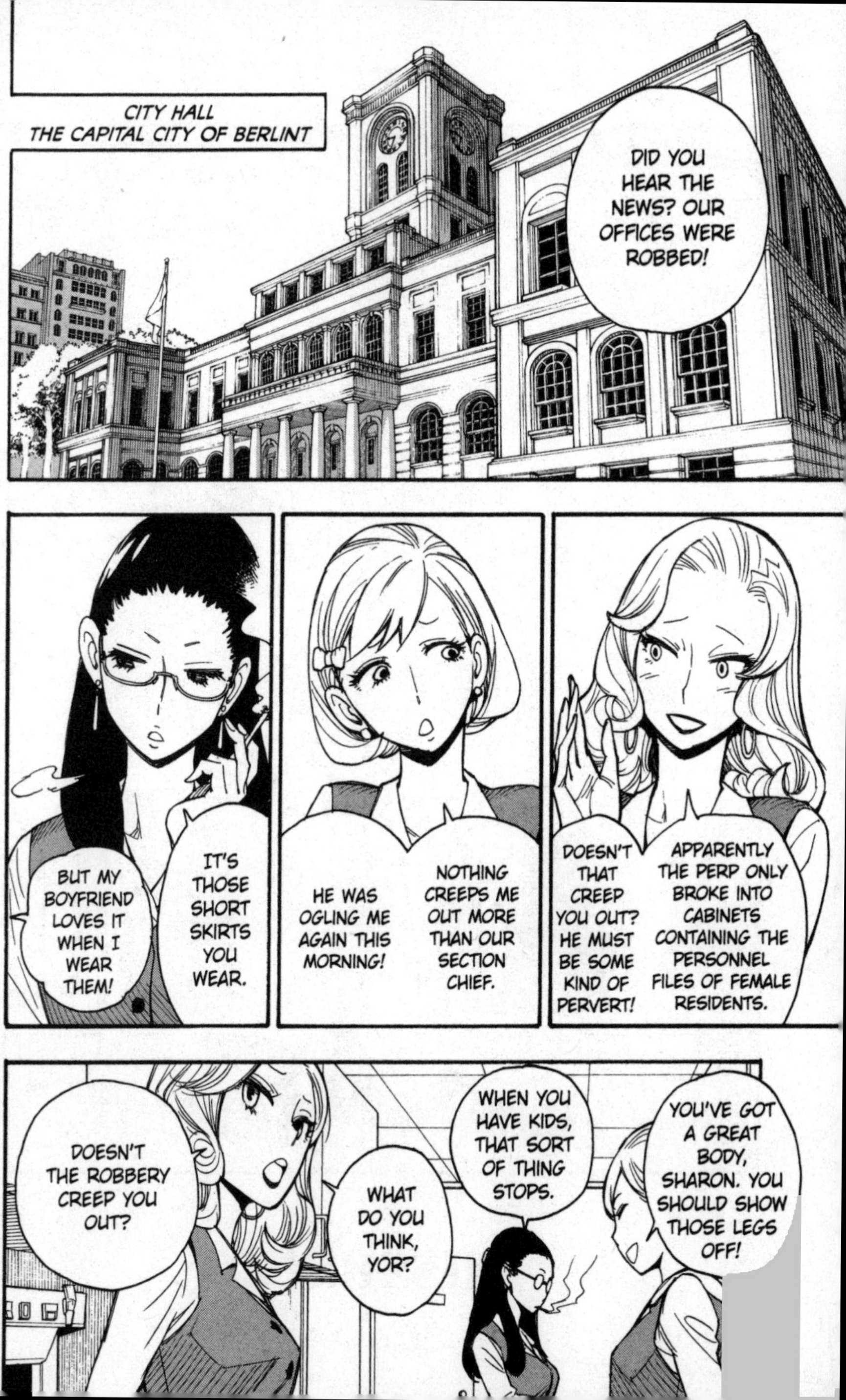
CITY HALL
THE CAPITAL CITY OF BERLINT
DID YOU HEAR THE NEWS? OUR OFFICES WERE ROBBED!
APPARENTLY THE PERP ONLY BROKE INTO CABINETS CONTAINING THE PERSONNEL FILES OF FEMALE RESIDENTS.
DOESN'T THAT CREEP YOU OUT? HE MUST BE SOME KIND OF PERVERT!
NOTHING CREEPS ME OUT MORE THAN OUR SECTION CHIEF.
HE WAS OGLING ME AGAIN THIS MORNING!
IT'S THOSE SHORT SKIRTS YOU WEAR.
BUT MY BOYFRIEND LOVES IT WHEN I WEAR THEM!
YOU'VE GOT A GREAT BODY, SHARON. YOU SHOULD SHOW THOSE LEGS OFF!
WHEN YOU HAVE KIDS, THAT SORT OF THING STOPS.
DOESN'T THE ROBBERY CREEP YOU OUT?
WHAT DO YOU THINK, YOR?

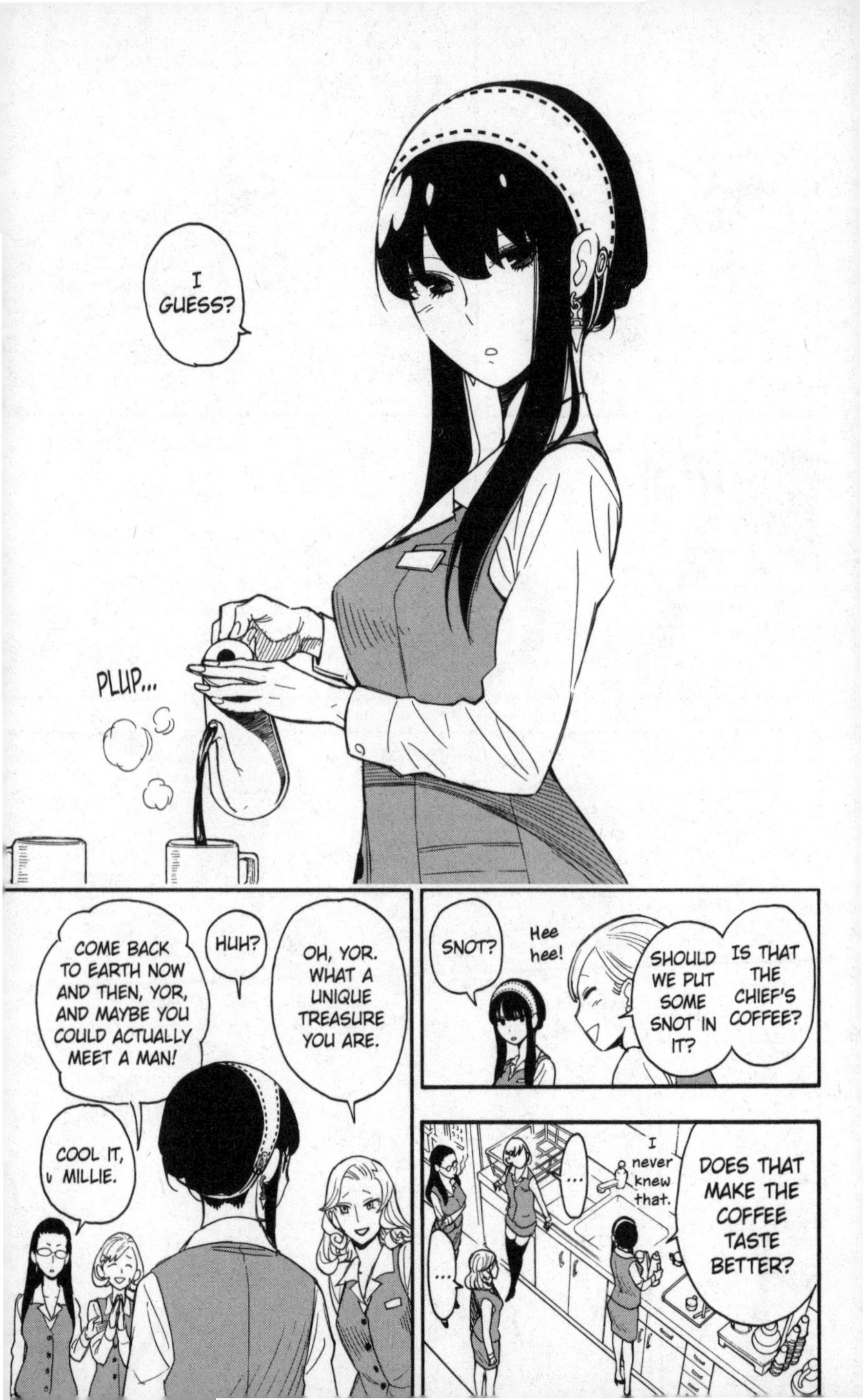
I GUESS?
PLUP...
IS THAT THE CHIEF'S COFFEE?
SHOULD WE PUT SOME SNOT IN IT?
Hee hee!
SNOT?
DOES THAT MAKE THE COFFEE TASTE BETTER?
I never knew that.
...
...
OH, YOR. WHAT A UNIQUE TREASURE YOU ARE.
HUH?
COME BACK TO EARTH NOW AND THEN, YOR, AND MAYBE YOU COULD ACTUALLY MEET A MAN!
COOL IT, MILLIE.

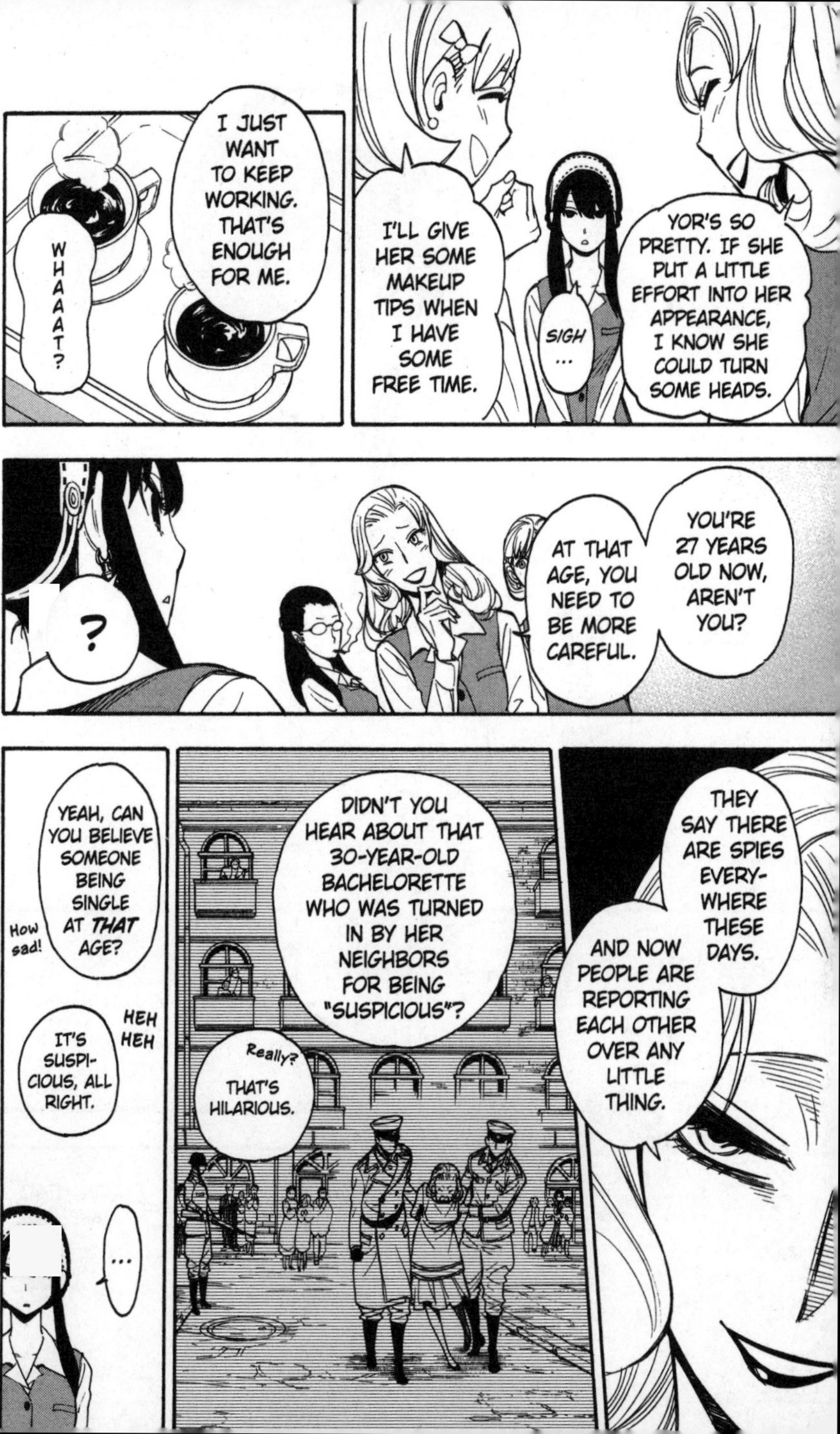
YOR'S SO PRETTY. IF SHE PUT A LITTLE EFFORT INTO HER APPEARANCE, I KNOW SHE COULD TURN SOME HEADS.
SIGH...
I'LL GIVE HER SOME MAKEUP TIPS WHEN I HAVE SOME FREE TIME.
I JUST WANT TO KEEP WORKING. THAT'S ENOUGH FOR ME.
WHAAAT?
YOU'RE 27 YEARS OLD NOW, AREN'T YOU?
AT THAT AGE, YOU NEED TO BE MORE CAREFUL.
?
THEY SAY THERE ARE SPIES EVERYWHERE THESE DAYS.
AND NOW PEOPLE ARE REPORTING EACH OTHER OVER ANY LITTLE THING.
DIDN'T YOU HEAR ABOUT THAT 30-YEAR-OLD BACHELORETTE WHO WAS TURNED IN BY HER NEIGHBORS FOR BEING "SUSPICIOUS"?
Really?
THAT'S HILARIOUS.
YEAH, CAN YOU BELIEVE SOMEONE BEING SINGLE AT *THAT* AGE?
How sad!
HEH HEH
IT'S SUSPICIOUS, ALL RIGHT.
...

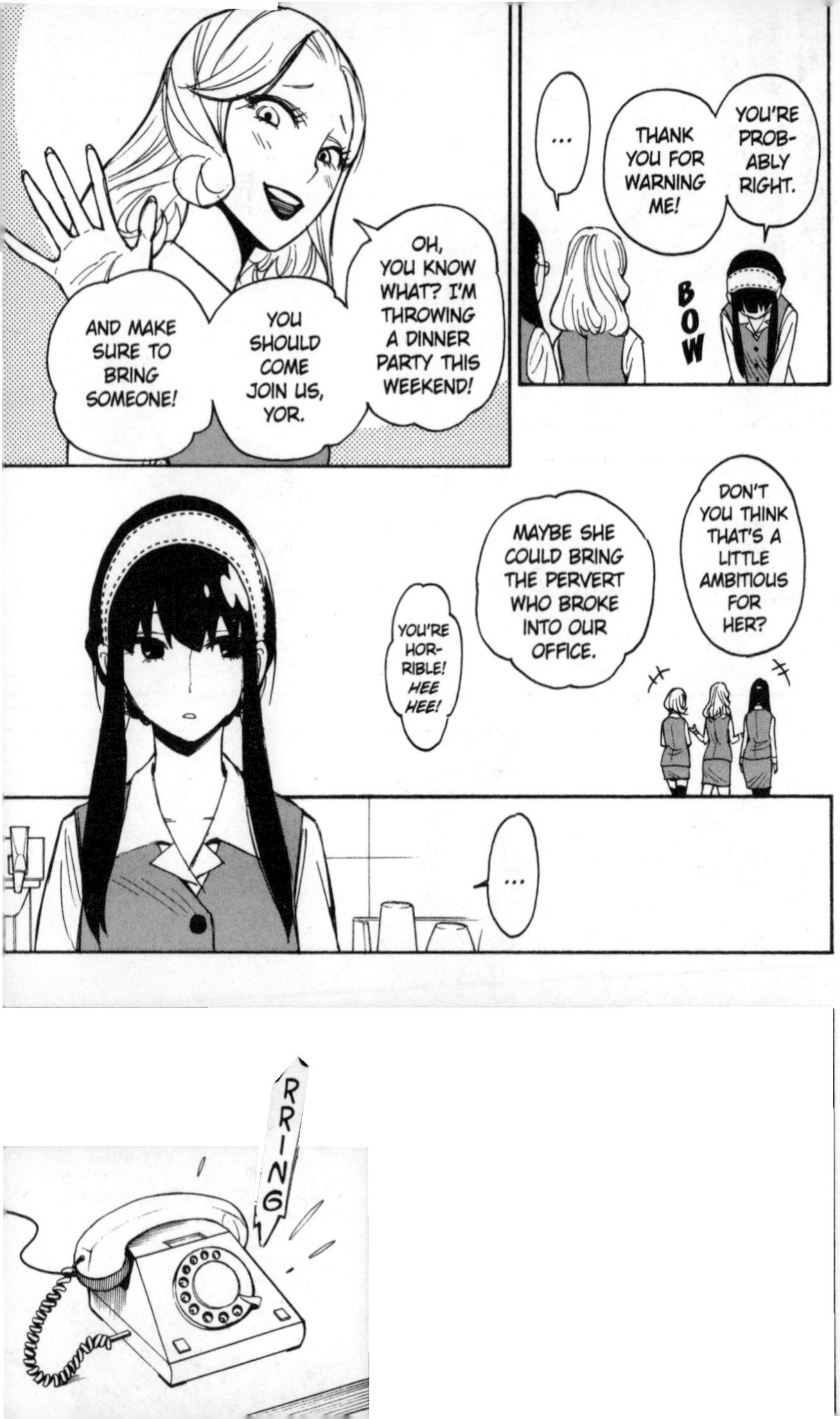
YOU'RE PROB-ABLY RIGHT.
THANK YOU FOR WARNING ME!
...
BOW
OH, YOU KNOW WHAT? I'M THROWING A DINNER PARTY THIS WEEKEND!
YOU SHOULD COME JOIN US, YOR.
AND MAKE SURE TO BRING SOMEONE!
DON'T YOU THINK THAT'S A LITTLE AMBITIOUS FOR HER?
MAYBE SHE COULD BRING THE PERVERT WHO BROKE INTO OUR OFFICE.
YOU'RE HOR-RIBLE! HEE HEE!
...
RRING

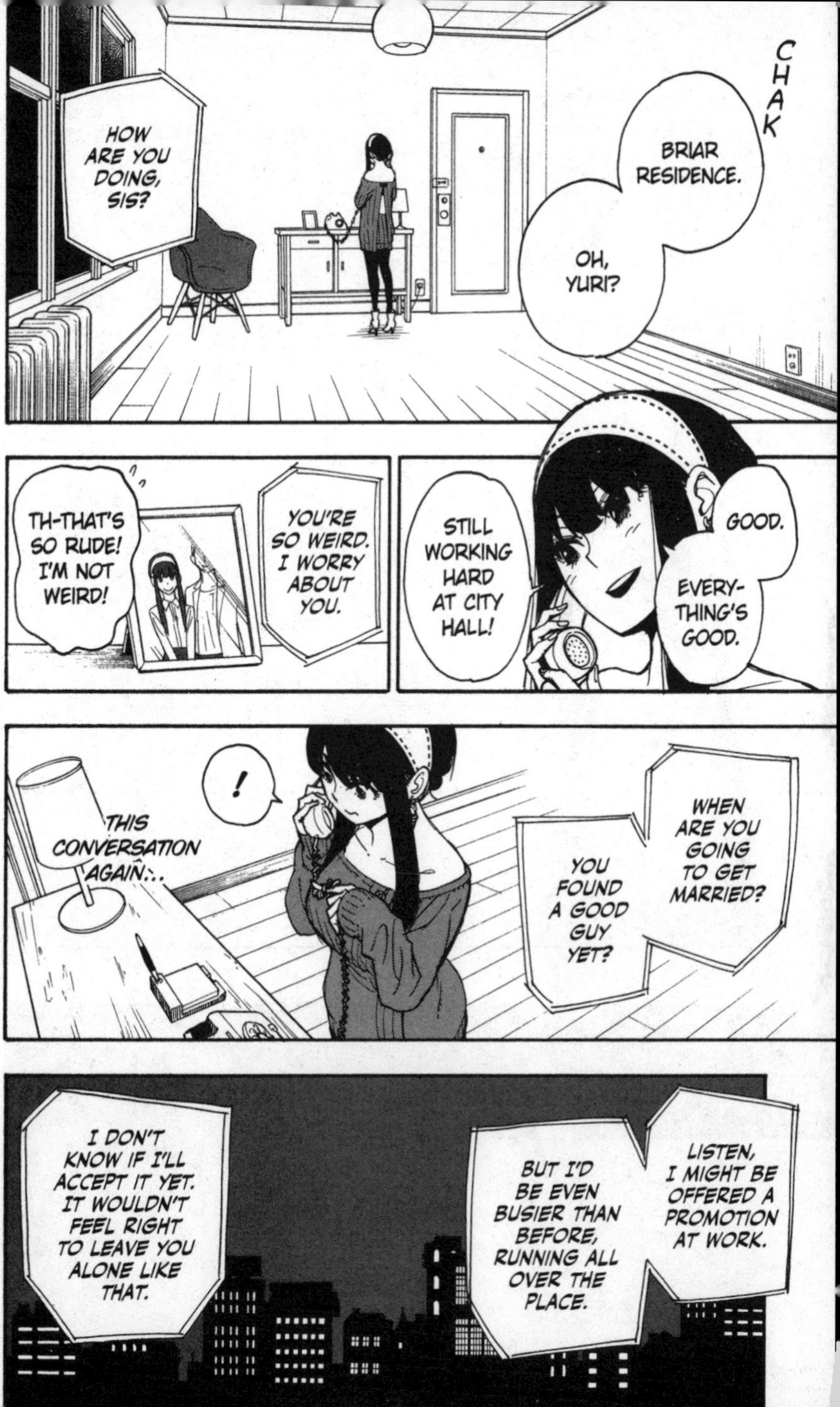
CHAK
BRIAR RESIDENCE.
OH, YURI?
HOW ARE YOU DOING, SIS?
GOOD.
EVERY-THING'S GOOD.
STILL WORKING HARD AT CITY HALL!
YOU'RE SO WEIRD. I WORRY ABOUT YOU.
TH-THAT'S SO RUDE! I'M NOT WEIRD!
WHEN ARE YOU GOING TO GET MARRIED?
YOU FOUND A GOOD GUY YET?
!
THIS CONVERSATION AGAIN...
LISTEN, I MIGHT BE OFFERED A PROMOTION AT WORK.
BUT I'D BE EVEN BUSIER THAN BEFORE, RUNNING ALL OVER THE PLACE.
I DON'T KNOW IF I'LL ACCEPT IT YET. IT WOULDN'T FEEL RIGHT TO LEAVE YOU ALONE LIKE THAT.

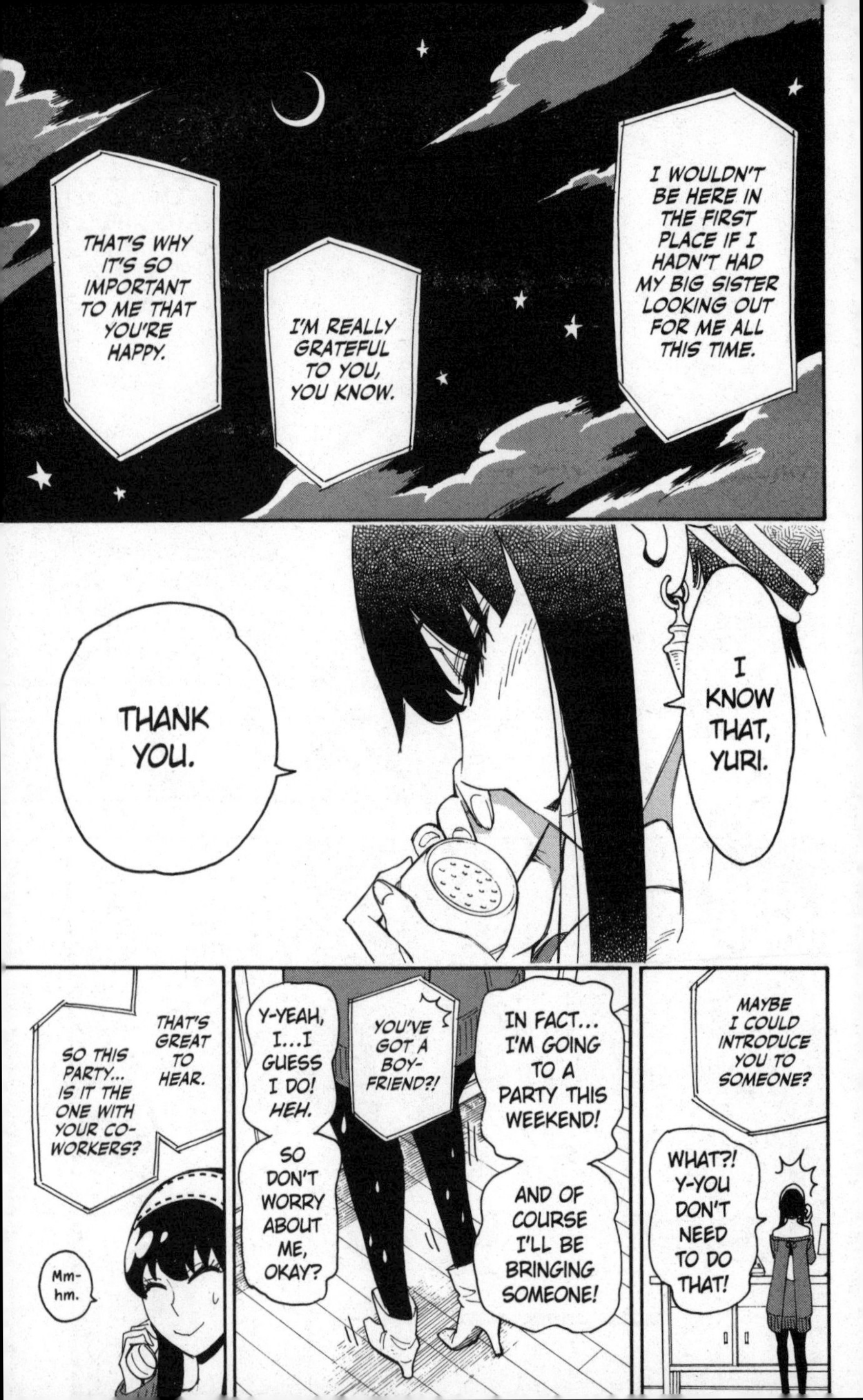
I WOULDN'T BE HERE IN THE FIRST PLACE IF I HADN'T HAD MY BIG SISTER LOOKING OUT FOR ME ALL THIS TIME.
I'M REALLY GRATEFUL TO YOU, YOU KNOW.
THAT'S WHY IT'S SO IMPORTANT TO ME THAT YOU'RE HAPPY.
I KNOW THAT, YURI.
THANK YOU.
MAYBE I COULD INTRODUCE YOU TO SOMEONE?
WHAT?! Y-YOU DON'T NEED TO DO THAT!
IN FACT... I'M GOING TO A PARTY THIS WEEKEND!
AND OF COURSE I'LL BE BRINGING SOMEONE!
YOU'VE GOT A BOY-FRIEND?!
Y-YEAH, I...I GUESS I DO! HEH.
SO DON'T WORRY ABOUT ME, OKAY?
THAT'S GREAT TO HEAR.
SO THIS PARTY... IS IT THE ONE WITH YOUR CO-WORKERS?
Mm-hm.

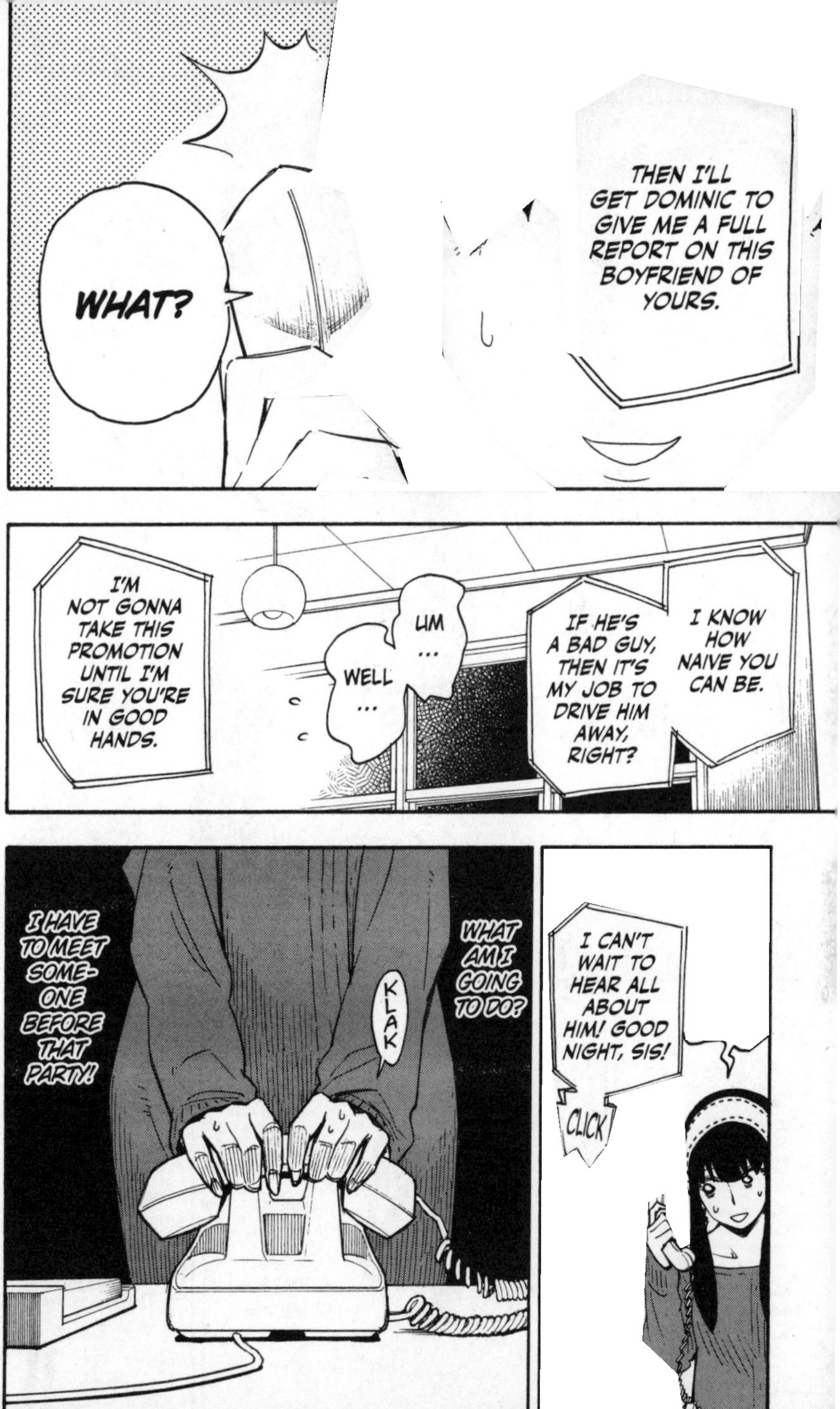
THEN I'LL GET DOMINIC TO GIVE ME A FULL REPORT ON THIS BOYFRIEND OF YOURS.
WHAT?
I KNOW HOW NAIVE YOU CAN BE.
IF HE'S A BAD GUY, THEN IT'S MY JOB TO DRIVE HIM AWAY, RIGHT?
UM ...
WELL ...
I'M NOT GONNA TAKE THIS PROMOTION UNTIL I'M SURE YOU'RE IN GOOD HANDS.
I CAN'T WAIT TO HEAR ALL ABOUT HIM! GOOD NIGHT, SIS!
CLICK
WHAT AM I GOING TO DO?
KLAK
I HAVE TO MEET SOME-ONE BEFORE THAT PARTY!

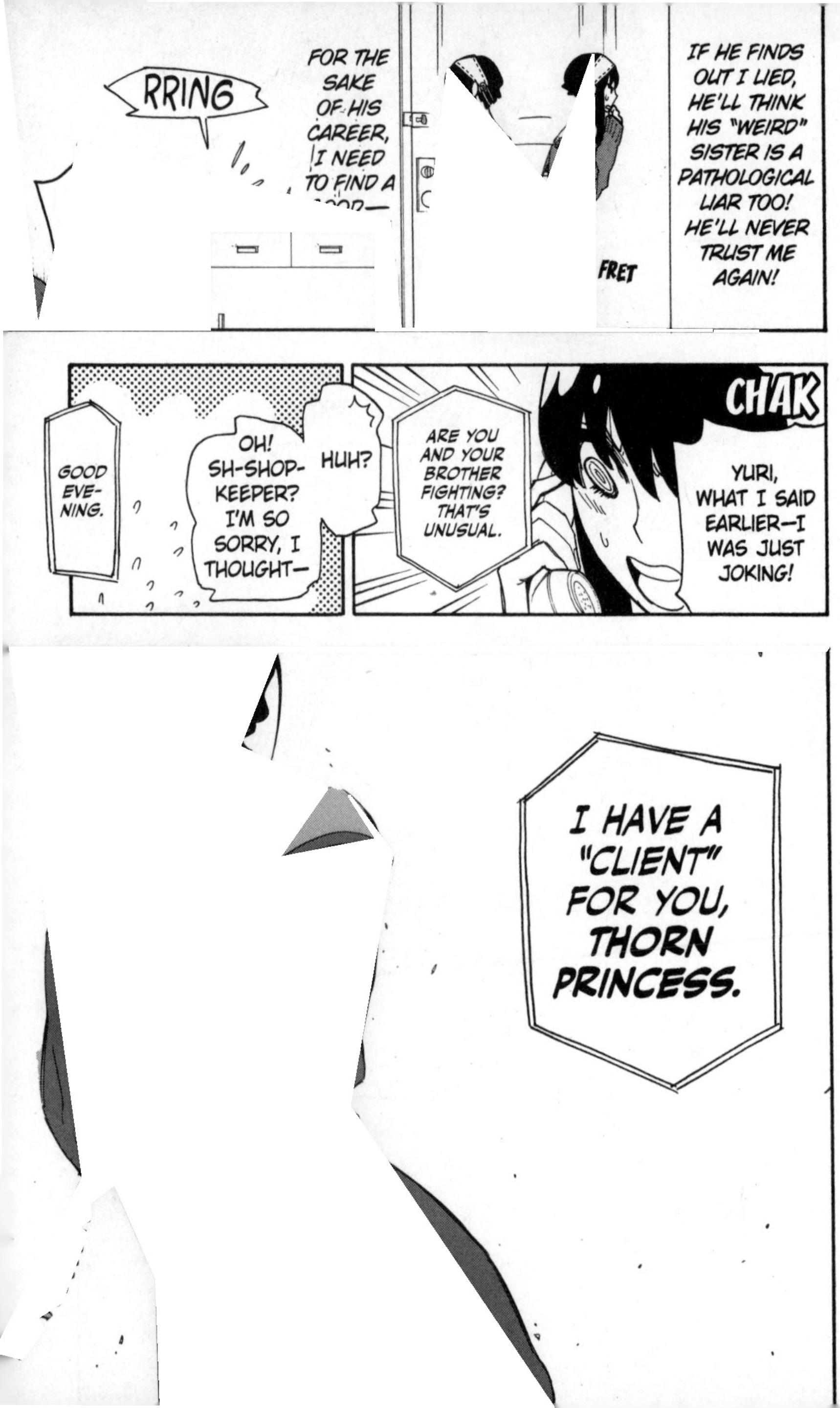
IF HE FINDS OUT I LIED, HE'LL THINK HIS "WEIRD" SISTER IS A PATHOLOGICAL LIAR TOO! HE'LL NEVER TRUST ME AGAIN!
FRET
FOR THE SAKE OF HIS CAREER, I NEED TO FIND A
RRING
CHAK
YURI, WHAT I SAID EARLIER—I WAS JUST JOKING!
ARE YOU AND YOUR BROTHER FIGHTING? THAT'S UNUSUAL.
HUH?
OH! SH-SHOP-KEEPER? I'M SO SORRY, I THOUGHT—
GOOD EVE-NING.
I HAVE A "CLIENT" FOR YOU, THORN PRINCESS.

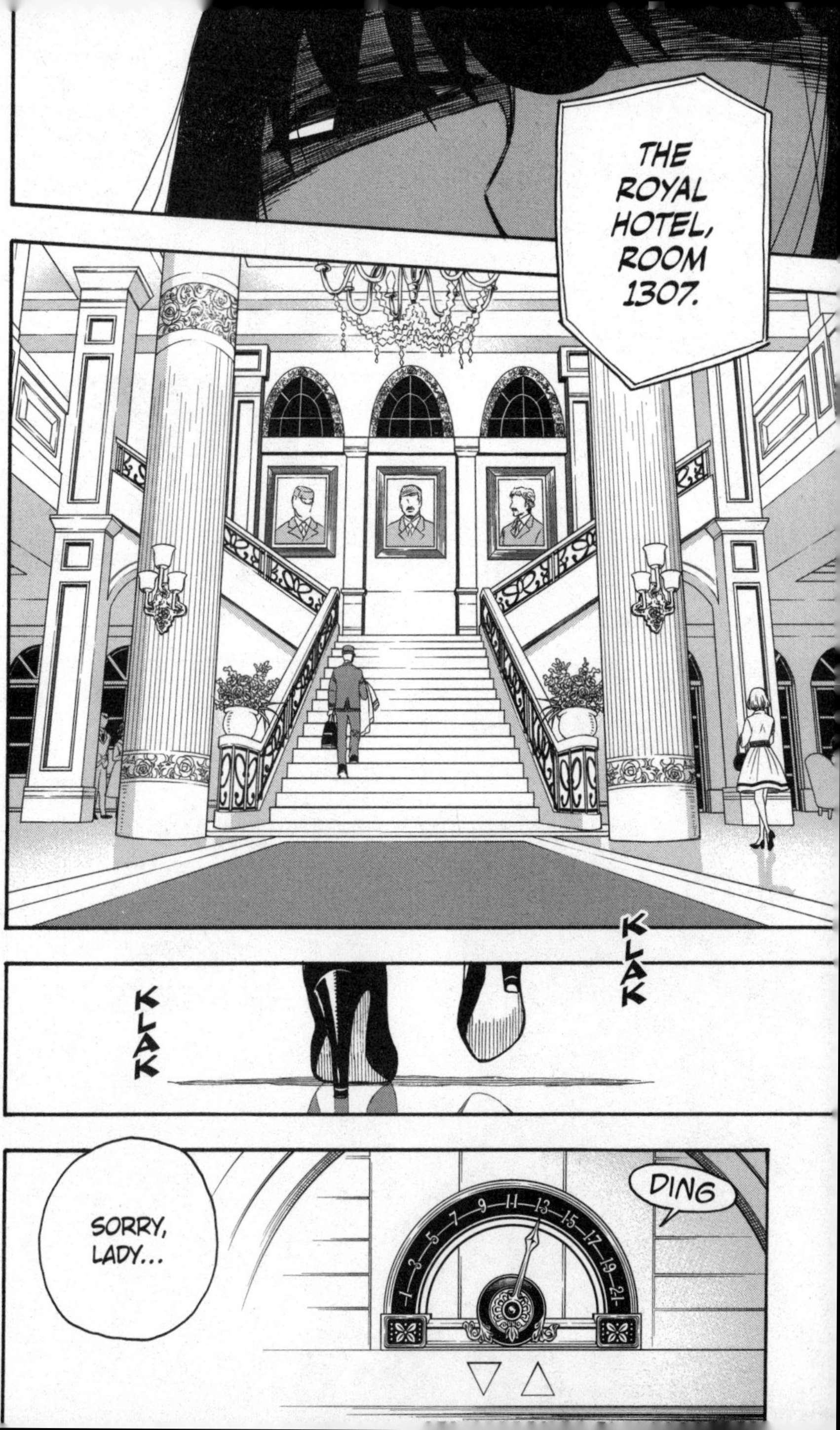
THE ROYAL HOTEL, ROOM 1307.
KLAK
KLAK
DING
SORRY, LADY...

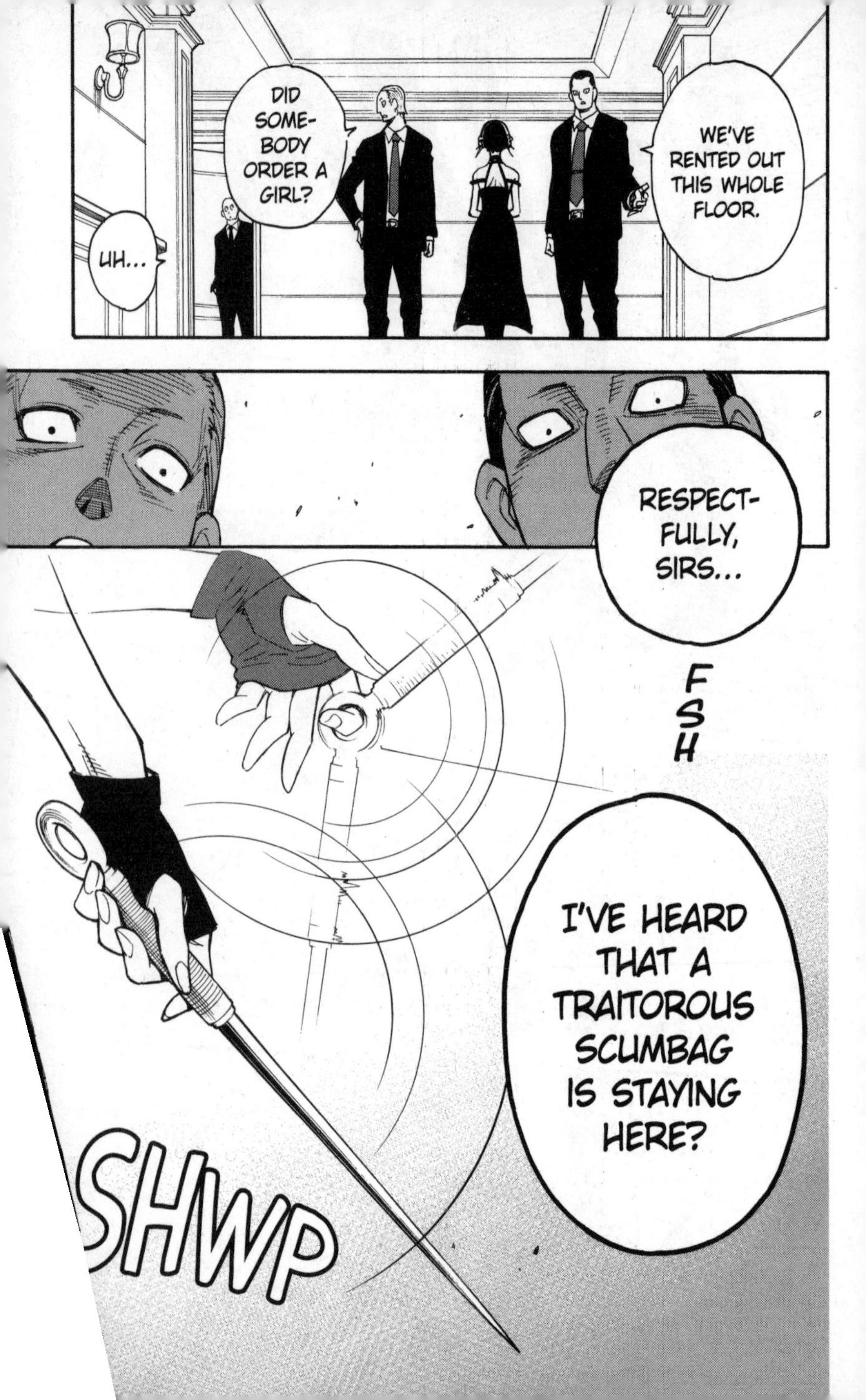
WE'VE RENTED OUT THIS WHOLE FLOOR.
DID SOME-BODY ORDER A GIRL?
UH...
RESPECT-FULLY, SIRS...
FSH
I'VE HEARD THAT A TRAITOROUS SCUMBAG IS STAYING HERE?
SHWP

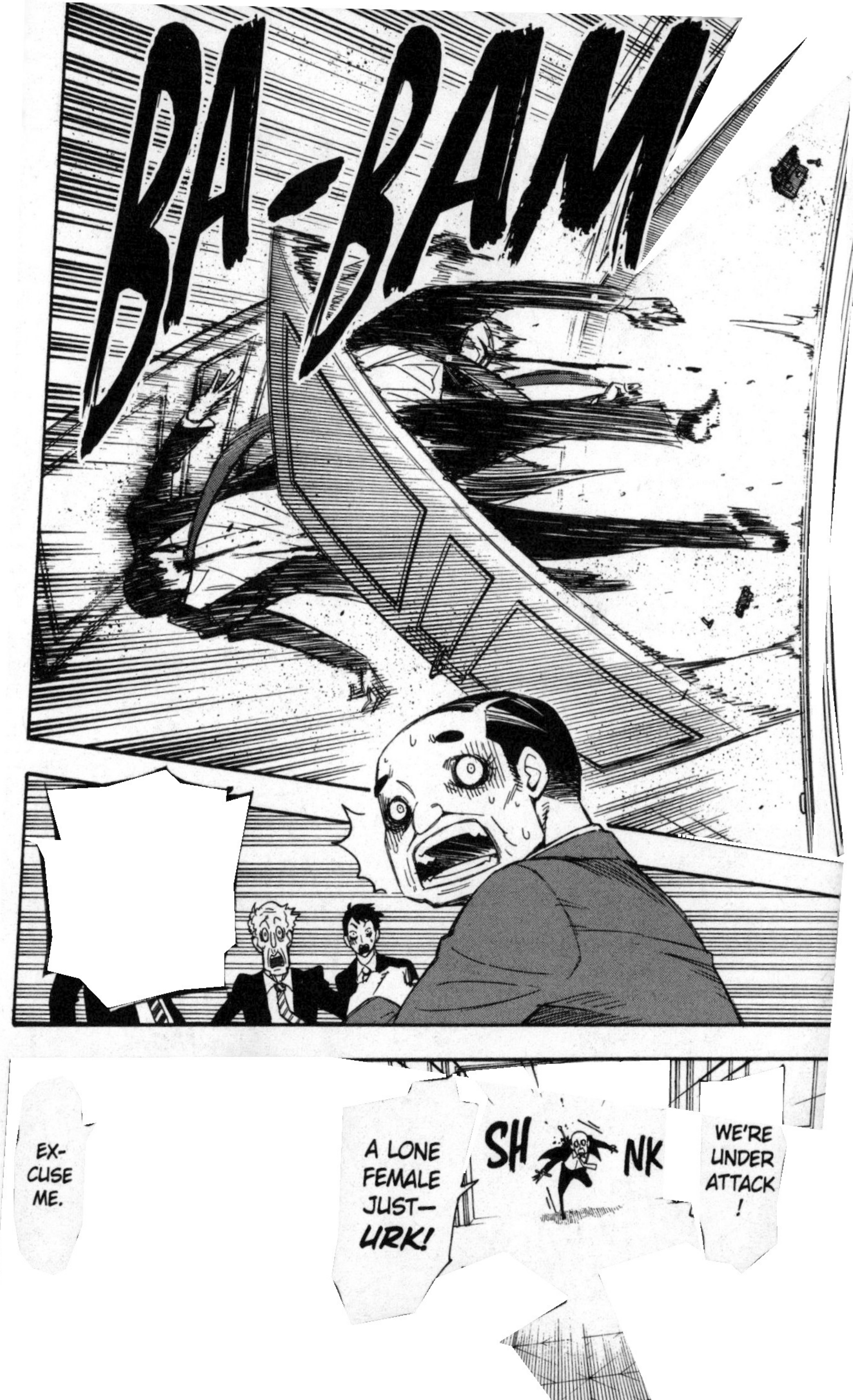
BA-BAM
WE'RE UNDER ATTACK!
SH NK
A LONE FEMALE JUST— URK!
EX-CUSE ME.

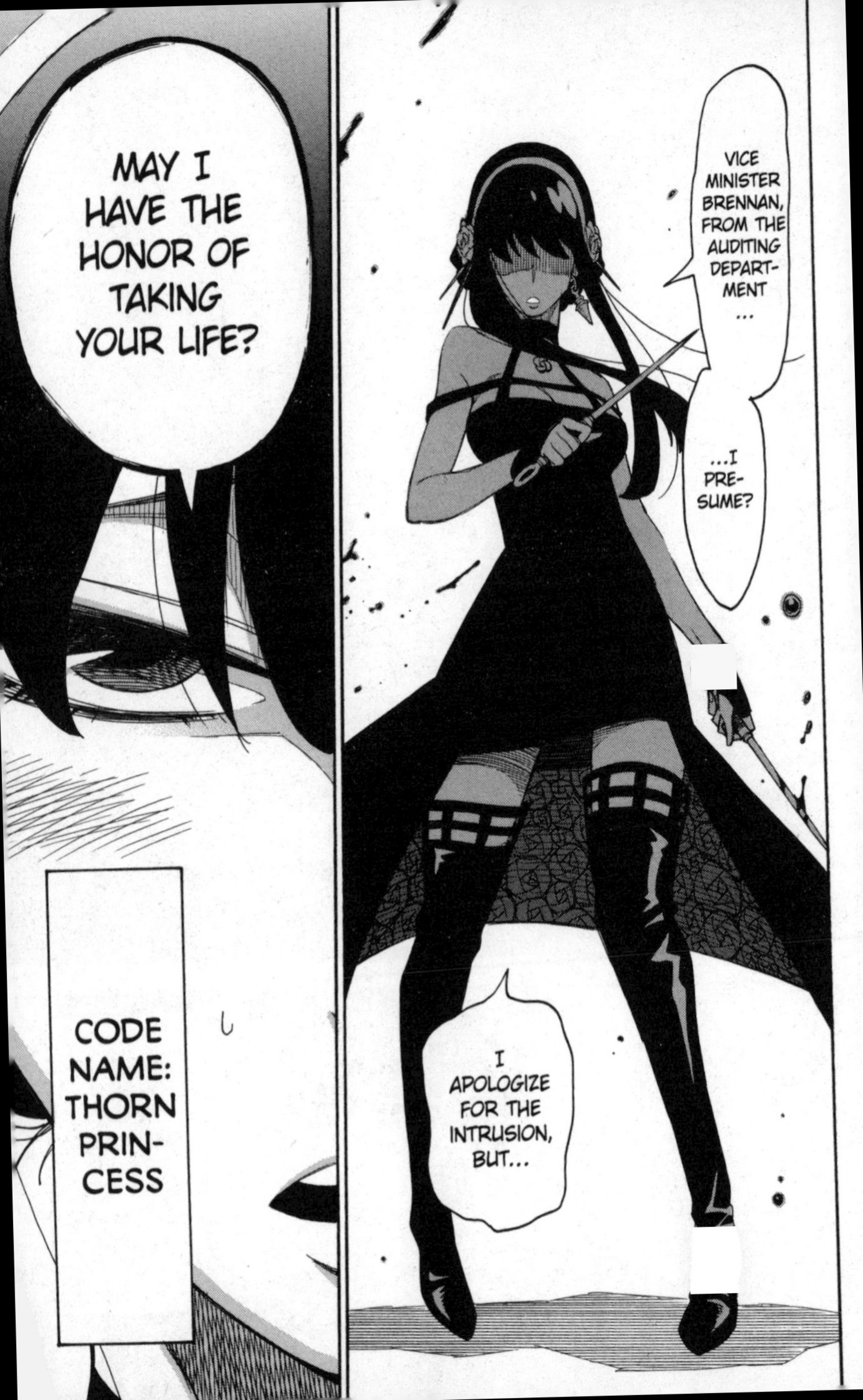
VICE MINISTER BRENNAN, FROM THE AUDITING DEPART-MENT...
...I PRE-SUME?
I APOLOGIZE FOR THE INTRUSION, BUT...
MAY I HAVE THE HONOR OF TAKING YOUR LIFE?
CODE NAME: THORN PRIN-CESS

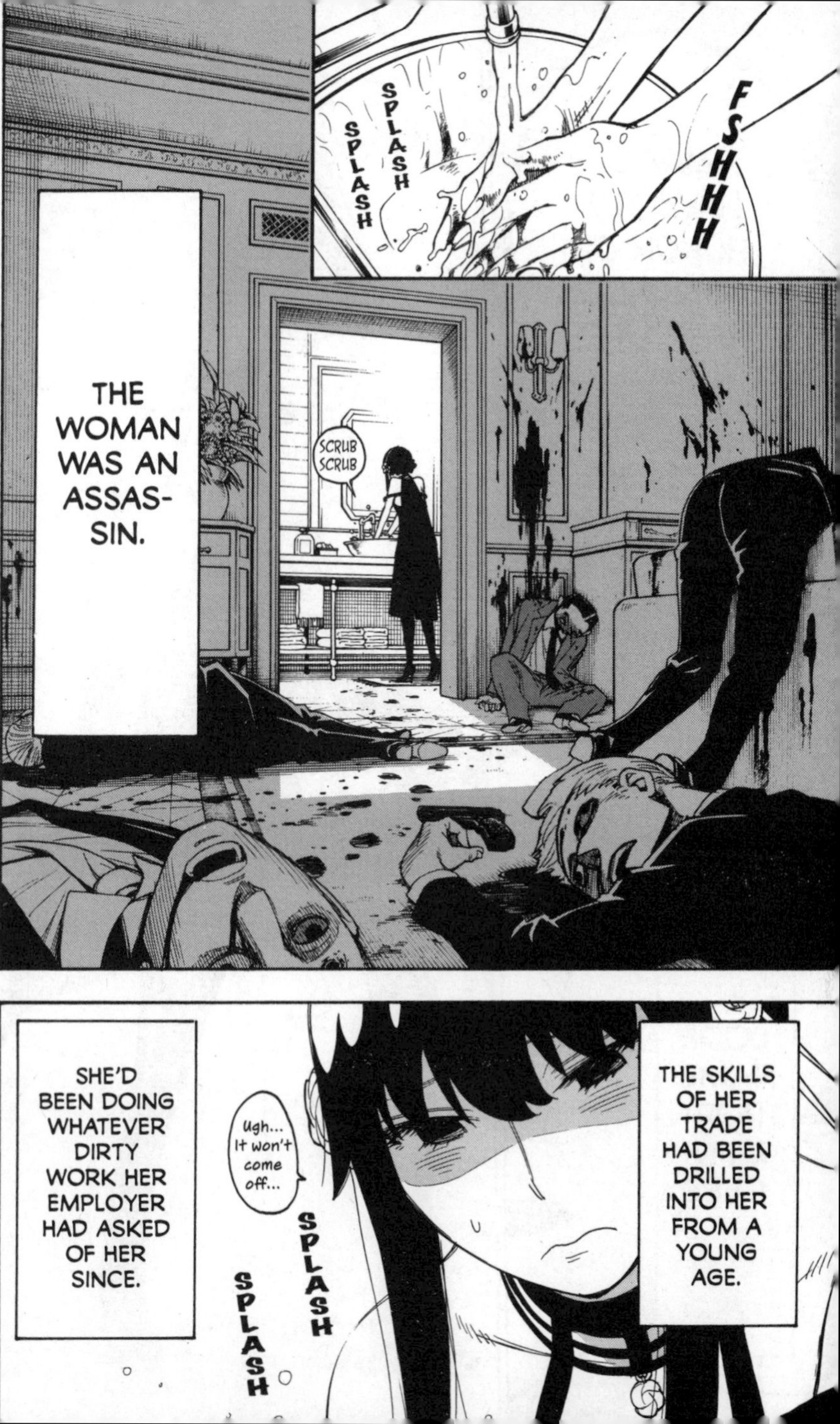
FSHHH
SPLASH
SPLASH
THE WOMAN WAS AN ASSAS-SIN.
SCRUB SCRUB
THE SKILLS OF HER TRADE HAD BEEN DRILLED INTO HER FROM A YOUNG AGE.
Ugh... It won't come off...
SPLASH
SPLASH
SHE'D BEEN DOING WHATEVER DIRTY WORK HER EMPLOYER HAD ASKED OF HER SINCE.

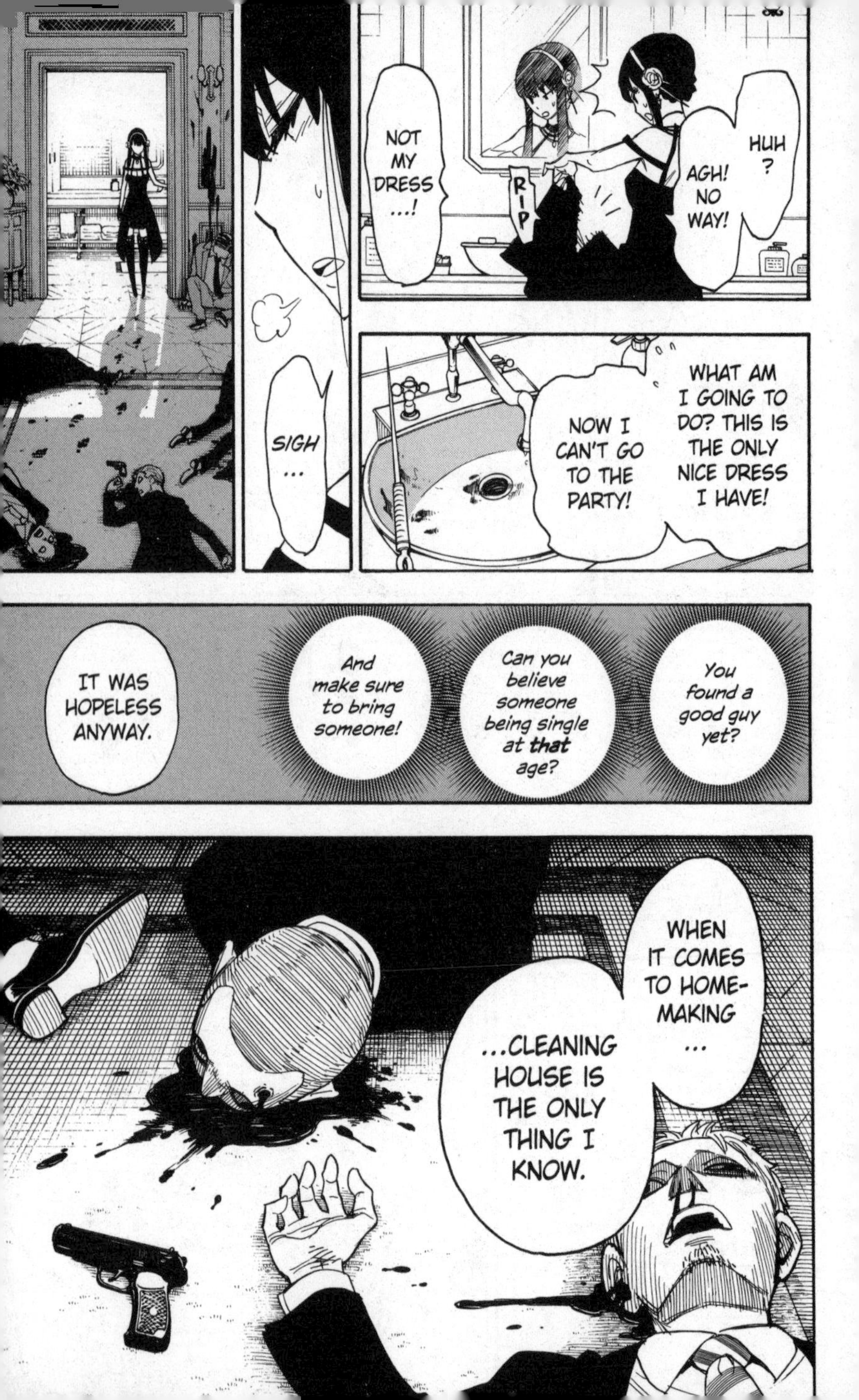
HUH?
AGH! NO WAY!
RIP
NOT MY DRESS ...!
WHAT AM I GOING TO DO? THIS IS THE ONLY NICE DRESS I HAVE!
NOW I CAN'T GO TO THE PARTY!
SIGH ...
You found a good guy yet?
Can you believe someone being single at **that** age?
And make sure to bring someone!
IT WAS HOPELESS ANYWAY.
WHEN IT COMES TO HOME-MAKING ...
...CLEANING HOUSE IS THE ONLY THING I KNOW.

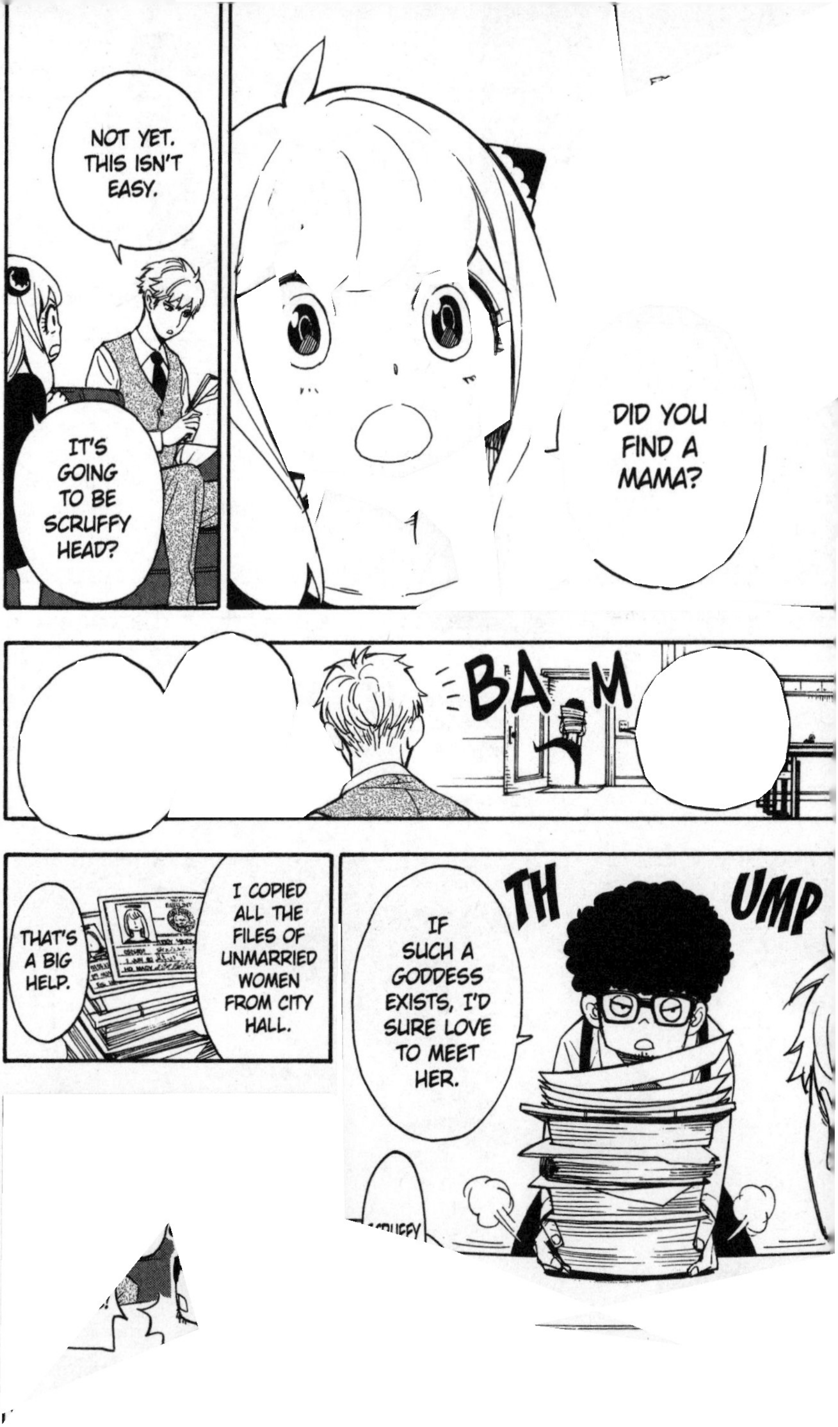
DID YOU FIND A MAMA?
NOT YET. THIS ISN'T EASY.
IT'S GOING TO BE SCRUFFY HEAD?
BAM
THUMP
IF SUCH A GODDESS EXISTS, I'D SURE LOVE TO MEET HER.
I COPIED ALL THE FILES OF UNMARRIED WOMEN FROM CITY HALL.
THAT'S A BIG HELP.

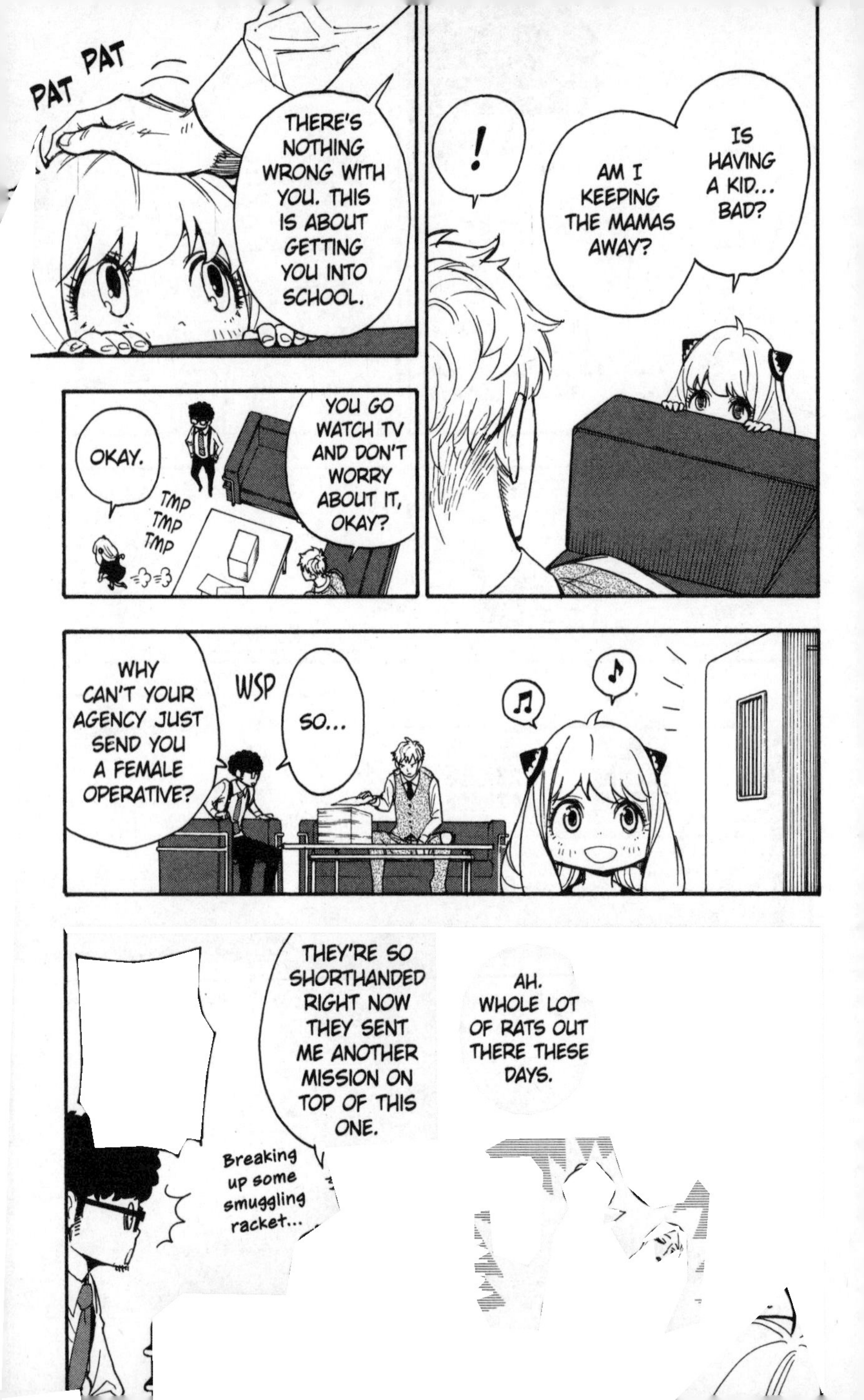
!
IS HAVING A KID... BAD?
AM I KEEPING THE MAMAS AWAY?
PAT PAT
THERE'S NOTHING WRONG WITH YOU. THIS IS ABOUT GETTING YOU INTO SCHOOL.
YOU GO WATCH TV AND DON'T WORRY ABOUT IT, OKAY?
OKAY.
TMP TMP TMP
♪
♪
SO...
WSP
WHY CAN'T YOUR AGENCY JUST SEND YOU A FEMALE OPERATIVE?
AH. WHOLE LOT OF RATS OUT THERE THESE DAYS.
THEY'RE SO SHORTHANDED RIGHT NOW THEY SENT ME ANOTHER MISSION ON TOP OF THIS ONE.
Breaking up some smuggling racket...

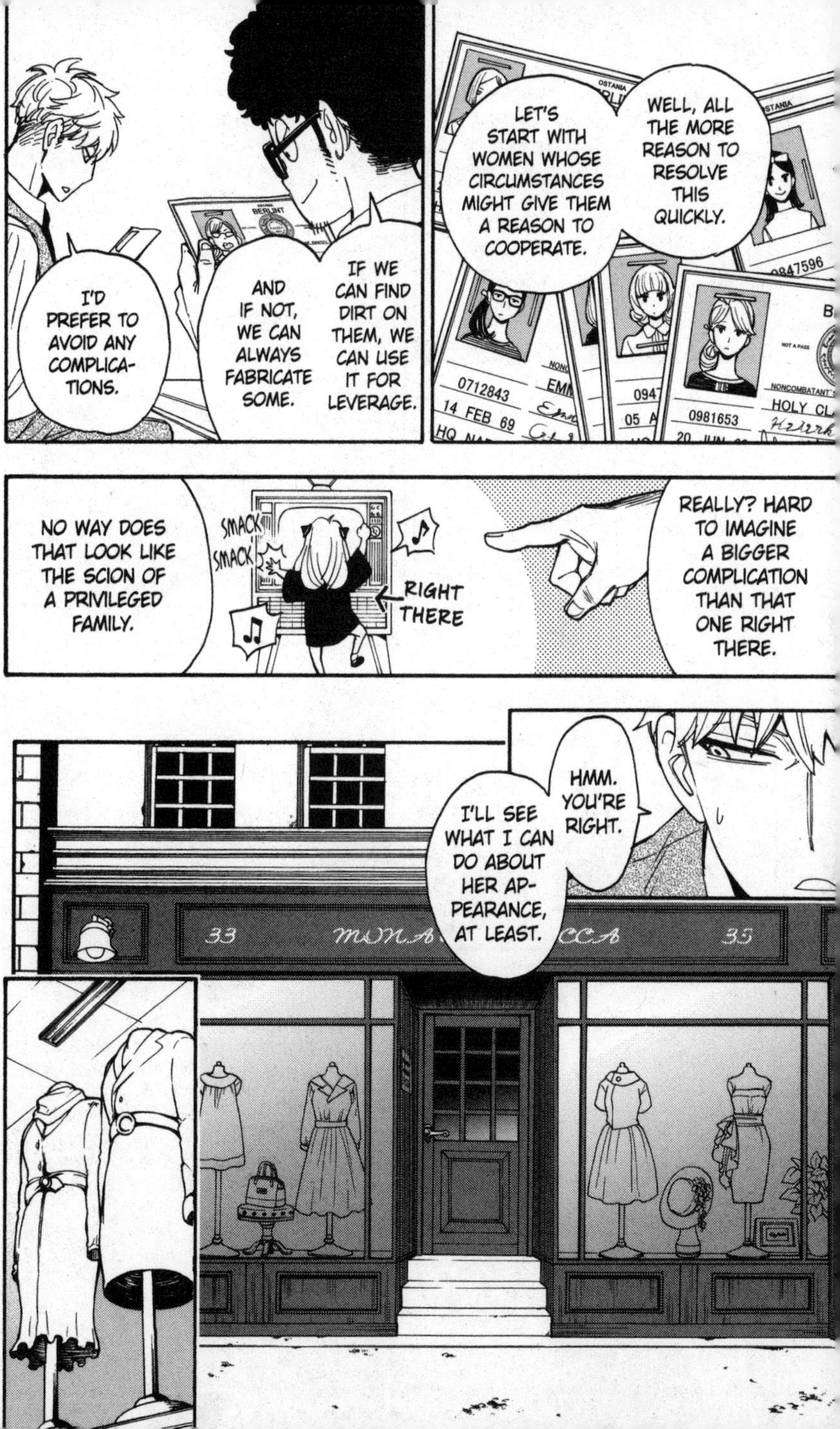
WELL, ALL THE MORE REASON TO RESOLVE THIS QUICKLY.
LET'S START WITH WOMEN WHOSE CIRCUMSTANCES MIGHT GIVE THEM A REASON TO COOPERATE.
IF WE CAN FIND DIRT ON THEM, WE CAN USE IT FOR LEVERAGE.
AND IF NOT, WE CAN ALWAYS FABRICATE SOME.
I'D PREFER TO AVOID ANY COMPLICATIONS.
REALLY? HARD TO IMAGINE A BIGGER COMPLICATION THAN THAT ONE RIGHT THERE.
RIGHT THERE
SMACK
SMACK
NO WAY DOES THAT LOOK LIKE THE SCION OF A PRIVILEGED FAMILY.
HMM. YOU'RE RIGHT.
I'LL SEE WHAT I CAN DO ABOUT HER APPEARANCE, AT LEAST.
33
35

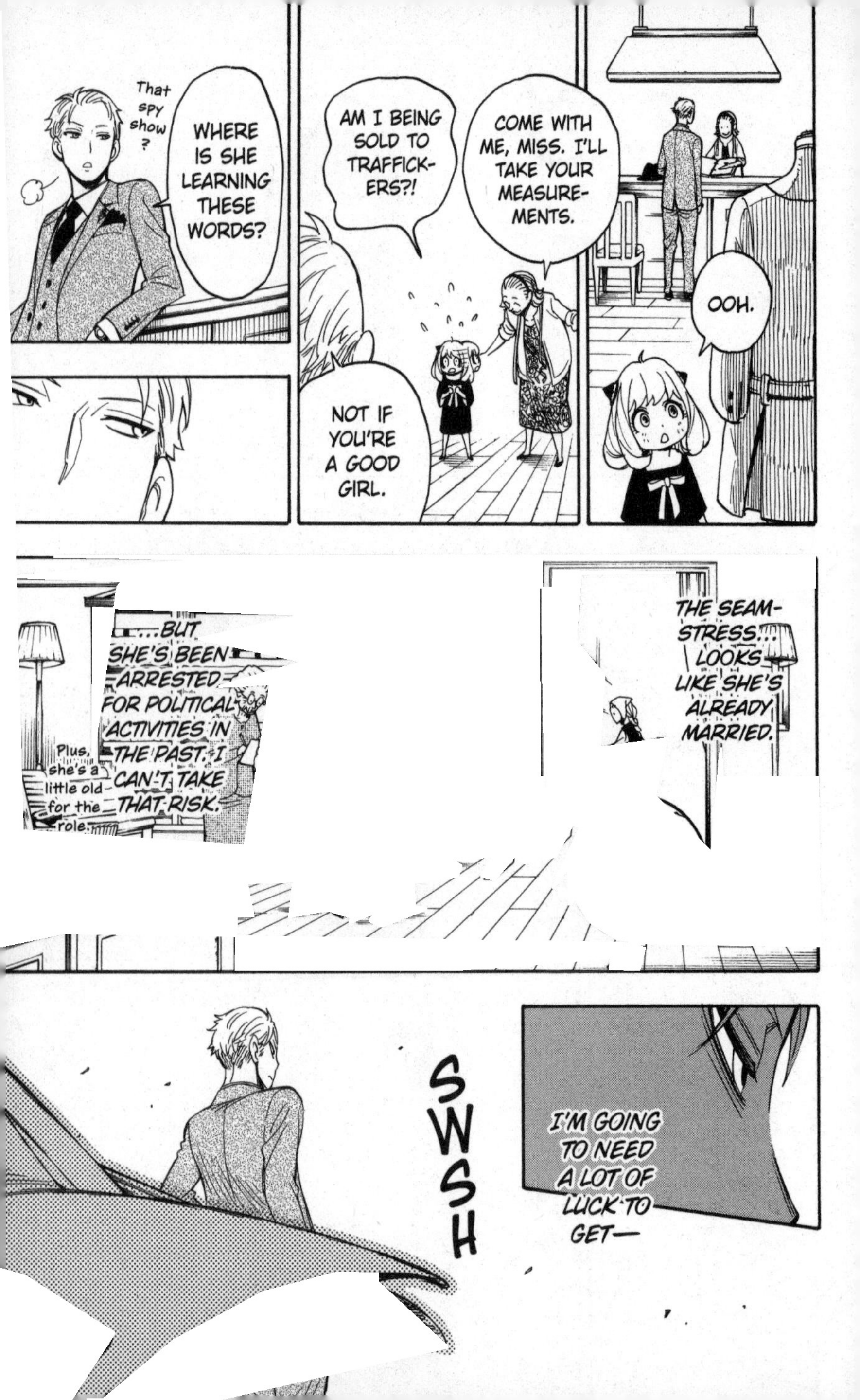
OOH.
COME WITH ME, MISS. I'LL TAKE YOUR MEASURE-MENTS.
AM I BEING SOLD TO TRAFFICK-ERS?!
NOT IF YOU'RE A GOOD GIRL.
WHERE IS SHE LEARNING THESE WORDS?
That spy show?
THE SEAM-STRESS... LOOKS LIKE SHE'S ALREADY MARRIED.
...BUT SHE'S BEEN ARRESTED FOR POLITICAL ACTIVITIES IN THE PAST. I CAN'T TAKE THAT RISK.
Plus, she's a little old for the role.
I'M GOING TO NEED A LOT OF LUCK TO GET—
SWSH

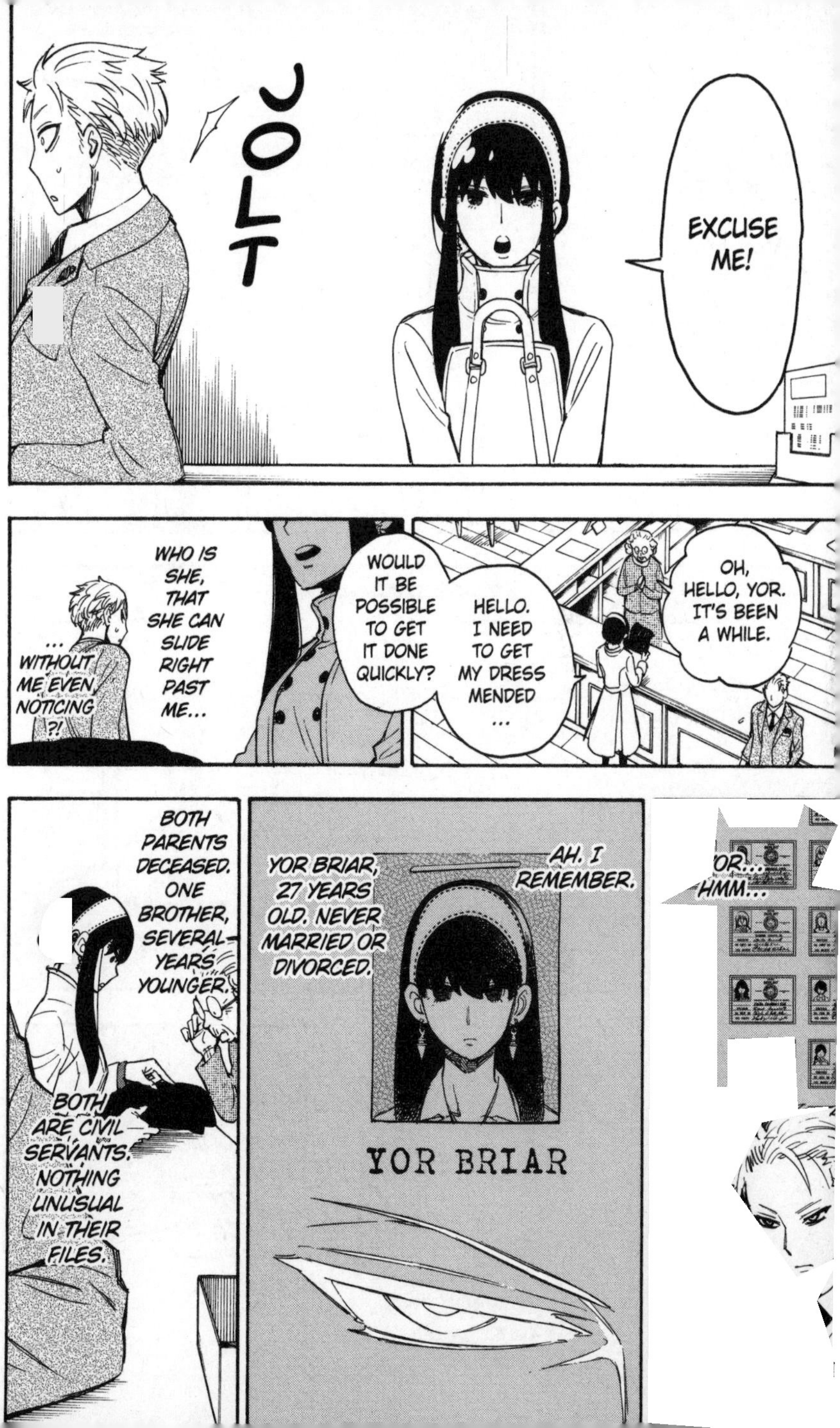
EXCUSE ME!
JOLT
OH, HELLO, YOR. IT'S BEEN A WHILE.
HELLO. I NEED TO GET MY DRESS MENDED...
WOULD IT BE POSSIBLE TO GET IT DONE QUICKLY?
WHO IS SHE, THAT SHE CAN SLIDE RIGHT PAST ME...
...WITHOUT ME EVEN NOTICING?!
OR... HMM...
AH. I REMEMBER.
YOR BRIAR, 27 YEARS OLD. NEVER MARRIED OR DIVORCED.
YOR BRIAR
BOTH PARENTS DECEASED. ONE BROTHER, SEVERAL YEARS YOUNGER.
BOTH ARE CIVIL SERVANTS. NOTHING UNUSUAL IN THEIR FILES.

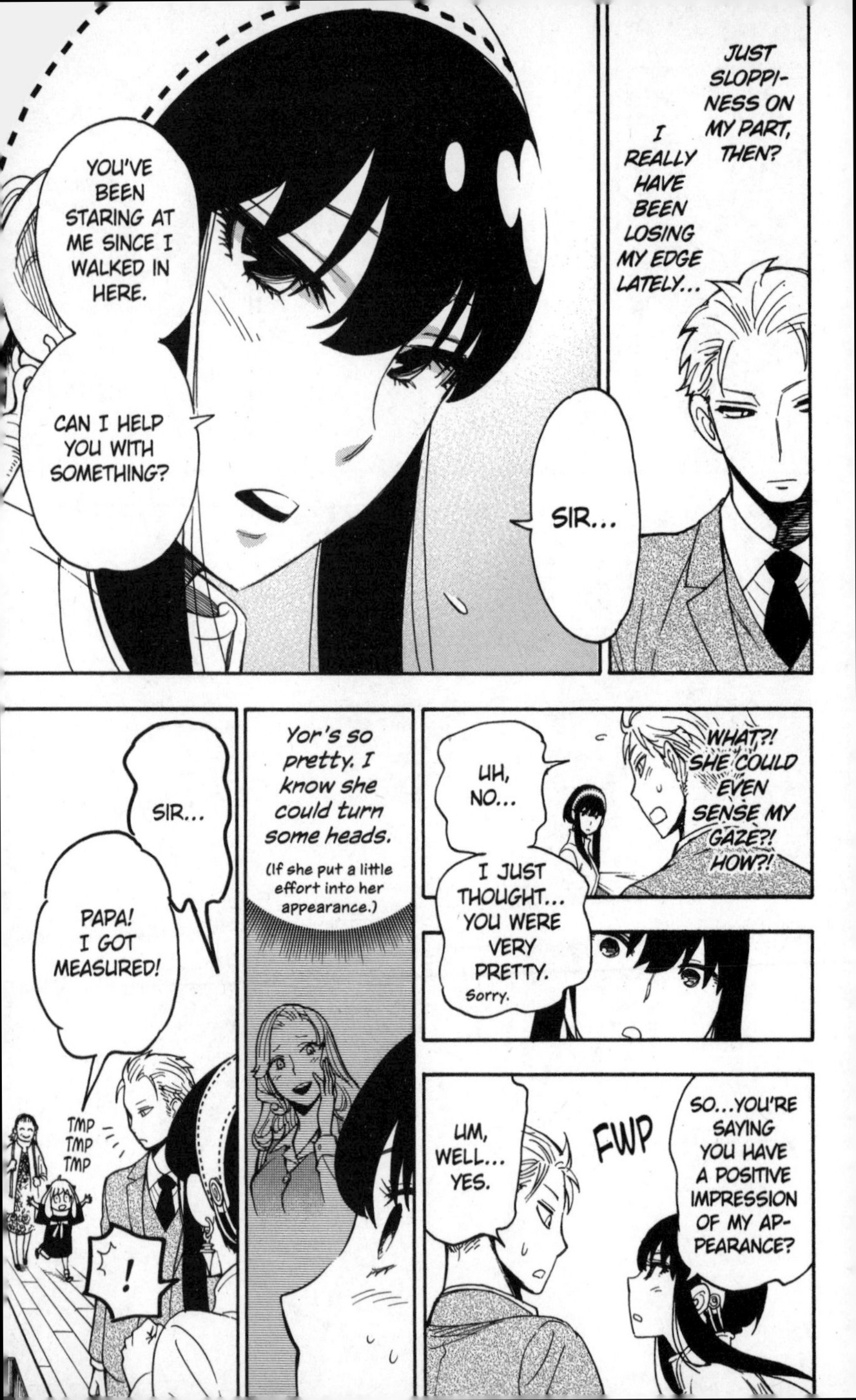
JUST SLOPPINESS ON MY PART, THEN?
I REALLY HAVE BEEN LOSING MY EDGE LATELY...
SIR...
YOU'VE BEEN STARING AT ME SINCE I WALKED IN HERE.
CAN I HELP YOU WITH SOMETHING?
WHAT?! SHE COULD EVEN SENSE MY GAZE?! HOW?!
UH, NO...
I JUST THOUGHT... YOU WERE VERY PRETTY.
Sorry.
SO...YOU'RE SAYING YOU HAVE A POSITIVE IMPRESSION OF MY APPEARANCE?
FWP
UM, WELL... YES.
Yor's so pretty. I know she could turn some heads.
(If she put a little effort into her appearance.)
SIR...
PAPA! I GOT MEASURED!
TMP TMP TMP
!

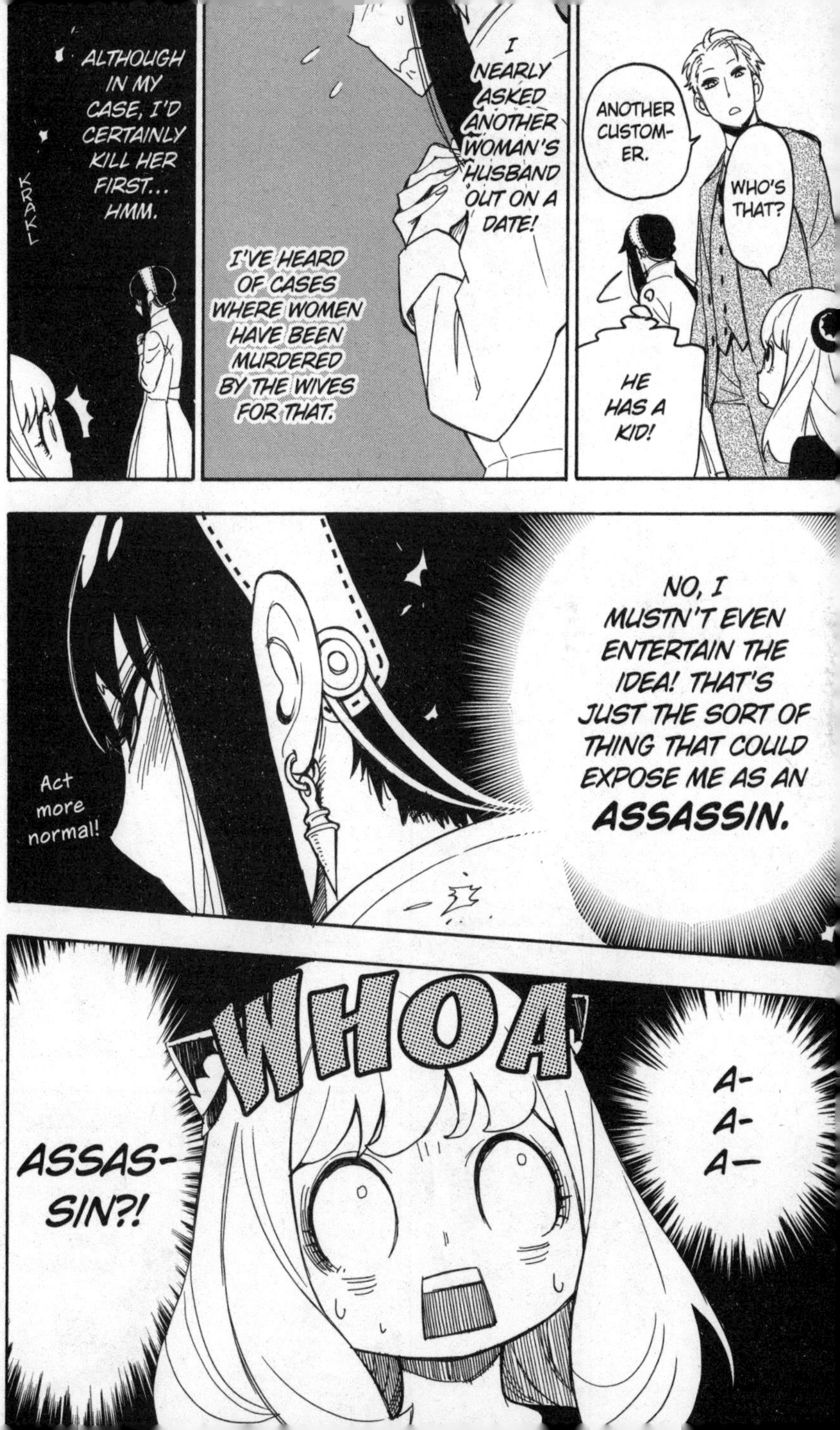
ANOTHER CUSTOM-ER.
WHO'S THAT?
HE HAS A KID!
I NEARLY ASKED ANOTHER WOMAN'S HUSBAND OUT ON A DATE!
I'VE HEARD OF CASES WHERE WOMEN HAVE BEEN MURDERED BY THE WIVES FOR THAT.
ALTHOUGH IN MY CASE, I'D CERTAINLY KILL HER FIRST... HMM.
KRAKL
NO, I MUSTN'T EVEN ENTERTAIN THE IDEA! THAT'S JUST THE SORT OF THING THAT COULD EXPOSE ME AS AN ASSASSIN.
Act more normal!
WHOA
A- A- A—
ASSAS-SIN?!

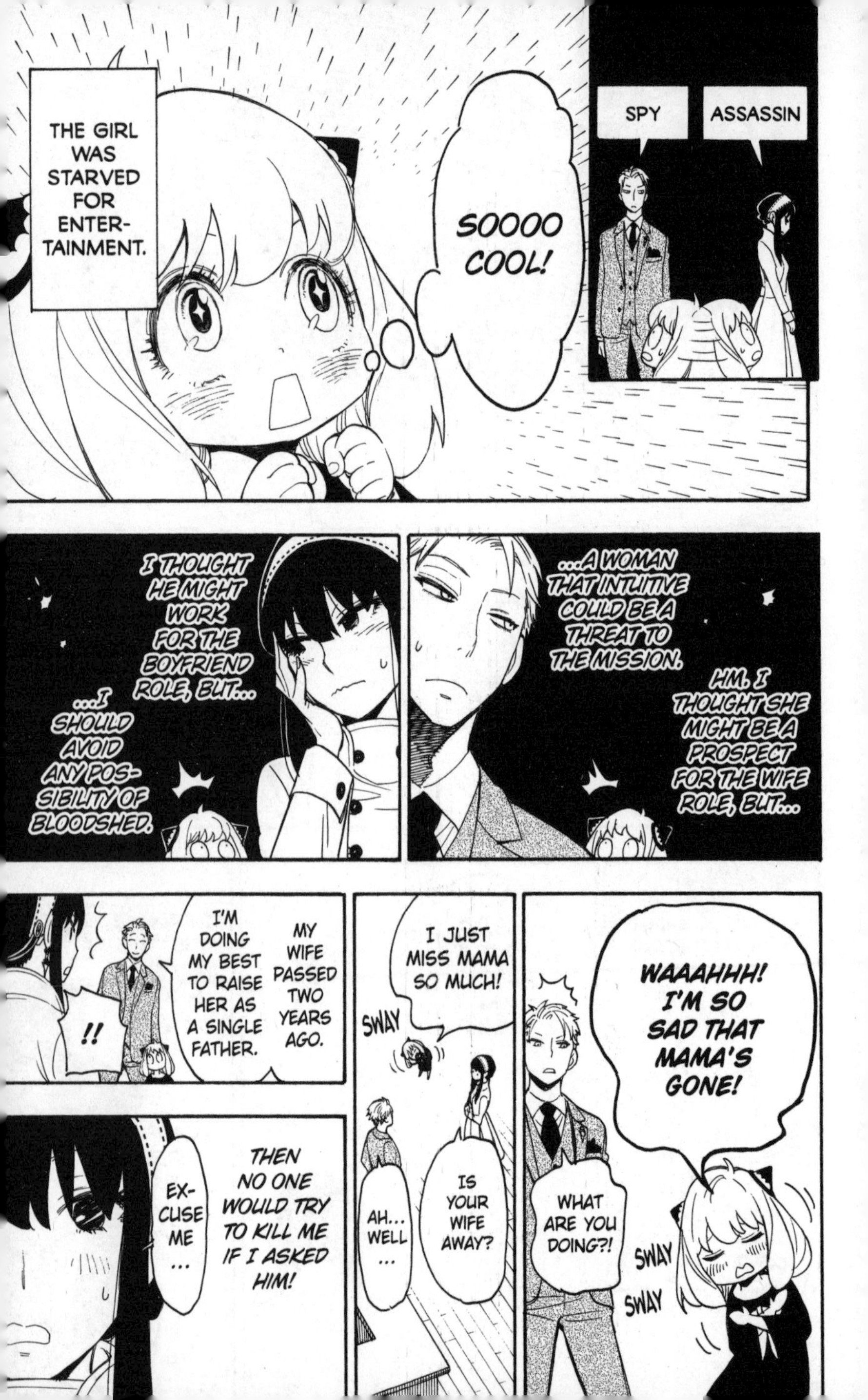
ASSASSIN
SPY
SOOOO COOL!
THE GIRL WAS STARVED FOR ENTER-TAINMENT.
HM. I THOUGHT SHE MIGHT BE A PROSPECT FOR THE WIFE ROLE, BUT...
...A WOMAN THAT INTUITIVE COULD BE A THREAT TO THE MISSION.
I THOUGHT HE MIGHT WORK FOR THE BOYFRIEND ROLE, BUT...
...I SHOULD AVOID ANY POS-SIBILITY OF BLOODSHED.
WAAAHHH! I'M SO SAD THAT MAMA'S GONE!
WHAT ARE YOU DOING?!
SWAY
SWAY
I JUST MISS MAMA SO MUCH!
SWAY
IS YOUR WIFE AWAY?
AH... WELL...
MY WIFE PASSED TWO YEARS AGO.
I'M DOING MY BEST TO RAISE HER AS A SINGLE FATHER.
!!
THEN NO ONE WOULD TRY TO KILL ME IF I ASKED HIM!
EX-CUSE ME...

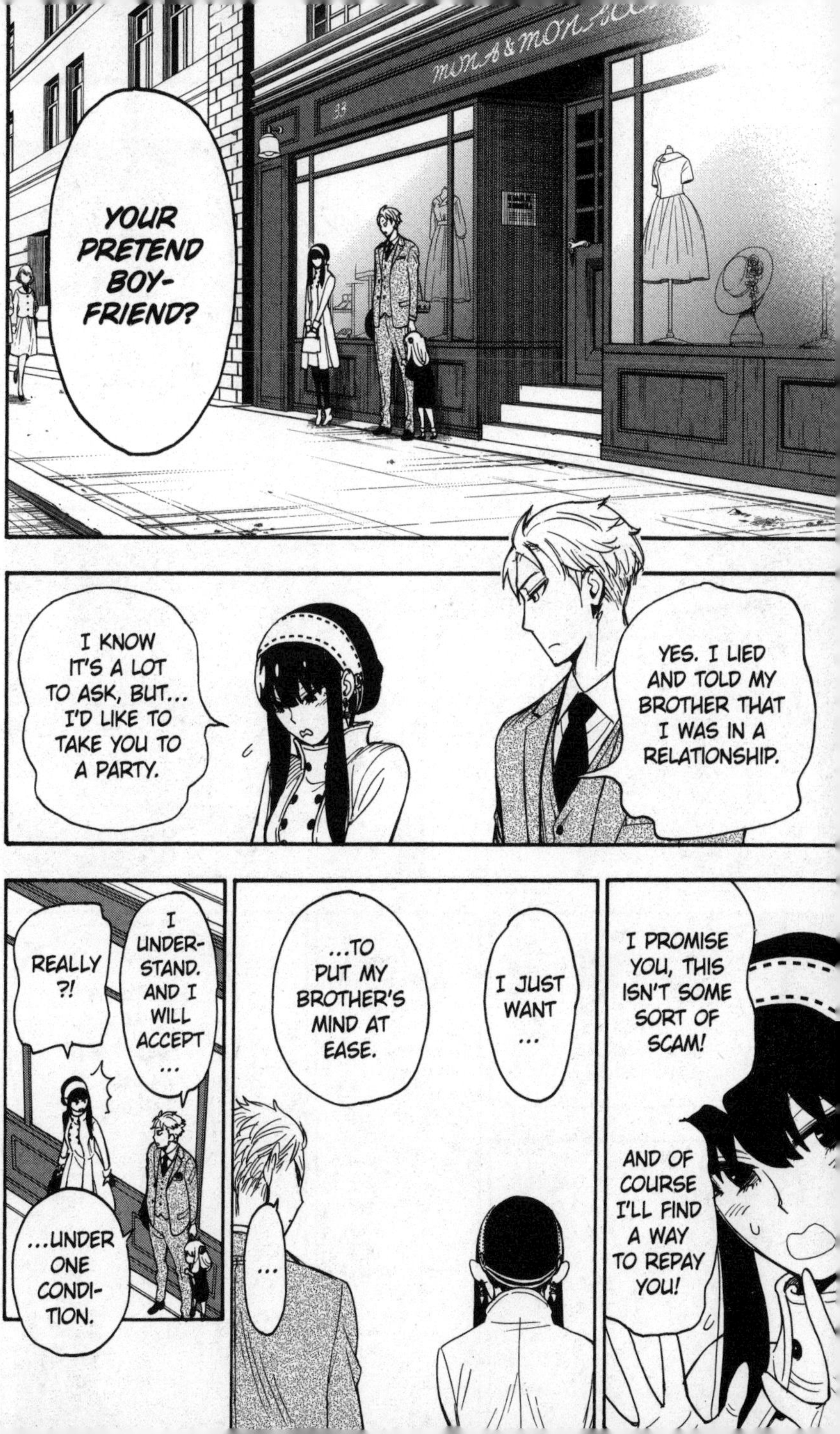
YOUR PRETEND BOY-FRIEND?
YES. I LIED AND TOLD MY BROTHER THAT I WAS IN A RELATIONSHIP.
I KNOW IT'S A LOT TO ASK, BUT... I'D LIKE TO TAKE YOU TO A PARTY.
I PROMISE YOU, THIS ISN'T SOME SORT OF SCAM!
AND OF COURSE I'LL FIND A WAY TO REPAY YOU!
I JUST WANT ...
...TO PUT MY BROTHER'S MIND AT EASE.
...
I UNDER-STAND. AND I WILL ACCEPT ...
REALLY ?!
...UNDER ONE CONDI-TION.

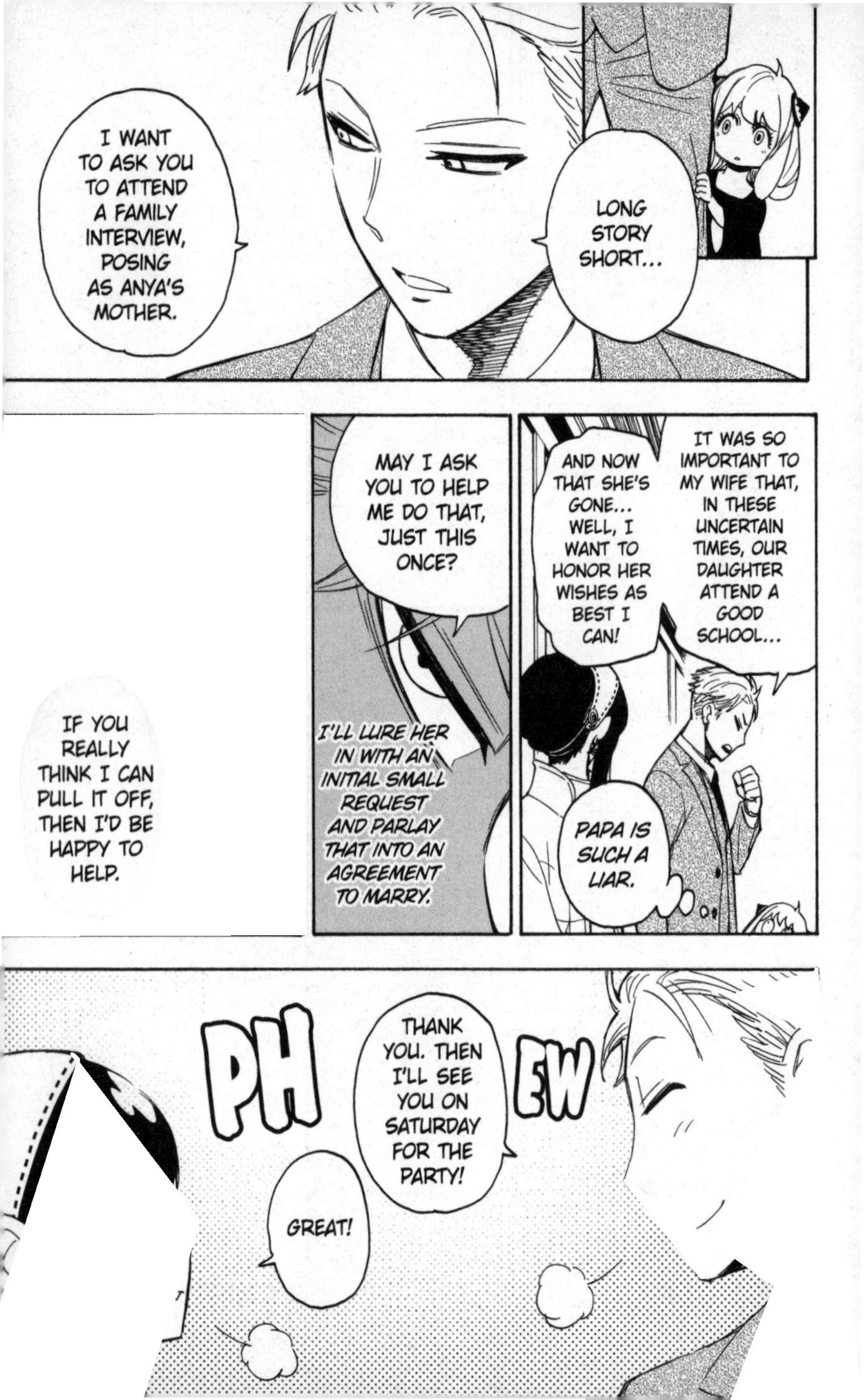
LONG STORY SHORT...
I WANT TO ASK YOU TO ATTEND A FAMILY INTERVIEW, POSING AS ANYA'S MOTHER.
IT WAS SO IMPORTANT TO MY WIFE THAT, IN THESE UNCERTAIN TIMES, OUR DAUGHTER ATTEND A GOOD SCHOOL...
AND NOW THAT SHE'S GONE... WELL, I WANT TO HONOR HER WISHES AS BEST I CAN!
PAPA IS SUCH A LIAR.
MAY I ASK YOU TO HELP ME DO THAT, JUST THIS ONCE?
I'LL LURE HER IN WITH AN INITIAL SMALL REQUEST AND PARLAY THAT INTO AN AGREEMENT TO MARRY.
IF YOU REALLY THINK I CAN PULL IT OFF, THEN I'D BE HAPPY TO HELP.
PHEW
THANK YOU. THEN I'LL SEE YOU ON SATURDAY FOR THE PARTY!
GREAT!

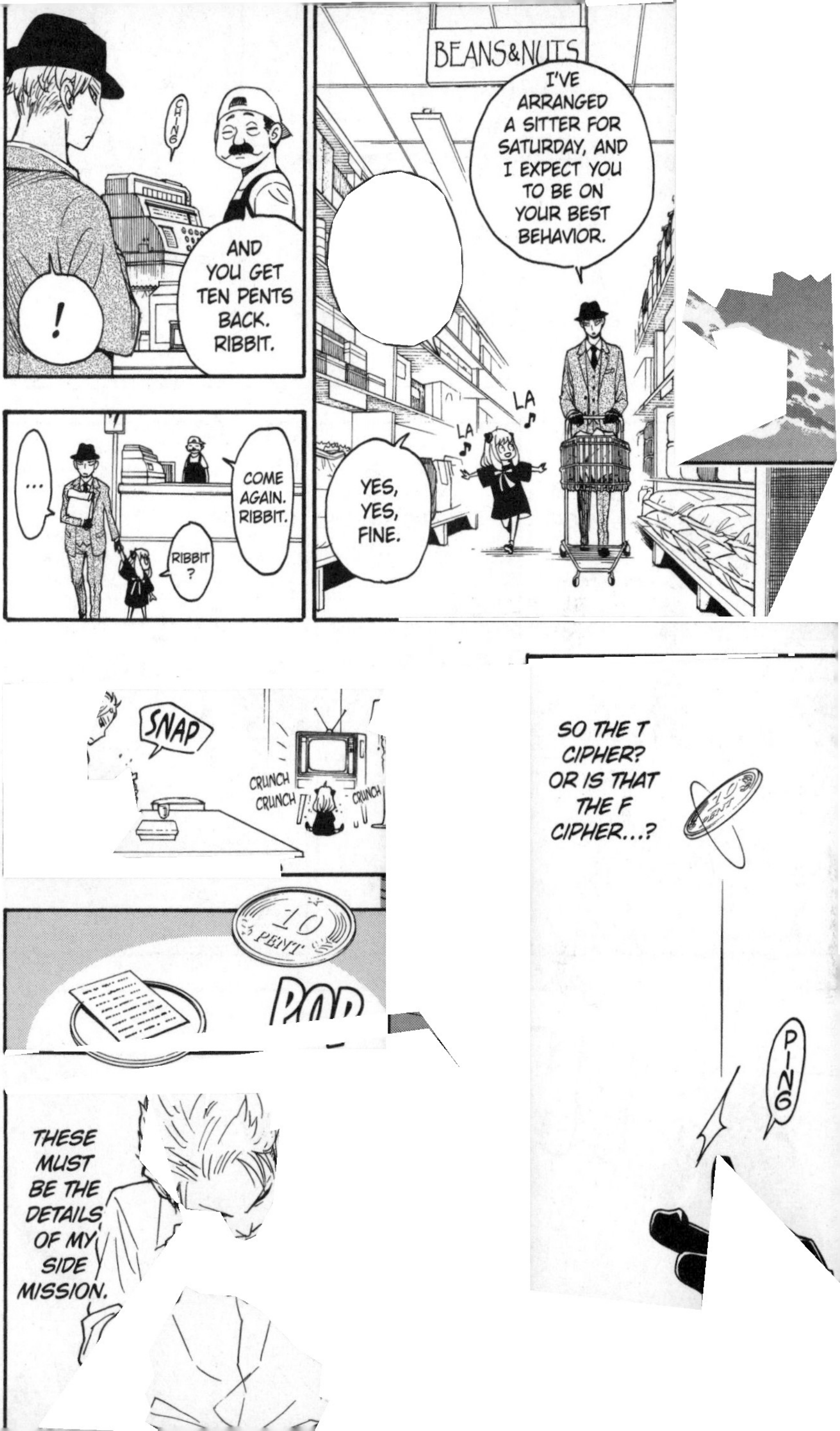
BEANS&NUTS
I'VE ARRANGED A SITTER FOR SATURDAY, AND I EXPECT YOU TO BE ON YOUR BEST BEHAVIOR.
LA
LA
YES, YES, FINE.
CHING
AND YOU GET TEN PENTS BACK. RIBBIT.
!
COME AGAIN. RIBBIT.
RIBBIT?
...
SO THE T CIPHER? OR IS THAT THE F CIPHER...?
10 PENT
PING
SNAP
CRUNCH CRUNCH
CRUNCH
10 PENT
POP
THESE MUST BE THE DETAILS OF MY SIDE MISSION.

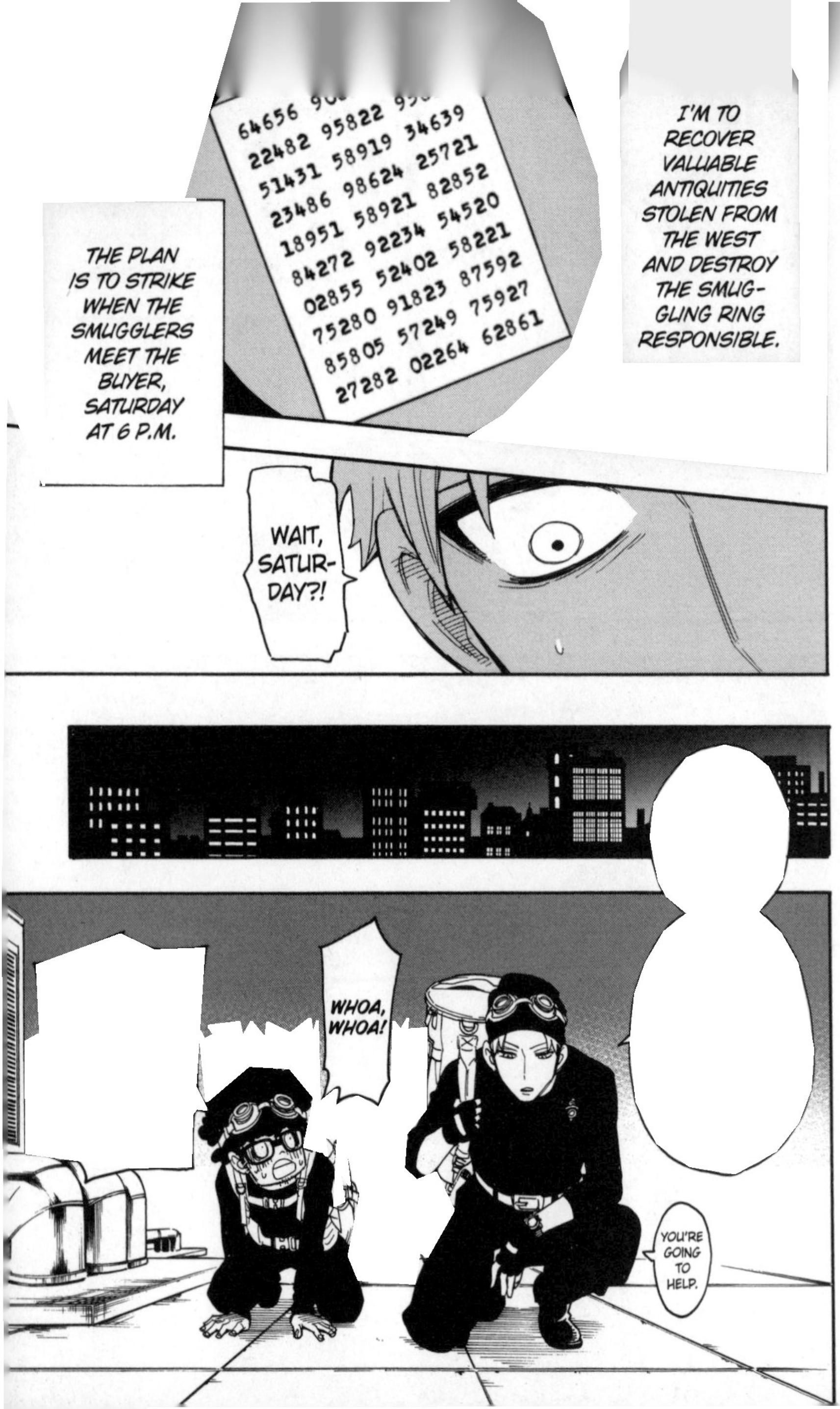
I'M TO RECOVER VALUABLE ANTIQUITIES STOLEN FROM THE WEST AND DESTROY THE SMUG-GLING RING RESPONSIBLE.
22482 95822 34639
51431 58919 25721
23486 98624 82852
18951 58921 54520
84272 92234 58221
02855 52402 87592
75280 91823 75927
85805 57249 62861
27282 02264
THE PLAN IS TO STRIKE WHEN THE SMUGGLERS MEET THE BUYER, SATURDAY AT 6 P.M.
WAIT, SATUR-DAY?!
YOU'RE GOING TO HELP.
WHOA, WHOA!

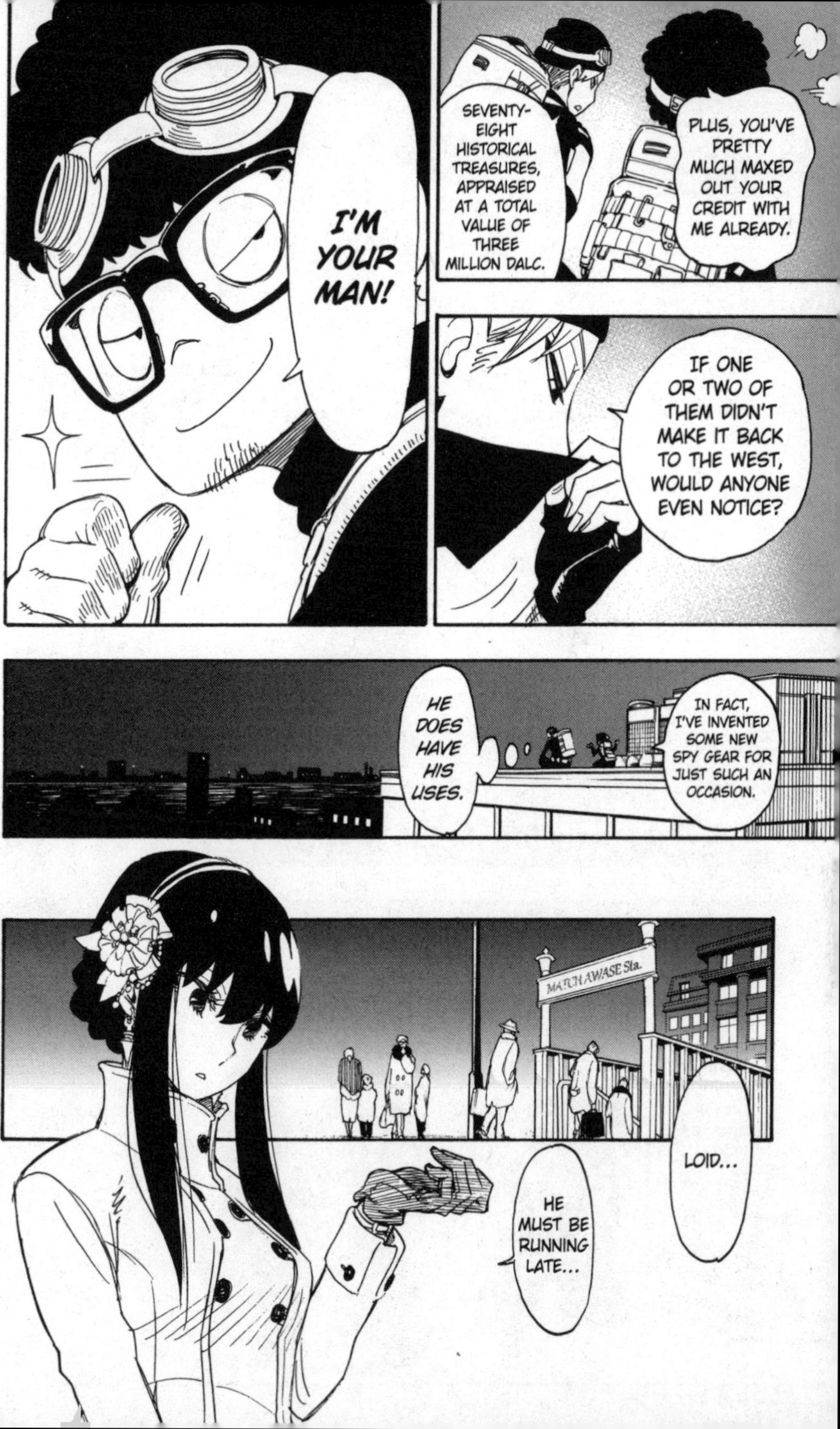
PLUS, YOU'VE PRETTY MUCH MAXED OUT YOUR CREDIT WITH ME ALREADY.
SEVENTY-EIGHT HISTORICAL TREASURES, APPRAISED AT A TOTAL VALUE OF THREE MILLION DALC.
IF ONE OR TWO OF THEM DIDN'T MAKE IT BACK TO THE WEST, WOULD ANYONE EVEN NOTICE?
I'M YOUR MAN!
IN FACT, I'VE INVENTED SOME NEW SPY GEAR FOR JUST SUCH AN OCCASION.
HE DOES HAVE HIS USES.
MATCHAWASE Sta.
LOID...
HE MUST BE RUNNING LATE...

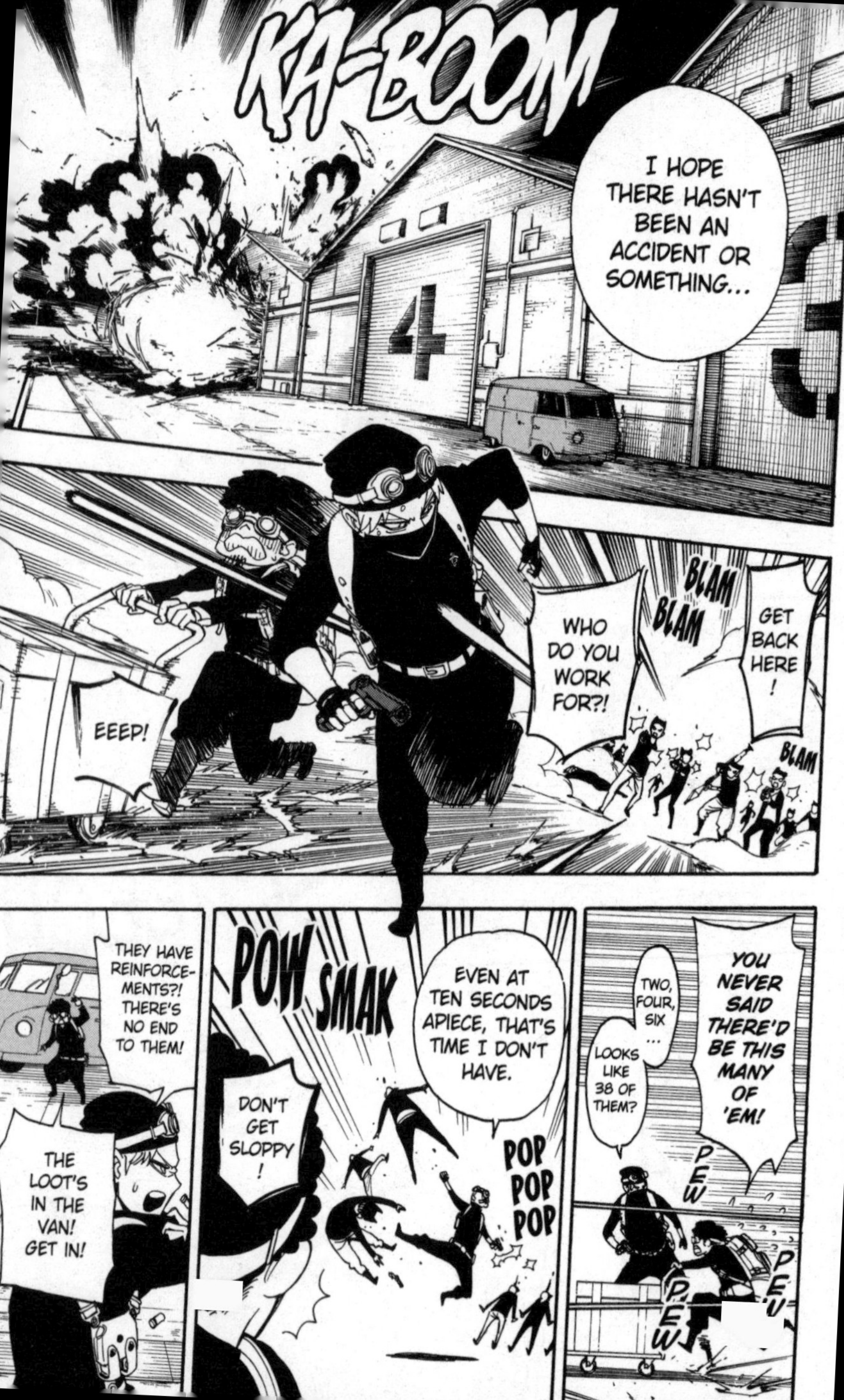
KA-BOOM
I HOPE THERE HASN'T BEEN AN ACCIDENT OR SOMETHING...
BLAM BLAM
GET BACK HERE!
WHO DO YOU WORK FOR?!
BLAM
EEEP!
YOU NEVER SAID THERE'D BE THIS MANY OF 'EM!
TWO, FOUR, SIX...
LOOKS LIKE 38 OF THEM?
PEW
PEW
PEW
EVEN AT TEN SECONDS APIECE, THAT'S TIME I DON'T HAVE.
POW
SMAK
DON'T GET SLOPPY!
POP POP POP
THEY HAVE REINFORCEMENTS?! THERE'S NO END TO THEM!
THE LOOT'S IN THE VAN! GET IN!

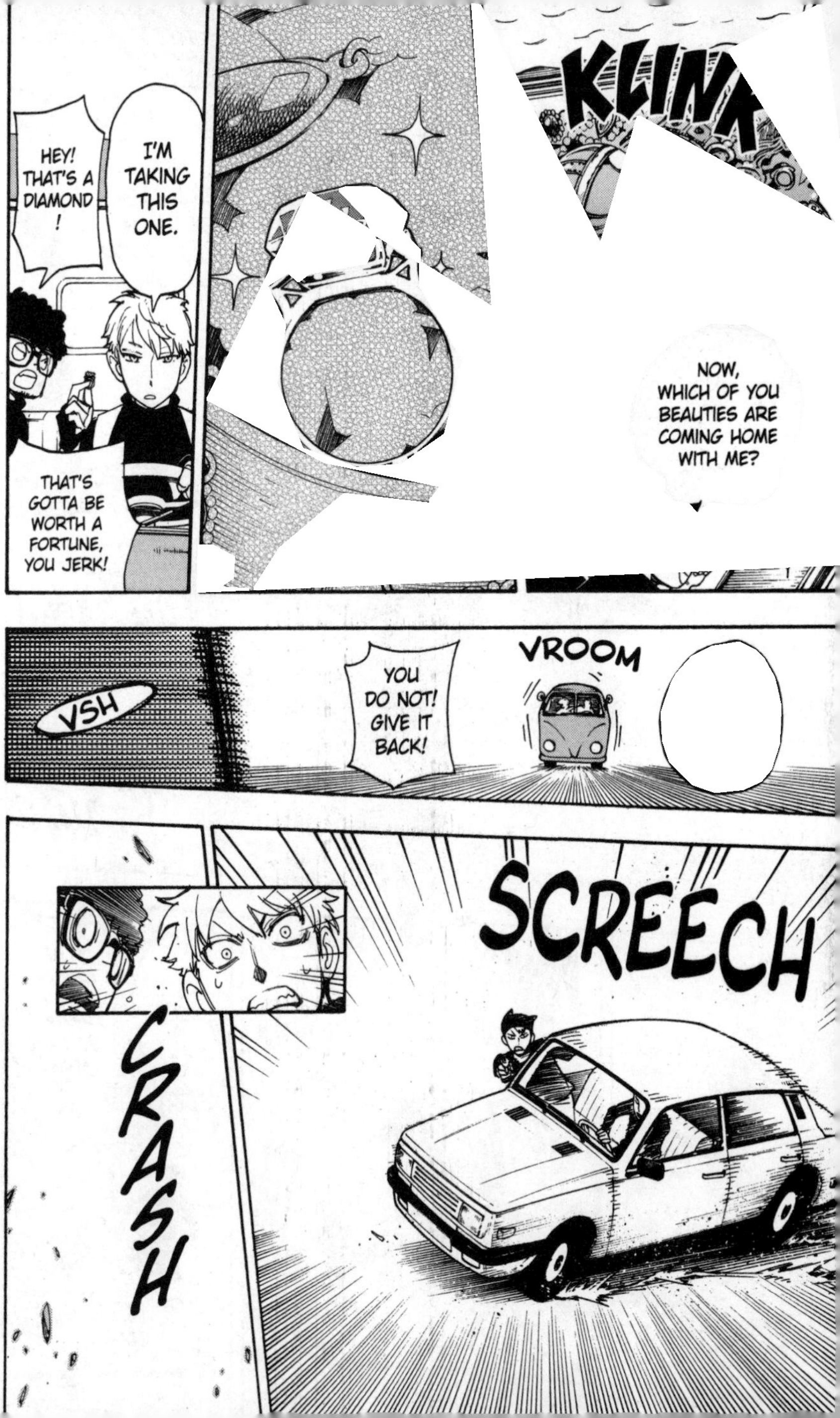
KLINK
NOW, WHICH OF YOU BEAUTIES ARE COMING HOME WITH ME?
I'M TAKING THIS ONE.
HEY! THAT'S A DIAMOND!
THAT'S GOTTA BE WORTH A FORTUNE, YOU JERK!
VROOM
YOU DO NOT! GIVE IT BACK!
VSH
SCREECH
CRASH

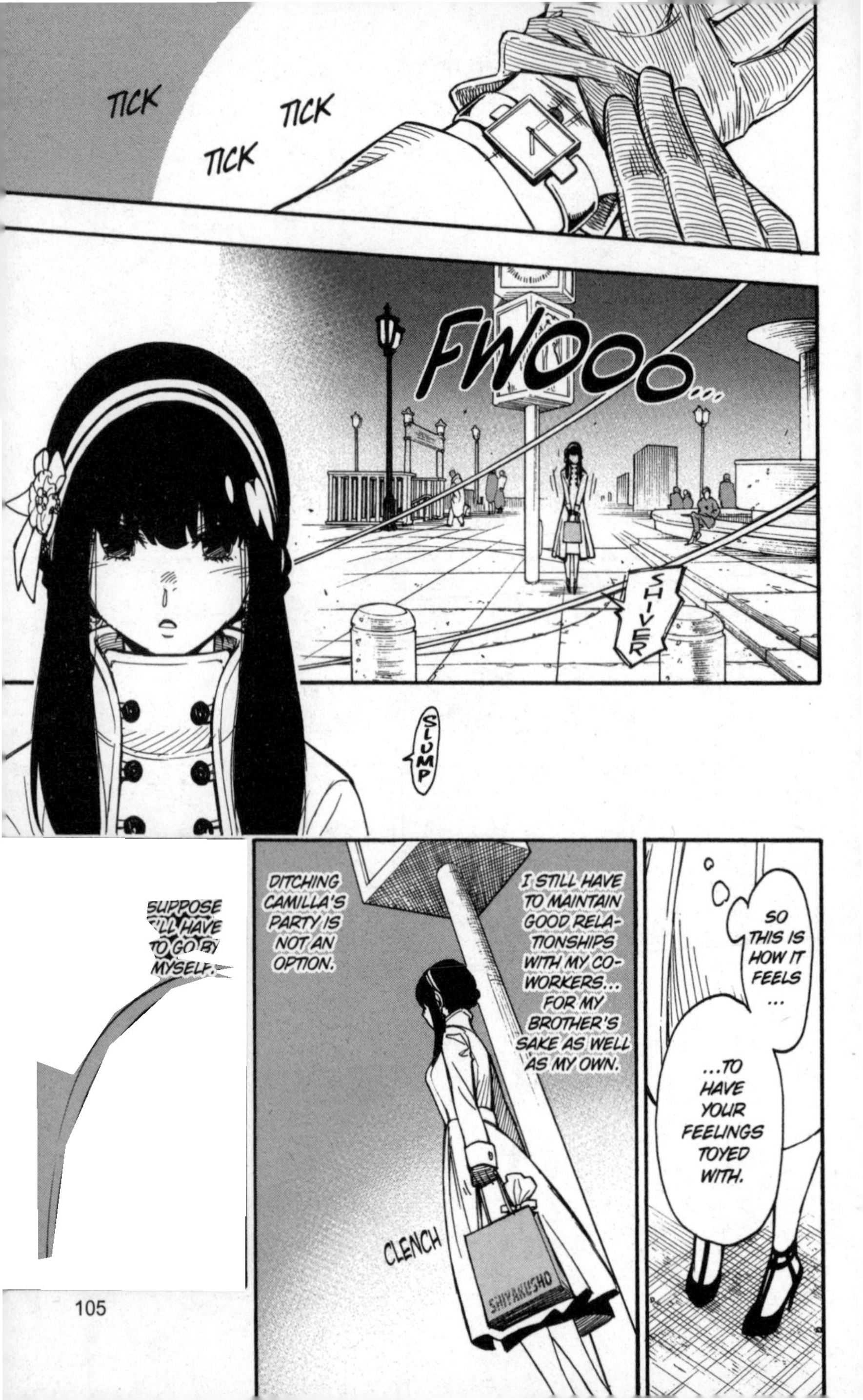
TICK
TICK
TICK
FWOOO...
SHIVER
SLUMP
SO THIS IS HOW IT FEELS...
...TO HAVE YOUR FEELINGS TOYED WITH.
I STILL HAVE TO MAINTAIN GOOD RELATIONSHIPS WITH MY CO-WORKERS... FOR MY BROTHER'S SAKE AS WELL AS MY OWN.
DITCHING CAMILLA'S PARTY IS NOT AN OPTION.
CLENCH
SHIYAKUSHO
SUPPOSE
LL HAVE
TO GO BY
MYSELF.

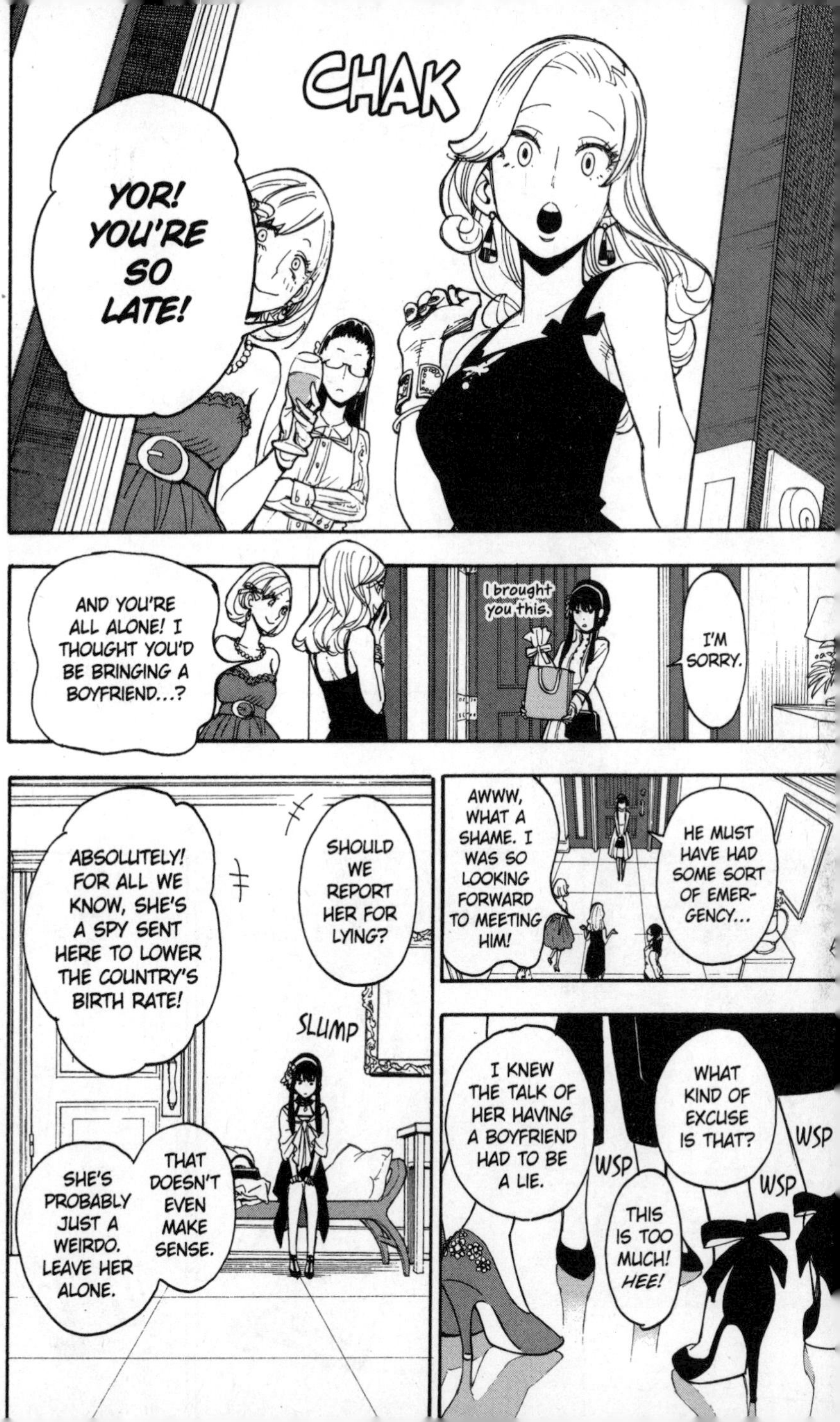
CHAK
YOR! YOU'RE SO LATE!
I'M SORRY.
I brought you this.
AND YOU'RE ALL ALONE! I THOUGHT YOU'D BE BRINGING A BOYFRIEND...?
HE MUST HAVE HAD SOME SORT OF EMERGENCY...
AWWW, WHAT A SHAME. I WAS SO LOOKING FORWARD TO MEETING HIM!
WHAT KIND OF EXCUSE IS THAT?
WSP
WSP
I KNEW THE TALK OF HER HAVING A BOYFRIEND HAD TO BE A LIE.
WSP
THIS IS TOO MUCH! HEE!
SHOULD WE REPORT HER FOR LYING?
ABSOLUTELY! FOR ALL WE KNOW, SHE'S A SPY SENT HERE TO LOWER THE COUNTRY'S BIRTH RATE!
SLUMP
THAT DOESN'T EVEN MAKE SENSE.
SHE'S PROBABLY JUST A WEIRDO. LEAVE HER ALONE.

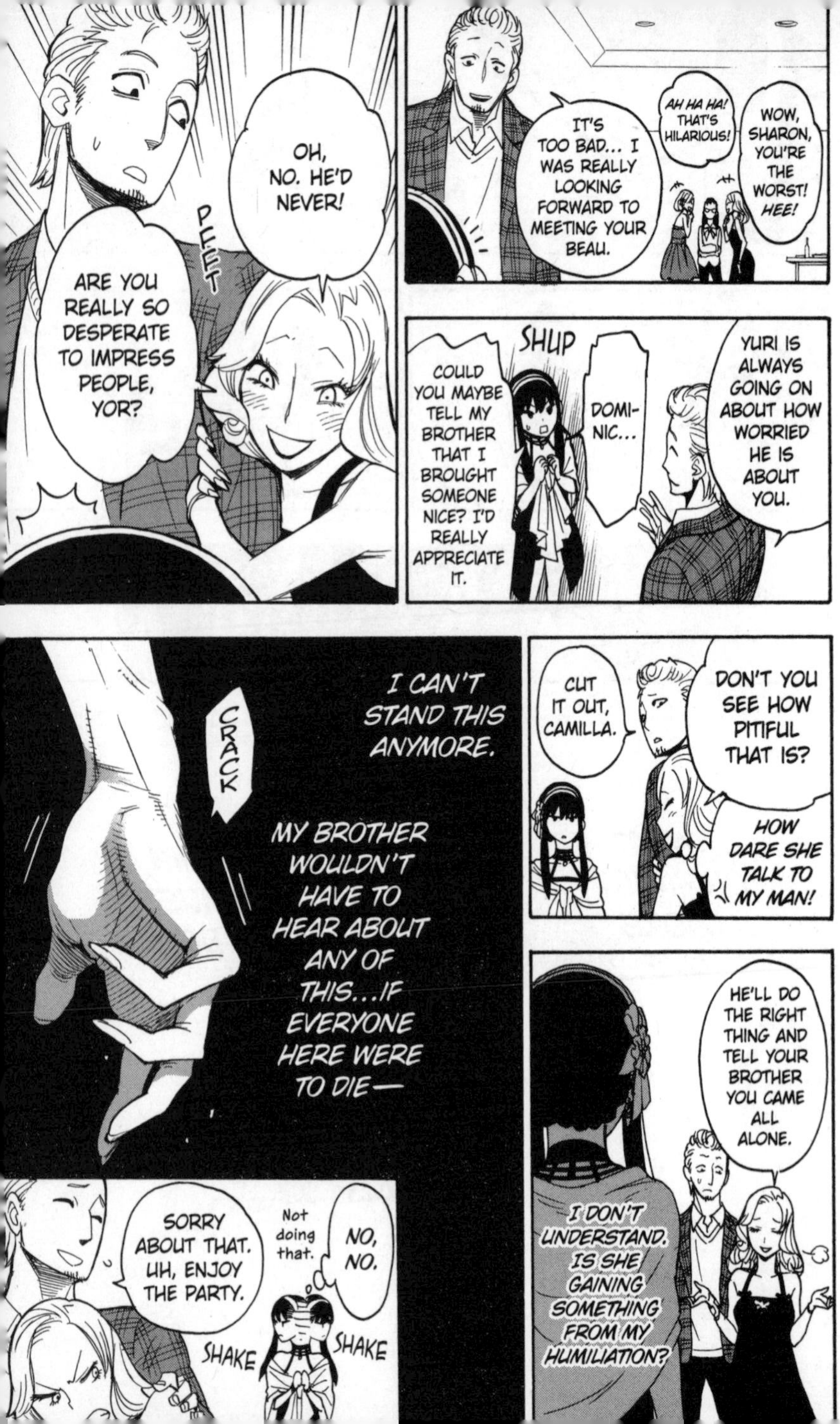
WOW, SHARON, YOU'RE THE WORST! HEE!
AH HA HA! THAT'S HILARIOUS!
IT'S TOO BAD... I WAS REALLY LOOKING FORWARD TO MEETING YOUR BEAU.
YURI IS ALWAYS GOING ON ABOUT HOW WORRIED HE IS ABOUT YOU.
DOMINIC...
SHUP
COULD YOU MAYBE TELL MY BROTHER THAT I BROUGHT SOMEONE NICE? I'D REALLY APPRECIATE IT.
OH, NO. HE'D NEVER!
PFFT
ARE YOU REALLY SO DESPERATE TO IMPRESS PEOPLE, YOR?
DON'T YOU SEE HOW PITIFUL THAT IS?
HOW DARE SHE TALK TO MY MAN!
CUT IT OUT, CAMILLA.
HE'LL DO THE RIGHT THING AND TELL YOUR BROTHER YOU CAME ALL ALONE.
I DON'T UNDERSTAND. IS SHE GAINING SOMETHING FROM MY HUMILIATION?
I CAN'T STAND THIS ANYMORE.
CRACK
MY BROTHER WOULDN'T HAVE TO HEAR ABOUT ANY OF THIS...IF EVERYONE HERE WERE TO DIE—
NO, NO.
Not doing that.
SORRY ABOUT THAT. UH, ENJOY THE PARTY.
SHAKE
SHAKE

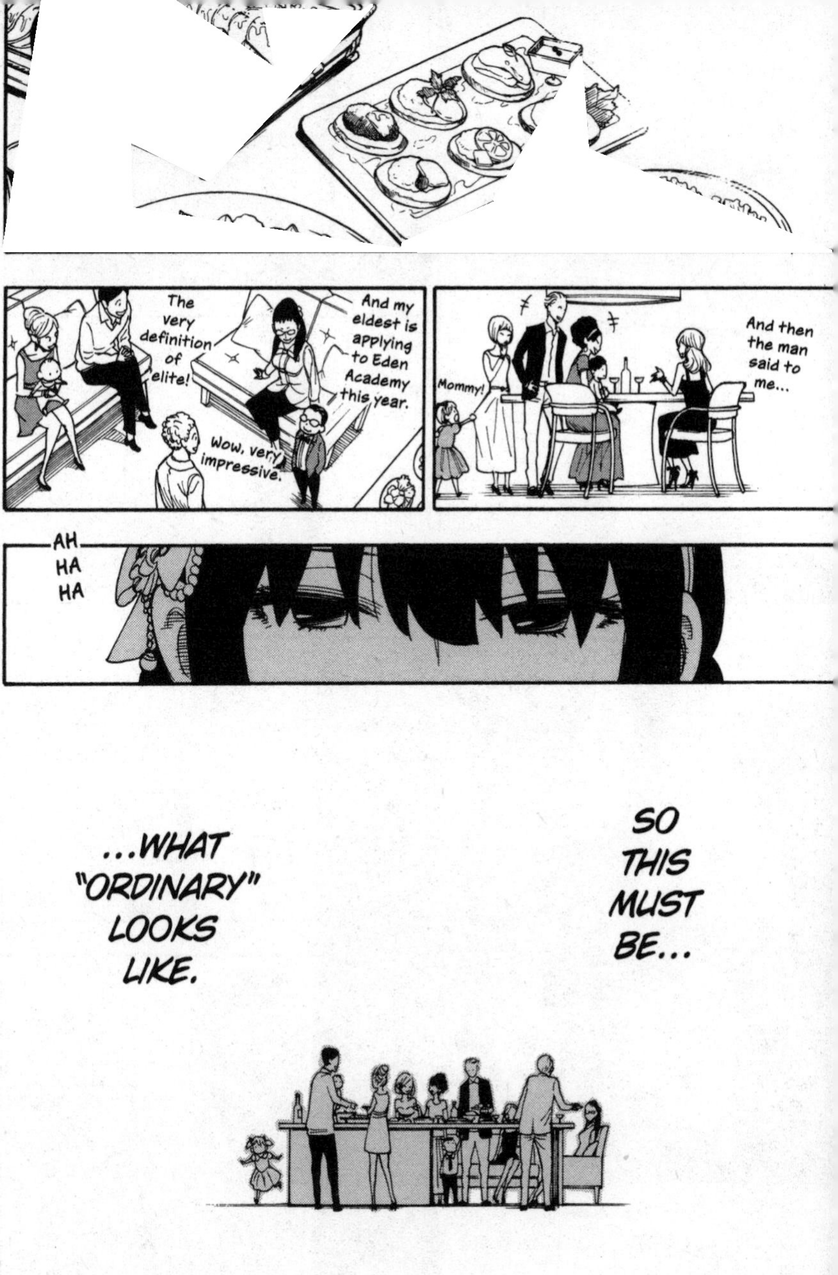
And then the man said to me...
Mommy!
And my eldest is applying to Eden Academy this year.
The very definition of elite!
Wow, very impressive.
AH HA HA
SO THIS MUST BE...
...WHAT "ORDINARY" LOOKS LIKE.

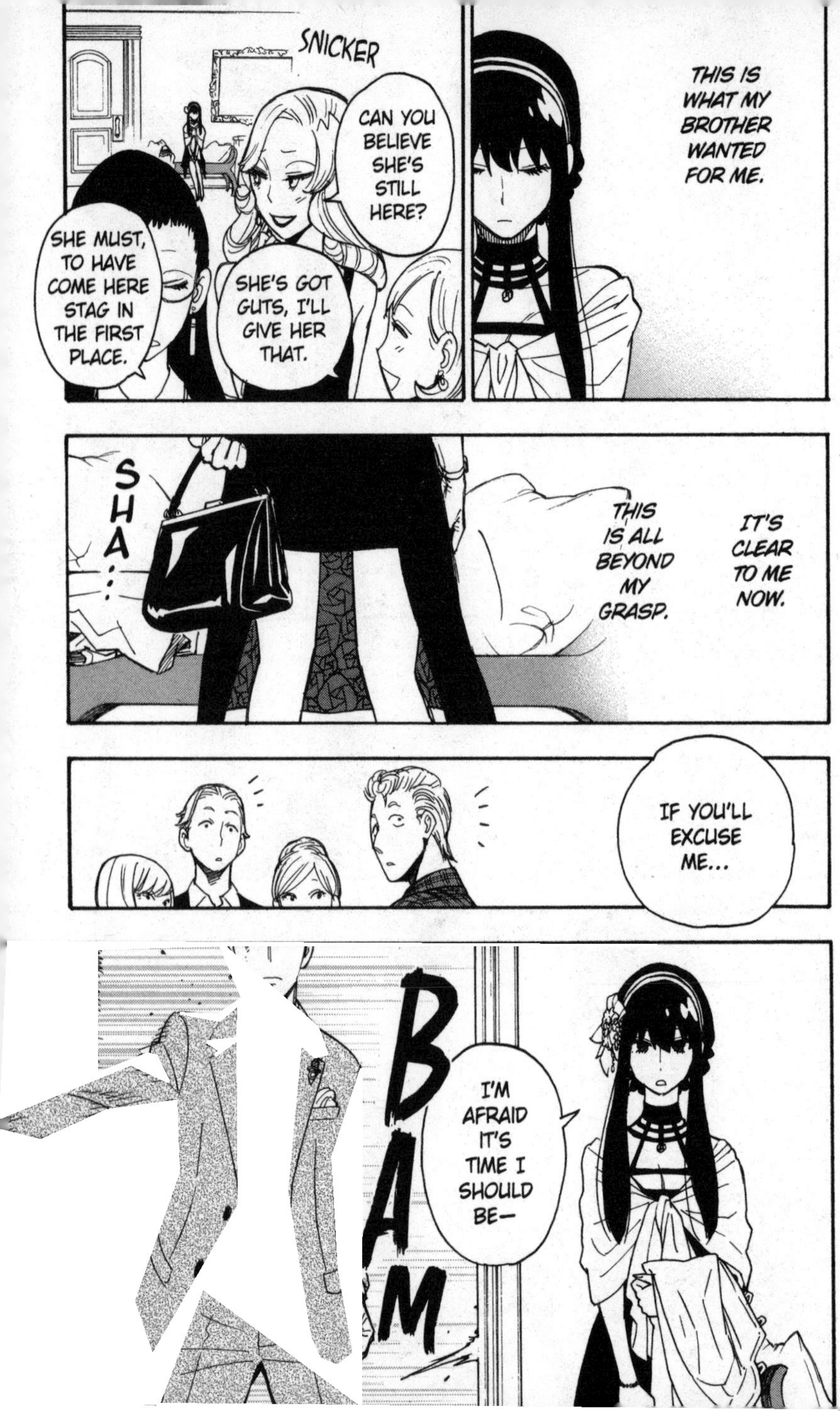
THIS IS WHAT MY BROTHER WANTED FOR ME.
SNICKER
CAN YOU BELIEVE SHE'S STILL HERE?
SHE'S GOT GUTS, I'LL GIVE HER THAT.
SHE MUST, TO HAVE COME HERE STAG IN THE FIRST PLACE.
IT'S CLEAR TO ME NOW.
THIS IS ALL BEYOND MY GRASP.
SHA...
IF YOU'LL EXCUSE ME...
I'M AFRAID IT'S TIME I SHOULD BE—
BAM

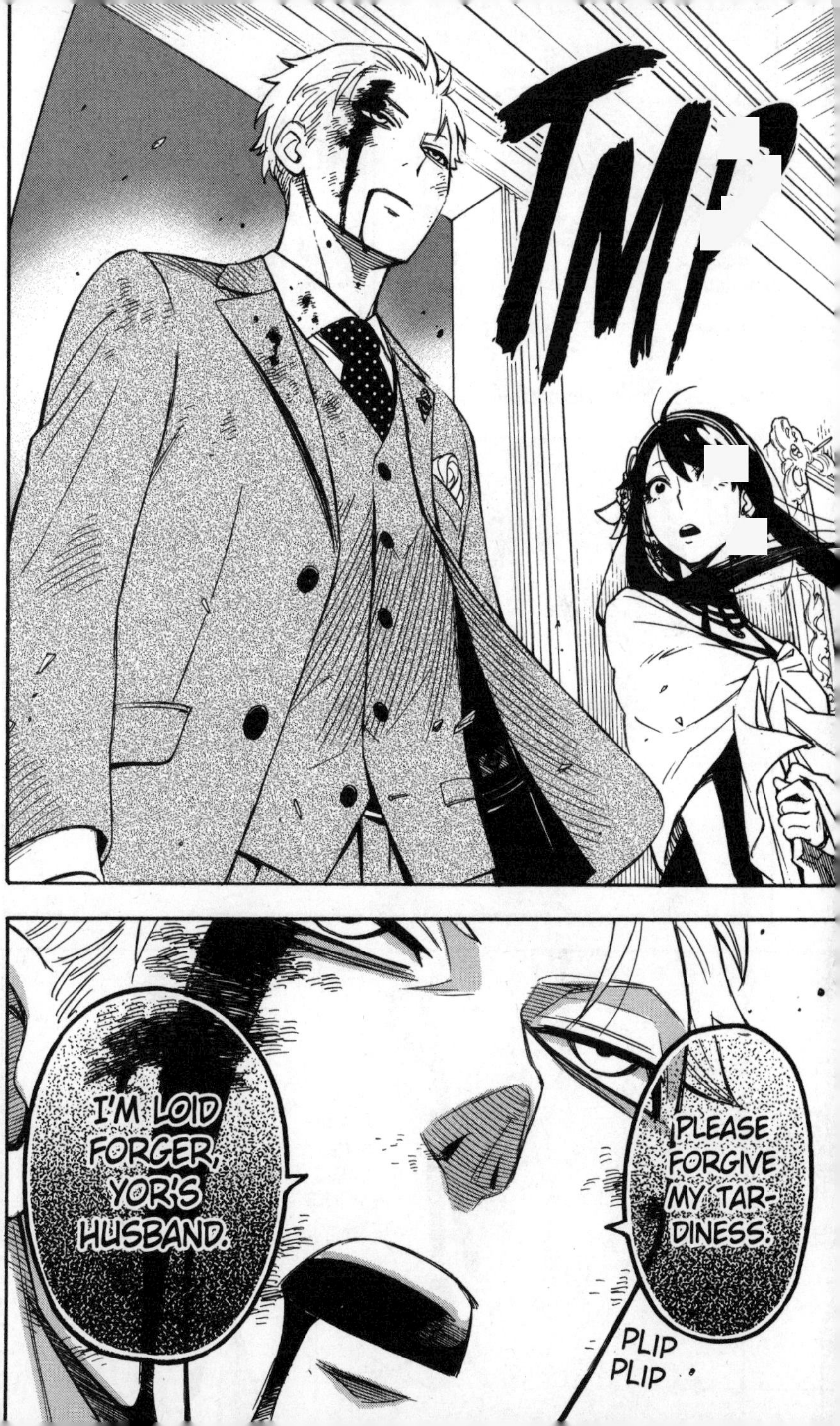
PLEASE FORGIVE MY TAR-DINESS.
I'M LOID FORGER, YOR'S HUSBAND.
PLIP PLIP

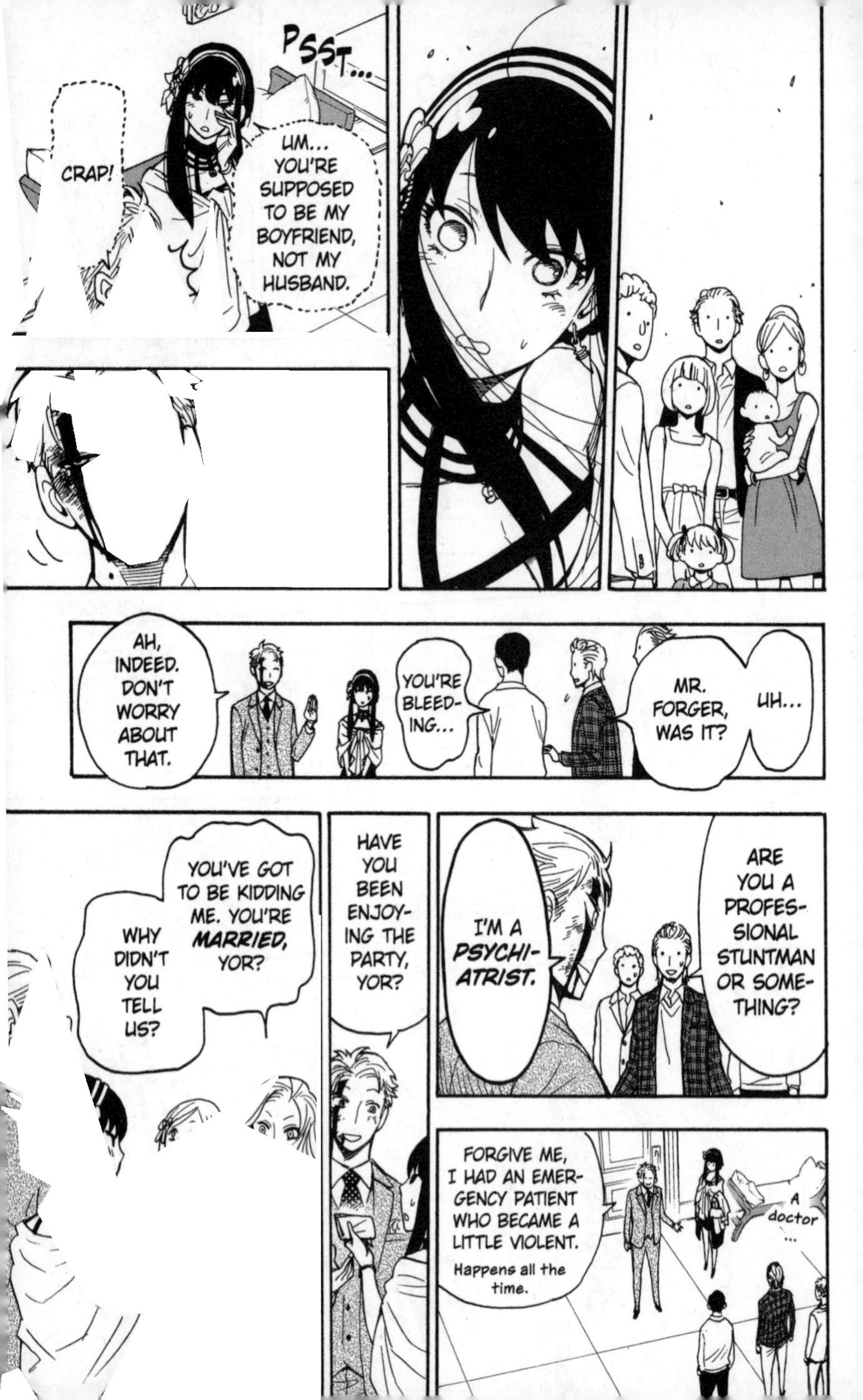
PSST...
UM... YOU'RE SUPPOSED TO BE MY BOYFRIEND, NOT MY HUSBAND.
CRAP!
UH...
MR. FORGER, WAS IT?
YOU'RE BLEEDING...
AH, INDEED. DON'T WORRY ABOUT THAT.
ARE YOU A PROFESSIONAL STUNTMAN OR SOMETHING?
I'M A ***PSYCHIATRIST.***
FORGIVE ME, I HAD AN EMERGENCY PATIENT WHO BECAME A LITTLE VIOLENT. Happens all the time.
A doctor...
HAVE YOU BEEN ENJOYING THE PARTY, YOR?
YOU'VE GOT TO BE KIDDING ME. YOU'RE ***MARRIED,*** YOR?
WHY DIDN'T YOU TELL US?

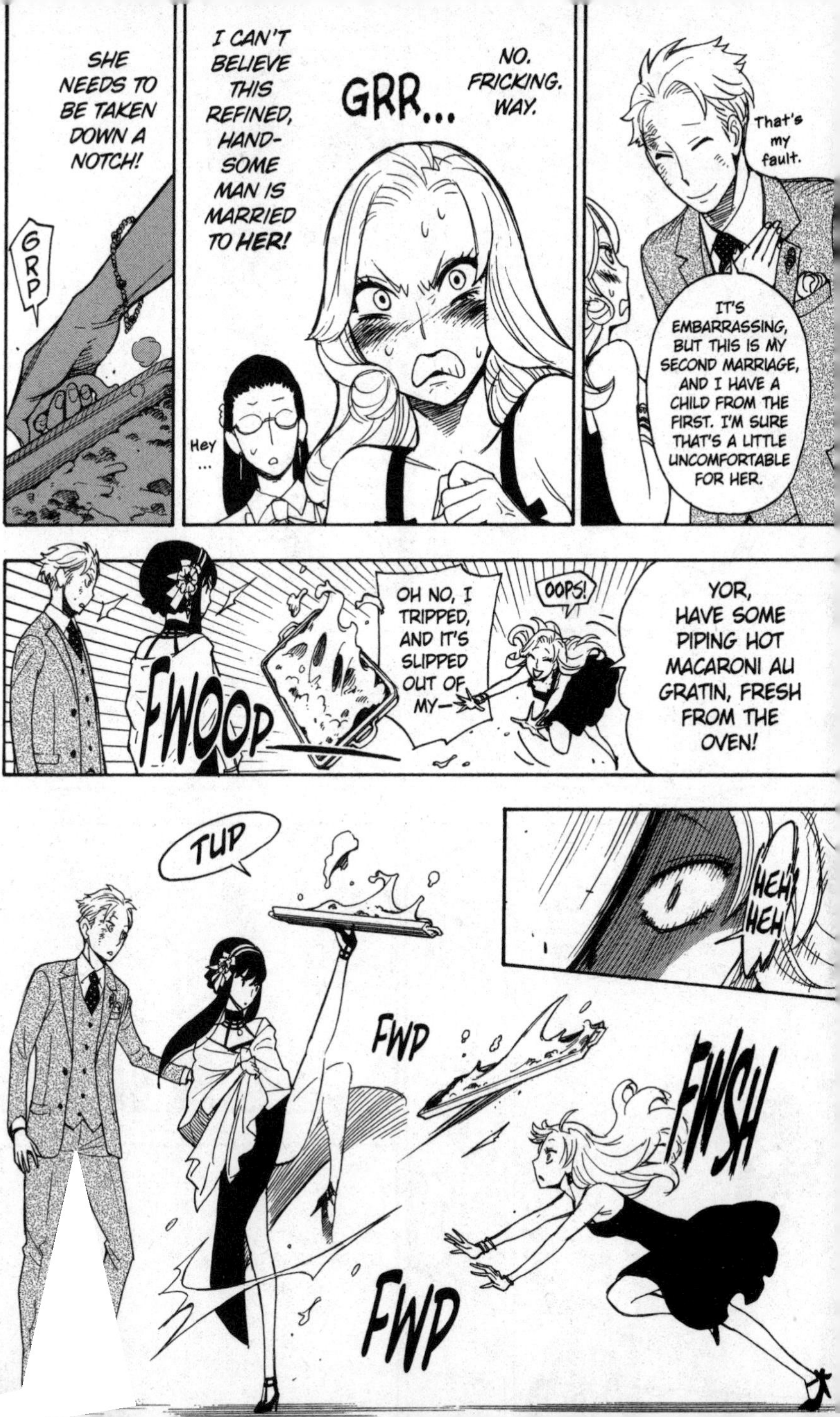

That's my fault.
IT'S EMBARRASSING, BUT THIS IS MY SECOND MARRIAGE, AND I HAVE A CHILD FROM THE FIRST. I'M SURE THAT'S A LITTLE UNCOMFORTABLE FOR HER.
NO. FRICKING. WAY.
GRR...
I CAN'T BELIEVE THIS REFINED, HAND-SOME MAN IS MARRIED TO HER!
Hey ...
SHE NEEDS TO BE TAKEN DOWN A NOTCH!
GRP
YOR, HAVE SOME PIPING HOT MACARONI AU GRATIN, FRESH FROM THE OVEN!
OOPS!
OH NO, I TRIPPED, AND IT'S SLIPPED OUT OF MY—
FWOOP
HEH HEH
FWSH
TUP
FWP
FWP

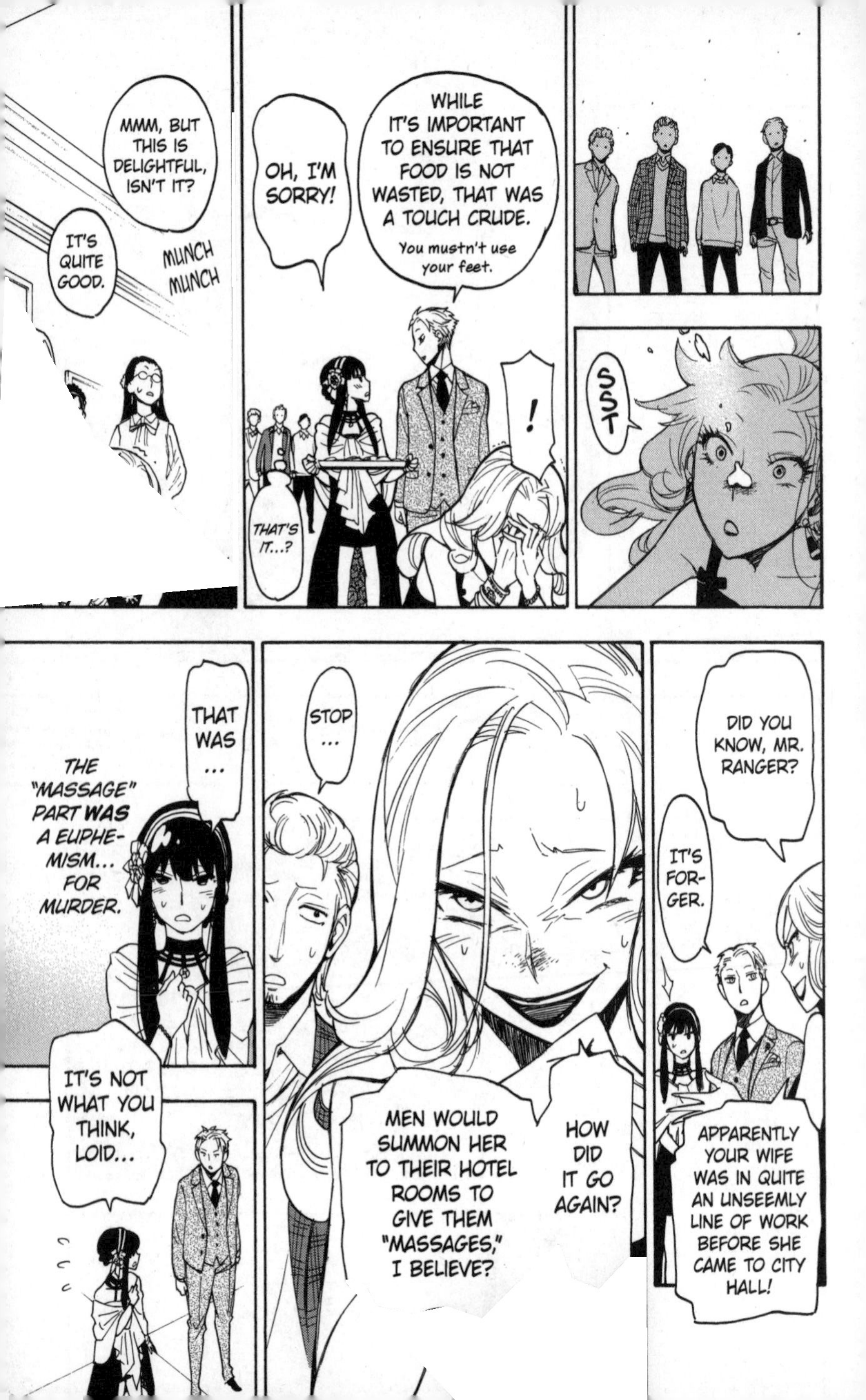
SST
WHILE IT'S IMPORTANT TO ENSURE THAT FOOD IS NOT WASTED, THAT WAS A TOUCH CRUDE.
You mustn't use your feet.
OH, I'M SORRY!
!
THAT'S IT...?
MMM, BUT THIS IS DELIGHTFUL, ISN'T IT?
IT'S QUITE GOOD.
MUNCH MUNCH
DID YOU KNOW, MR. RANGER?
IT'S FORGER.
APPARENTLY YOUR WIFE WAS IN QUITE AN UNSEEMLY LINE OF WORK BEFORE SHE CAME TO CITY HALL!
STOP...
HOW DID IT GO AGAIN?
MEN WOULD SUMMON HER TO THEIR HOTEL ROOMS TO GIVE THEM "MASSAGES," I BELIEVE?
THAT WAS...
THE "MASSAGE" PART WAS A EUPHEMISM... FOR MURDER.
IT'S NOT WHAT YOU THINK, LOID...

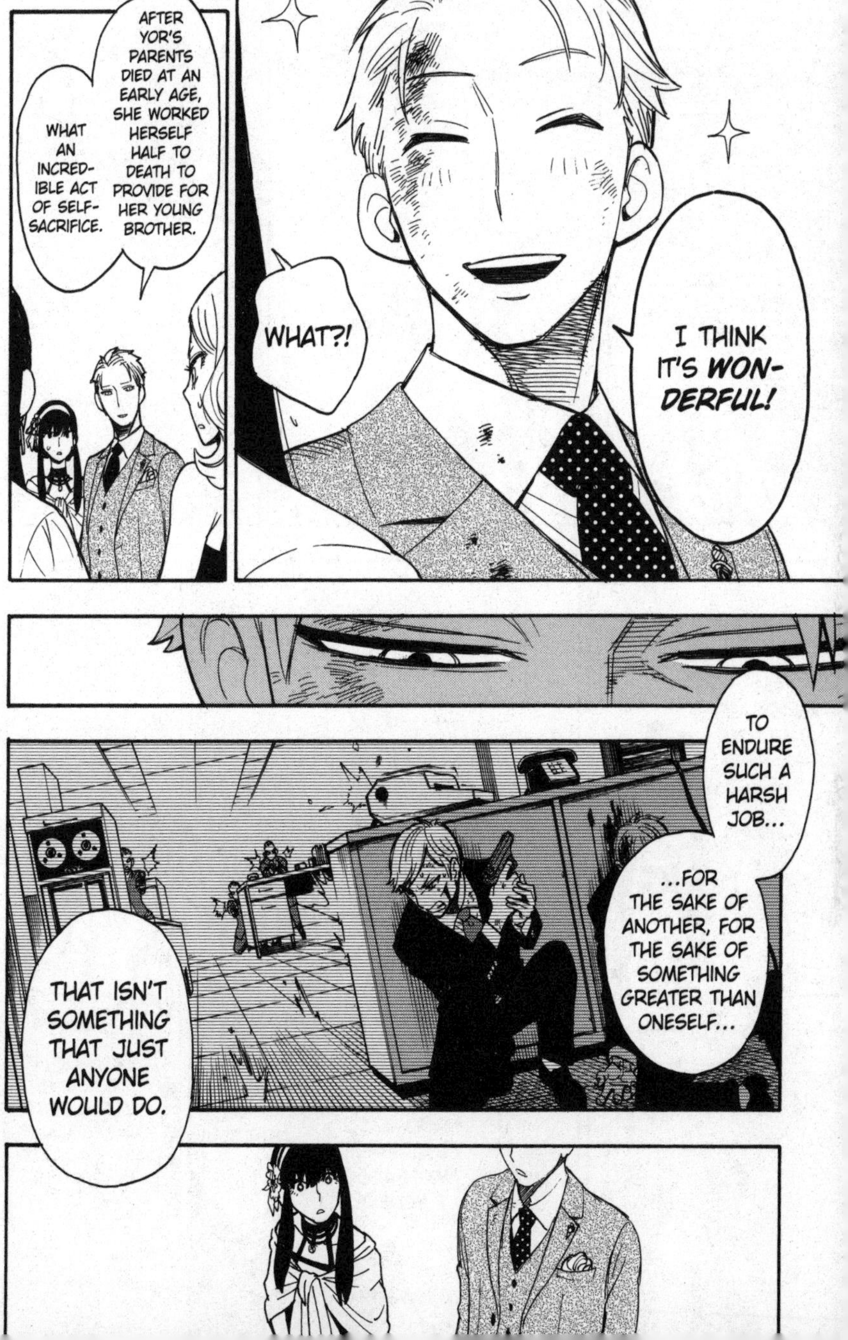
I THINK IT'S **WON-DERFUL!**
WHAT?!
AFTER YOR'S PARENTS DIED AT AN EARLY AGE, SHE WORKED HERSELF HALF TO DEATH TO PROVIDE FOR HER YOUNG BROTHER.
WHAT AN INCRED-IBLE ACT OF SELF-SACRIFICE.
TO ENDURE SUCH A HARSH JOB...
...FOR THE SAKE OF ANOTHER, FOR THE SAKE OF SOMETHING GREATER THAN ONESELF...
THAT ISN'T SOMETHING THAT JUST ANYONE WOULD DO.

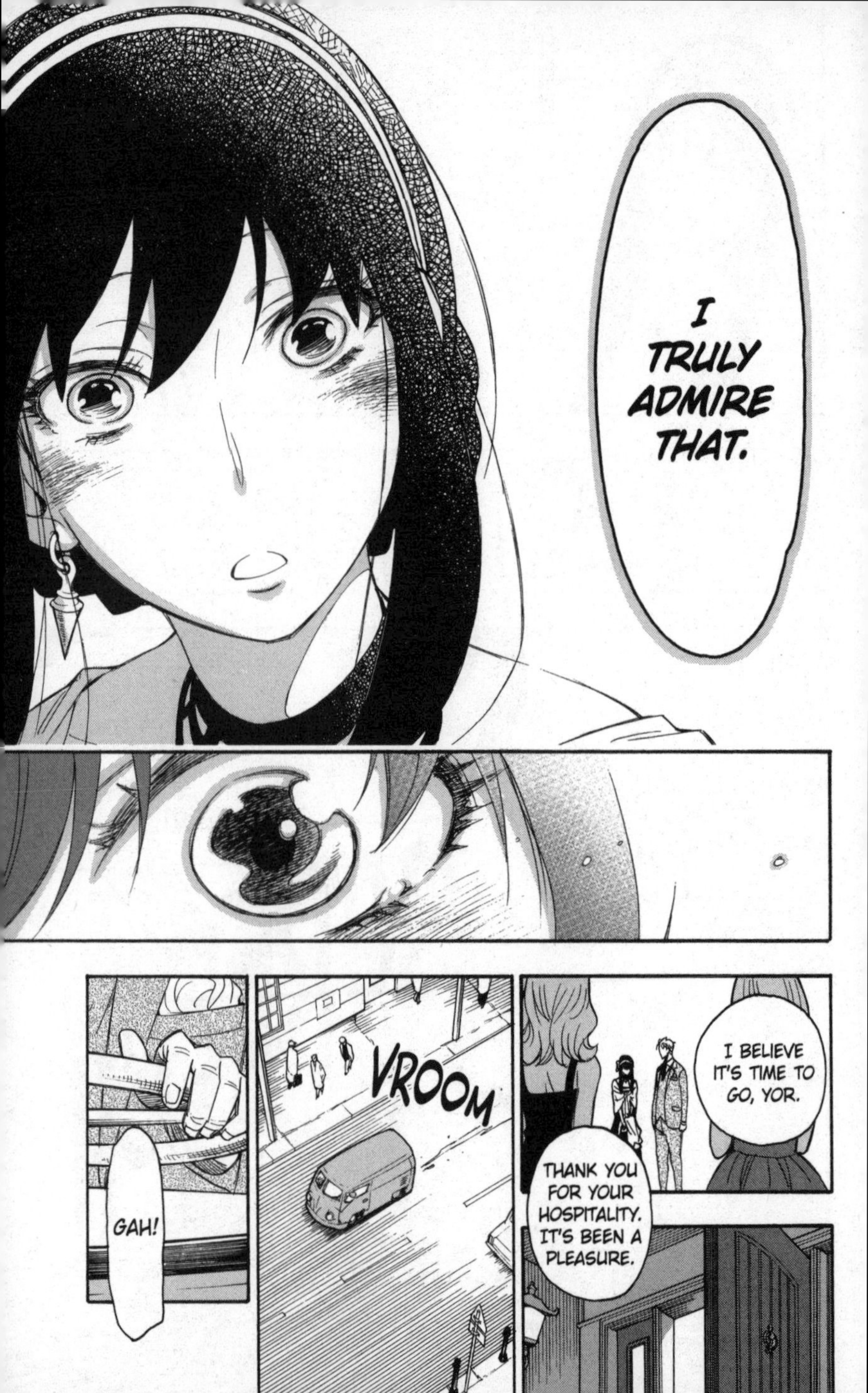
I TRULY ADMIRE THAT.
I BELIEVE IT'S TIME TO GO, YOR.
THANK YOU FOR YOUR HOSPITALITY. IT'S BEEN A PLEASURE.
VROOM
GAH!

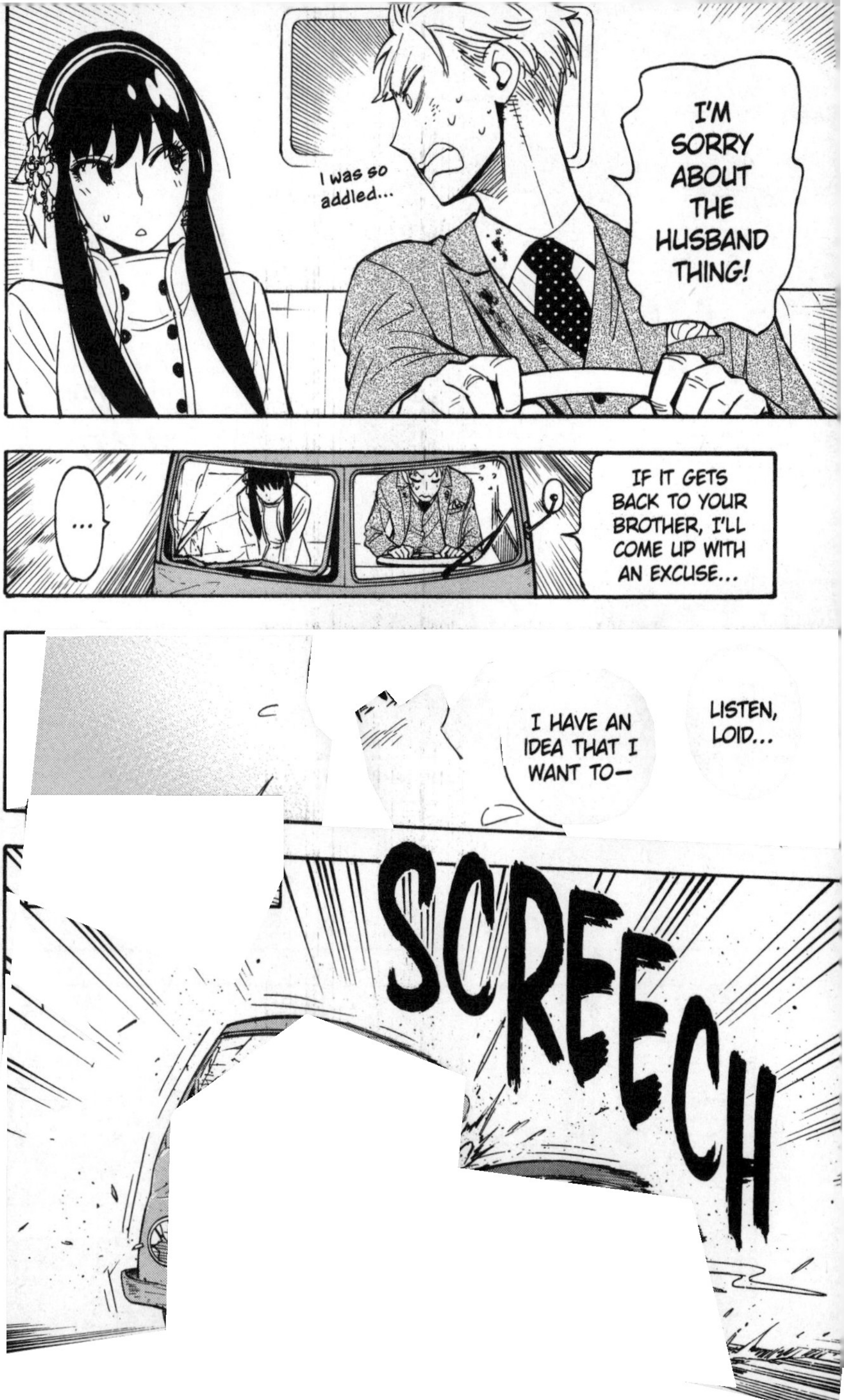
I'M SORRY ABOUT THE HUSBAND THING!
I was so addled...
IF IT GETS BACK TO YOUR BROTHER, I'LL COME UP WITH AN EXCUSE...
...
LISTEN, LOID...
I HAVE AN IDEA THAT I WANT TO—
SCREECH

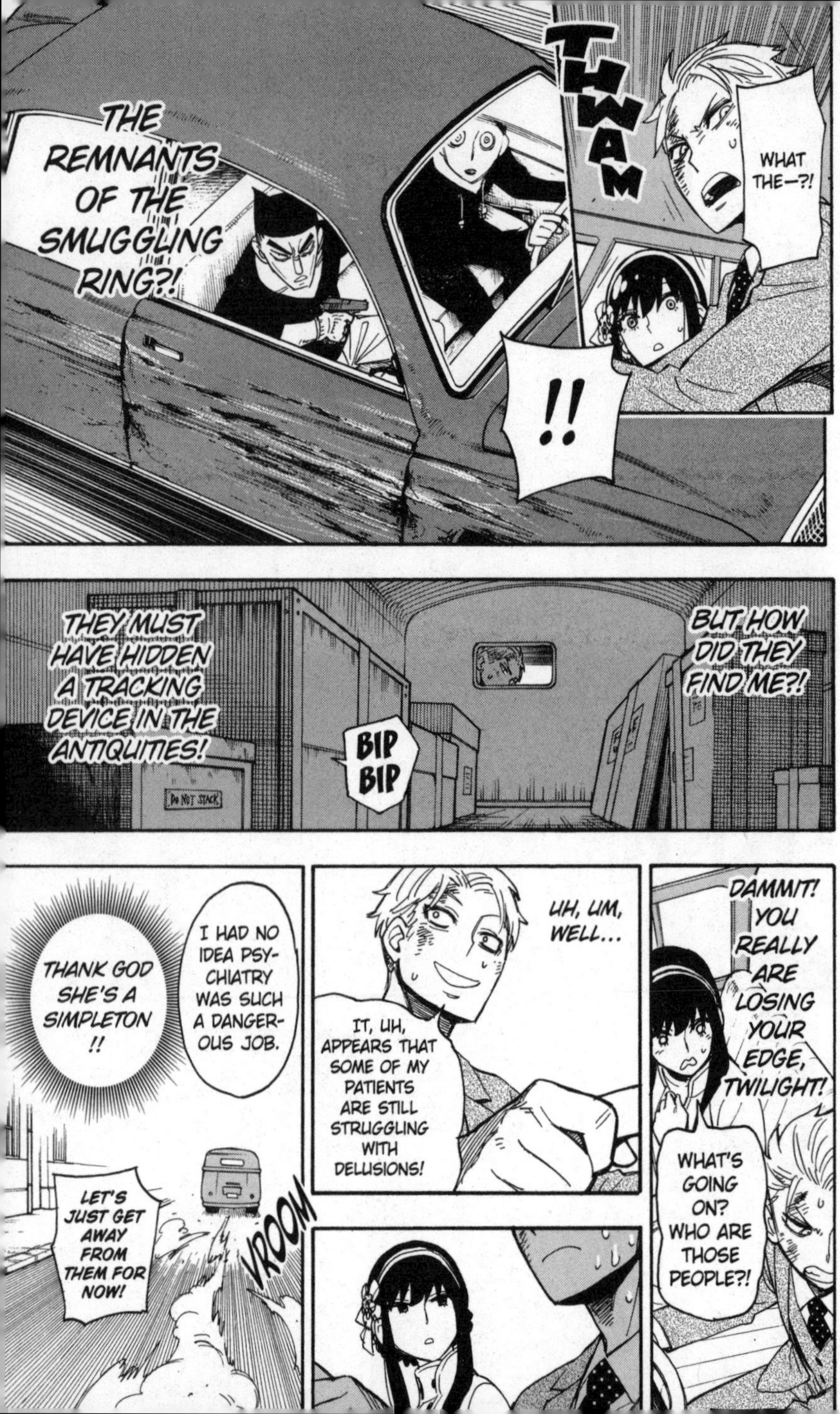
THWAM
WHAT THE—?!
THE REMNANTS OF THE SMUGGLING RING?!
!!
BUT HOW DID THEY FIND ME?!
THEY MUST HAVE HIDDEN A TRACKING DEVICE IN THE ANTIQUITIES!
BIP BIP
DO NOT STACK
DAMMIT! YOU REALLY ARE LOSING YOUR EDGE, TWILIGHT!
WHAT'S GOING ON? WHO ARE THOSE PEOPLE?!
UH, UM, WELL...
IT, UH, APPEARS THAT SOME OF MY PATIENTS ARE STILL STRUGGLING WITH DELUSIONS!
I HAD NO IDEA PSY-CHIATRY WAS SUCH A DANGER-OUS JOB.
THANK GOD SHE'S A SIMPLETON !!
LET'S JUST GET AWAY FROM THEM FOR NOW!
VROOM

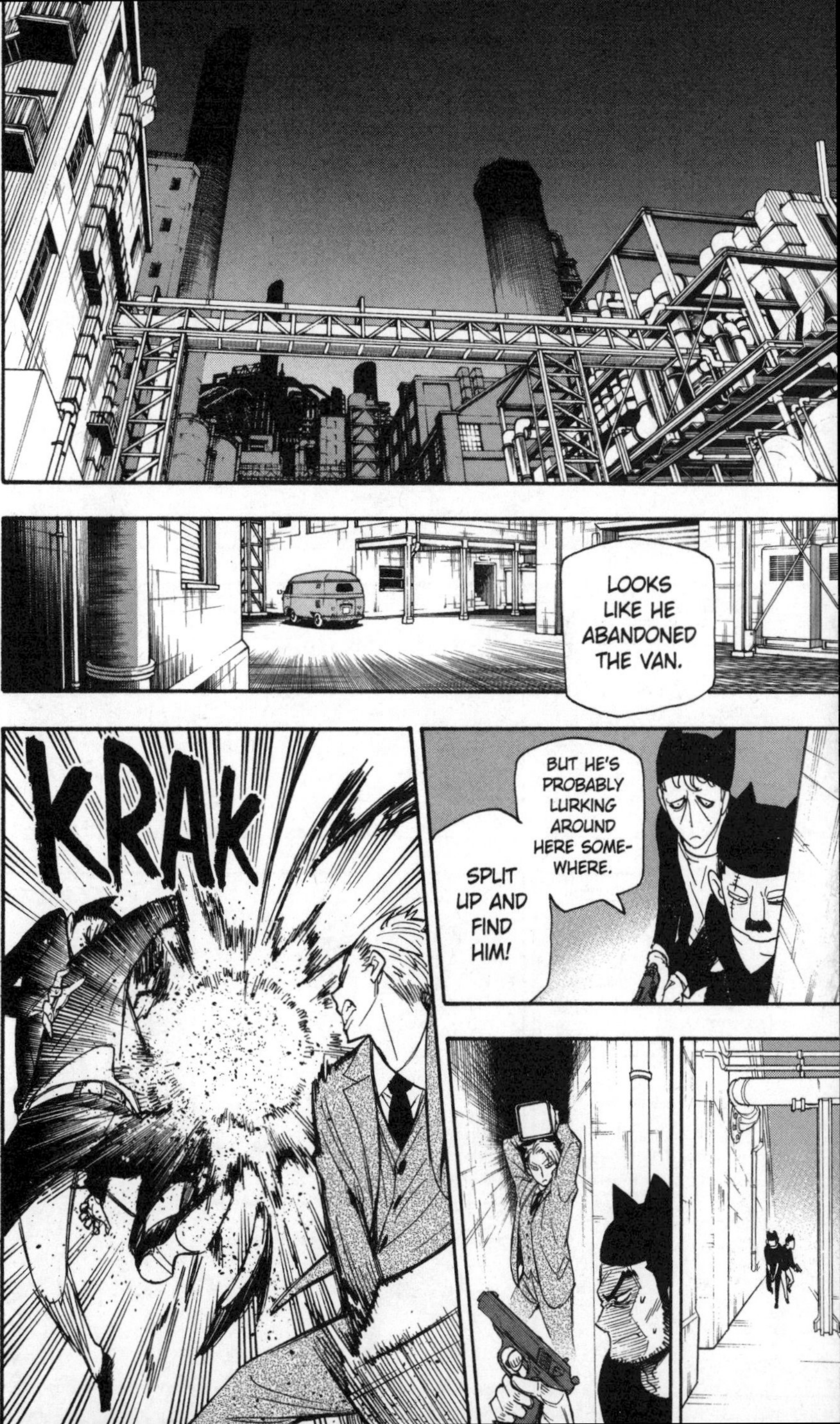

LOOKS LIKE HE ABANDONED THE VAN.
BUT HE'S PROBABLY LURKING AROUND HERE SOME-WHERE.
SPLIT UP AND FIND HIM!
KRAK

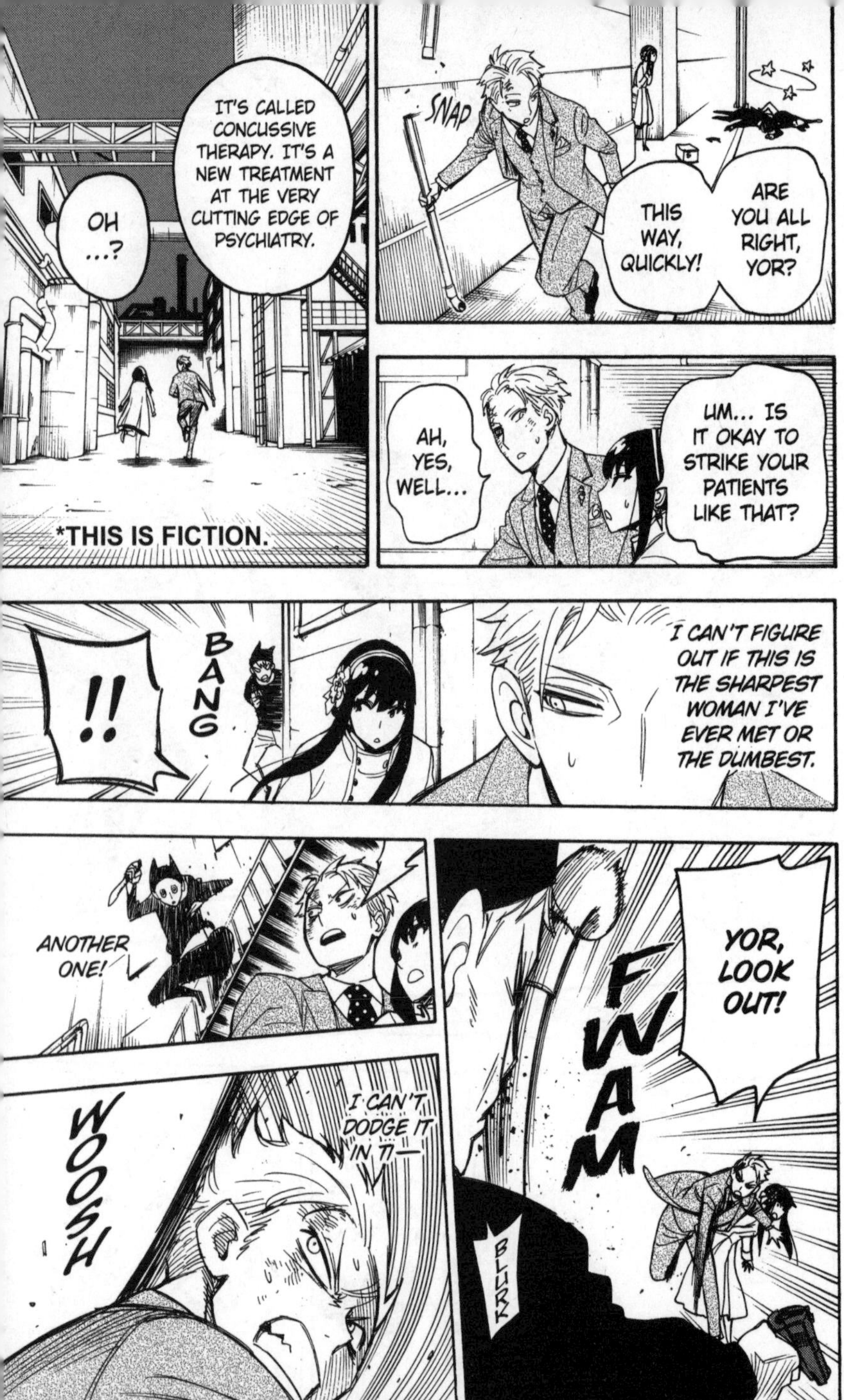
SNAP
ARE YOU ALL RIGHT, YOR?
THIS WAY, QUICKLY!
UM... IS IT OKAY TO STRIKE YOUR PATIENTS LIKE THAT?
AH, YES, WELL...
IT'S CALLED CONCUSSIVE THERAPY. IT'S A NEW TREATMENT AT THE VERY CUTTING EDGE OF PSYCHIATRY.
OH ...?
*THIS IS FICTION.
I CAN'T FIGURE OUT IF THIS IS THE SHARPEST WOMAN I'VE EVER MET OR THE DUMBEST.
BANG
!!
YOR, LOOK OUT!
FWAM
BLURK
ANOTHER ONE!
I CAN'T DODGE IT IN TI—
WOOOSH

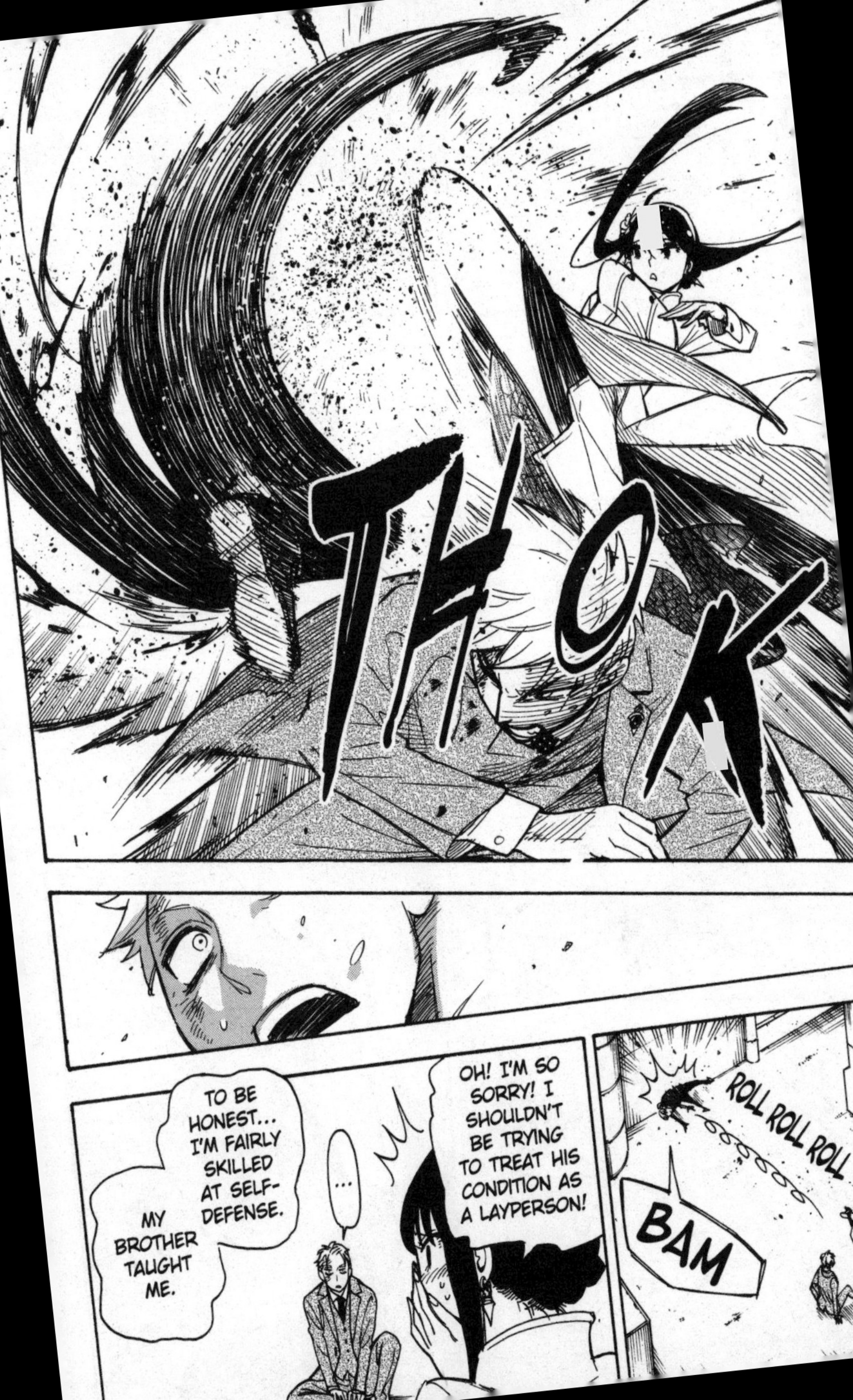
THOK
ROLL ROLL ROLL
BAM
OH! I'M SO SORRY! I SHOULDN'T BE TRYING TO TREAT HIS CONDITION AS A LAYPERSON!
...
TO BE HONEST... I'M FAIRLY SKILLED AT SELF-DEFENSE.
MY BROTHER TAUGHT ME.

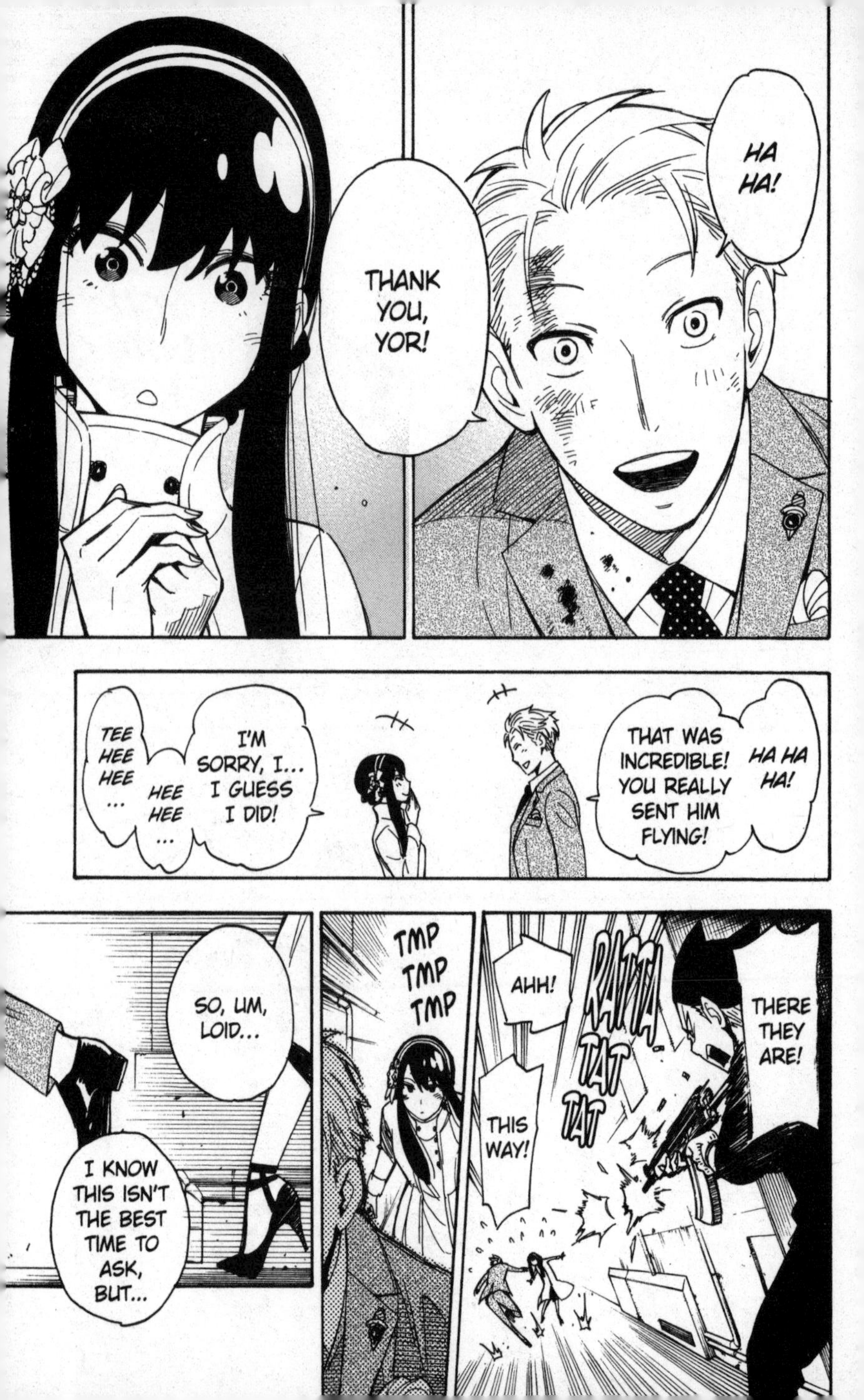
HA HA!
THANK YOU, YOR!
HA HA HA!
THAT WAS INCREDIBLE! YOU REALLY SENT HIM FLYING!
I'M SORRY, I... I GUESS I DID!
HEE HEE...
TEE HEE HEE...
THERE THEY ARE!
RATTA TAT TAT
AHH!
THIS WAY!
TMP TMP TMP
SO, UM, LOID...
I KNOW THIS ISN'T THE BEST TIME TO ASK, BUT...

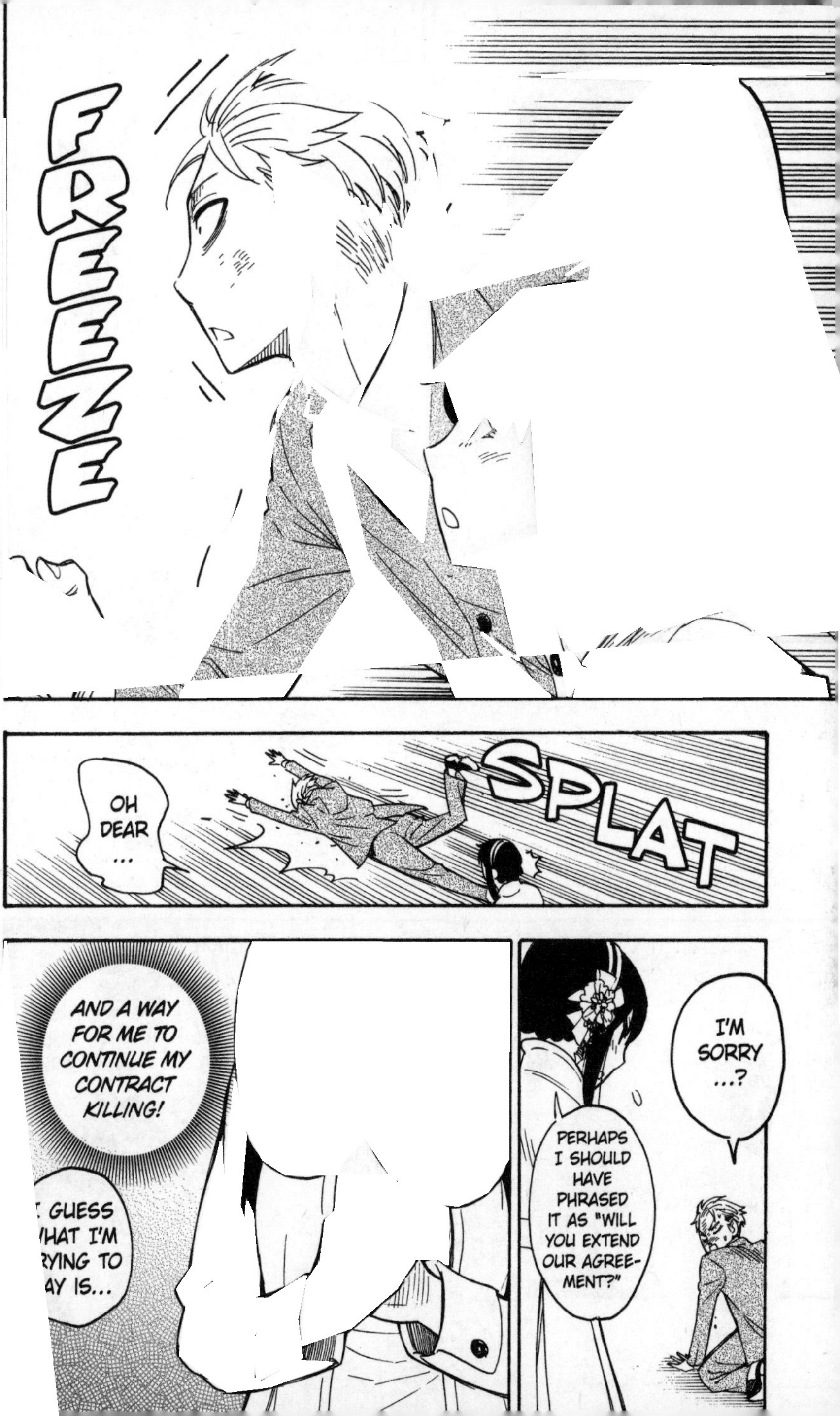
FREEZE
SPLAT
OH DEAR...
I'M SORRY...?
PERHAPS I SHOULD HAVE PHRASED IT AS "WILL YOU EXTEND OUR AGREEMENT?"
AND A WAY FOR ME TO CONTINUE MY CONTRACT KILLING!
I GUESS WHAT I'M TRYING TO SAY IS...

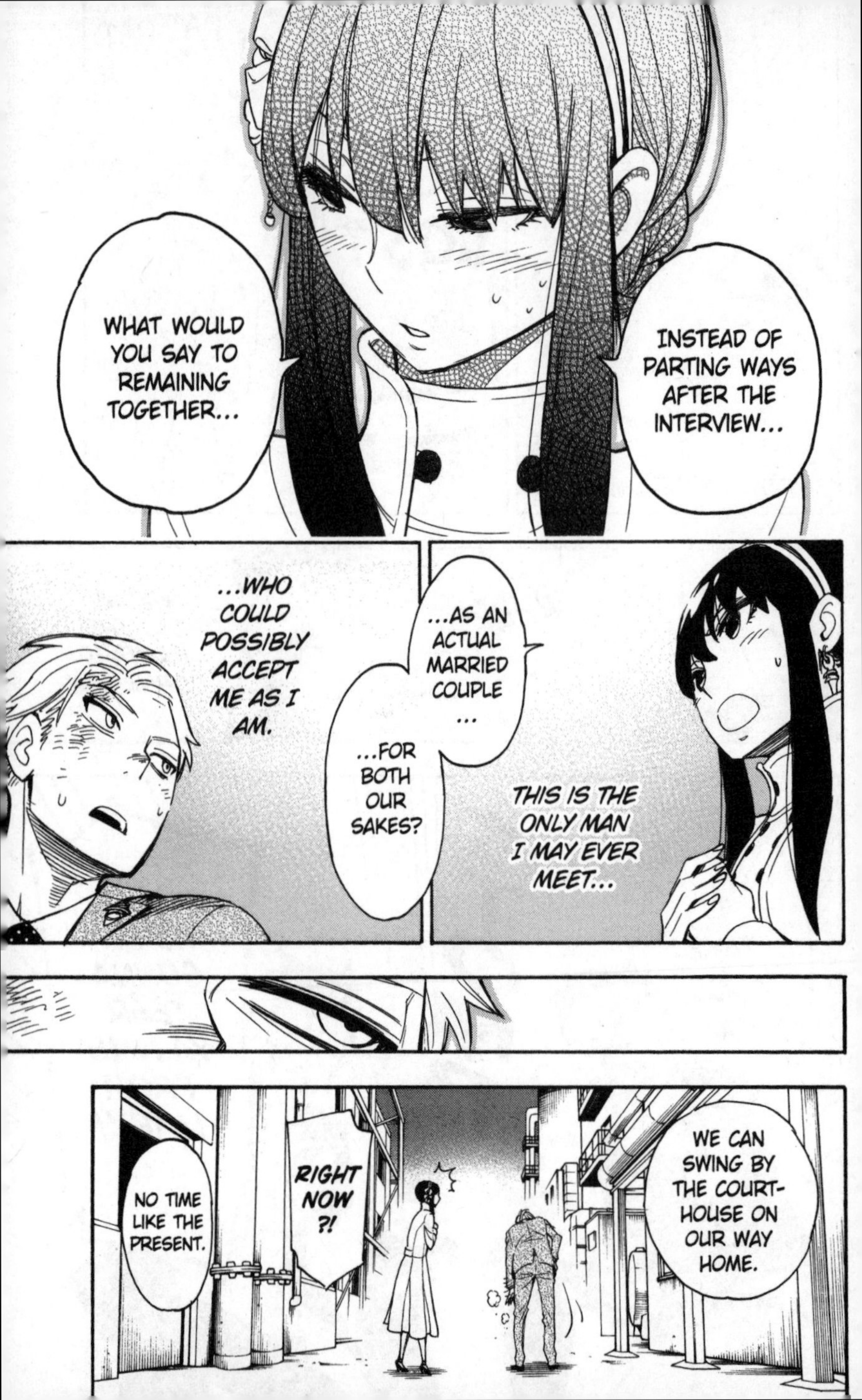
INSTEAD OF PARTING WAYS AFTER THE INTERVIEW...
WHAT WOULD YOU SAY TO REMAINING TOGETHER...
...AS AN ACTUAL MARRIED COUPLE ...
...FOR BOTH OUR SAKES?
THIS IS THE ONLY MAN I MAY EVER MEET...
...WHO COULD POSSIBLY ACCEPT ME AS I AM.
WE CAN SWING BY THE COURT-HOUSE ON OUR WAY HOME.
RIGHT NOW ?!
NO TIME LIKE THE PRESENT.

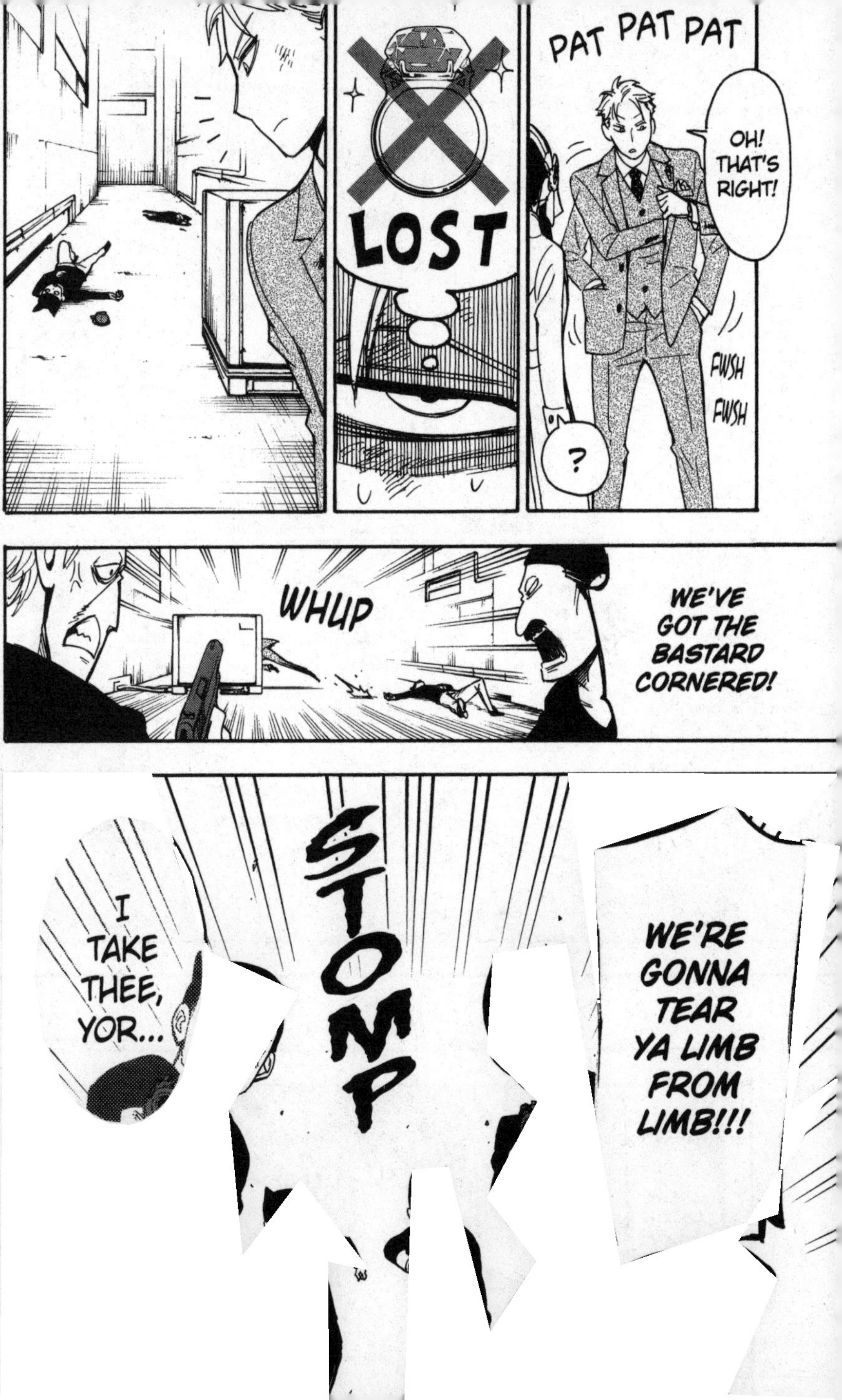
PAT PAT PAT
OH! THAT'S RIGHT!
FWSH FWSH
?
LOST
WE'VE GOT THE BASTARD CORNERED!
WHUP
WE'RE GONNA TEAR YA LIMB FROM LIMB!!!
STOMP
I TAKE THEE, YOR...

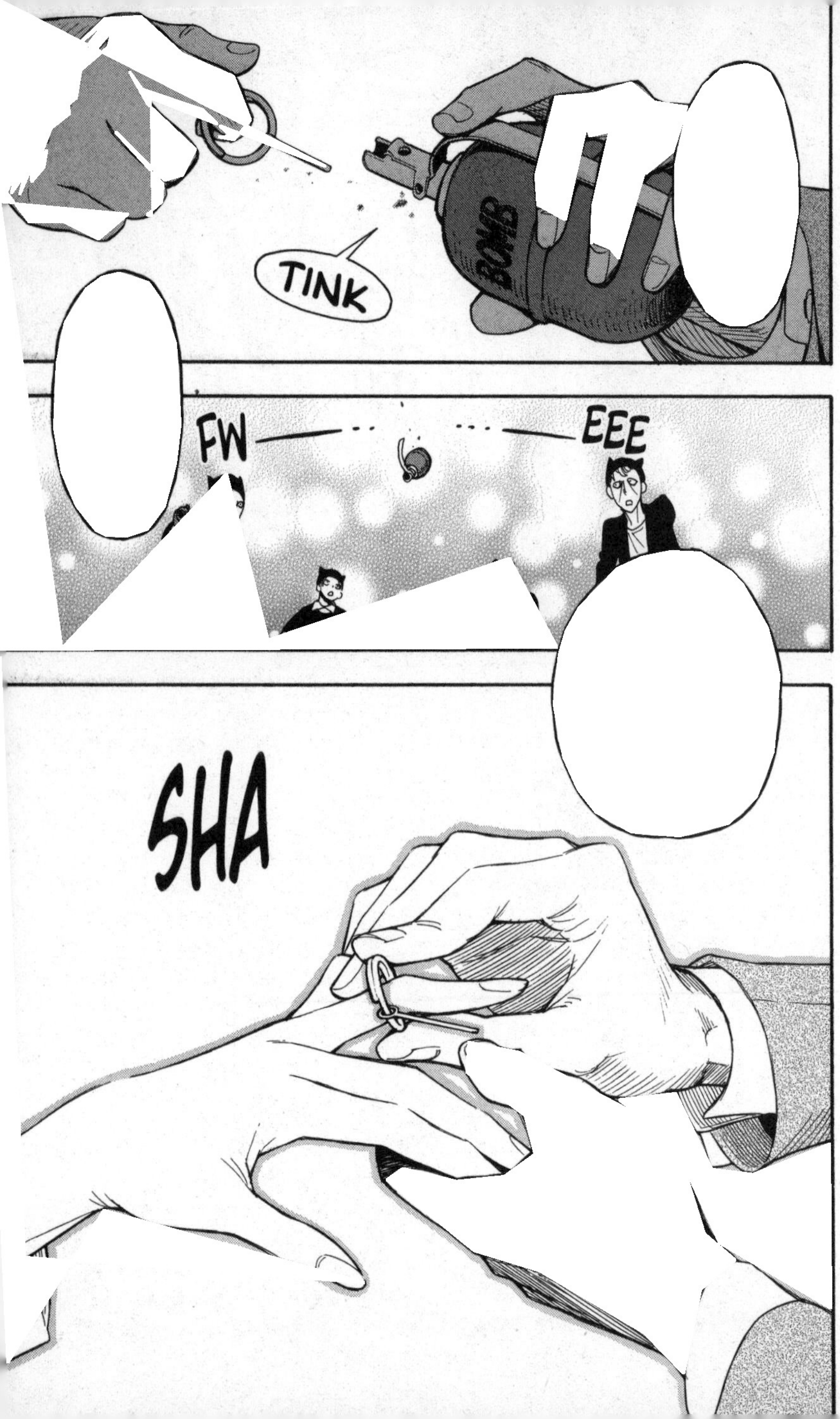
TINK
FW——EEE
SHA

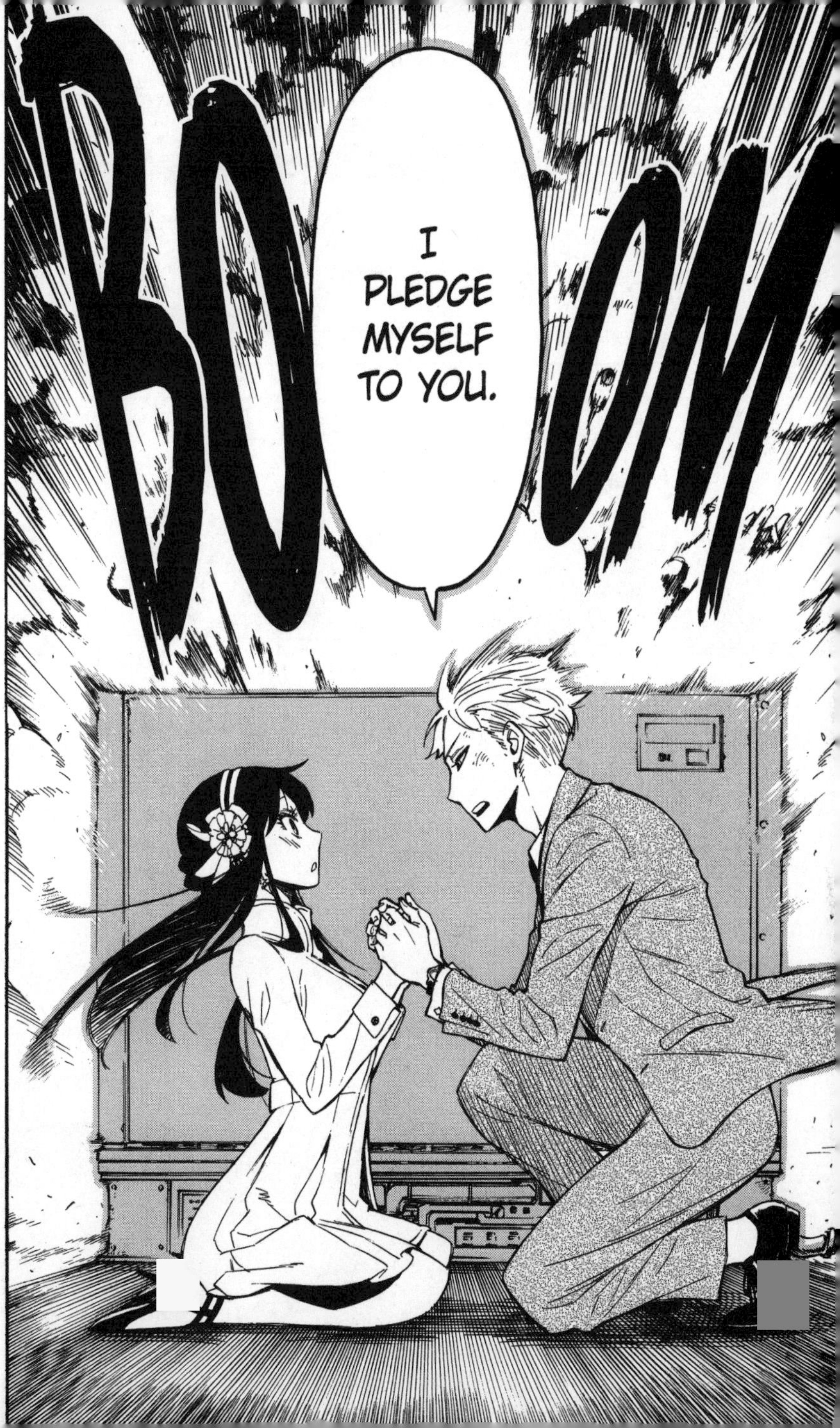
BOOOM
I PLEDGE MYSELF TO YOU.

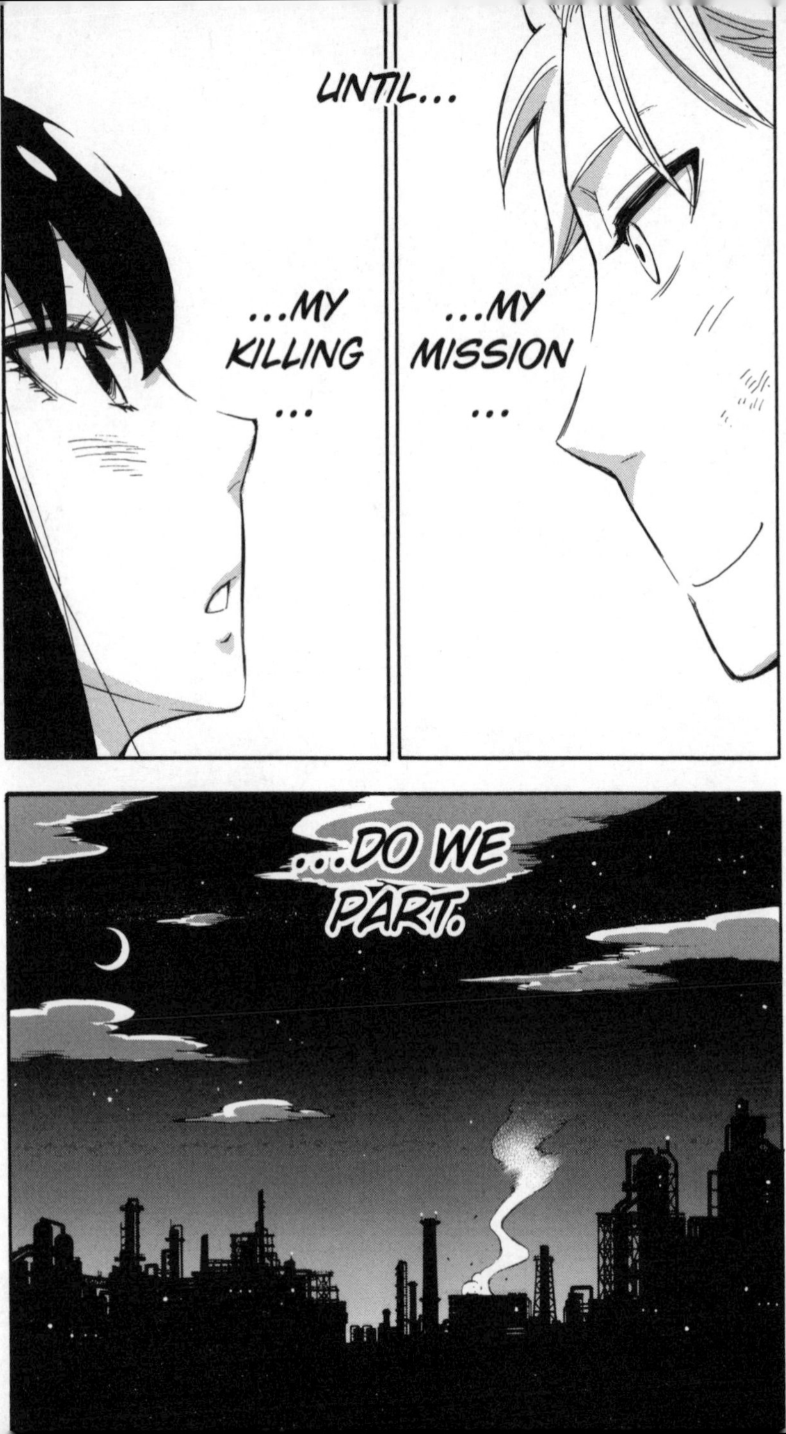
UNTIL...
...MY MISSION ...
...MY KILLING ...
...DO WE PART.

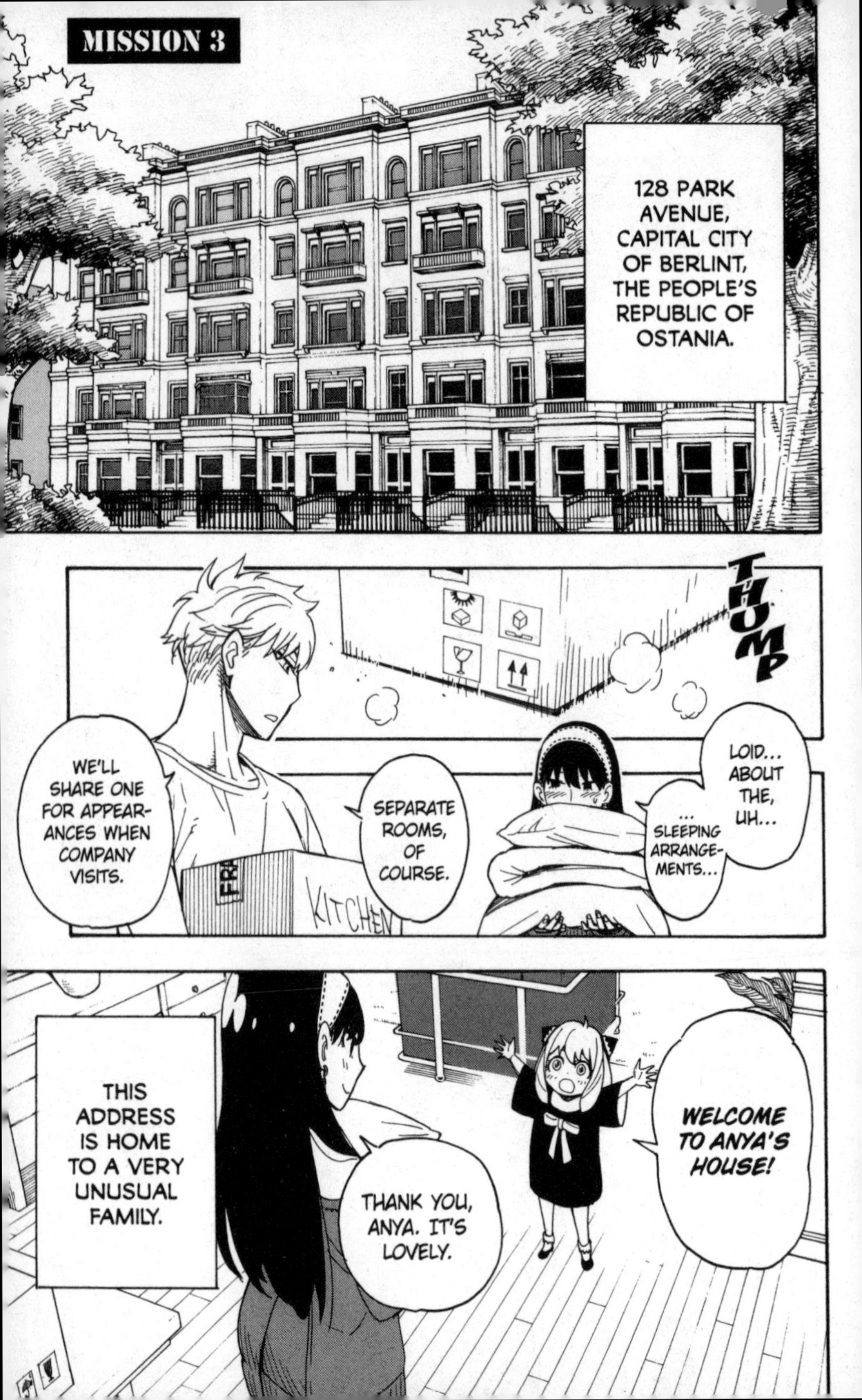
MISSION 3
128 PARK AVENUE, CAPITAL CITY OF BERLINT, THE PEOPLE'S REPUBLIC OF OSTANIA.
THUMP
LOID... ABOUT THE, UH...
...SLEEPING ARRANGEMENTS...
SEPARATE ROOMS, OF COURSE.
WE'LL SHARE ONE FOR APPEARANCES WHEN COMPANY VISITS.
KITCHEN
WELCOME TO ANYA'S HOUSE!
THANK YOU, ANYA. IT'S LOVELY.
THIS ADDRESS IS HOME TO A VERY UNUSUAL FAMILY.

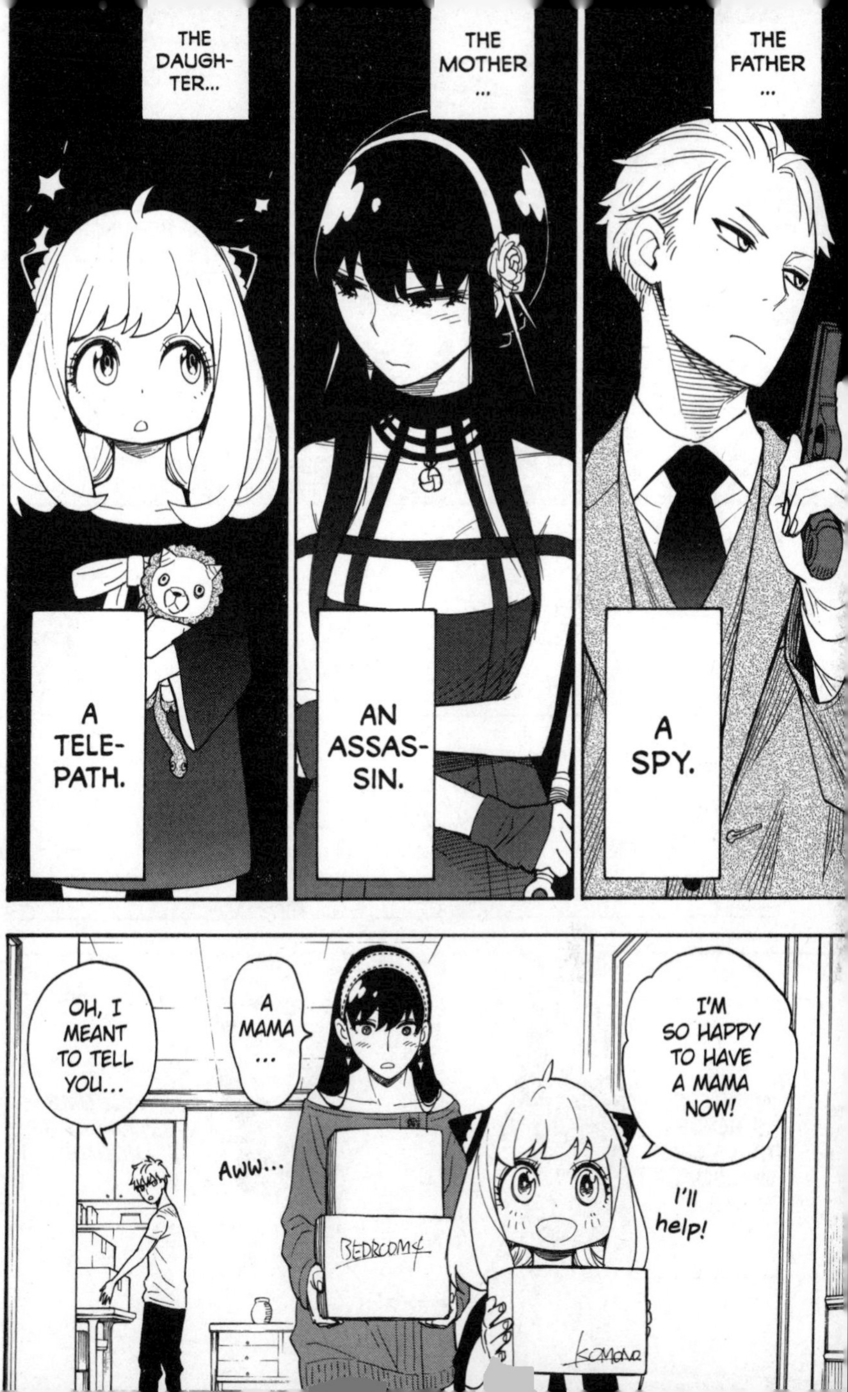
THE FATHER ...
A SPY.
THE MOTHER ...
AN ASSAS-SIN.
THE DAUGH-TER...
A TELE-PATH.
I'M SO HAPPY TO HAVE A MAMA NOW!
I'll help!
A MAMA ...
AWW...
BEDROOM
komono
OH, I MEANT TO TELL YOU...

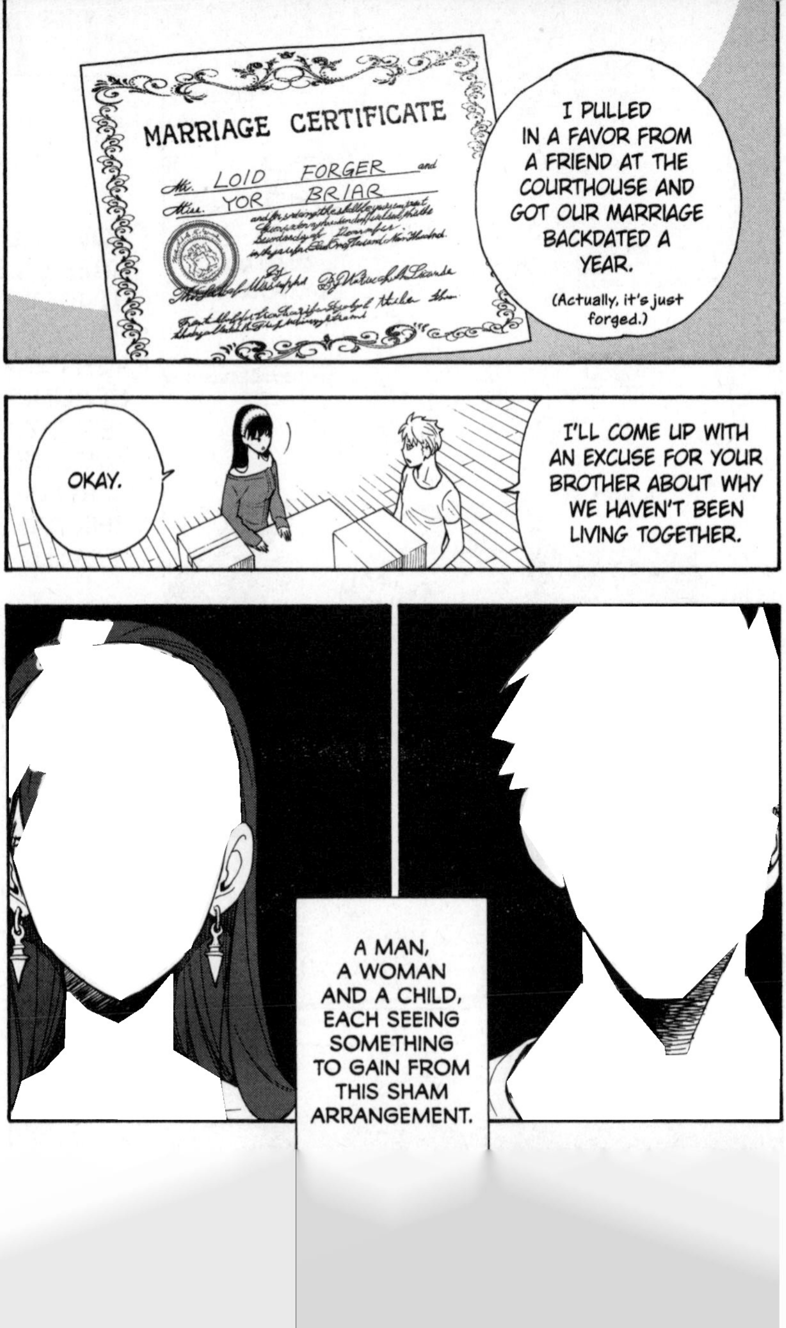
I PULLED IN A FAVOR FROM A FRIEND AT THE COURTHOUSE AND GOT OUR MARRIAGE BACKDATED A YEAR.
(Actually, it's just forged.)
MARRIAGE CERTIFICATE
Mr. LOID FORGER and
Miss. YOR BRIAR
I'LL COME UP WITH AN EXCUSE FOR YOUR BROTHER ABOUT WHY WE HAVEN'T BEEN LIVING TOGETHER.
OKAY.
A MAN, A WOMAN AND A CHILD, EACH SEEING SOMETHING TO GAIN FROM THIS SHAM ARRANGEMENT.

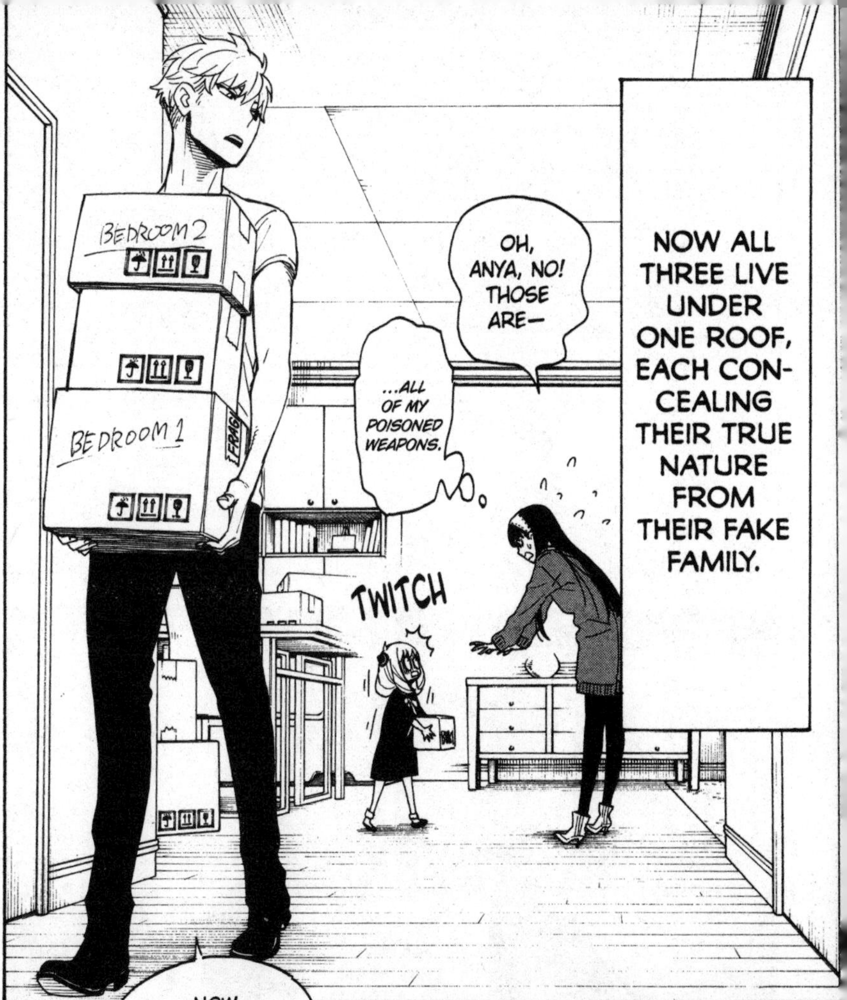
NOW ALL THREE LIVE UNDER ONE ROOF, EACH CON-CEALING THEIR TRUE NATURE FROM THEIR FAKE FAMILY.
OH, ANYA, NO! THOSE ARE—
...ALL OF MY POISONED WEAPONS.
TWITCH
BEDROOM 2
BEDROOM 1
NOW THAT WE'VE SORTED OUT THE BOXES, SHALL WE PRACTICE FOR THE INTERVIEW?
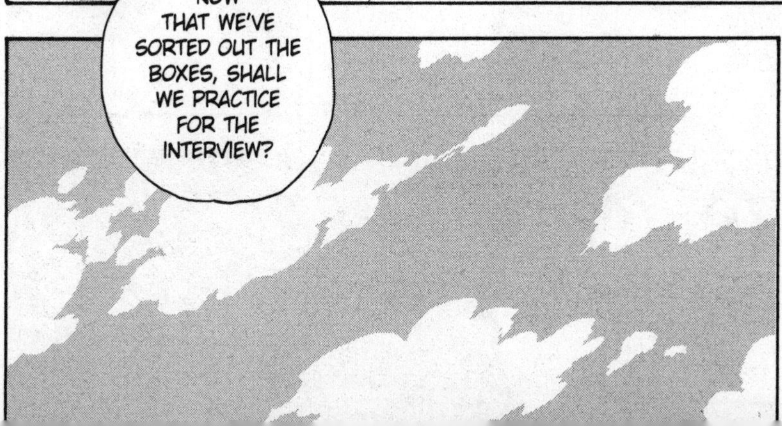

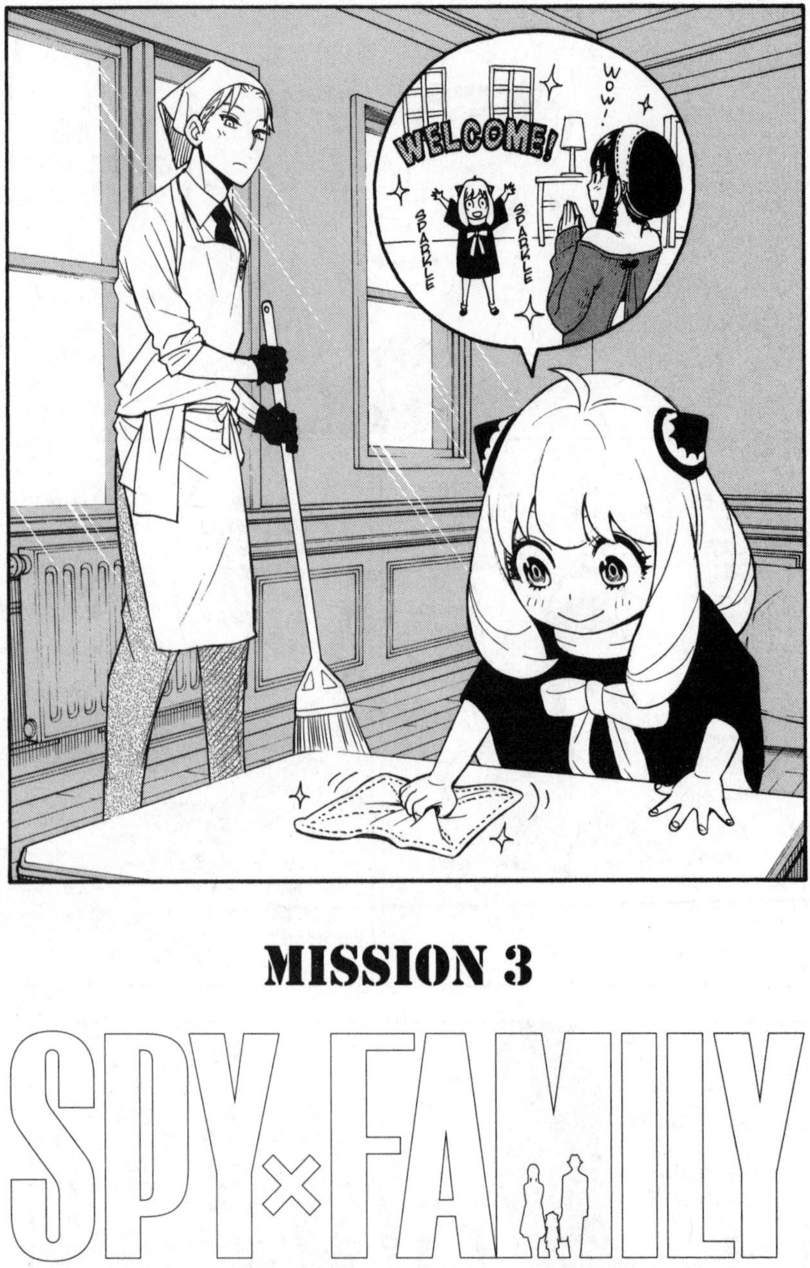
WOW!
WELCOME!
SPARKLE
SPARKLE

MISSION 3

SPY×FAMILY

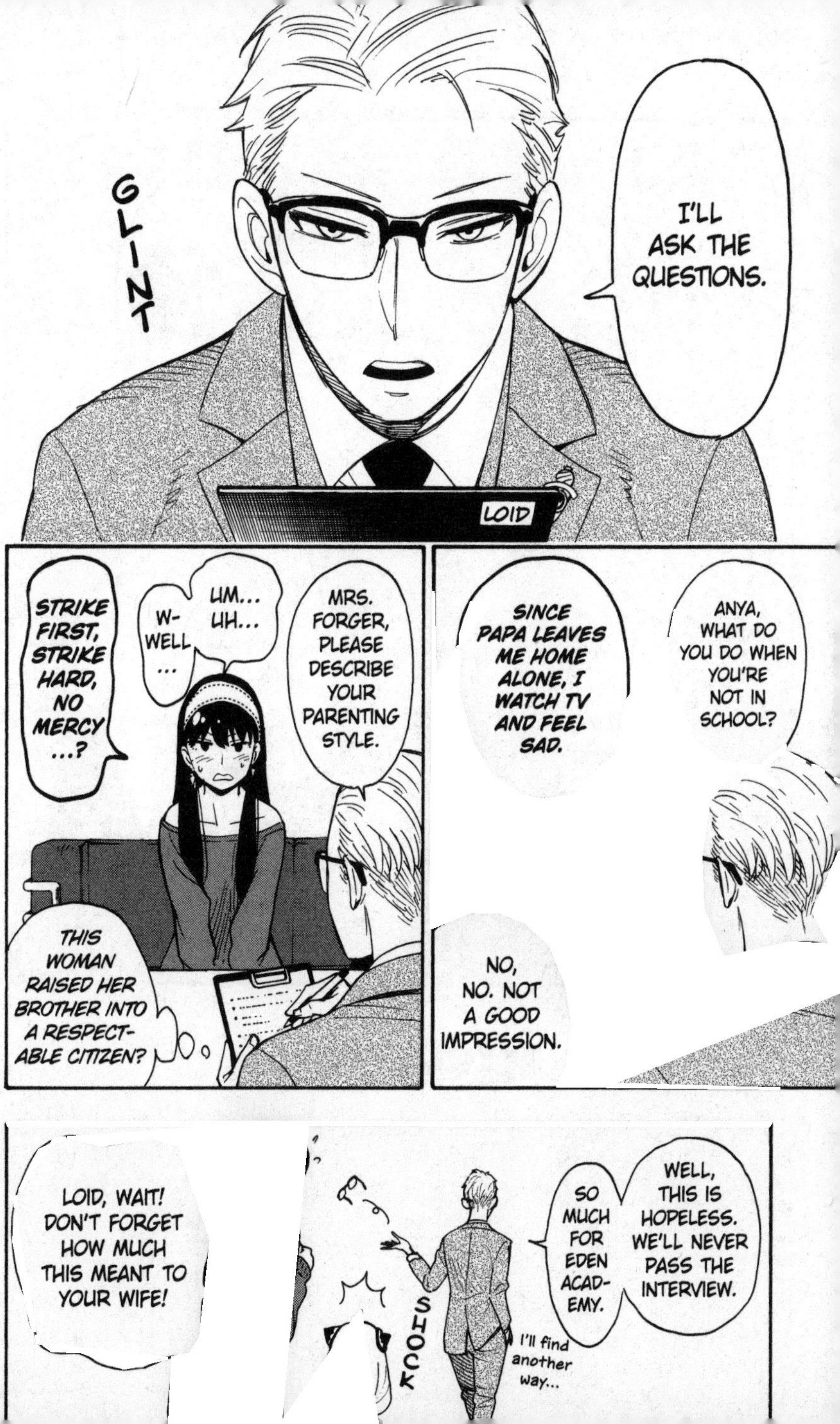
I'LL ASK THE QUESTIONS.
GLINT
LOID
ANYA, WHAT DO YOU DO WHEN YOU'RE NOT IN SCHOOL?
SINCE PAPA LEAVES ME HOME ALONE, I WATCH TV AND FEEL SAD.
NO, NO. NOT A GOOD IMPRESSION.
MRS. FORGER, PLEASE DESCRIBE YOUR PARENTING STYLE.
UM... UH...
W-WELL...
STRIKE FIRST, STRIKE HARD, NO MERCY...?
THIS WOMAN RAISED HER BROTHER INTO A RESPECTABLE CITIZEN?
WELL, THIS IS HOPELESS. WE'LL NEVER PASS THE INTERVIEW.
SO MUCH FOR EDEN ACADEMY.
I'll find another way...
SHOCK
LOID, WAIT! DON'T FORGET HOW MUCH THIS MEANT TO YOUR WIFE!

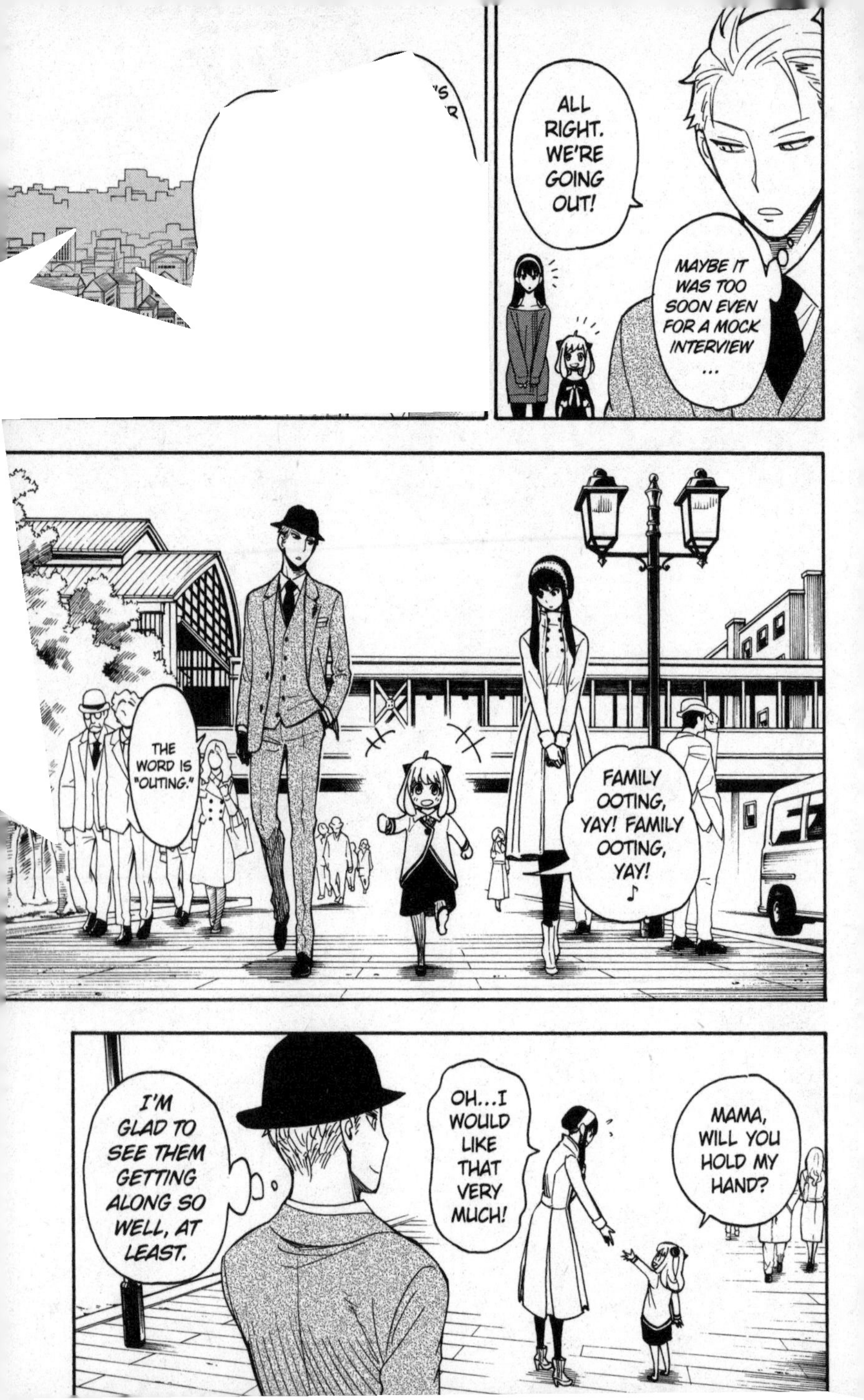
MAYBE IT WAS TOO SOON EVEN FOR A MOCK INTERVIEW...
ALL RIGHT. WE'RE GOING OUT!
FAMILY OOTING, YAY! FAMILY OOTING, YAY! ♪
THE WORD IS "OUTING."
MAMA, WILL YOU HOLD MY HAND?
OH...I WOULD LIKE THAT VERY MUCH!
I'M GLAD TO SEE THEM GETTING ALONG SO WELL, AT LEAST.

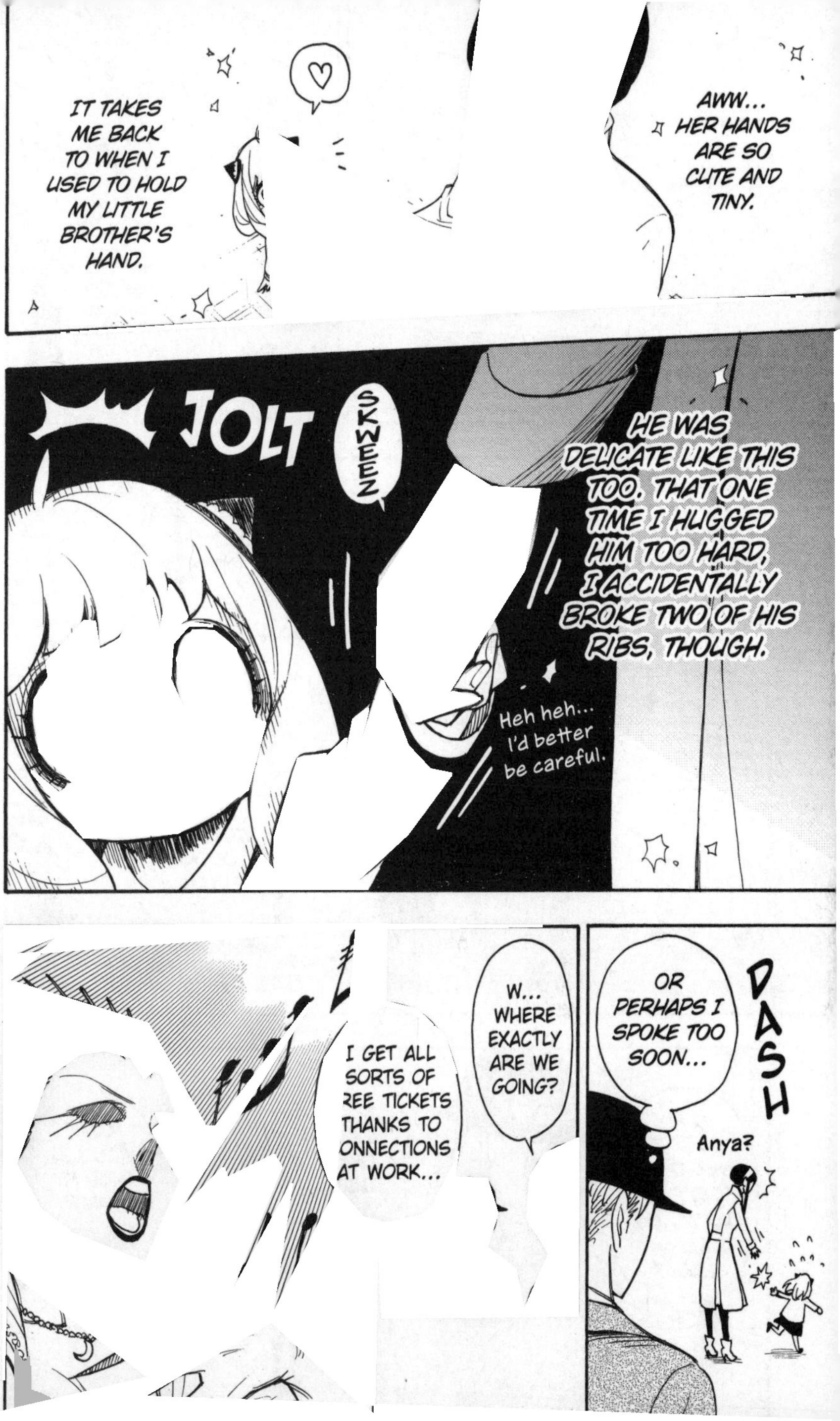
AWW... HER HANDS ARE SO CUTE AND TINY.
IT TAKES ME BACK TO WHEN I USED TO HOLD MY LITTLE BROTHER'S HAND.
HE WAS DELICATE LIKE THIS TOO. THAT ONE TIME I HUGGED HIM TOO HARD, I ACCIDENTALLY BROKE TWO OF HIS RIBS, THOUGH.
Heh heh... I'd better be careful.
SKWEEZ
JOLT
DASH
OR PERHAPS I SPOKE TOO SOON...
Anya?
W... WHERE EXACTLY ARE WE GOING?
I GET ALL SORTS OF REE TICKETS THANKS TO ONNECTIONS AT WORK...

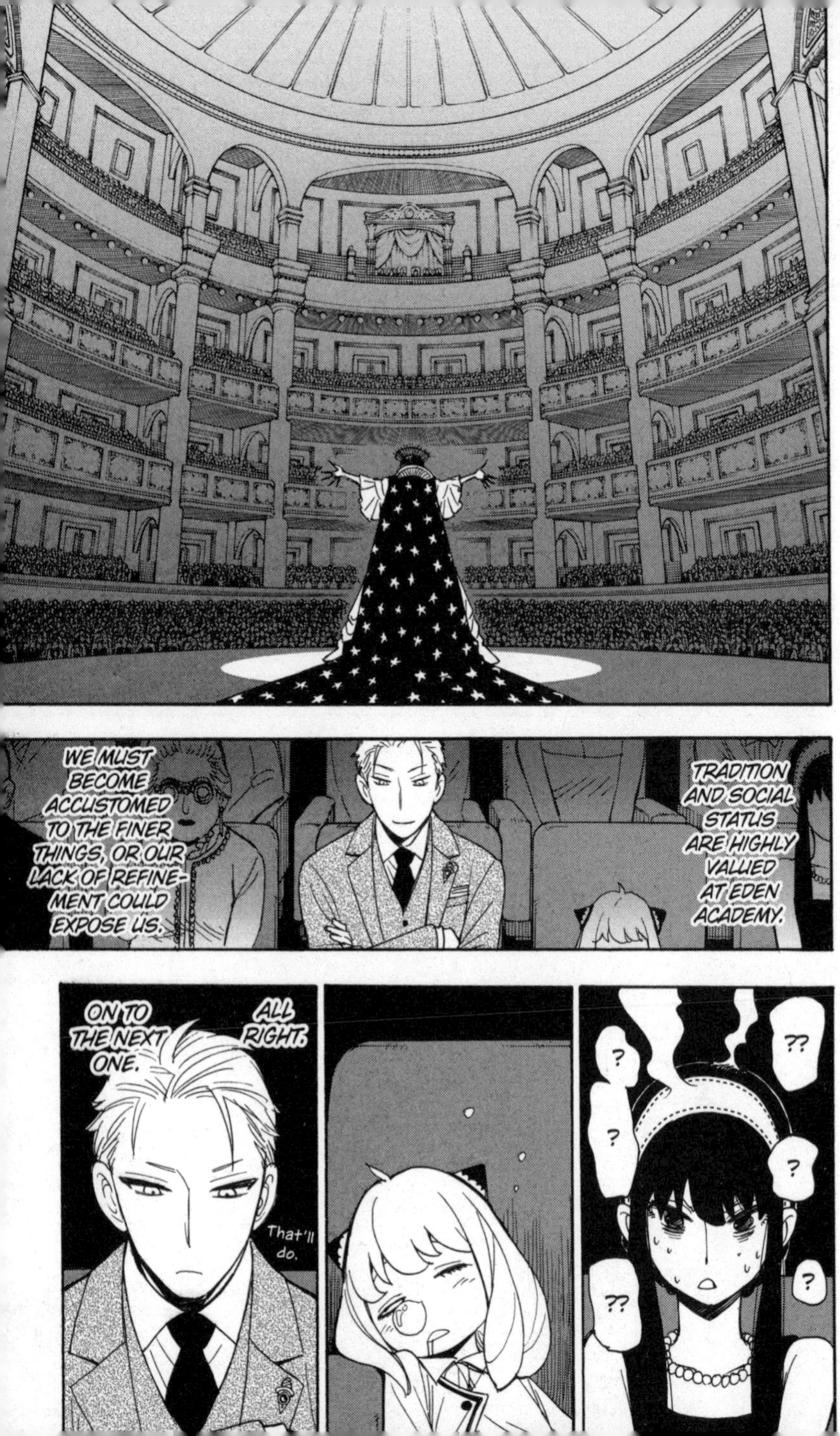
TRADITION AND SOCIAL STATUS ARE HIGHLY VALUED AT EDEN ACADEMY.
WE MUST BECOME ACCUSTOMED TO THE FINER THINGS, OR OUR LACK OF REFINEMENT COULD EXPOSE US.
??
?
?
?
?
??
ALL RIGHT.
ON TO THE NEXT ONE.
That'll do.

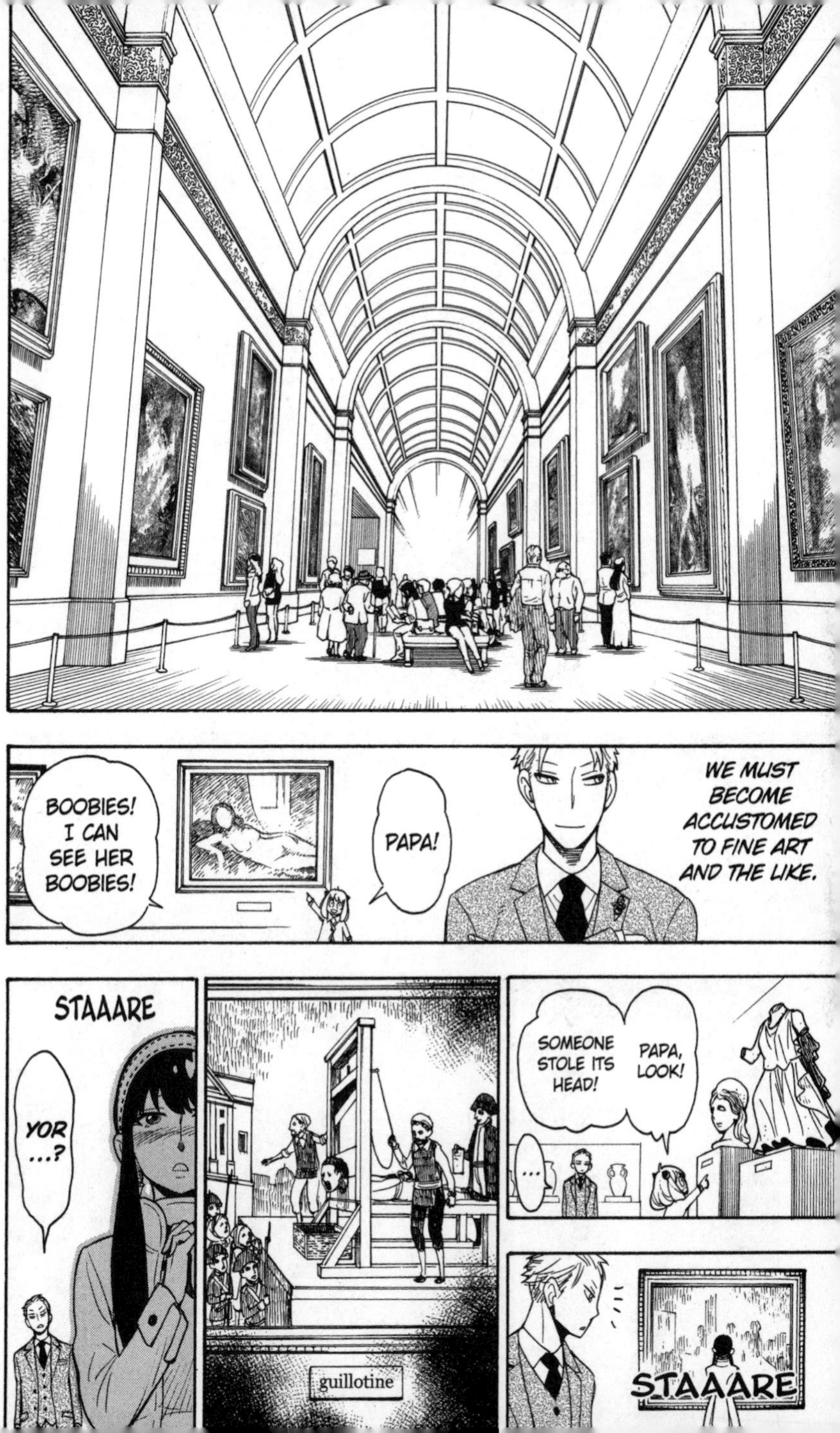
WE MUST BECOME ACCUSTOMED TO FINE ART AND THE LIKE.
PAPA!
BOOBIES! I CAN SEE HER BOOBIES!
PAPA, LOOK!
SOMEONE STOLE ITS HEAD!
...
STAAARE
guillotine
STAAARE
YOR ...?

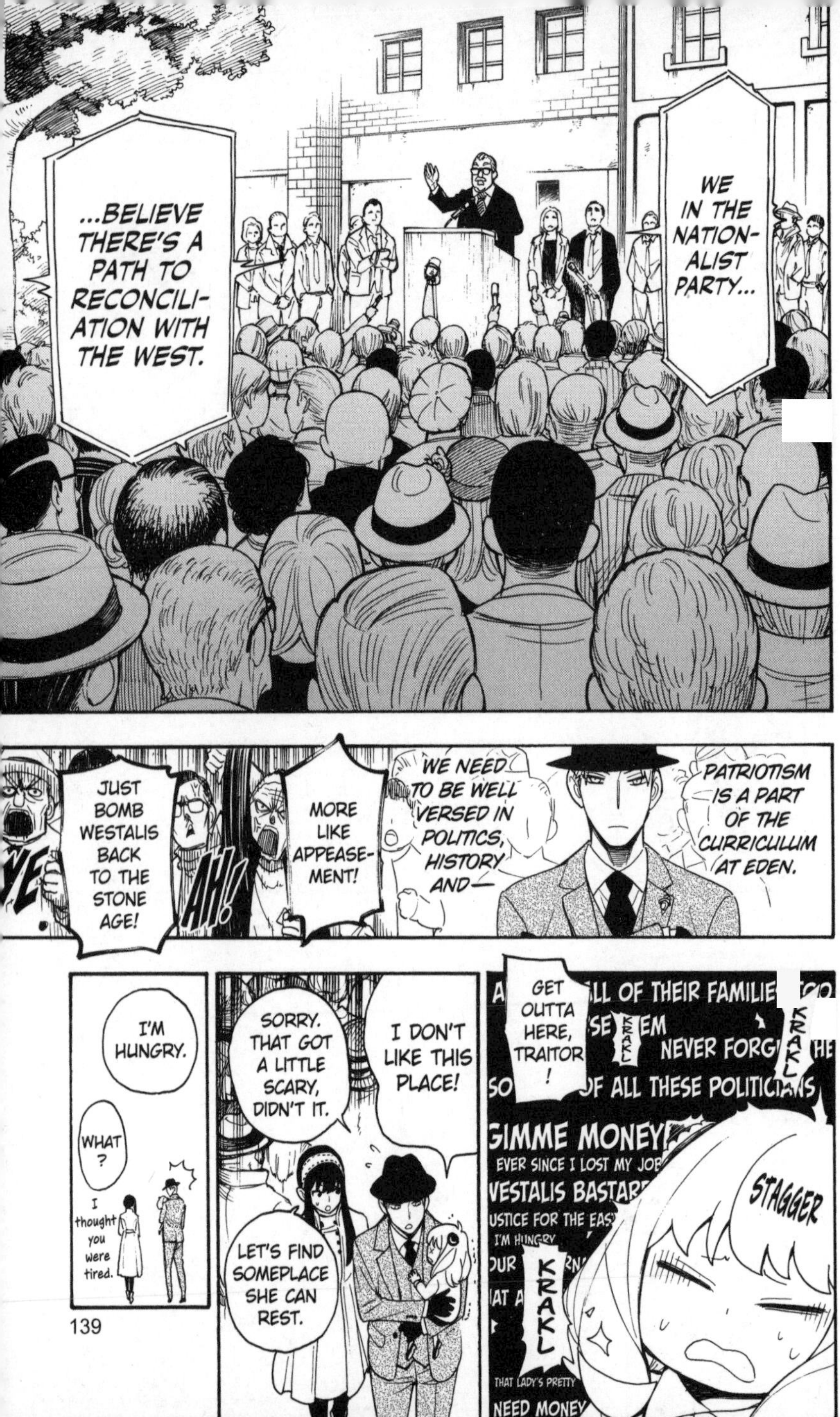
WE IN THE NATION-ALIST PARTY...
...BELIEVE THERE'S A PATH TO RECONCILI-ATION WITH THE WEST.
PATRIOTISM IS A PART OF THE CURRICULUM AT EDEN.
WE NEED TO BE WELL VERSED IN POLITICS, HISTORY AND—
MORE LIKE APPEASE-MENT!
AH!
JUST BOMB WESTALIS BACK TO THE STONE AGE!
GET OUTTA HERE, TRAITOR!
KRAKL
KRAKL
GIMME MONEY
EVER SINCE I LOST MY JOB
I'M HUNGRY
KRAKL
THAT LADY'S PRETTY
NEED MONEY
STAGGER
I DON'T LIKE THIS PLACE!
SORRY. THAT GOT A LITTLE SCARY, DIDN'T IT.
LET'S FIND SOMEPLACE SHE CAN REST.
I'M HUNGRY.
WHAT?
I thought you were tired.

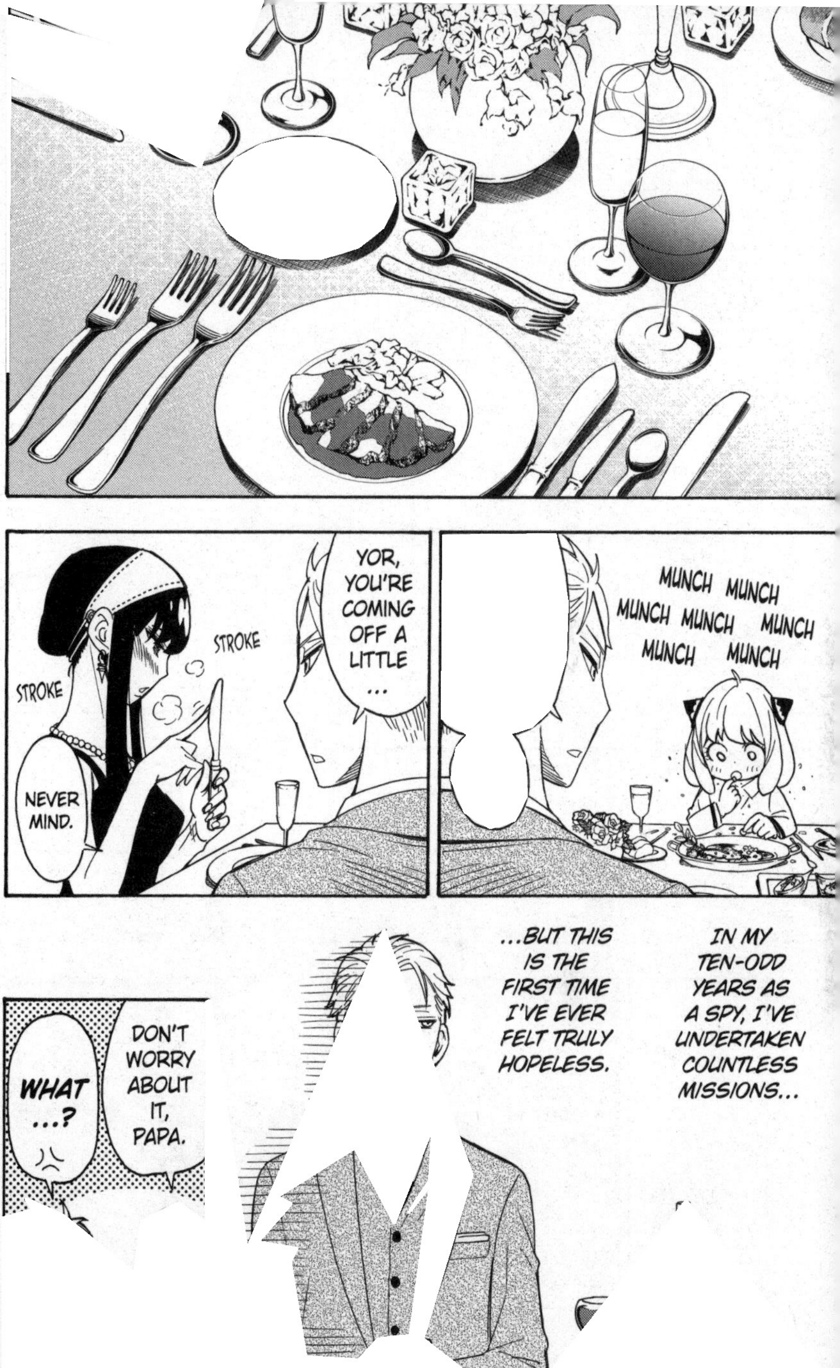
MUNCH MUNCH MUNCH MUNCH MUNCH MUNCH MUNCH
YOR, YOU'RE COMING OFF A LITTLE ...
STROKE
STROKE
NEVER MIND.
IN MY TEN-ODD YEARS AS A SPY, I'VE UNDERTAKEN COUNTLESS MISSIONS...
...BUT THIS IS THE FIRST TIME I'VE EVER FELT TRULY HOPELESS.
DON'T WORRY ABOUT IT, PAPA.
WHAT ...?

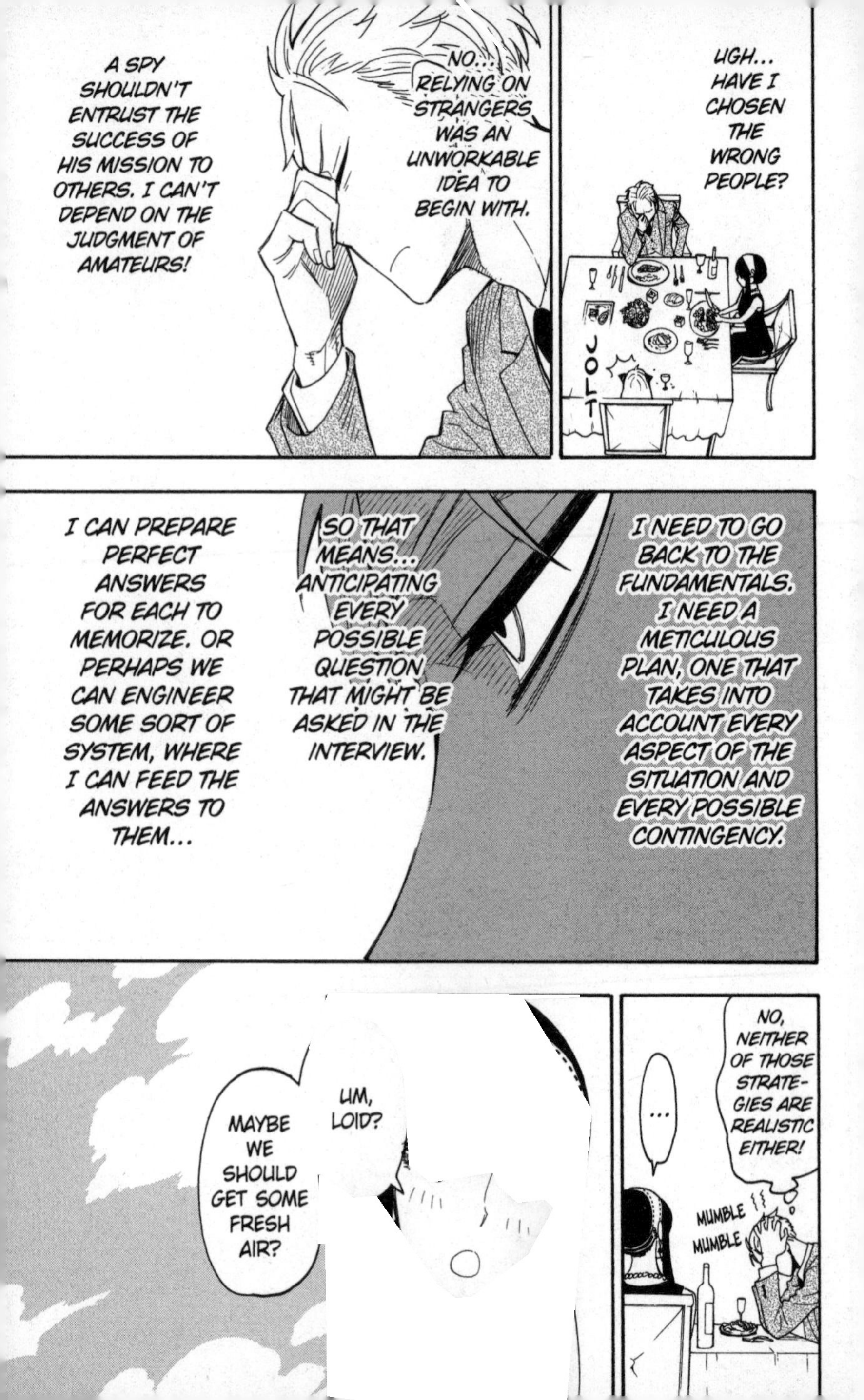
UGH... HAVE I CHOSEN THE WRONG PEOPLE?
JOLT
NO... RELYING ON STRANGERS WAS AN UNWORKABLE IDEA TO BEGIN WITH.
A SPY SHOULDN'T ENTRUST THE SUCCESS OF HIS MISSION TO OTHERS. I CAN'T DEPEND ON THE JUDGMENT OF AMATEURS!
I NEED TO GO BACK TO THE FUNDAMENTALS. I NEED A METICULOUS PLAN, ONE THAT TAKES INTO ACCOUNT EVERY ASPECT OF THE SITUATION AND EVERY POSSIBLE CONTINGENCY.
SO THAT MEANS... ANTICIPATING EVERY POSSIBLE QUESTION THAT MIGHT BE ASKED IN THE INTERVIEW.
I CAN PREPARE PERFECT ANSWERS FOR EACH TO MEMORIZE. OR PERHAPS WE CAN ENGINEER SOME SORT OF SYSTEM, WHERE I CAN FEED THE ANSWERS TO THEM...
NO, NEITHER OF THOSE STRATE-GIES ARE REALISTIC EITHER!
...
MUMBLE MUMBLE
UM, LOID?
MAYBE WE SHOULD GET SOME FRESH AIR?

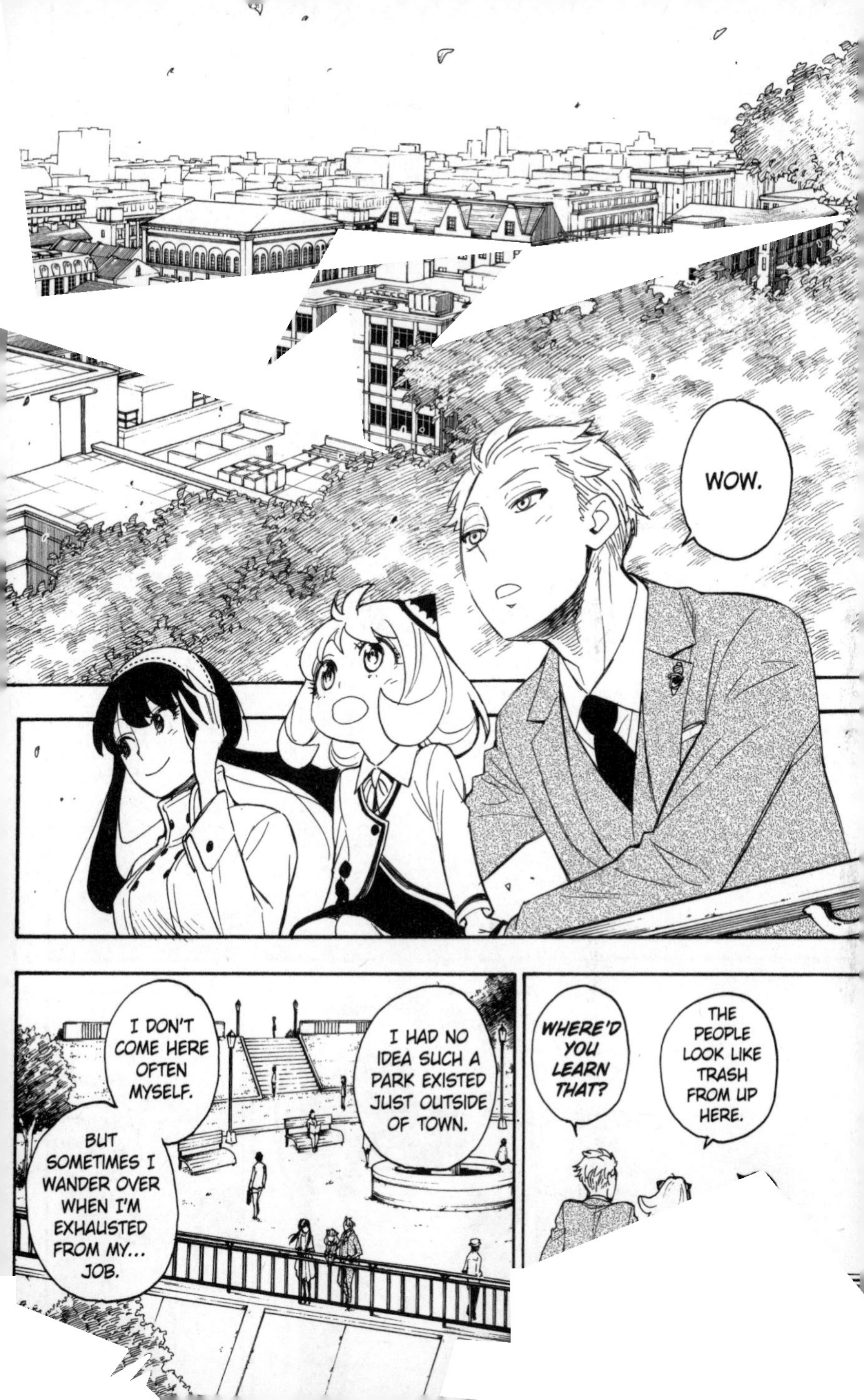
WOW.
THE PEOPLE LOOK LIKE TRASH FROM UP HERE.
WHERE'D YOU LEARN THAT?
I HAD NO IDEA SUCH A PARK EXISTED JUST OUTSIDE OF TOWN.
I DON'T COME HERE OFTEN MYSELF.
BUT SOMETIMES I WANDER OVER WHEN I'M EXHAUSTED FROM MY... JOB.

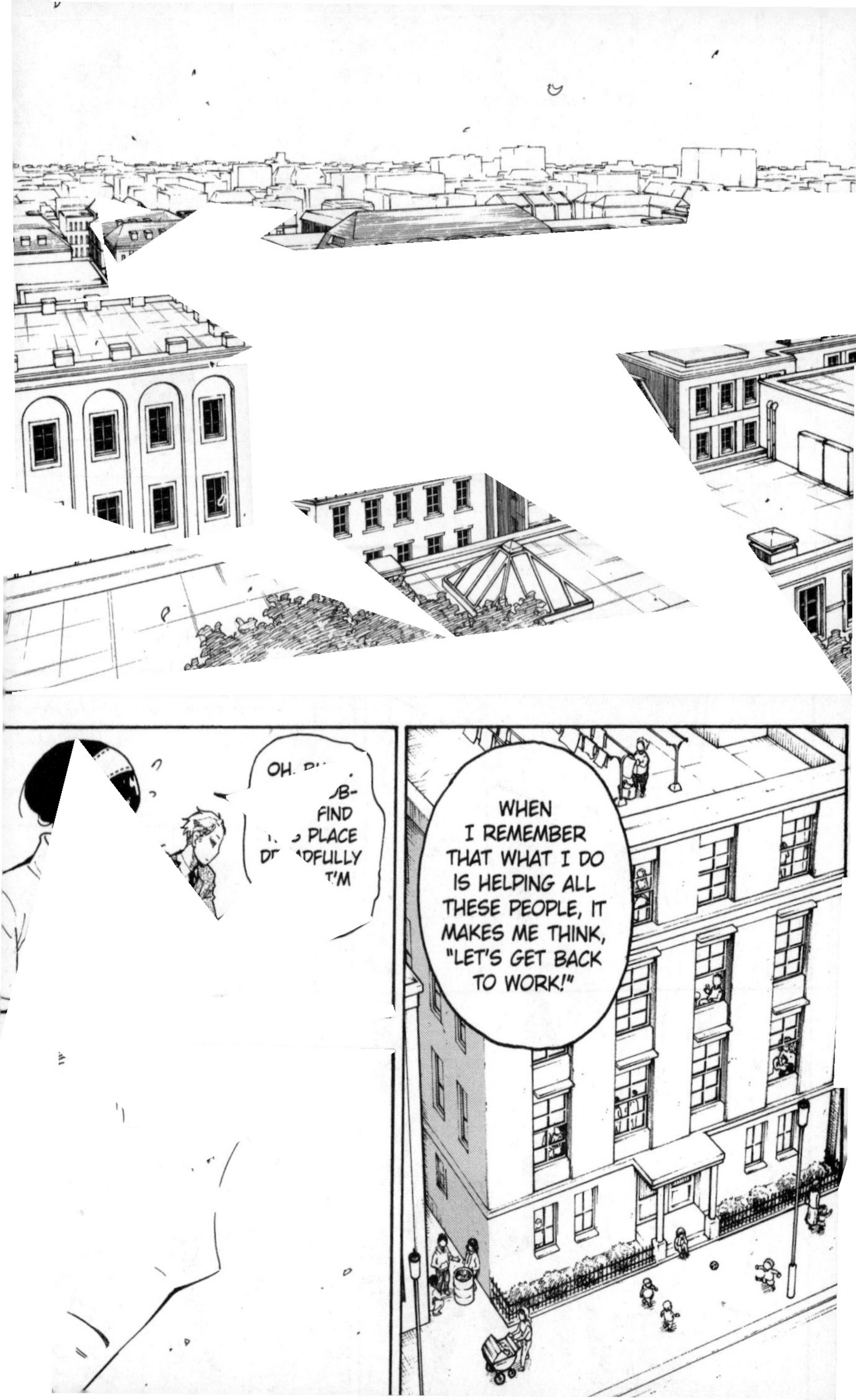
WHEN I REMEMBER THAT WHAT I DO IS HELPING ALL THESE PEOPLE, IT MAKES ME THINK, "LET'S GET BACK TO WORK!"

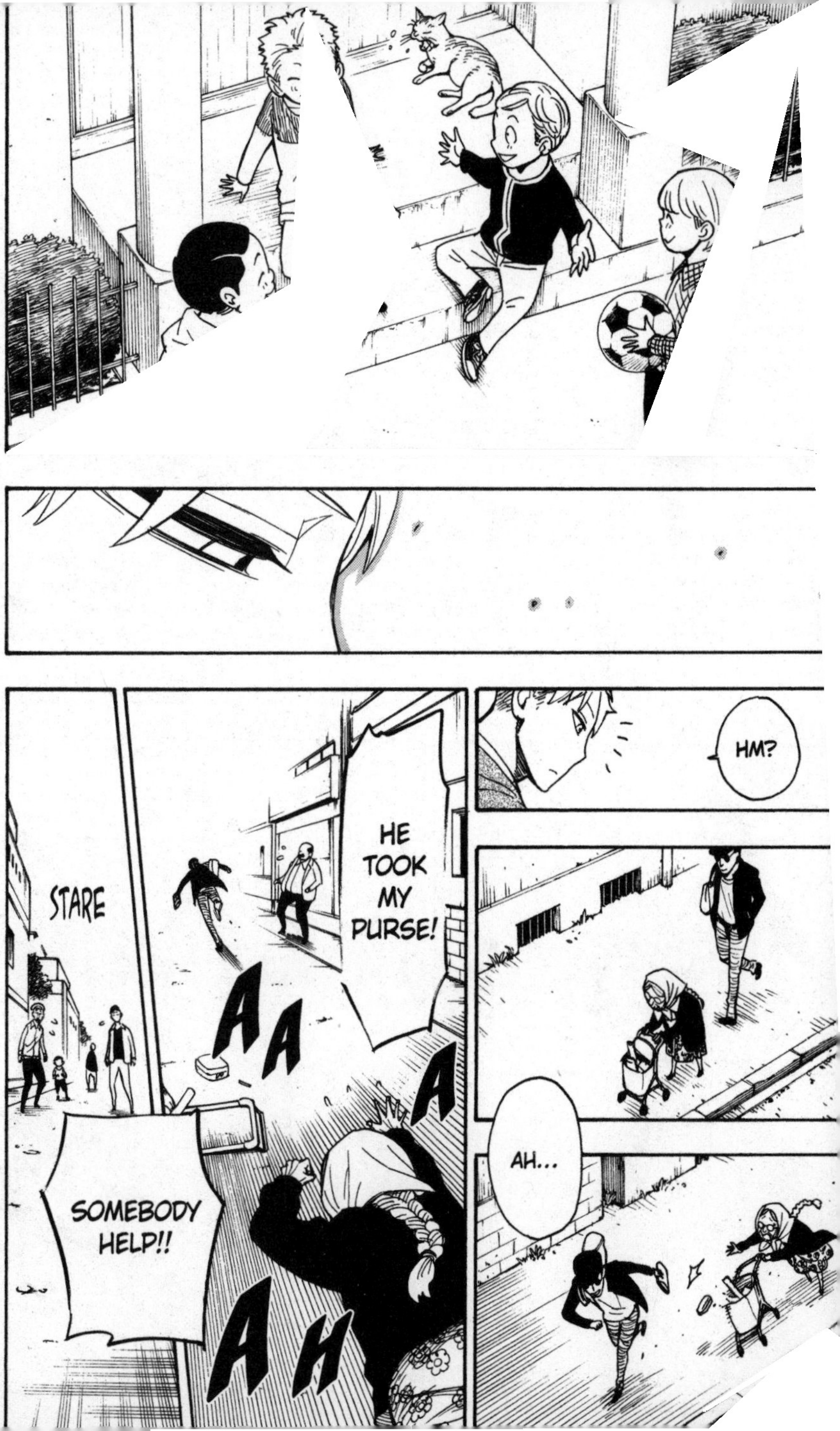
HM?
AH...
HE TOOK MY PURSE!
AAAAH
SOMEBODY HELP!!
STARE

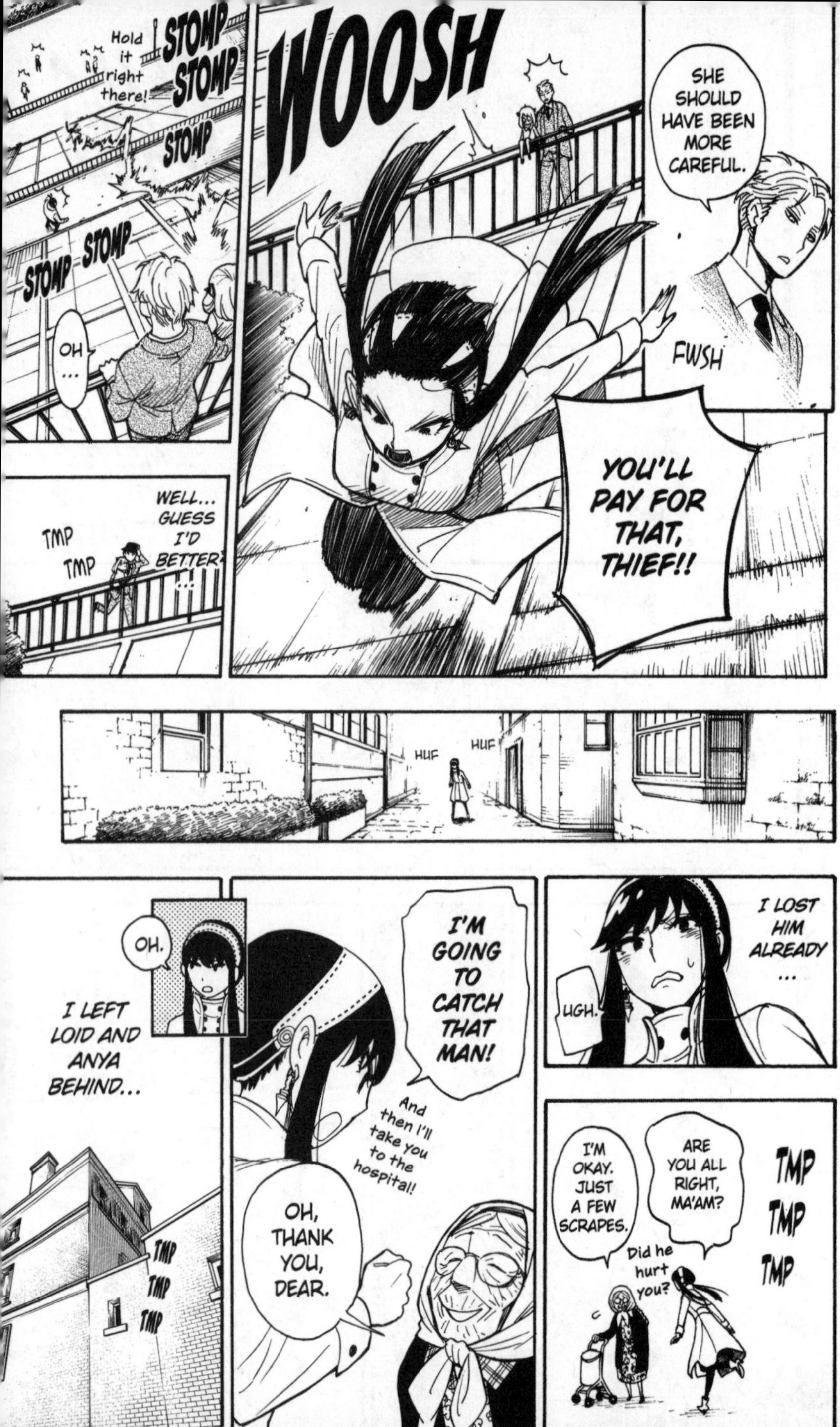

SHE SHOULD HAVE BEEN MORE CAREFUL.
FWSH
WOOSH
YOU'LL PAY FOR THAT, THIEF!!
STOMP
STOMP
STOMP
Hold it right there!
STOMP STOMP
OH...
WELL... GUESS I'D BETTER...
TMP
TMP
HUF
HUF
I LOST HIM ALREADY...
UGH.
TMP
TMP
TMP
ARE YOU ALL RIGHT, MA'AM?
I'M OKAY. JUST A FEW SCRAPES.
Did he hurt you?
I'M GOING TO CATCH THAT MAN!
And then I'll take you to the hospital!
OH, THANK YOU, DEAR.
OH.
I LEFT LOID AND ANYA BEHIND...
TMP
TMP
TMP

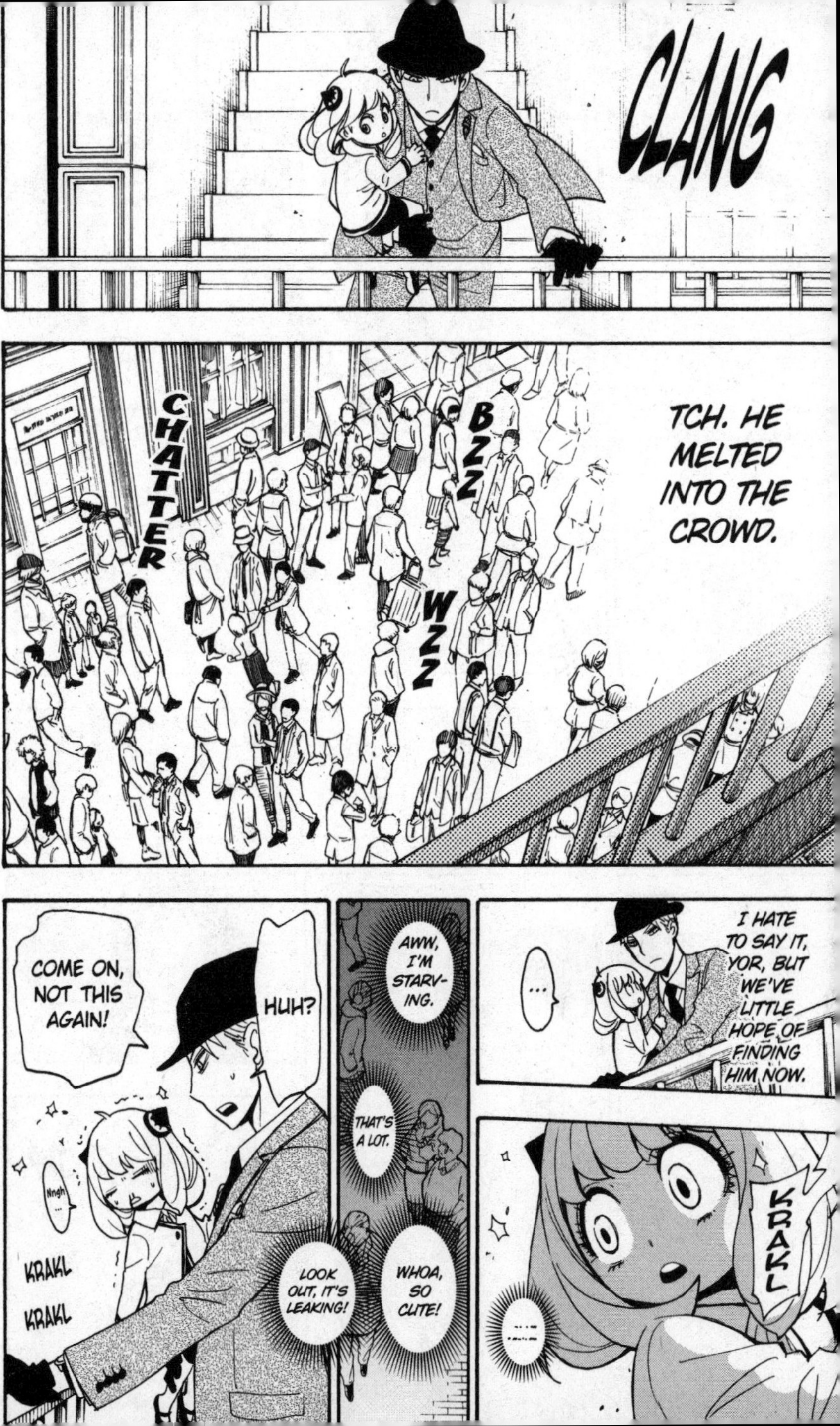
CLANG
TCH. HE MELTED INTO THE CROWD.
BZZ
WZZ
CHATTER
I HATE TO SAY IT, YOR, BUT WE'VE LITTLE HOPE OF FINDING HIM NOW.
...
KRAKL
AWW, I'M STARV-ING.
THAT'S A LOT.
WHOA, SO CUTE!
LOOK OUT, IT'S LEAKING!
HUH?
COME ON, NOT THIS AGAIN!
Nngh...
KRAKL
KRAKL

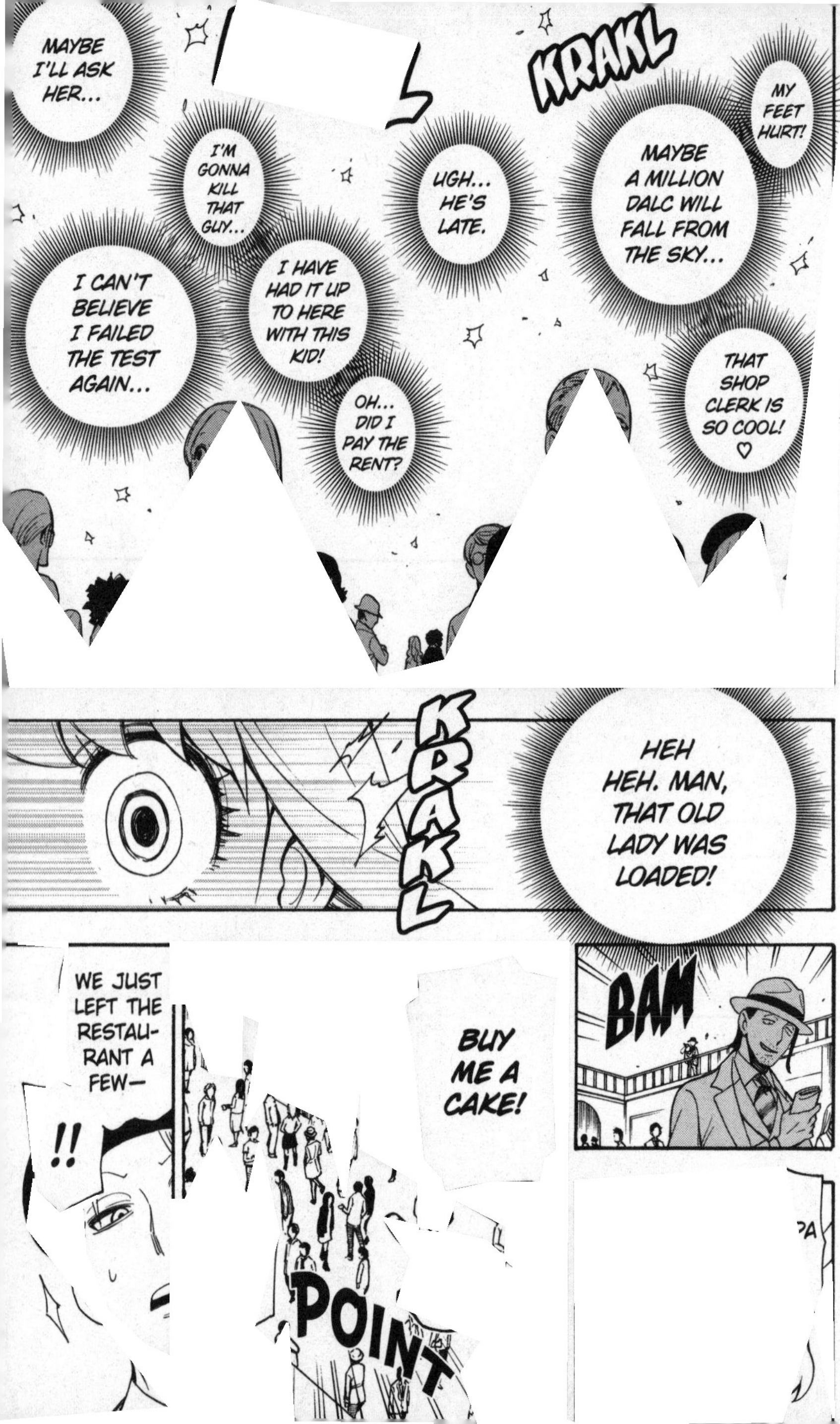
KRAKL
MY FEET HURT!
MAYBE A MILLION DALC WILL FALL FROM THE SKY...
THAT SHOP CLERK IS SO COOL! ♡
UGH... HE'S LATE.
OH... DID I PAY THE RENT?
I HAVE HAD IT UP TO HERE WITH THIS KID!
I'M GONNA KILL THAT GUY...
MAYBE I'LL ASK HER...
I CAN'T BELIEVE I FAILED THE TEST AGAIN...
HEH HEH. MAN, THAT OLD LADY WAS LOADED!
KRAKL
BAM
BUY ME A CAKE!
WE JUST LEFT THE RESTAU-RANT A FEW—
!!
POINT

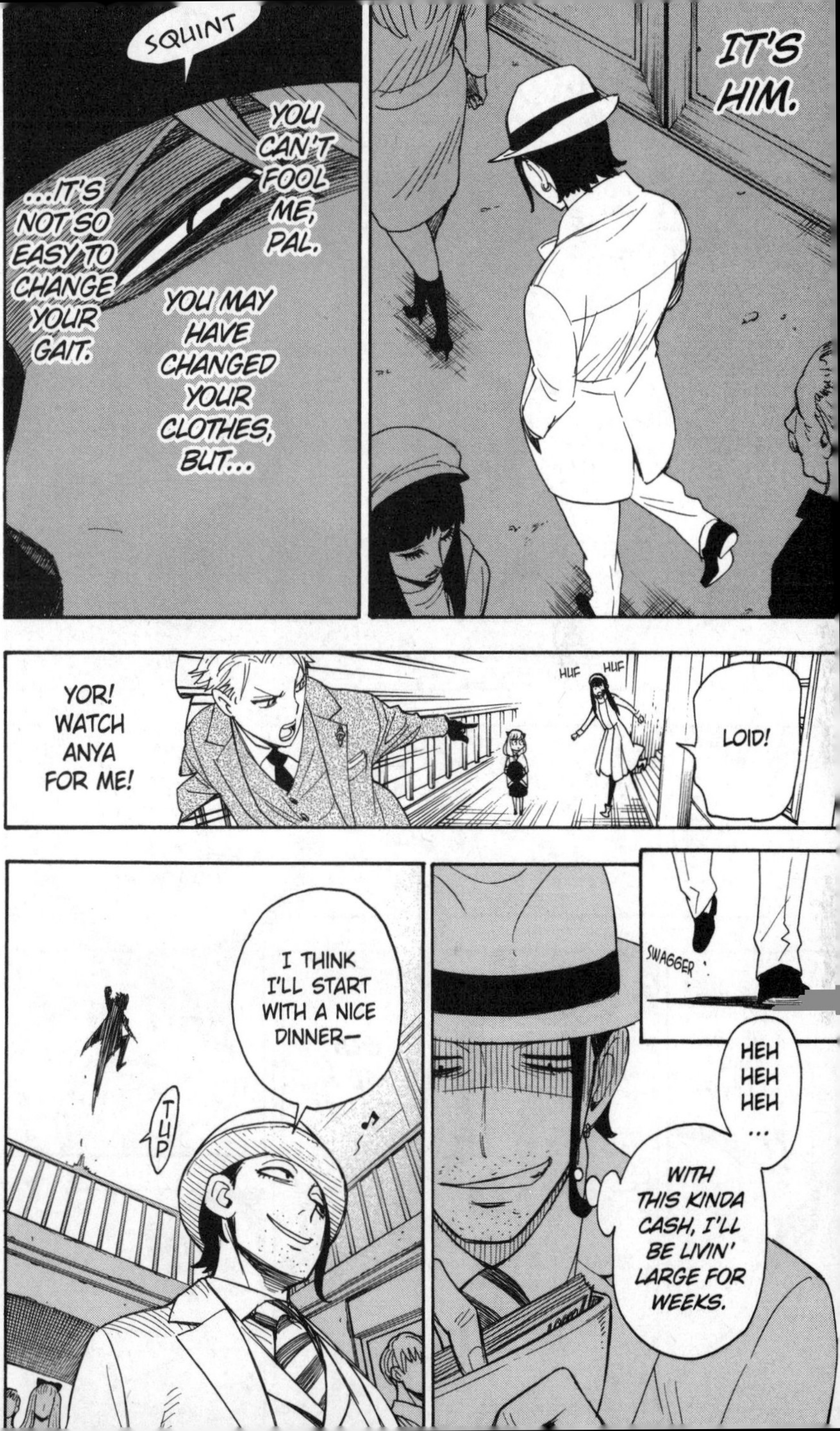
IT'S HIM.
SQUINT
YOU CAN'T FOOL ME, PAL.
...IT'S NOT SO EASY TO CHANGE YOUR GAIT.
YOU MAY HAVE CHANGED YOUR CLOTHES, BUT...
LOID!
HUF HUF
YOR! WATCH ANYA FOR ME!
SWAGGER
HEH HEH HEH...
WITH THIS KINDA CASH, I'LL BE LIVIN' LARGE FOR WEEKS.
I THINK I'LL START WITH A NICE DINNER—
THUP

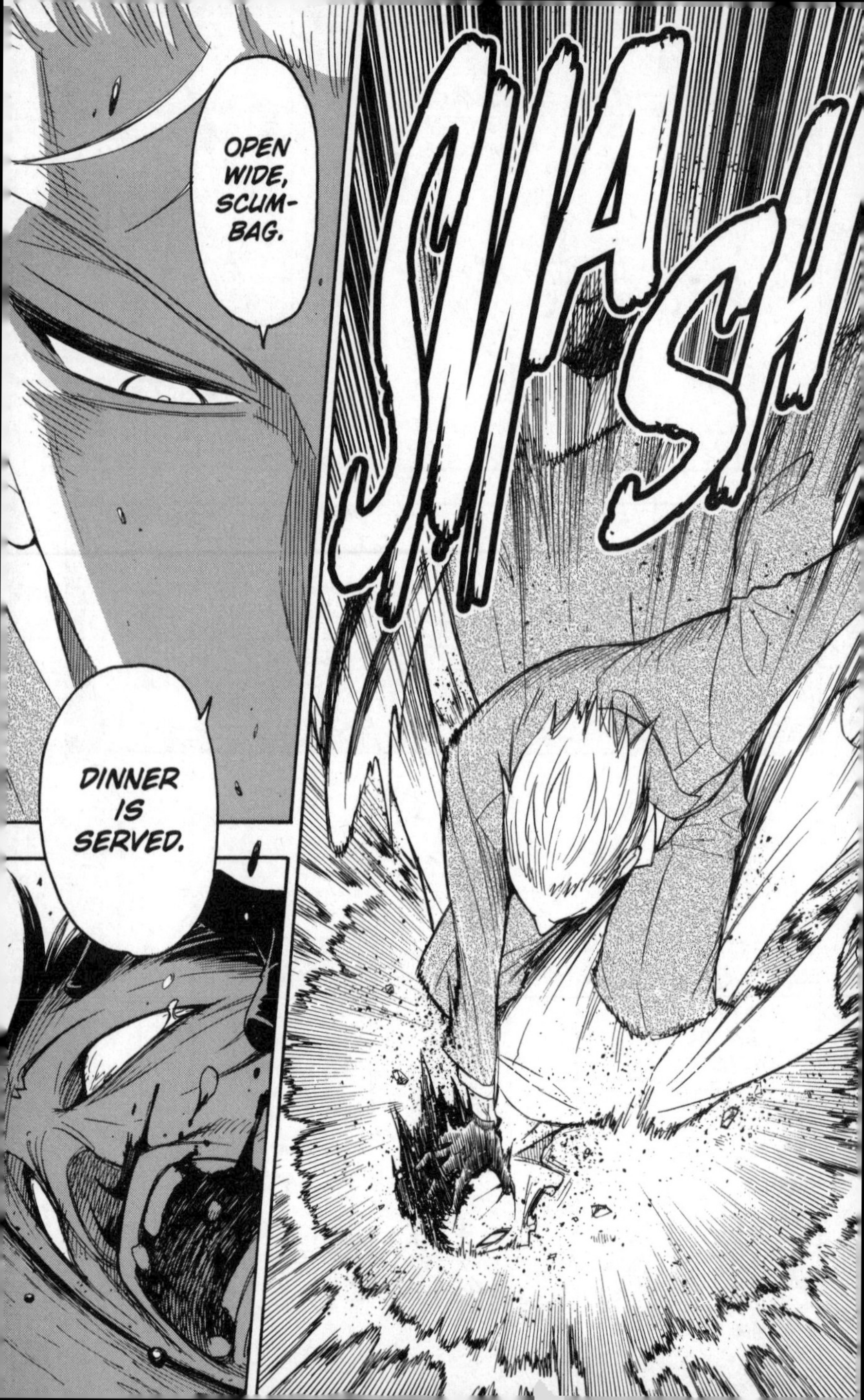
SMASH
OPEN WIDE, SCUMBAG.
DINNER IS SERVED.

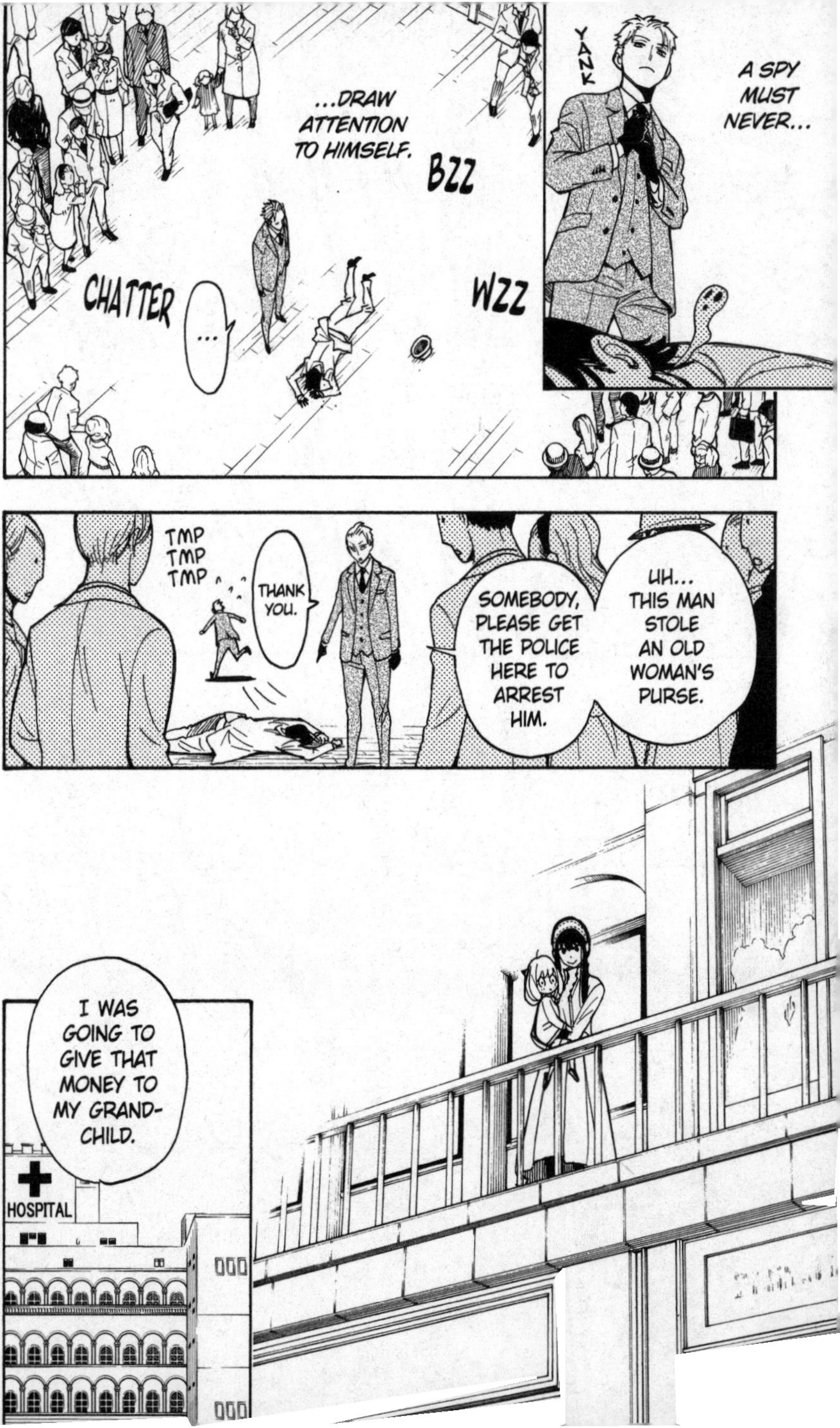
YANK
A SPY MUST NEVER...
...DRAW ATTENTION TO HIMSELF.
BZZ
WZZ
...
CHATTER
UH... THIS MAN STOLE AN OLD WOMAN'S PURSE.
SOMEBODY, PLEASE GET THE POLICE HERE TO ARREST HIM.
THANK YOU.
TMP TMP TMP
I WAS GOING TO GIVE THAT MONEY TO MY GRAND-CHILD.
HOSPITAL

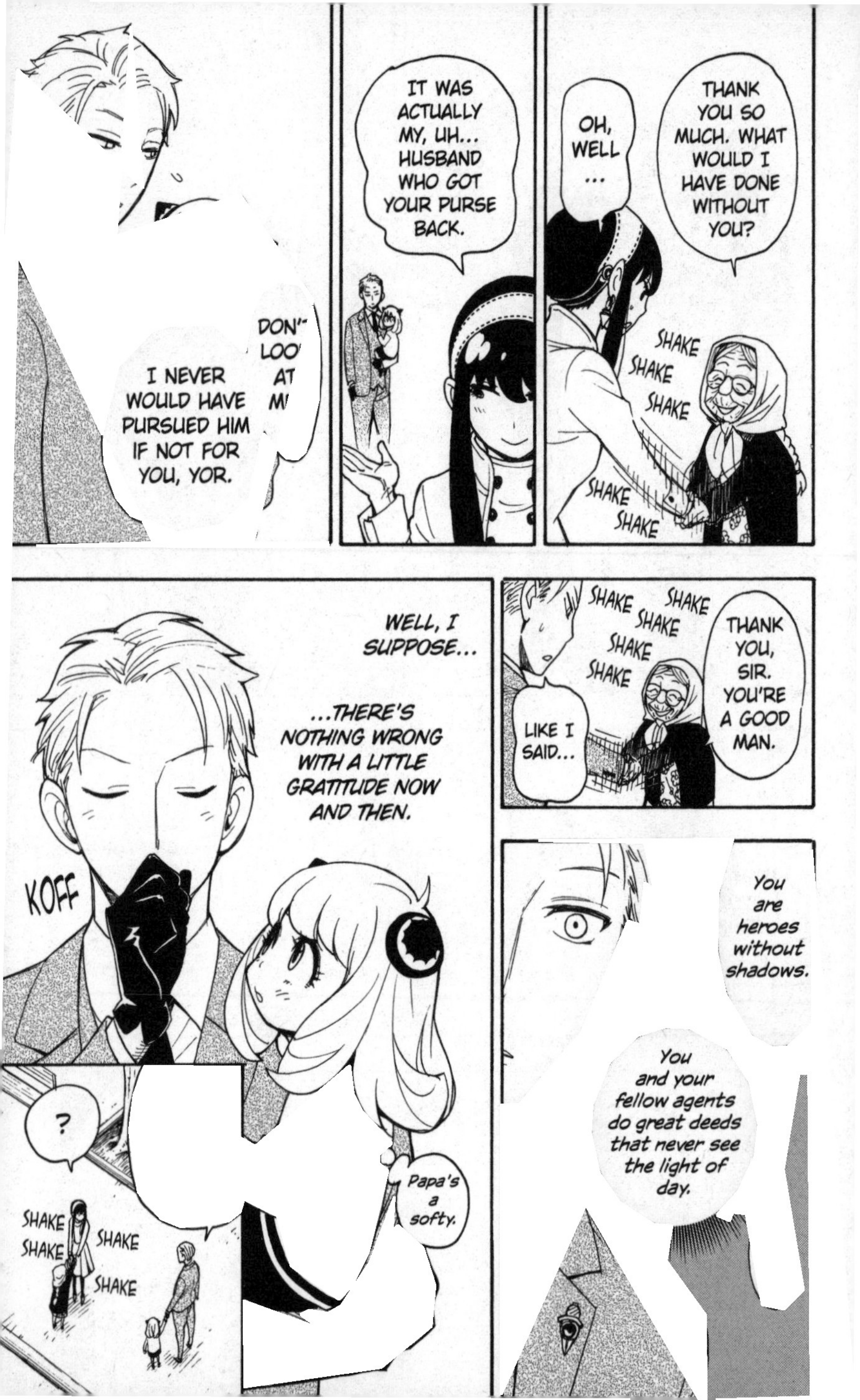
THANK YOU SO MUCH. WHAT WOULD I HAVE DONE WITHOUT YOU?
OH, WELL...
SHAKE SHAKE SHAKE
SHAKE SHAKE
IT WAS ACTUALLY MY, UH... HUSBAND WHO GOT YOUR PURSE BACK.
DON' LOO AT
I NEVER WOULD HAVE PURSUED HIM IF NOT FOR YOU, YOR.
SHAKE SHAKE SHAKE SHAKE SHAKE
THANK YOU, SIR. YOU'RE A GOOD MAN.
LIKE I SAID...
You are heroes without shadows.
You and your fellow agents do great deeds that never see the light of day.
WELL, I SUPPOSE...
...THERE'S NOTHING WRONG WITH A LITTLE GRATITUDE NOW AND THEN.
KOFF
Papa's a softy.
?
SHAKE SHAKE SHAKE SHAKE

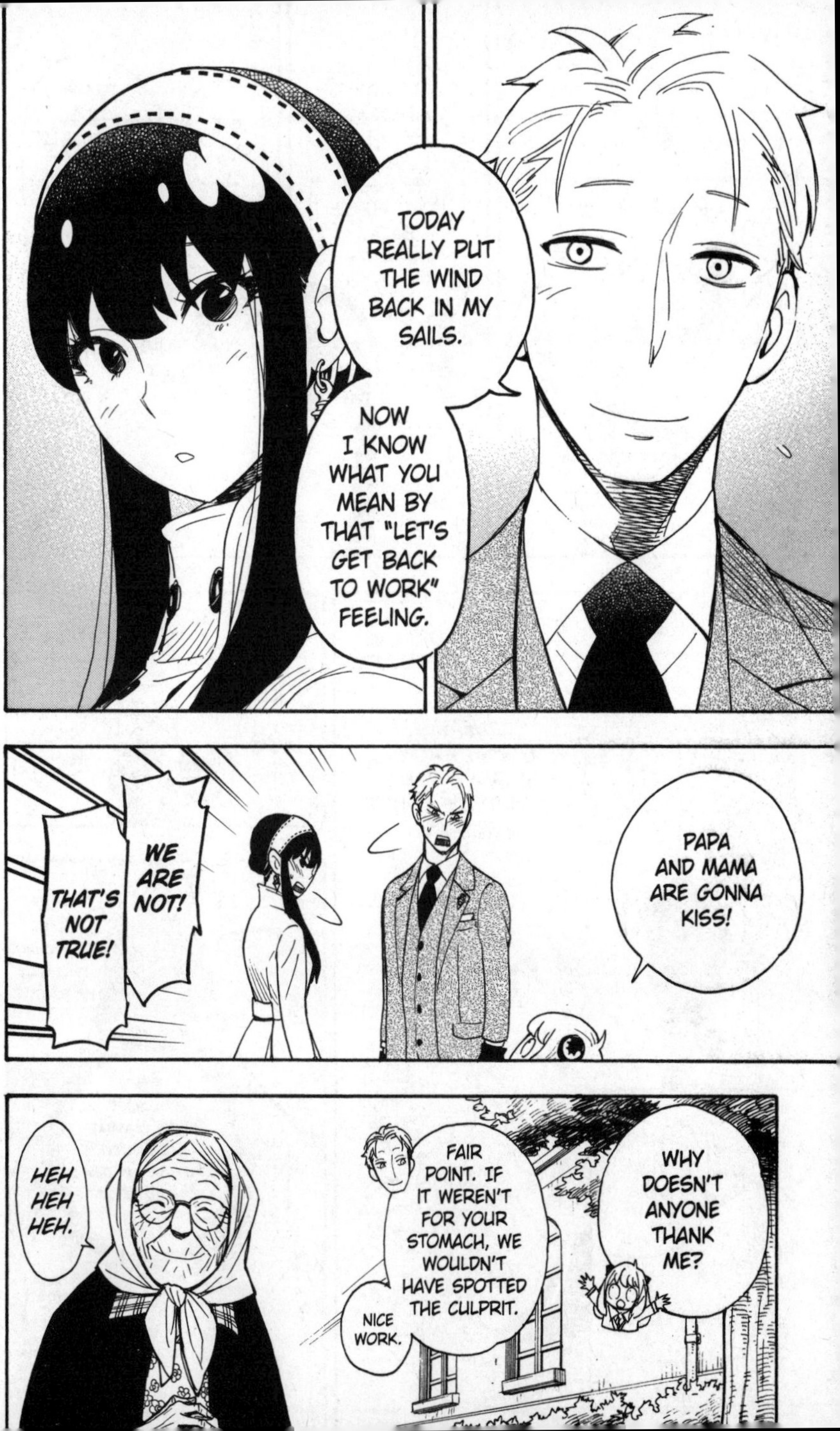
TODAY REALLY PUT THE WIND BACK IN MY SAILS.
NOW I KNOW WHAT YOU MEAN BY THAT "LET'S GET BACK TO WORK" FEELING.
PAPA AND MAMA ARE GONNA KISS!
WE ARE NOT!
THAT'S NOT TRUE!
WHY DOESN'T ANYONE THANK ME?
FAIR POINT. IF IT WEREN'T FOR YOUR STOMACH, WE WOULDN'T HAVE SPOTTED THE CULPRIT.
NICE WORK.
HEH HEH HEH.

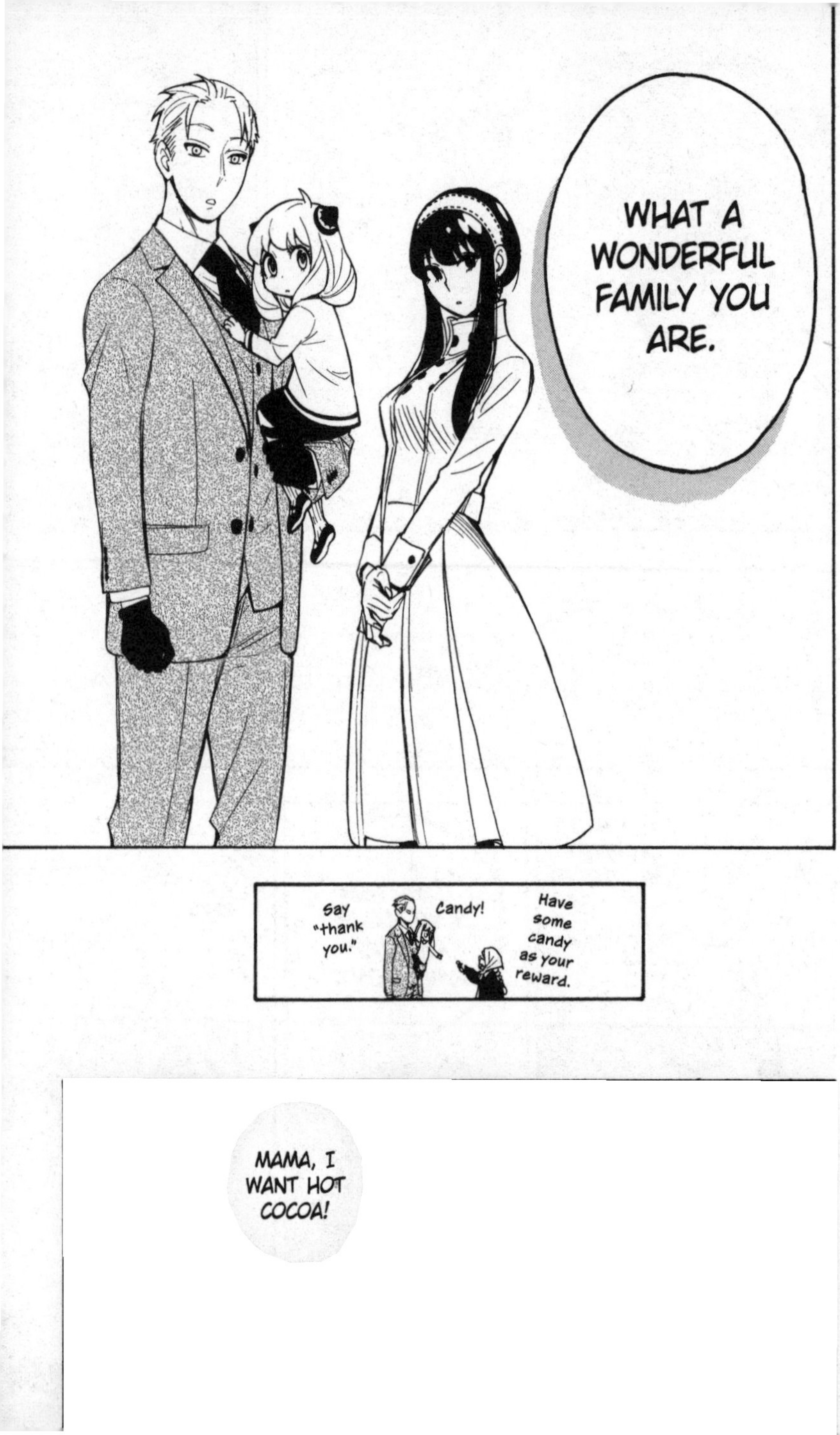
WHAT A WONDERFUL FAMILY YOU ARE.
Have some candy as your reward.
Candy!
Say "thank you."
MAMA, I WANT HOT COCOA!

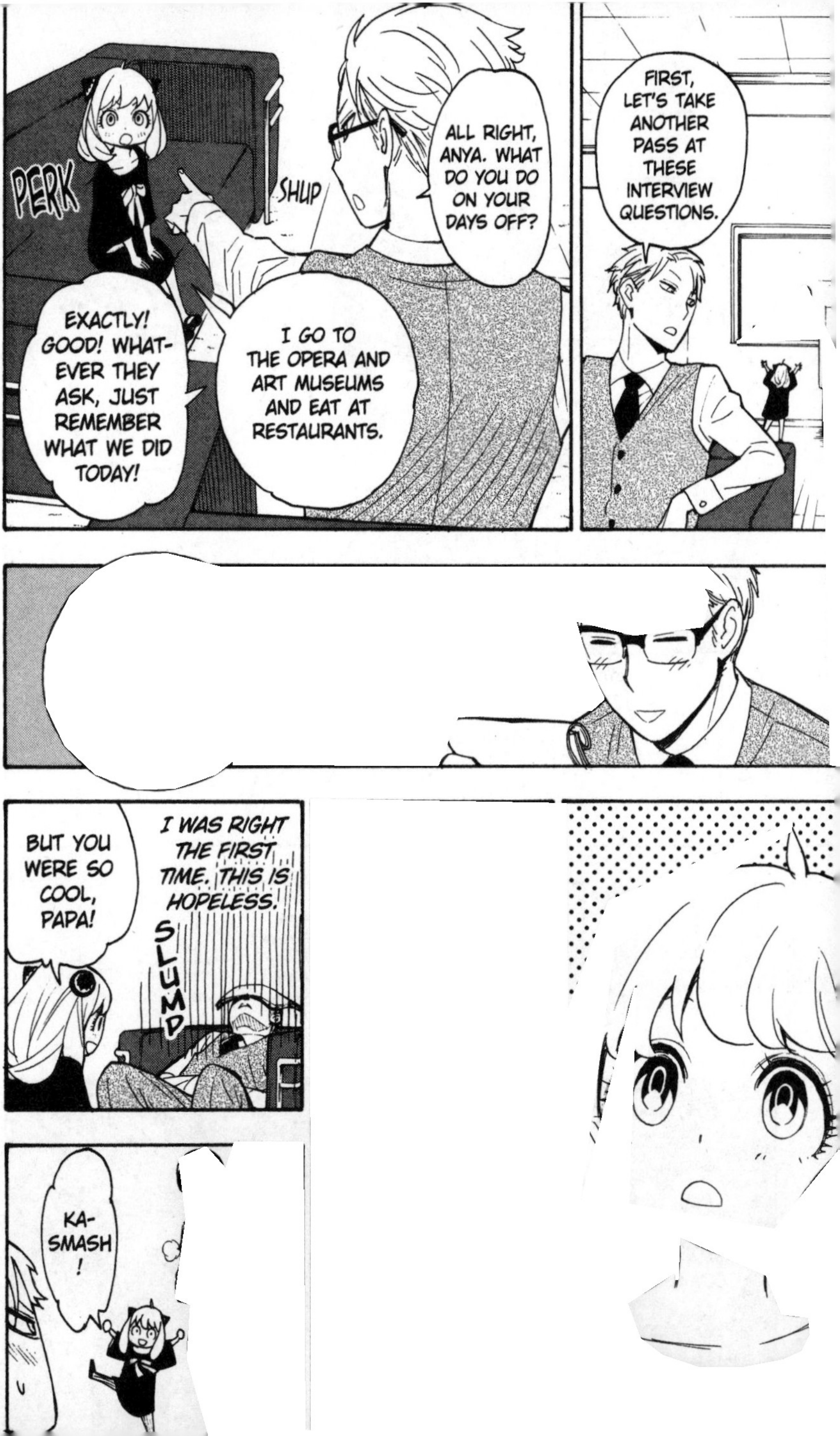
FIRST, LET'S TAKE ANOTHER PASS AT THESE INTERVIEW QUESTIONS.
ALL RIGHT, ANYA. WHAT DO YOU DO ON YOUR DAYS OFF?
SHUP
PERK
I GO TO THE OPERA AND ART MUSEUMS AND EAT AT RESTAURANTS.
EXACTLY! GOOD! WHAT-EVER THEY ASK, JUST REMEMBER WHAT WE DID TODAY!
I WAS RIGHT THE FIRST TIME. THIS IS HOPELESS.
SLUMP
BUT YOU WERE SO COOL, PAPA!
KA-SMASH!

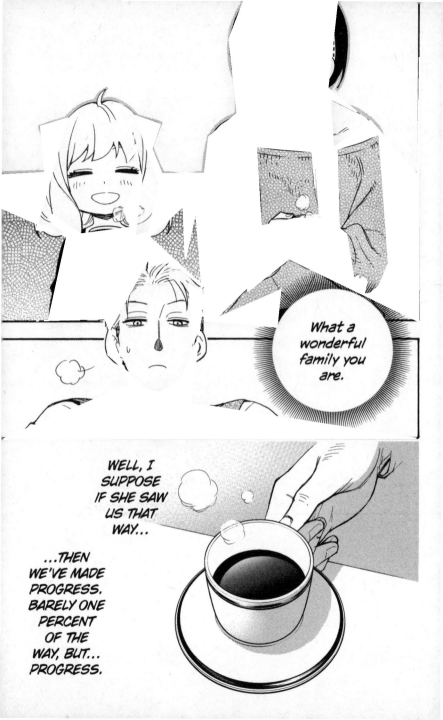

What a wonderful family you are.

WELL, I SUPPOSE IF SHE SAW US THAT WAY...

...THEN WE'VE MADE PROGRESS. BARELY ONE PERCENT OF THE WAY, BUT... PROGRESS.

SPY×FAMILY

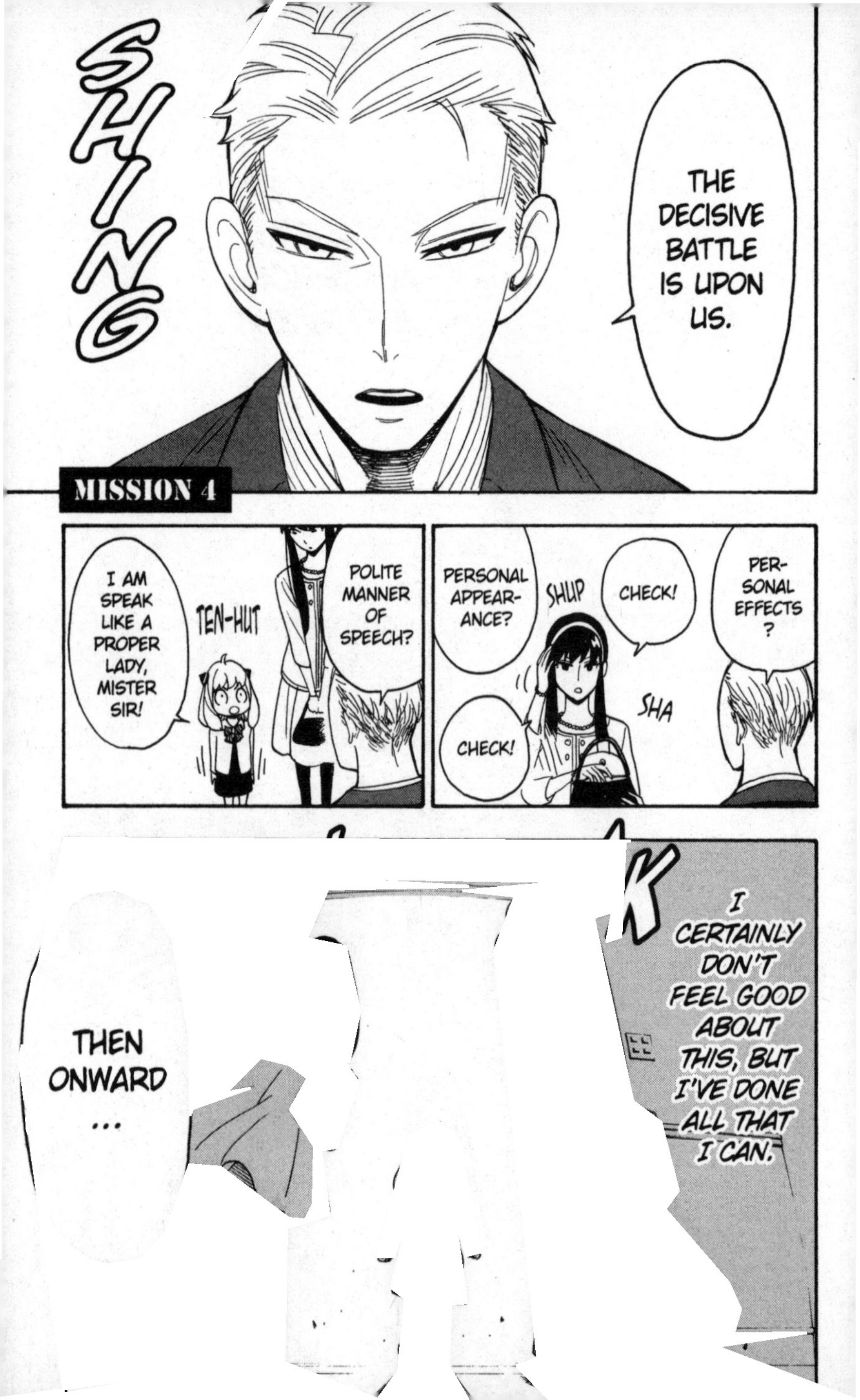
SHING
THE DECISIVE BATTLE IS UPON US.
MISSION 4
PER-SONAL EFFECTS?
CHECK!
SHUP
PERSONAL APPEAR-ANCE?
SHA
CHECK!
POLITE MANNER OF SPEECH?
TEN-HUT
I AM SPEAK LIKE A PROPER LADY, MISTER SIR!
I CERTAINLY DON'T FEEL GOOD ABOUT THIS, BUT I'VE DONE ALL THAT I CAN.
THEN ONWARD ...

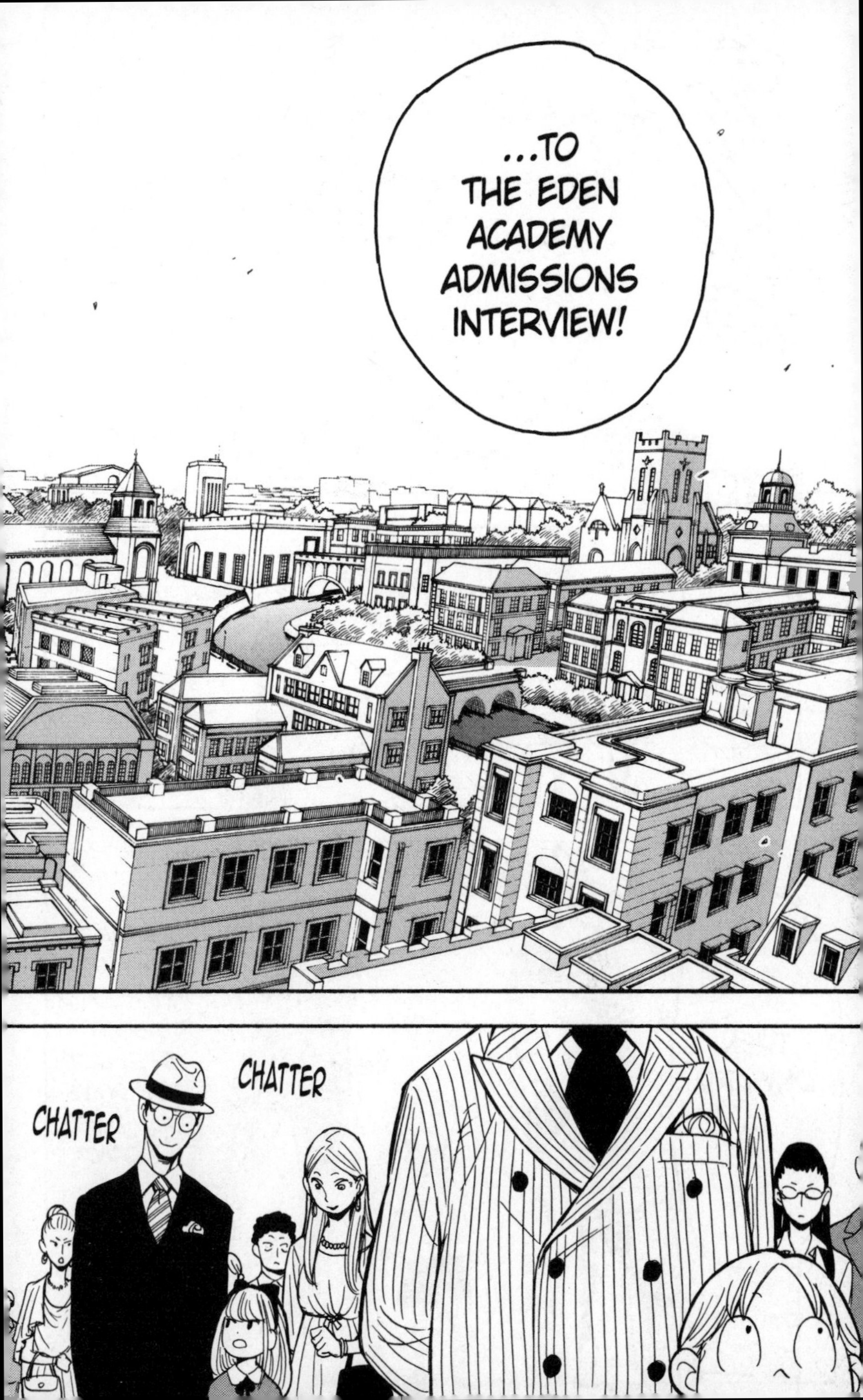
...TO THE EDEN ACADEMY ADMISSIONS INTERVIEW!
CHATTER
CHATTER

MISSION 4

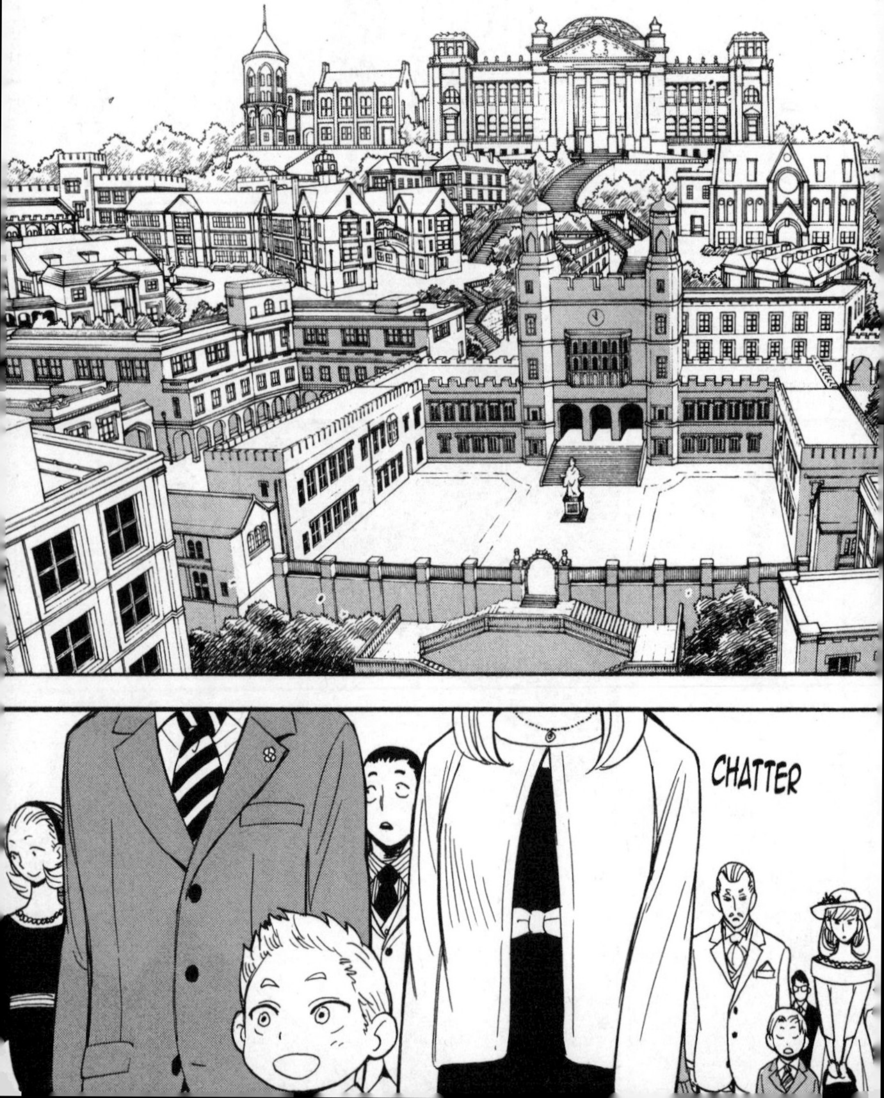
CHATTER

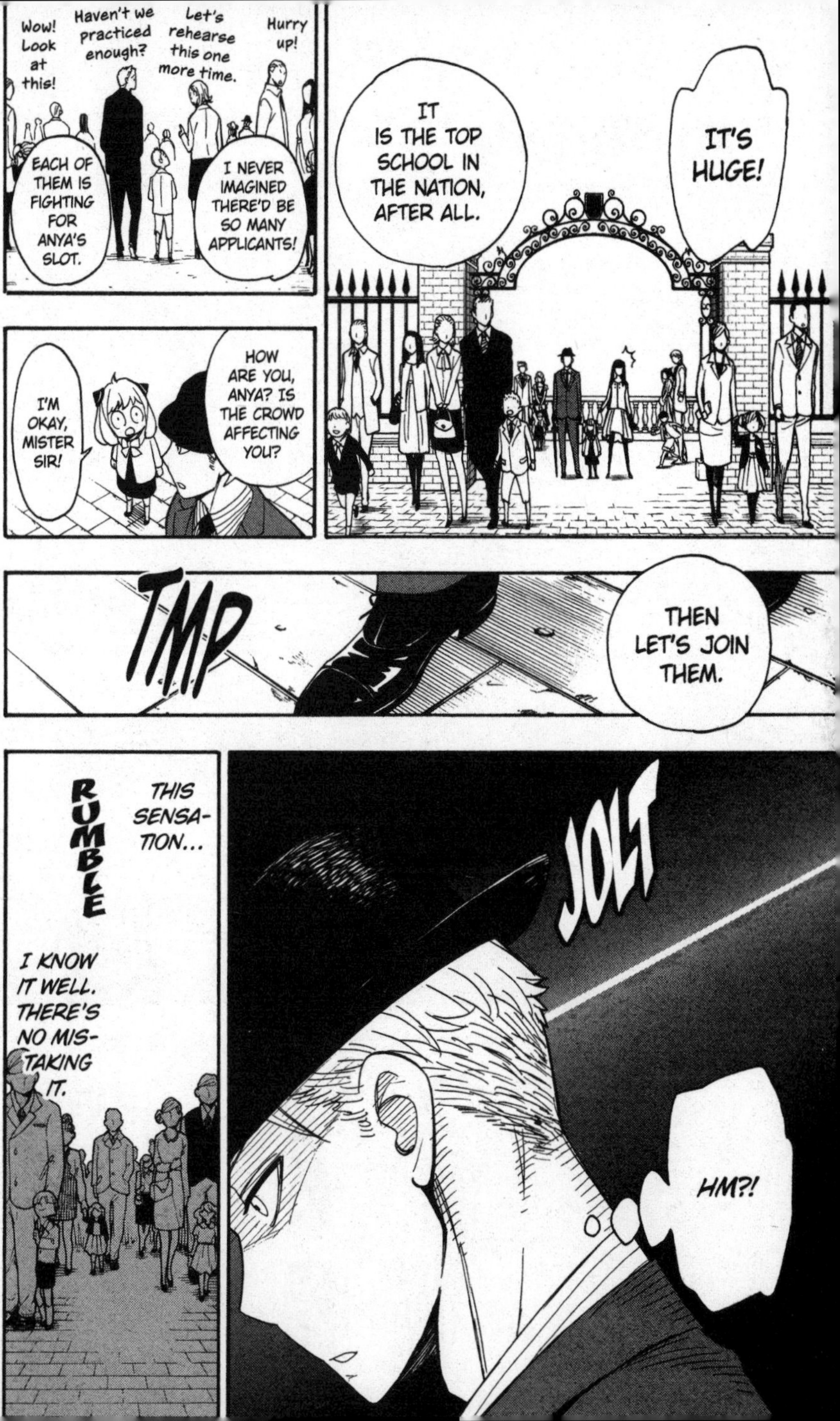

IT'S HUGE!
IT IS THE TOP SCHOOL IN THE NATION, AFTER ALL.
Hurry up!
Let's rehearse this one more time.
Haven't we practiced enough?
Wow! Look at this!
I NEVER IMAGINED THERE'D BE SO MANY APPLICANTS!
EACH OF THEM IS FIGHTING FOR ANYA'S SLOT.
HOW ARE YOU, ANYA? IS THE CROWD AFFECTING YOU?
I'M OKAY, MISTER SIR!
THEN LET'S JOIN THEM.
TMP
JOLT
HM?!
THIS SENSATION...
RUMBLE
I KNOW IT WELL. THERE'S NO MISTAKING IT.

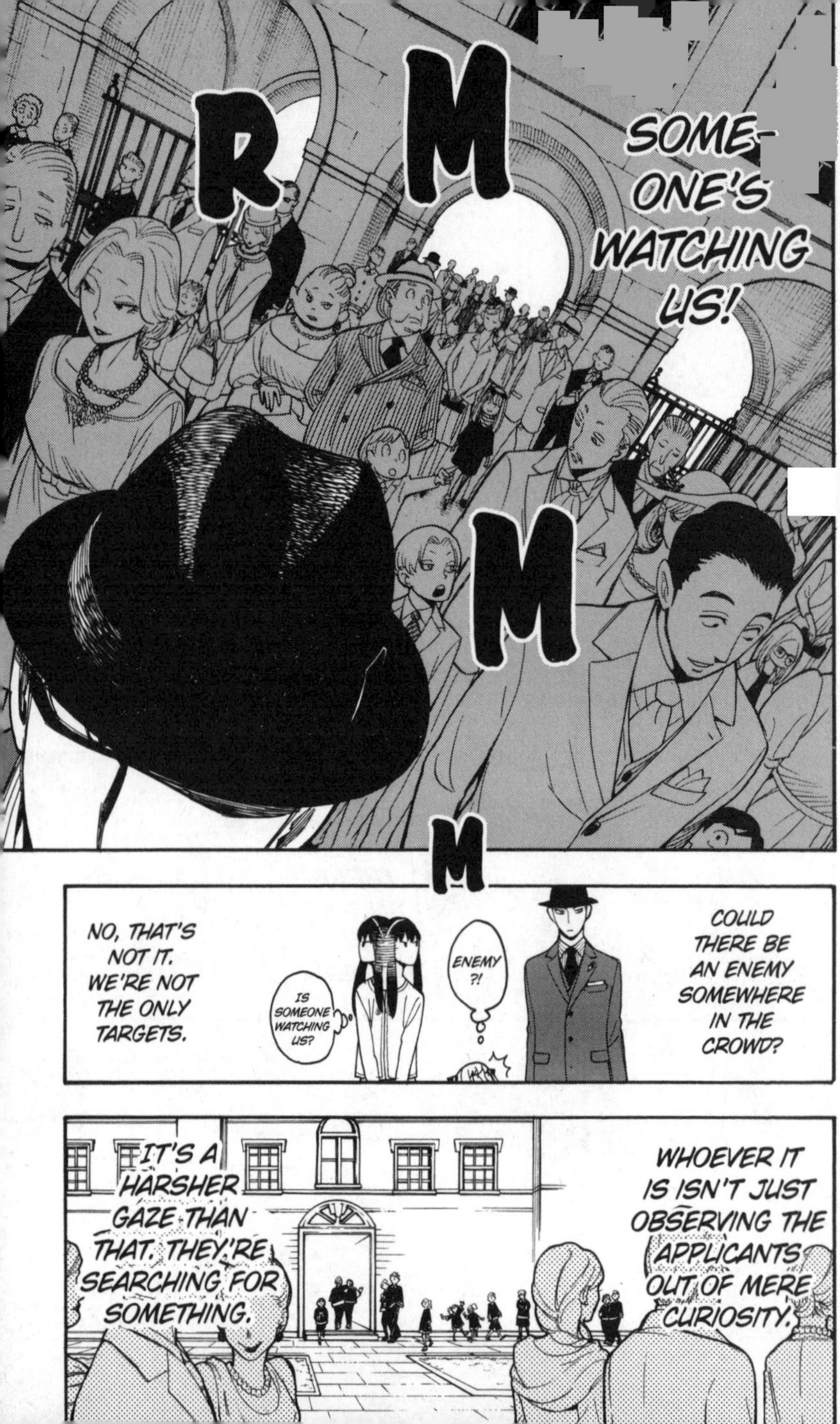
RMMM
SOME-ONE'S WATCHING US!
COULD THERE BE AN ENEMY SOMEWHERE IN THE CROWD?
ENEMY ?!
IS SOMEONE WATCHING US?
NO, THAT'S NOT IT. WE'RE NOT THE ONLY TARGETS.
WHOEVER IT IS ISN'T JUST OBSERVING THE APPLICANTS OUT OF MERE CURIOSITY.
IT'S A HARSHER GAZE THAN THAT. THEY'RE SEARCHING FOR SOMETHING.

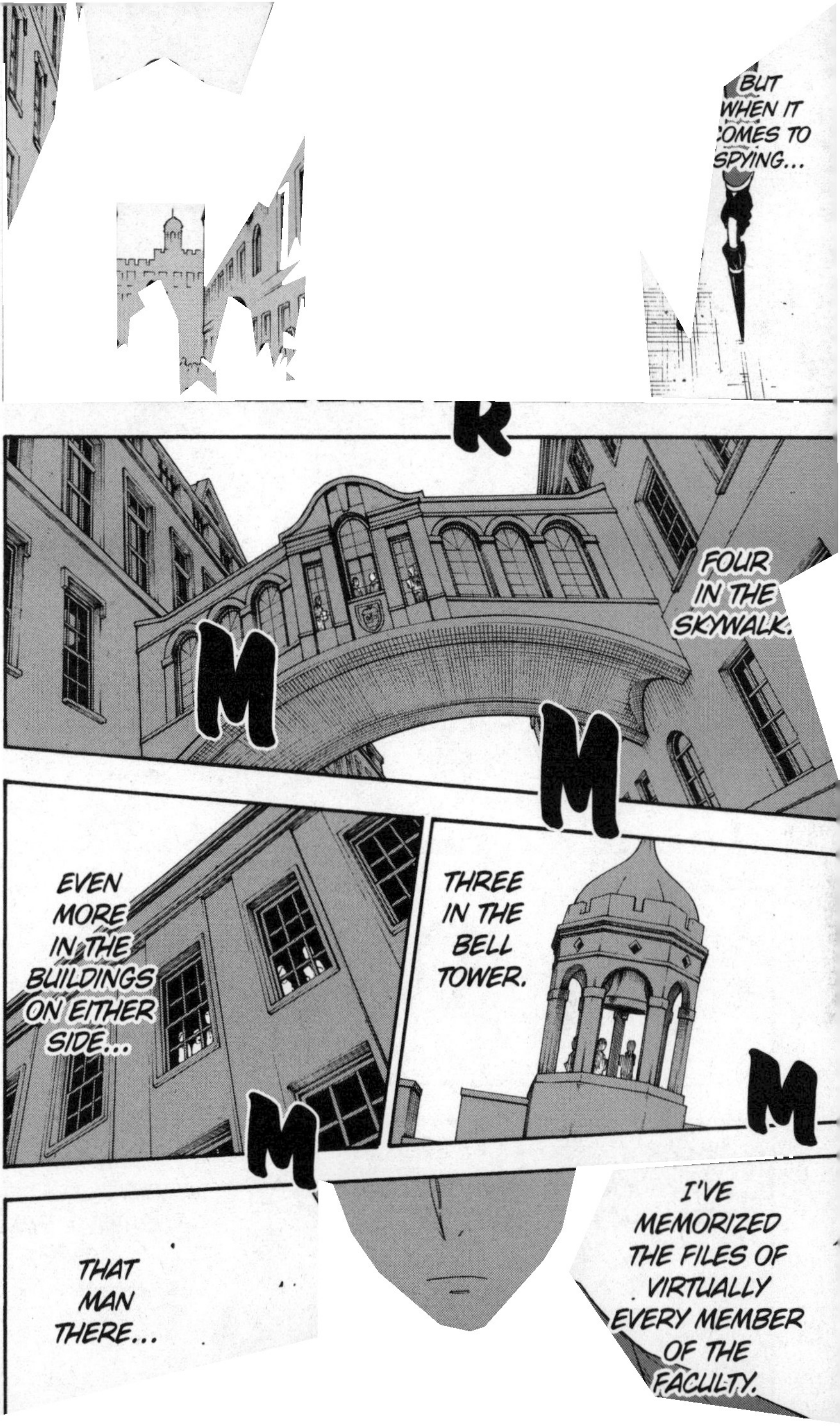
BUT WHEN IT COMES TO SPYING...
R
FOUR IN THE SKYWALK.
M
M
THREE IN THE BELL TOWER.
M
EVEN MORE IN THE BUILDINGS ON EITHER SIDE...
M
I'VE MEMORIZED THE FILES OF VIRTUALLY EVERY MEMBER OF THE FACULTY.
THAT MAN THERE...

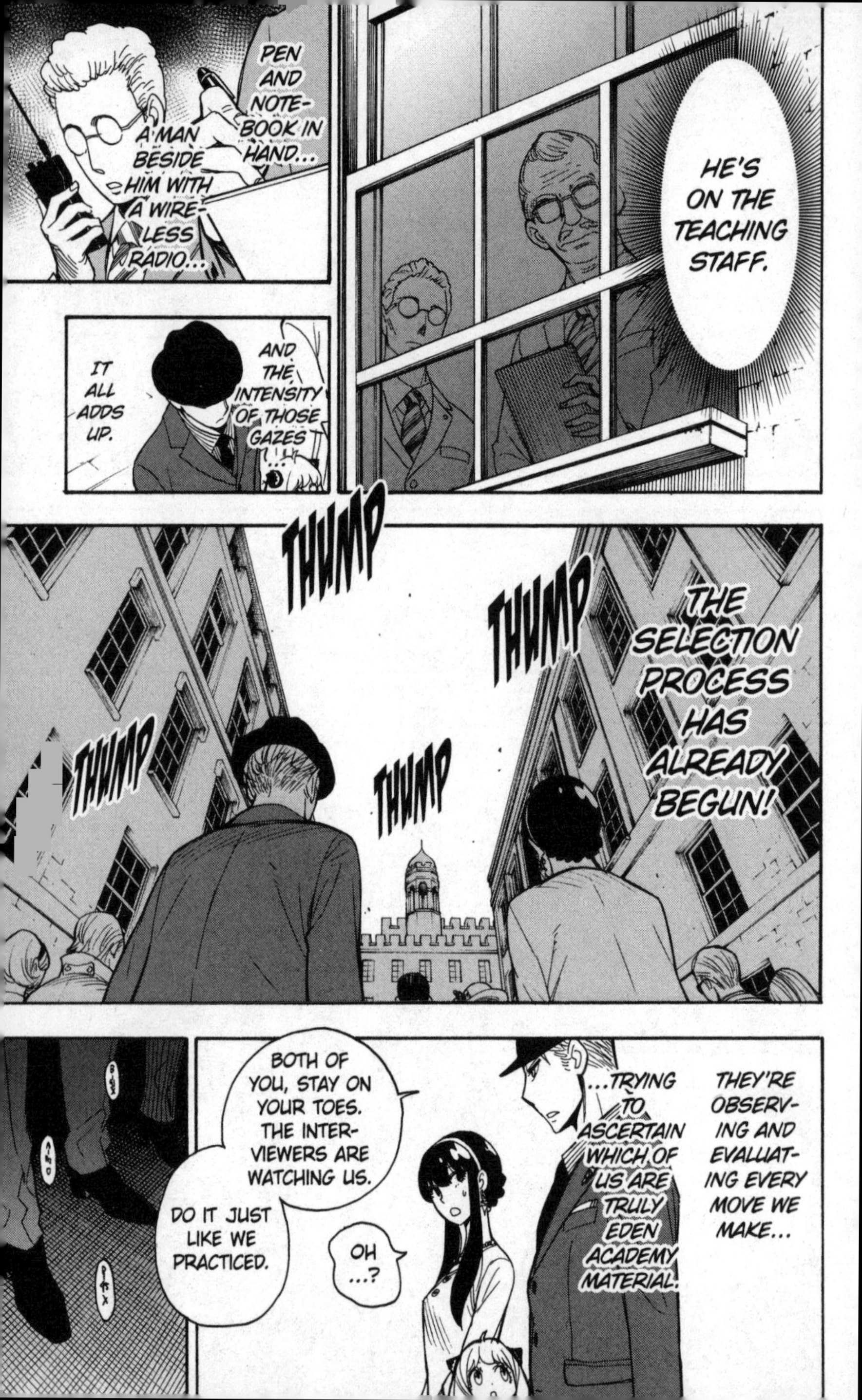
HE'S ON THE TEACHING STAFF.
PEN AND NOTE-BOOK IN HAND...
A MAN BESIDE HIM WITH A WIRE-LESS RADIO...
AND THE INTENSITY OF THOSE GAZES...
IT ALL ADDS UP.
THE SELECTION PROCESS HAS ALREADY BEGUN!
THUMP
THUMP
THUMP
THUMP
THEY'RE OBSERV-ING AND EVALUAT-ING EVERY MOVE WE MAKE...
...TRYING TO ASCERTAIN WHICH OF US ARE TRULY EDEN ACADEMY MATERIAL.
BOTH OF YOU, STAY ON YOUR TOES. THE INTER-VIEWERS ARE WATCHING US.
OH ...?
DO IT JUST LIKE WE PRACTICED.

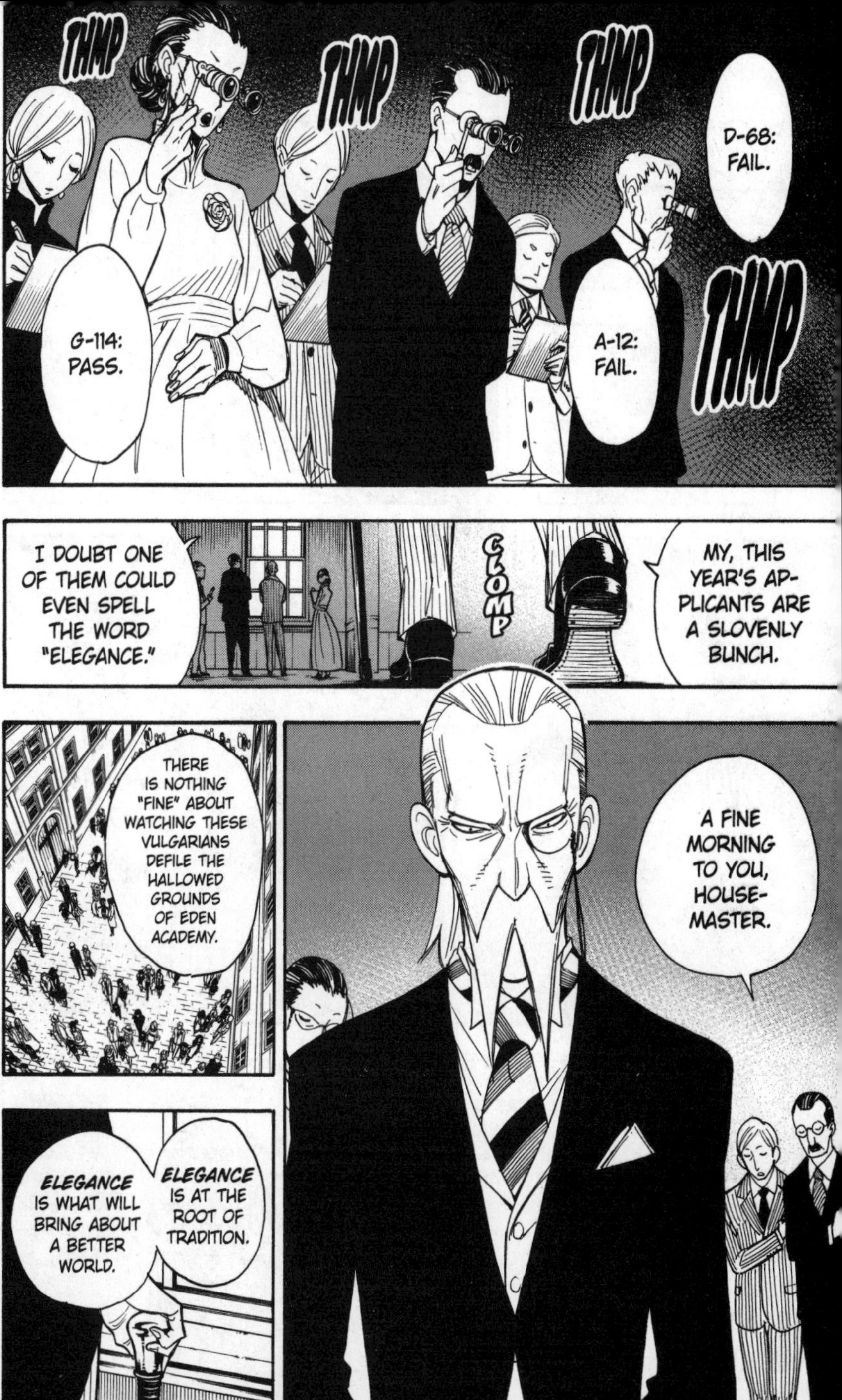
THMP
D-68: FAIL.
THMP
THMP
A-12: FAIL.
THMP
G-114: PASS.
THMP
MY, THIS YEAR'S AP- PLICANTS ARE A SLOVENLY BUNCH.
CLOMP
I DOUBT ONE OF THEM COULD EVEN SPELL THE WORD "ELEGANCE."
A FINE MORNING TO YOU, HOUSE- MASTER.
THERE IS NOTHING "FINE" ABOUT WATCHING THESE VULGARIANS DEFILE THE HALLOWED GROUNDS OF EDEN ACADEMY.
ELEGANCE IS AT THE ROOT OF TRADITION.
ELEGANCE IS WHAT WILL BRING ABOUT A BETTER WORLD.

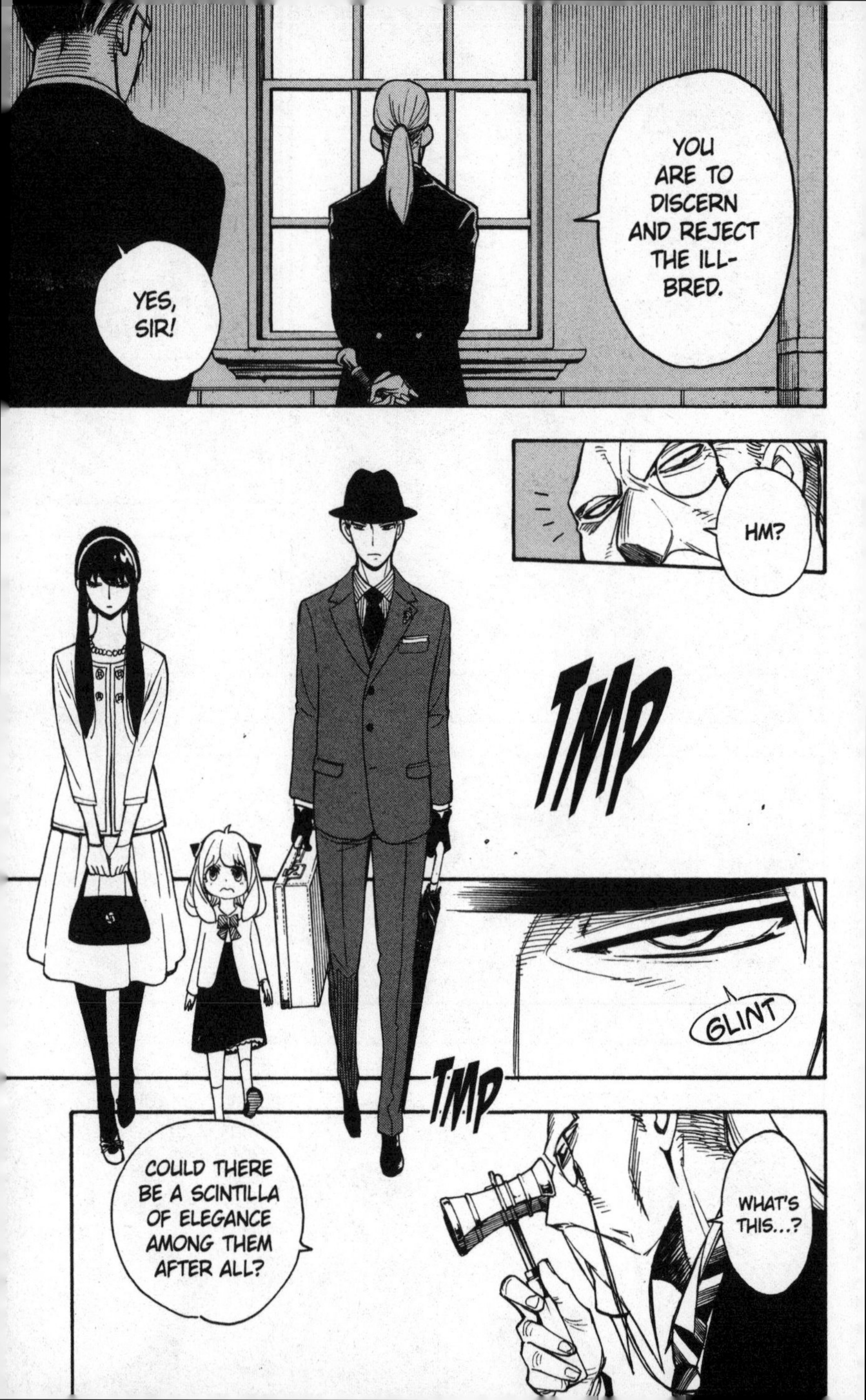
YOU ARE TO DISCERN AND REJECT THE ILL-BRED.
YES, SIR!
HM?
TMP
GLINT
TMP
WHAT'S THIS...?
COULD THERE BE A SCINTILLA OF ELEGANCE AMONG THEM AFTER ALL?

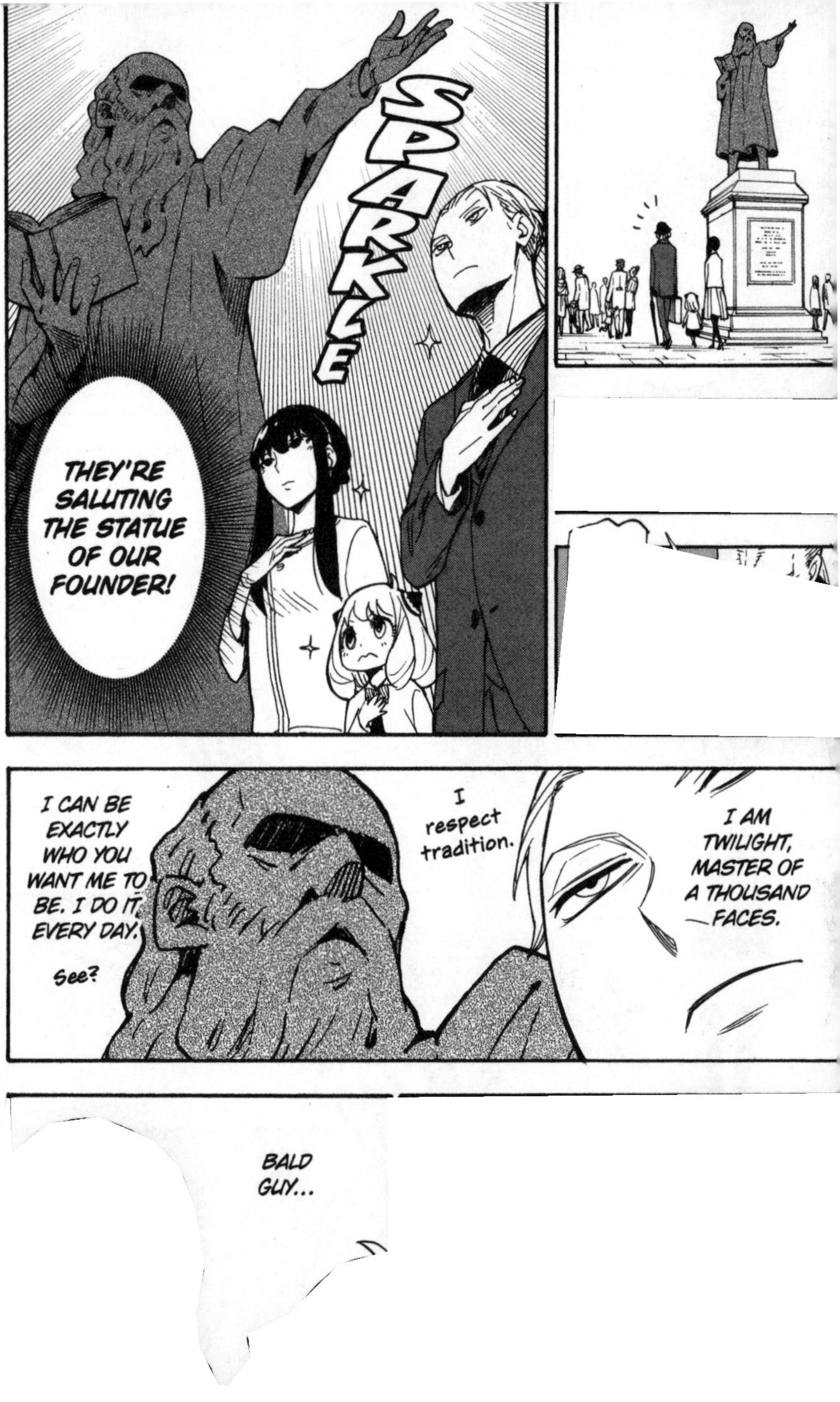
SPARKLE
THEY'RE SALUTING THE STATUE OF OUR FOUNDER!
I AM TWILIGHT, MASTER OF A THOUSAND FACES.
I respect tradition.
I CAN BE EXACTLY WHO YOU WANT ME TO BE. I DO IT EVERY DAY.
See?
BALD GUY...

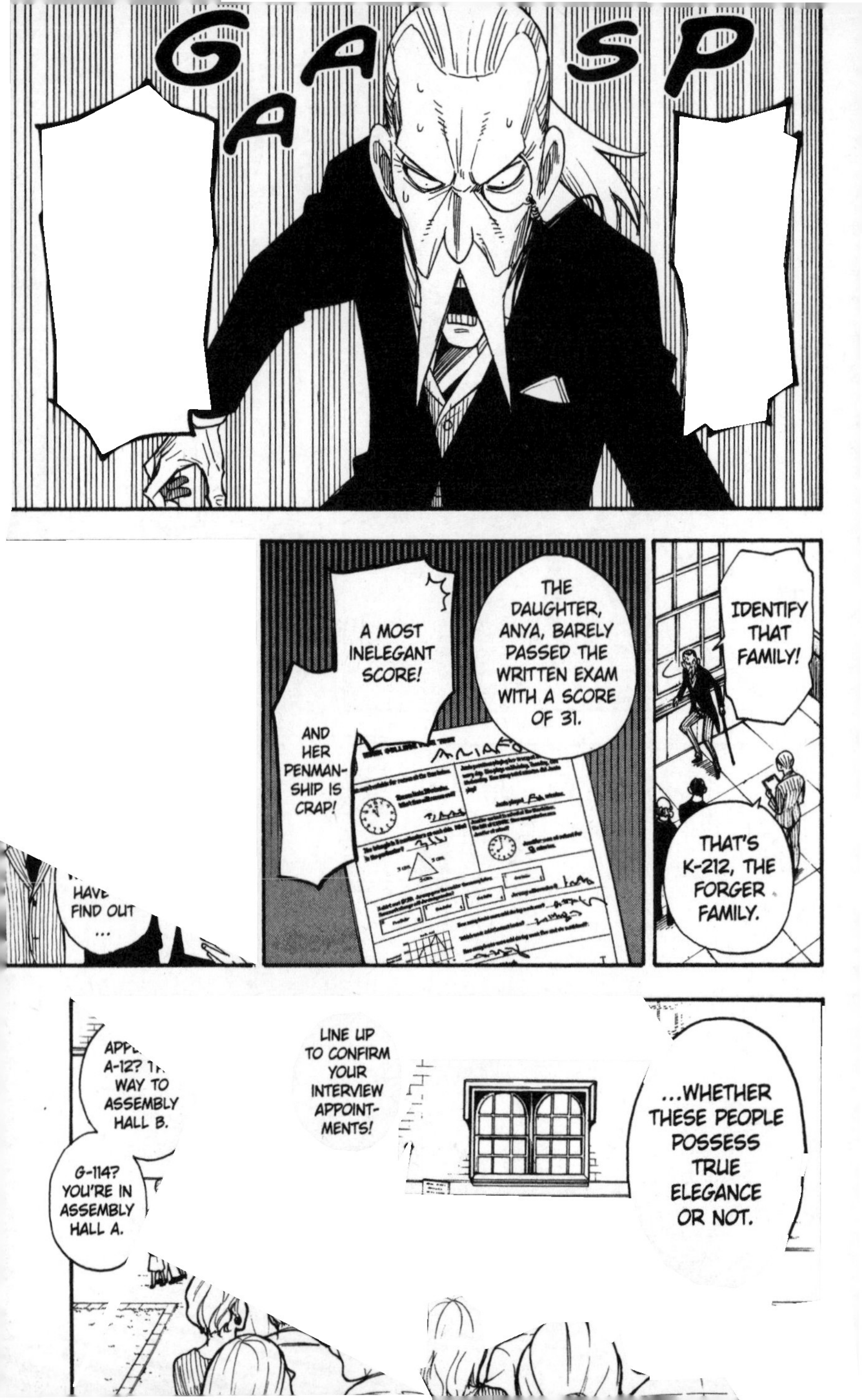
GASP
IDENTIFY THAT FAMILY!
THAT'S K-212, THE FORGER FAMILY.
THE DAUGHTER, ANYA, BARELY PASSED THE WRITTEN EXAM WITH A SCORE OF 31.
A MOST INELEGANT SCORE!
AND HER PENMANSHIP IS CRAP!
HAVE FIND OUT ...
...WHETHER THESE PEOPLE POSSESS TRUE ELEGANCE OR NOT.
LINE UP TO CONFIRM YOUR INTERVIEW APPOINTMENTS!
A-12? WAY TO ASSEMBLY HALL B.
G-114? YOU'RE IN ASSEMBLY HALL A.

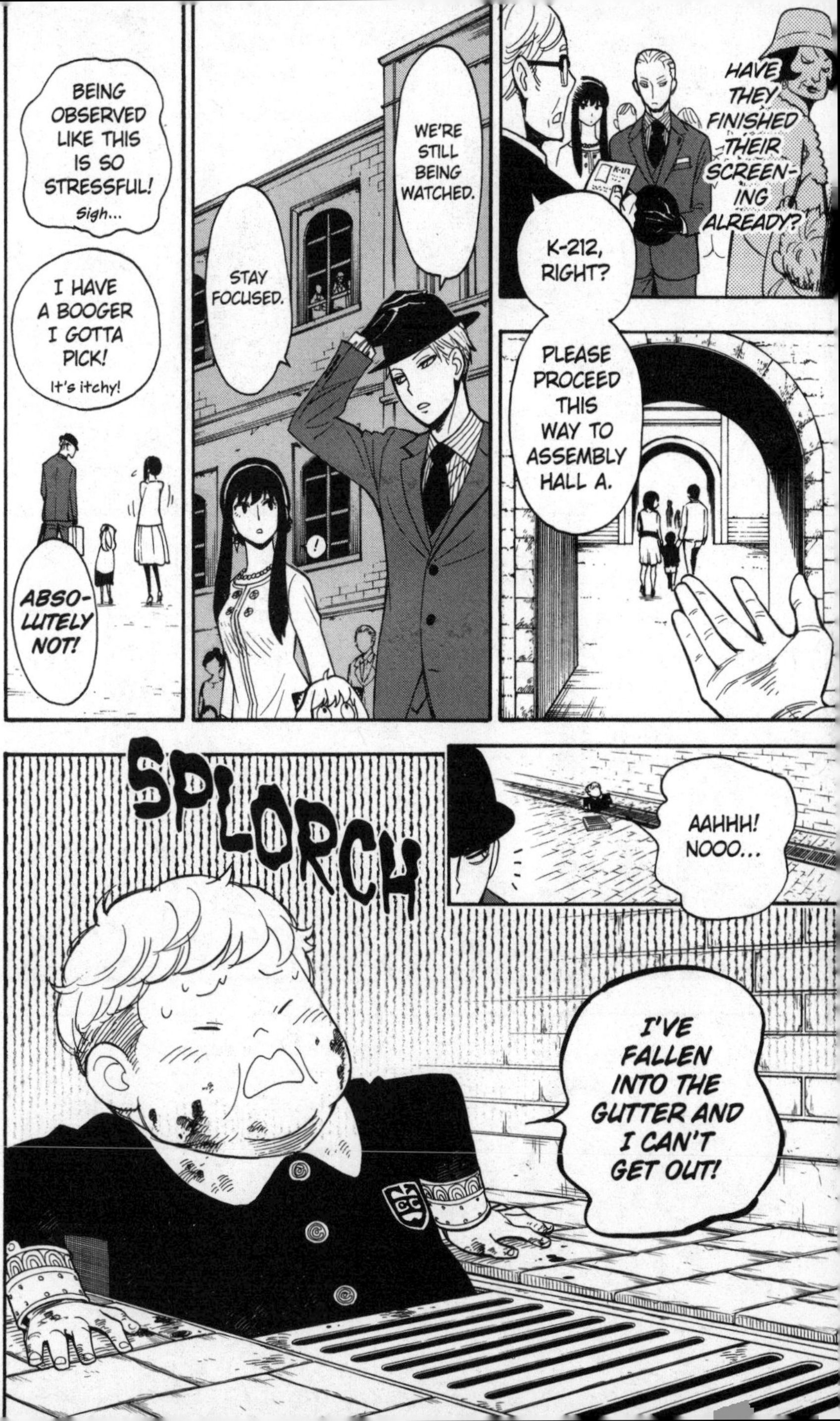
HAVE THEY FINISHED THEIR SCREEN-ING ALREADY?
K-212, RIGHT?
PLEASE PROCEED THIS WAY TO ASSEMBLY HALL A.
WE'RE STILL BEING WATCHED.
STAY FOCUSED.
BEING OBSERVED LIKE THIS IS SO STRESSFUL!
Sigh...
I HAVE A BOOGER I GOTTA PICK!
It's itchy!
ABSO-LUTELY NOT!
AAHHH! NOOO...
SPLORCH
I'VE FALLEN INTO THE GUTTER AND I CAN'T GET OUT!

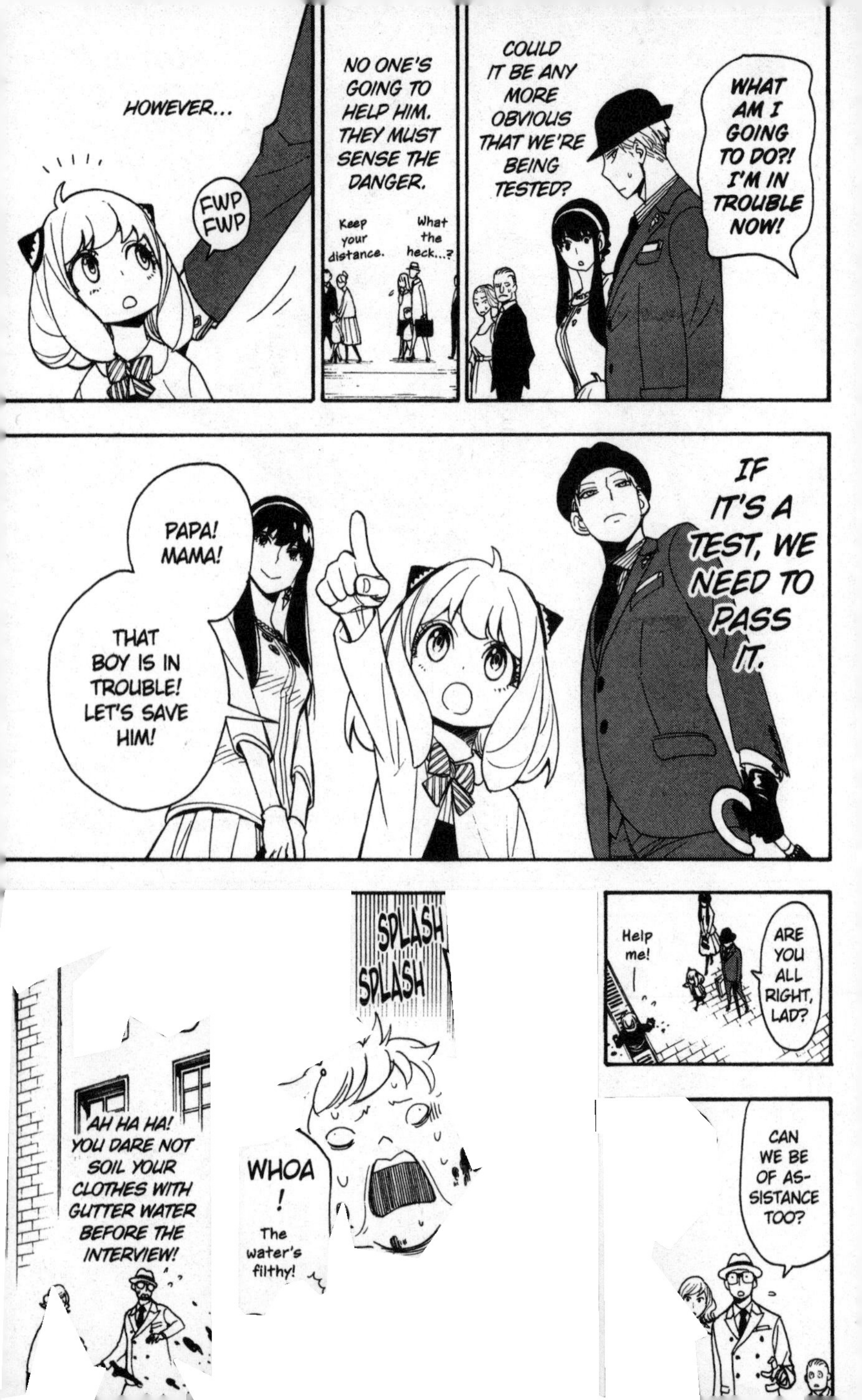
WHAT AM I GOING TO DO?! I'M IN TROUBLE NOW!
COULD IT BE ANY MORE OBVIOUS THAT WE'RE BEING TESTED?
NO ONE'S GOING TO HELP HIM. THEY MUST SENSE THE DANGER.
What the heck...?
Keep your distance.
HOWEVER...
FWP FWP
IF IT'S A TEST, WE NEED TO PASS IT.
PAPA! MAMA!
THAT BOY IS IN TROUBLE! LET'S SAVE HIM!
ARE YOU ALL RIGHT, LAD?
Help me!
CAN WE BE OF AS-SISTANCE TOO?
SPLASH
SPLASH
WHOA!
The water's filthy!
AH HA HA! YOU DARE NOT SOIL YOUR CLOTHES WITH GUTTER WATER BEFORE THE INTERVIEW!

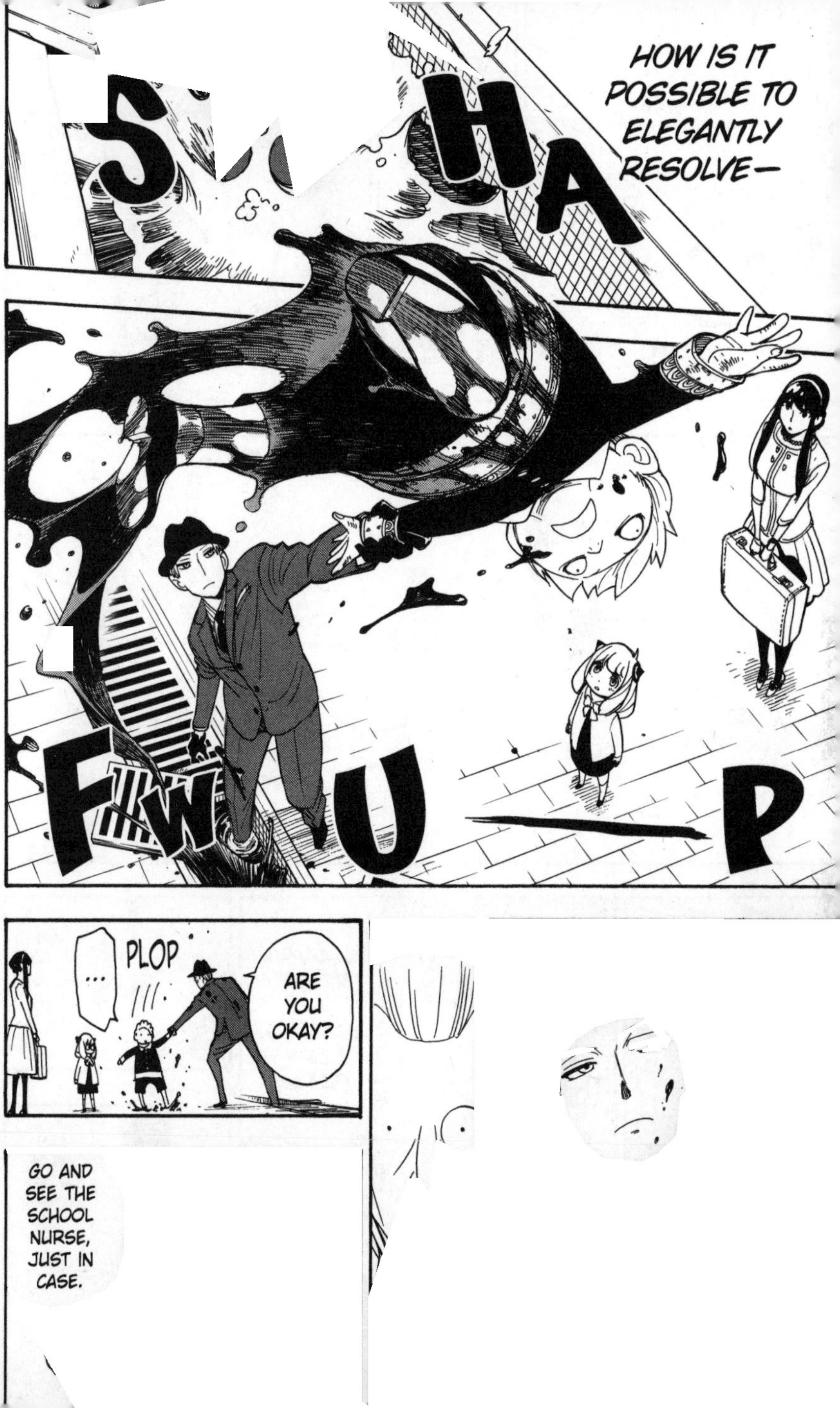

HOW IS IT POSSIBLE TO ELEGANTLY RESOLVE—
S HA
FW U P
ARE YOU OKAY?
PLOP
...
GO AND SEE THE SCHOOL NURSE, JUST IN CASE.

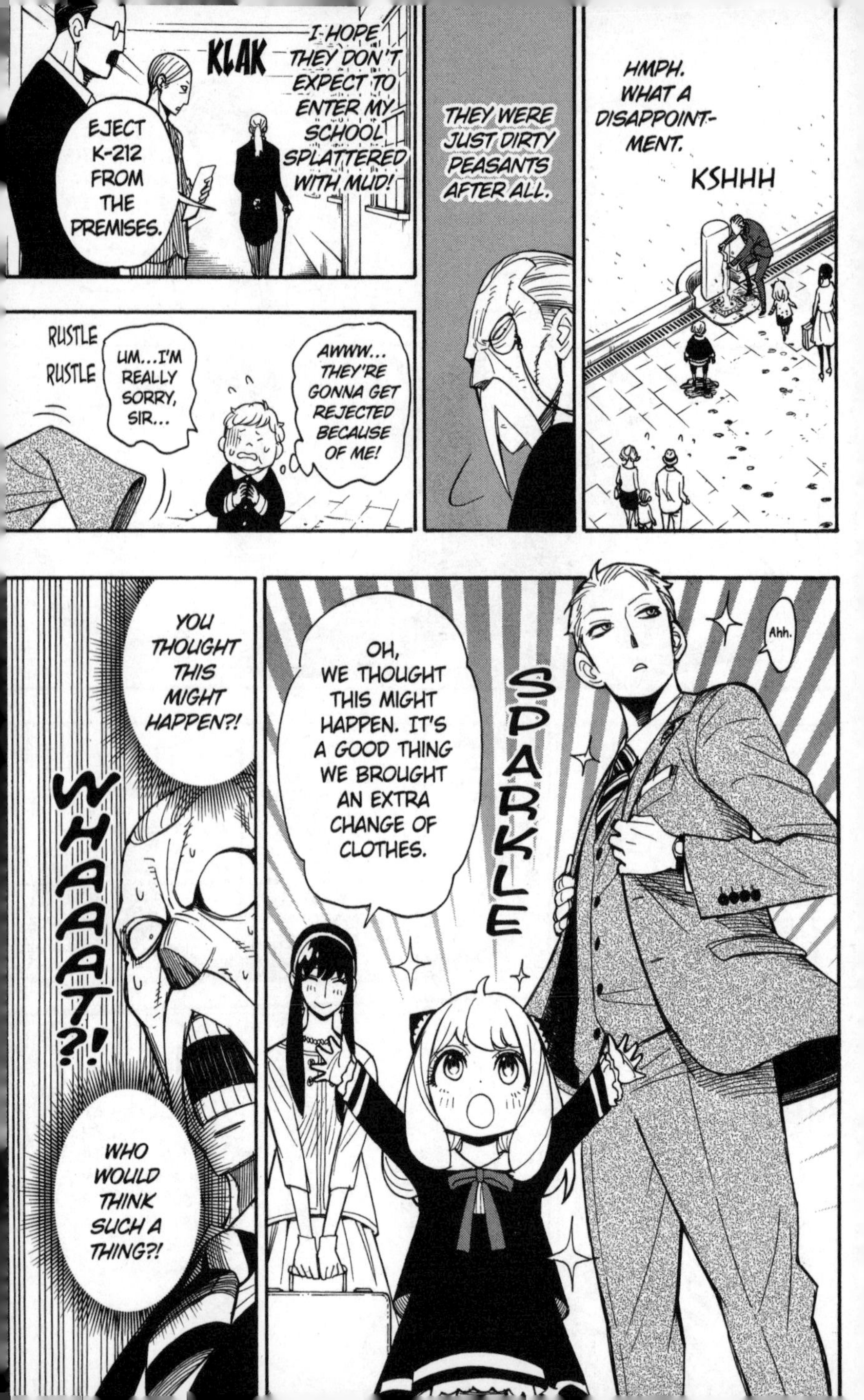
HMPH. WHAT A DISAPPOINT-MENT.
KSHHH
THEY WERE JUST DIRTY PEASANTS AFTER ALL.
I HOPE THEY DON'T EXPECT TO ENTER MY SCHOOL SPLATTERED WITH MUD!
KLAK
EJECT K-212 FROM THE PREMISES.
AWWW... THEY'RE GONNA GET REJECTED BECAUSE OF ME!
UM...I'M REALLY SORRY, SIR...
RUSTLE
RUSTLE
Ahh.
SPARKLE
OH, WE THOUGHT THIS MIGHT HAPPEN. IT'S A GOOD THING WE BROUGHT AN EXTRA CHANGE OF CLOTHES.
YOU THOUGHT THIS MIGHT HAPPEN?!
WHAAAT?!
WHO WOULD THINK SUCH A THING?!

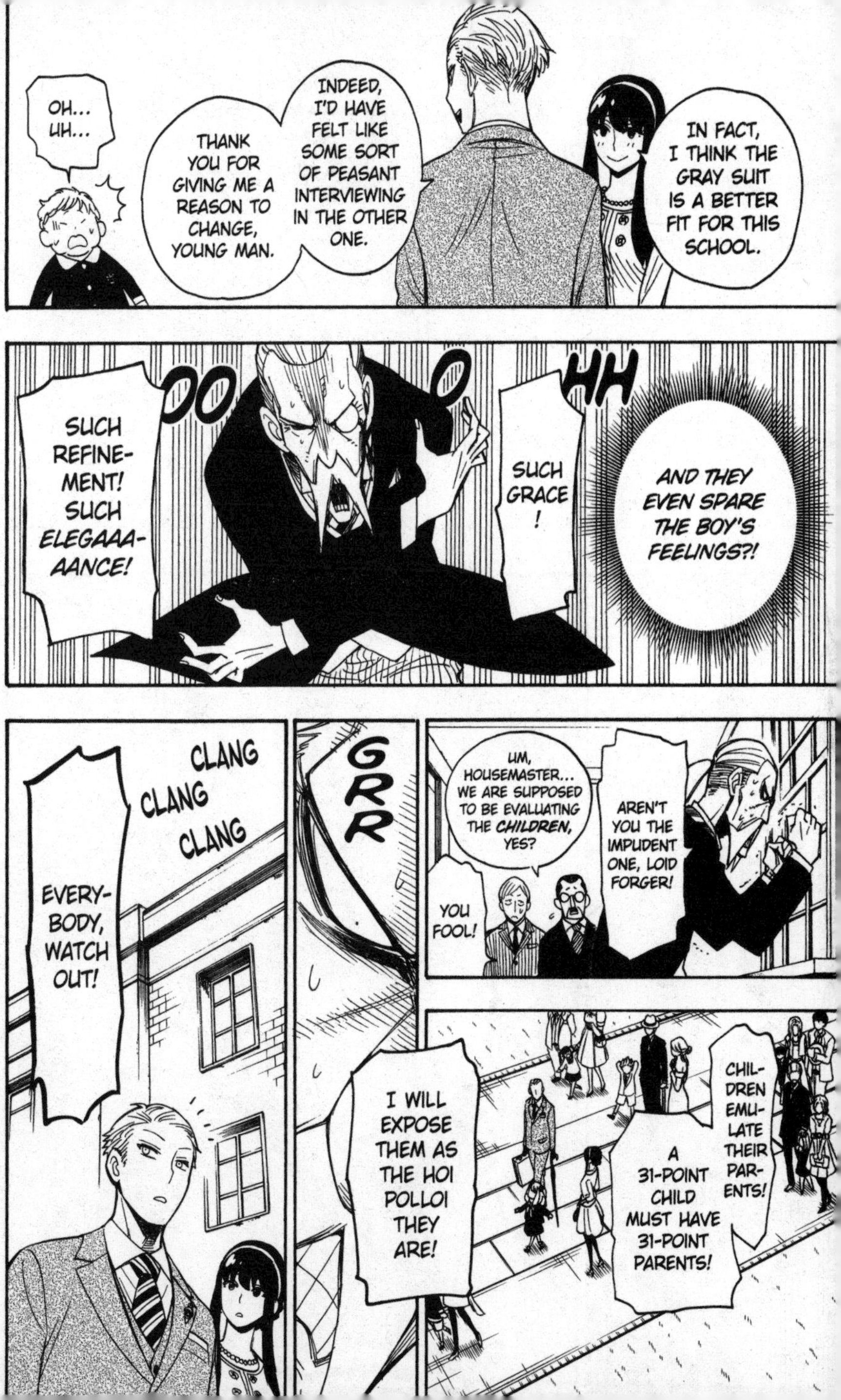
IN FACT, I THINK THE GRAY SUIT IS A BETTER FIT FOR THIS SCHOOL.
INDEED, I'D HAVE FELT LIKE SOME SORT OF PEASANT INTERVIEWING IN THE OTHER ONE.
THANK YOU FOR GIVING ME A REASON TO CHANGE, YOUNG MAN.
OH... UH...
AND THEY EVEN SPARE THE BOY'S FEELINGS?!
SUCH GRACE!
OOOHH
SUCH REFINE-MENT! SUCH ELEGAAAA-AANCE!
AREN'T YOU THE IMPUDENT ONE, LOID FORGER!
UM, HOUSEMASTER... WE ARE SUPPOSED TO BE EVALUATING THE CHILDREN, YES?
YOU FOOL!
CHIL-DREN EMU-LATE THEIR PAR-ENTS!
A 31-POINT CHILD MUST HAVE 31-POINT PARENTS!
GRR
I WILL EXPOSE THEM AS THE HOI POLLOI THEY ARE!
CLANG
CLANG
CLANG
EVERY-BODY, WATCH OUT!

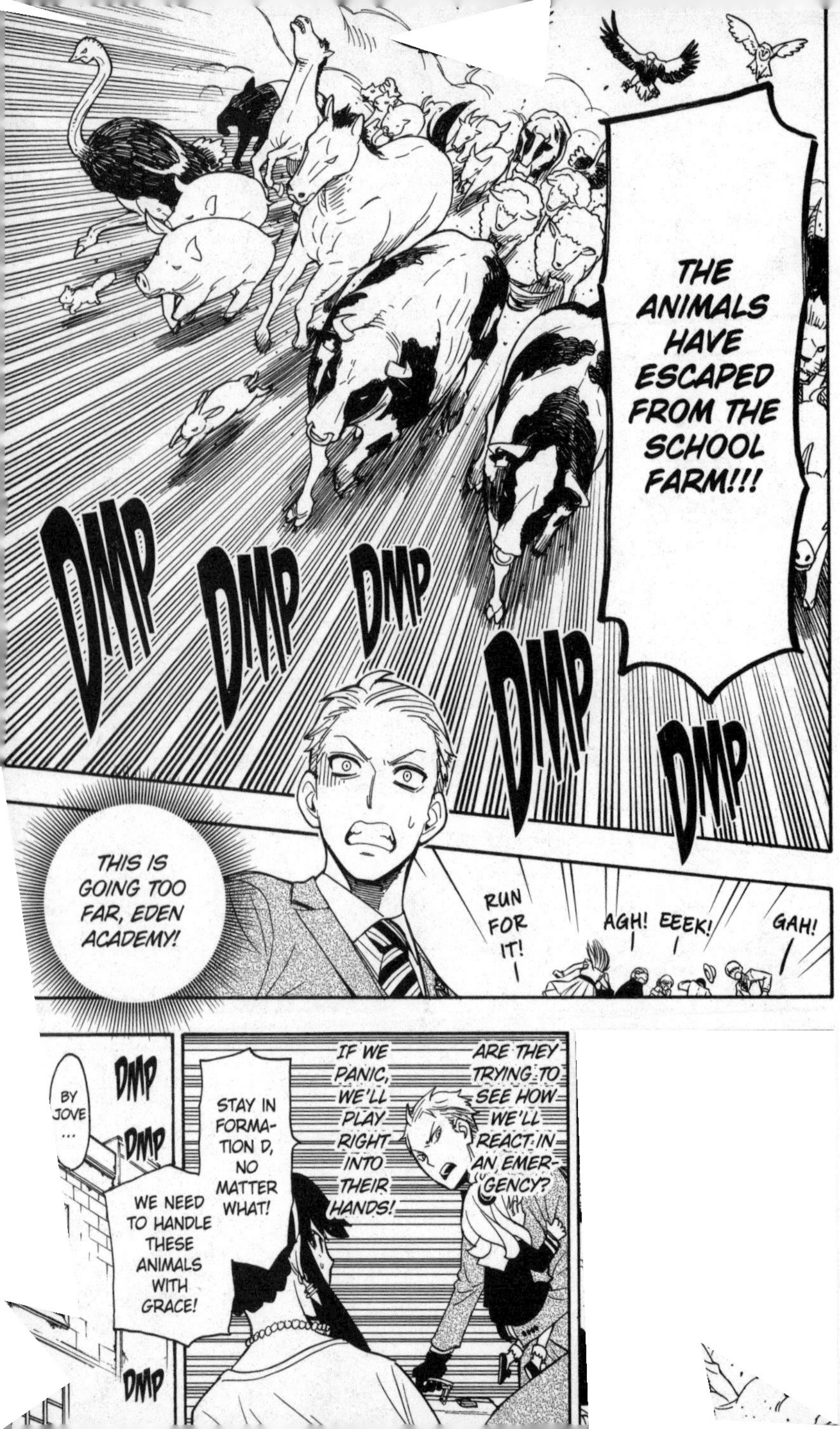
THE ANIMALS HAVE ESCAPED FROM THE SCHOOL FARM!!!
DMP DMP DMP DMP DMP
GAH!
EEEK!
AGH!
RUN FOR IT!
THIS IS GOING TOO FAR, EDEN ACADEMY!
ARE THEY TRYING TO SEE HOW WE'LL REACT IN AN EMERGENCY?
IF WE PANIC, WE'LL PLAY RIGHT INTO THEIR HANDS!
STAY IN FORMATION D, NO MATTER WHAT!
WE NEED TO HANDLE THESE ANIMALS WITH GRACE!
DMP DMP
BY JOVE...
DMP

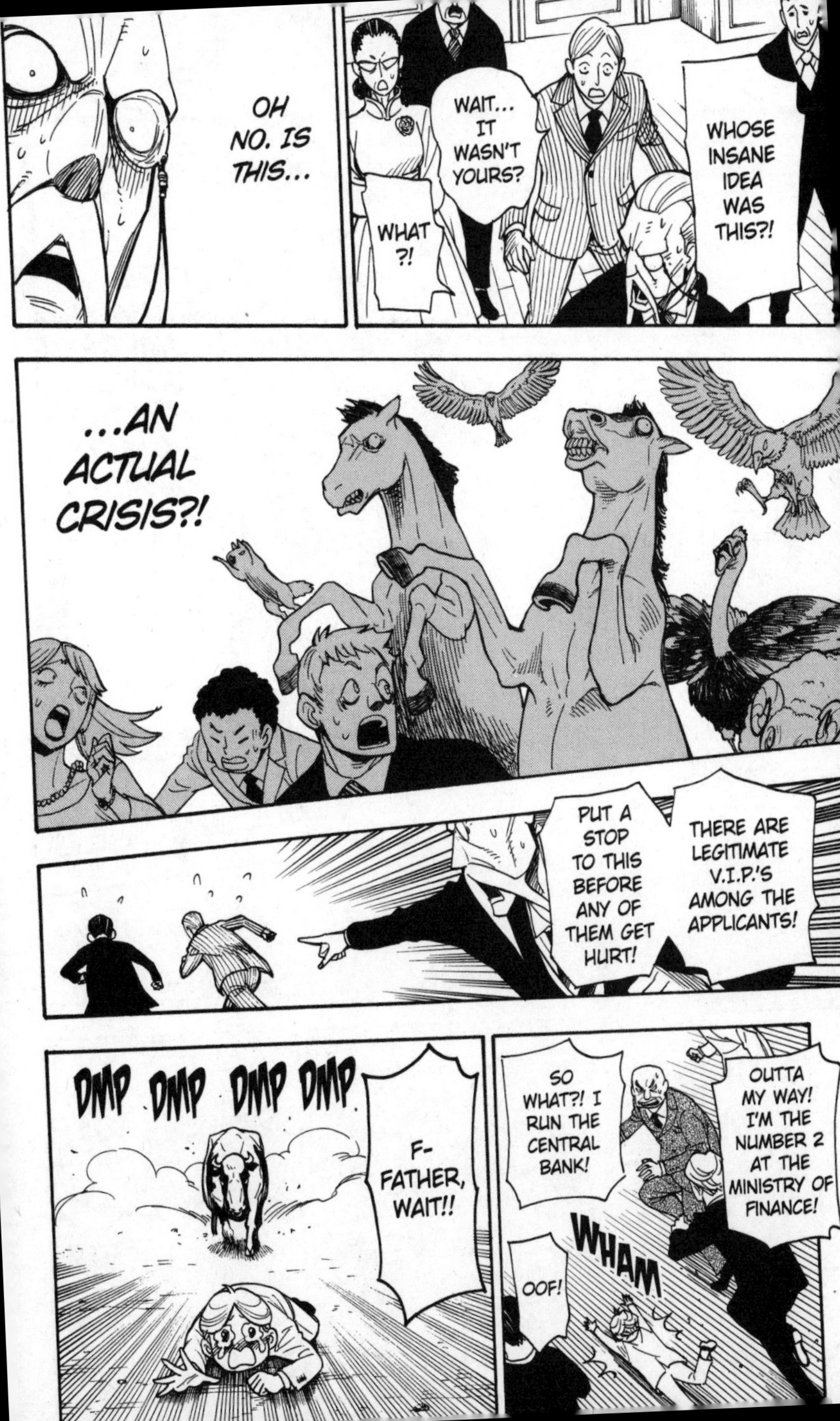

WHOSE INSANE IDEA WAS THIS?!
WAIT... IT WASN'T YOURS?
WHAT?!
OH NO. IS THIS...
...AN ACTUAL CRISIS?!
THERE ARE LEGITIMATE V.I.P.'S AMONG THE APPLICANTS!
PUT A STOP TO THIS BEFORE ANY OF THEM GET HURT!
OUTTA MY WAY! I'M THE NUMBER 2 AT THE MINISTRY OF FINANCE!
SO WHAT?! I RUN THE CENTRAL BANK!
WHAM
OOF!
F-FATHER, WAIT!!
DMP DMP DMP DMP

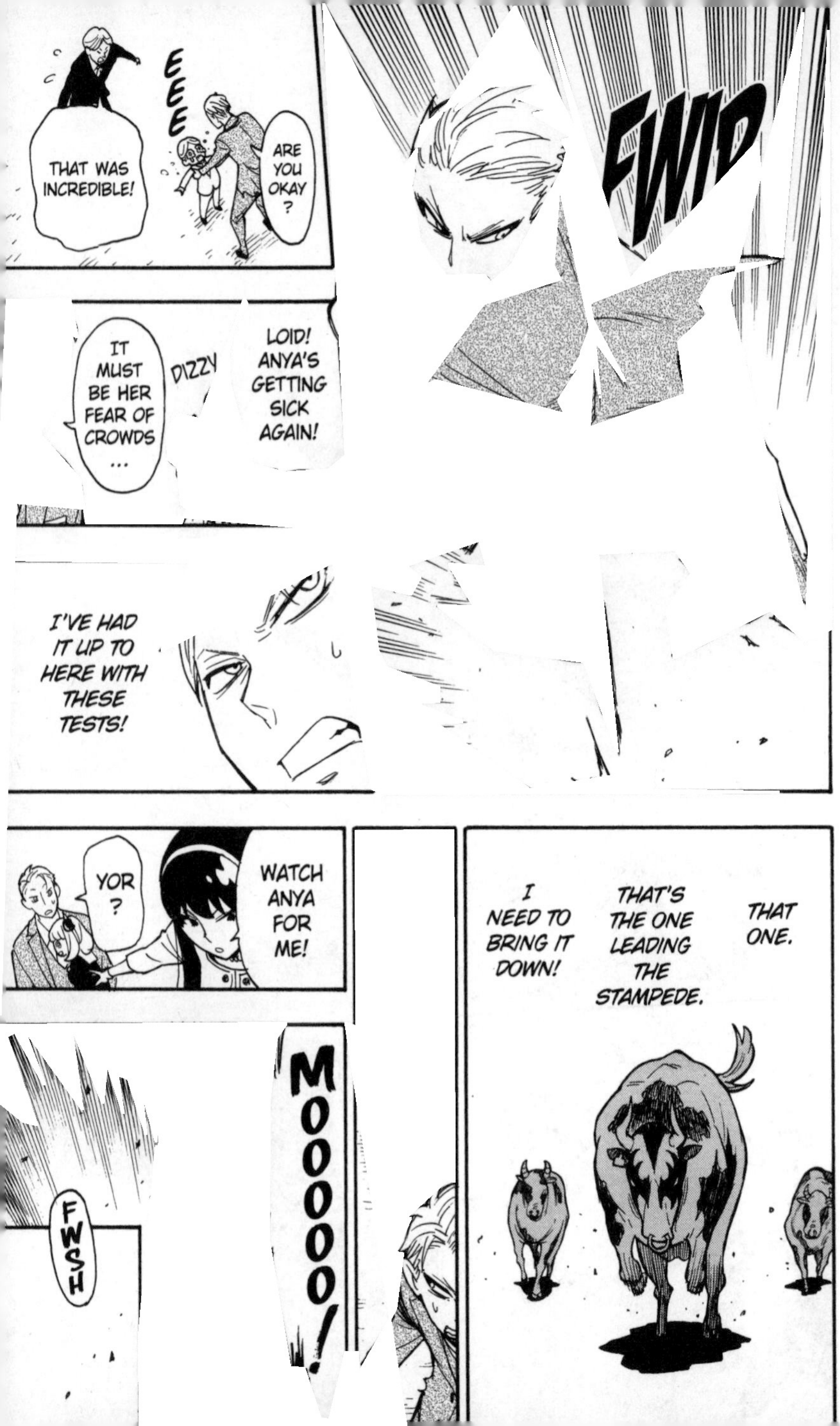
FWIP
ARE YOU OKAY?
EEE
THAT WAS INCREDIBLE!
LOID! ANYA'S GETTING SICK AGAIN!
DIZZY
IT MUST BE HER FEAR OF CROWDS...
I'VE HAD IT UP TO HERE WITH THESE TESTS!
THAT ONE.
THAT'S THE ONE LEADING THE STAMPEDE.
I NEED TO BRING IT DOWN!
WATCH ANYA FOR ME!
YOR?
MOOOOOO!
FWSH

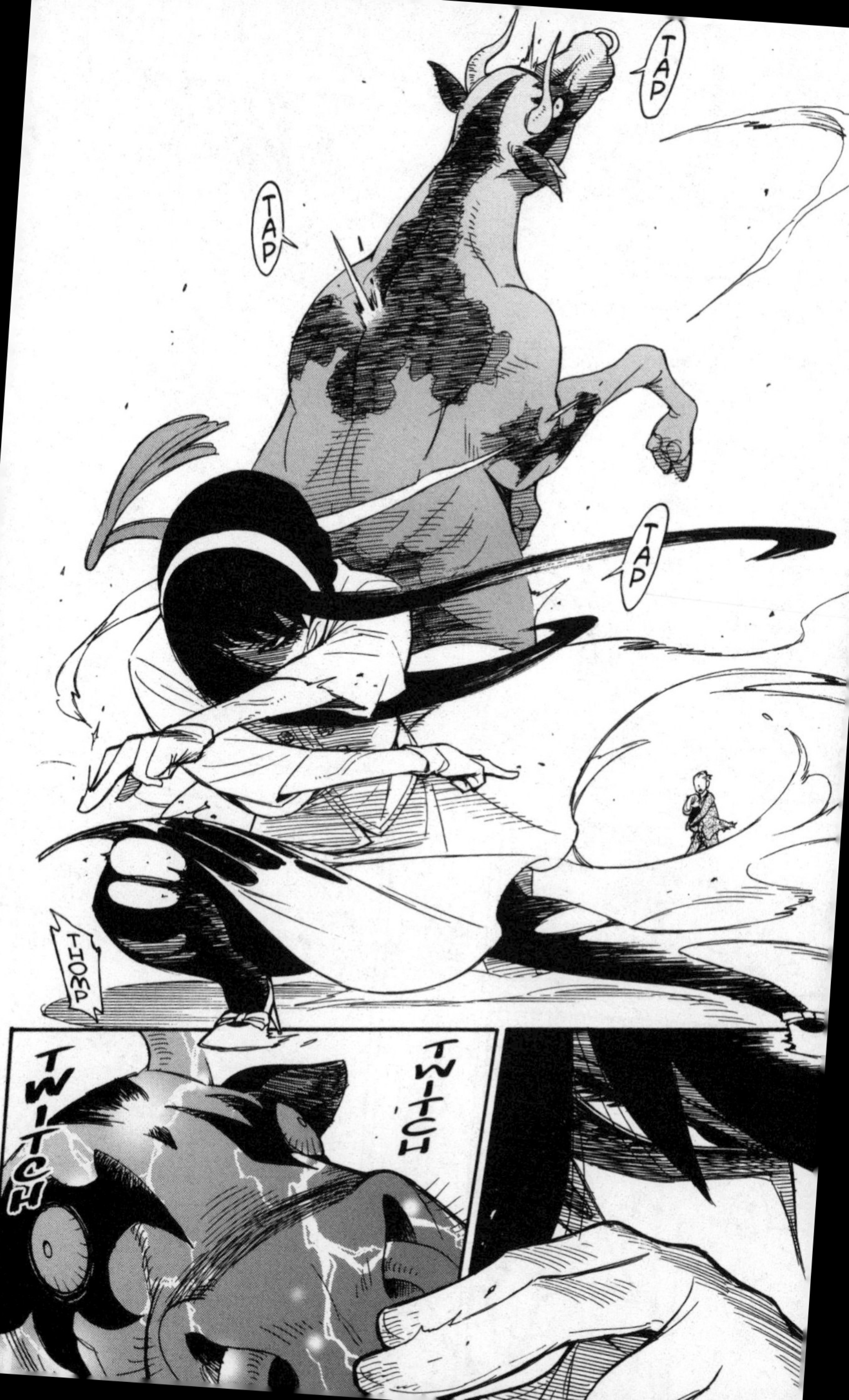
TAP
TAP
TAP
THOMP
TWITCH
TWITCH

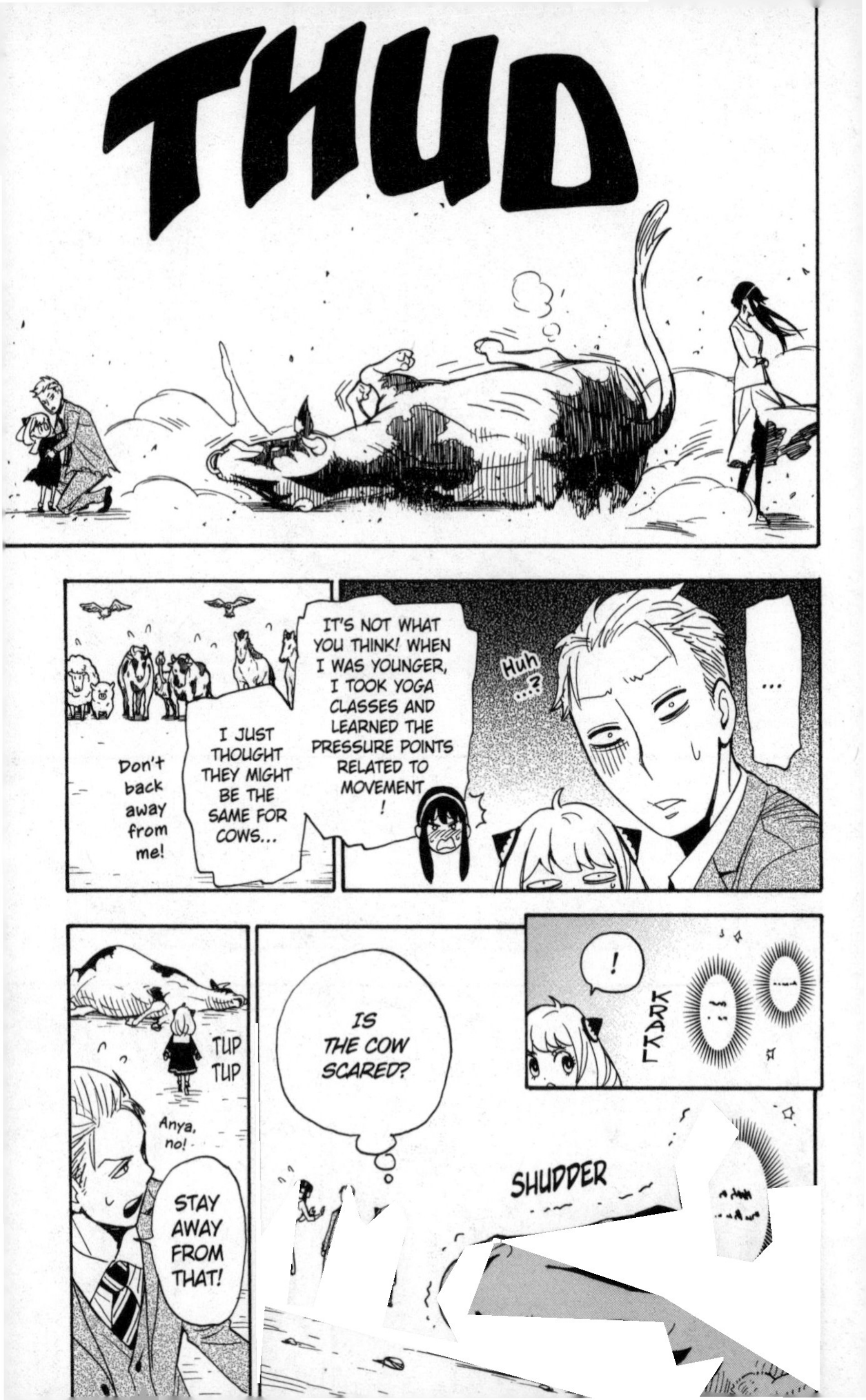
THUD
...
Huh ...?
IT'S NOT WHAT YOU THINK! WHEN I WAS YOUNGER, I TOOK YOGA CLASSES AND LEARNED THE PRESSURE POINTS RELATED TO MOVEMENT!
I JUST THOUGHT THEY MIGHT BE THE SAME FOR COWS...
Don't back away from me!
!
KRAKL
IS THE COW SCARED?
SHUDDER
TUP TUP
Anya, no!
STAY AWAY FROM THAT!

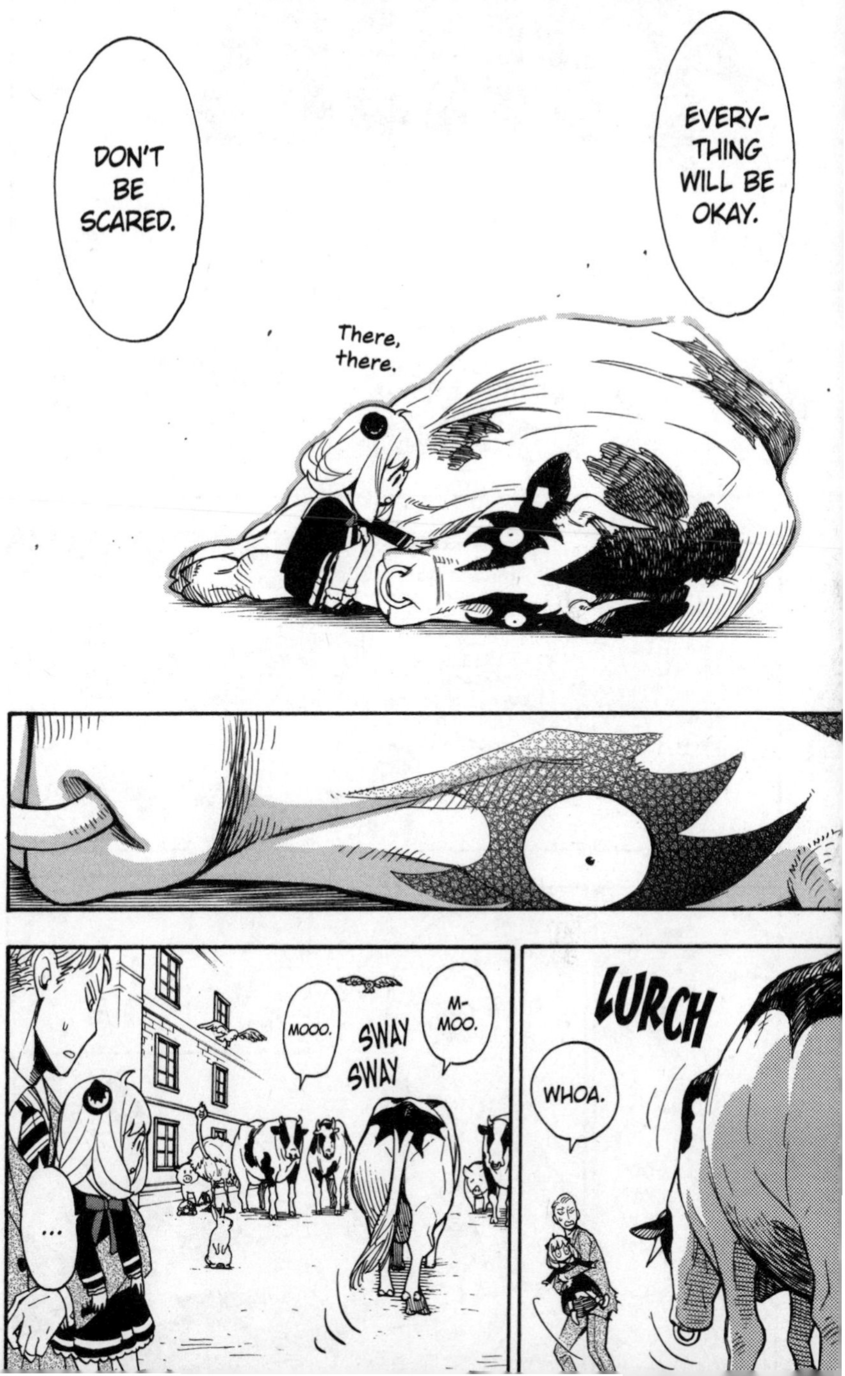
EVERY-THING WILL BE OKAY.
DON'T BE SCARED.
There, there.
LURCH
WHOA.
M-MOO.
SWAY SWAY
MOOO.
...

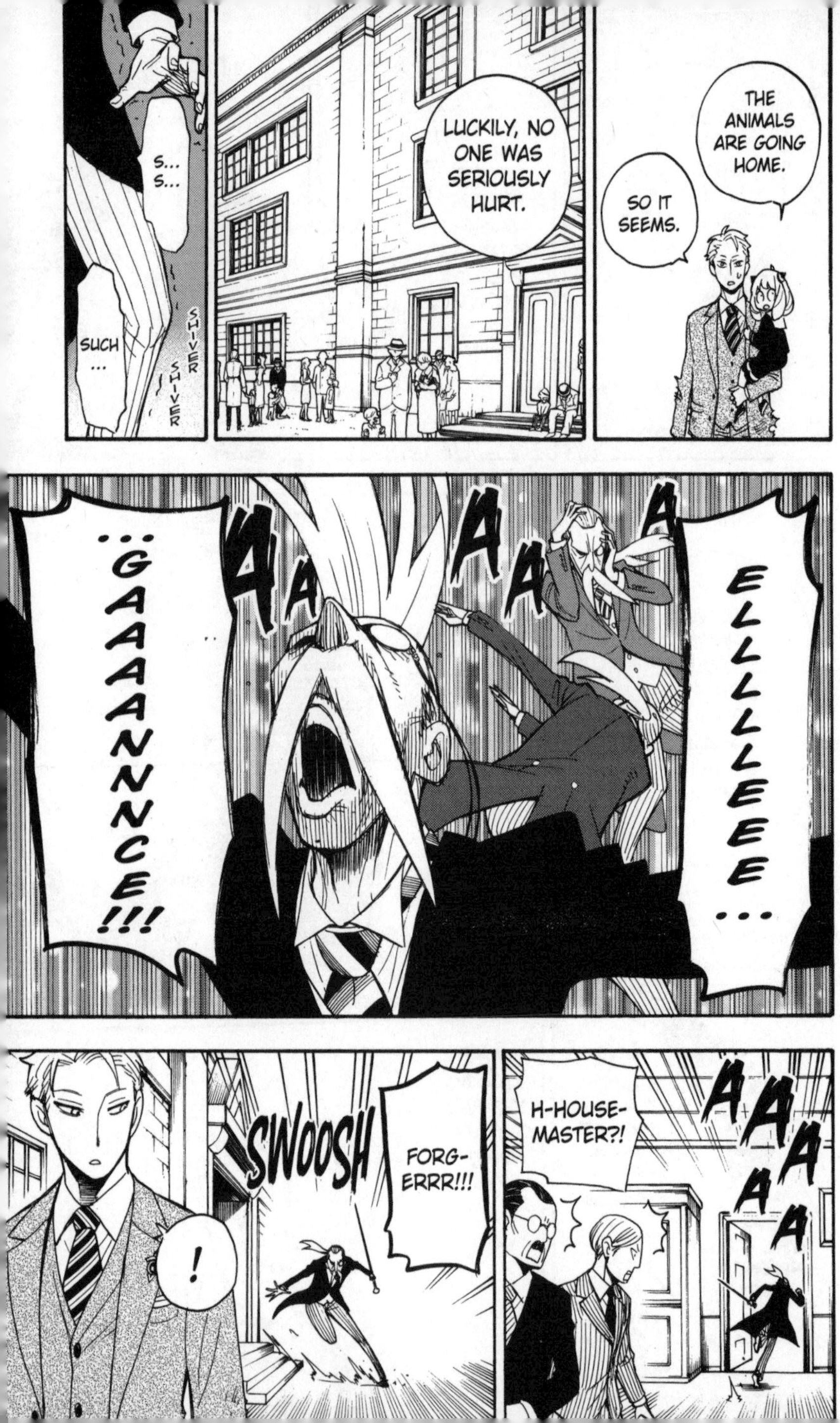
THE ANIMALS ARE GOING HOME.
SO IT SEEMS.
LUCKILY, NO ONE WAS SERIOUSLY HURT.
S... S...
SHIVER SHIVER
SUCH ...
ELLLLLEEE...
AAAAA
..GAAAANNNCE!!!
H-HOUSE-MASTER?!
AAAAAA
FORG-ERRR!!!
SWOOSH
!

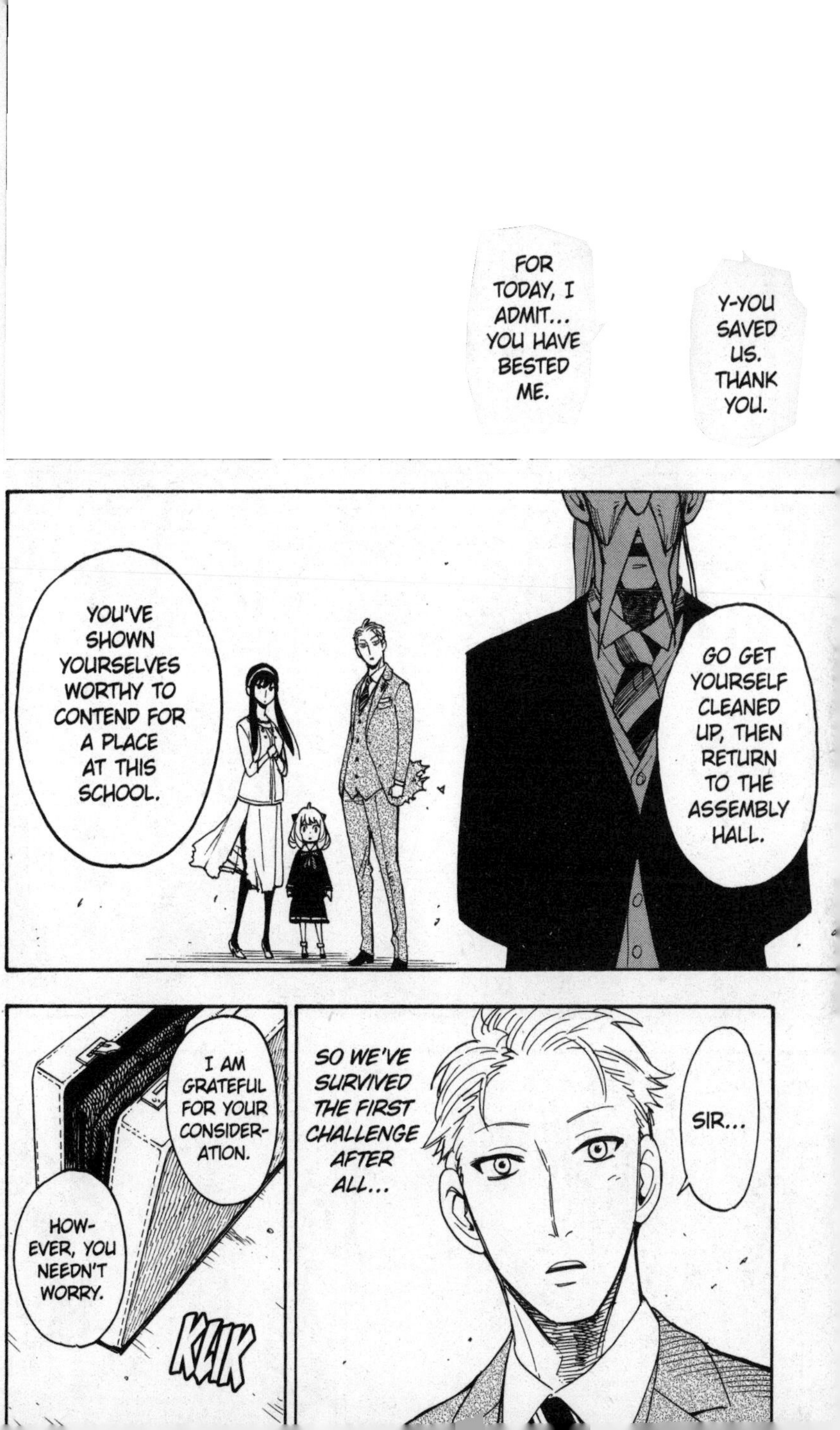
Y-YOU SAVED US. THANK YOU.
FOR TODAY, I ADMIT... YOU HAVE BESTED ME.
GO GET YOURSELF CLEANED UP, THEN RETURN TO THE ASSEMBLY HALL.
YOU'VE SHOWN YOURSELVES WORTHY TO CONTEND FOR A PLACE AT THIS SCHOOL.
SIR...
SO WE'VE SURVIVED THE FIRST CHALLENGE AFTER ALL...
I AM GRATEFUL FOR YOUR CONSIDER-ATION.
HOW-EVER, YOU NEEDN'T WORRY.
KLIK

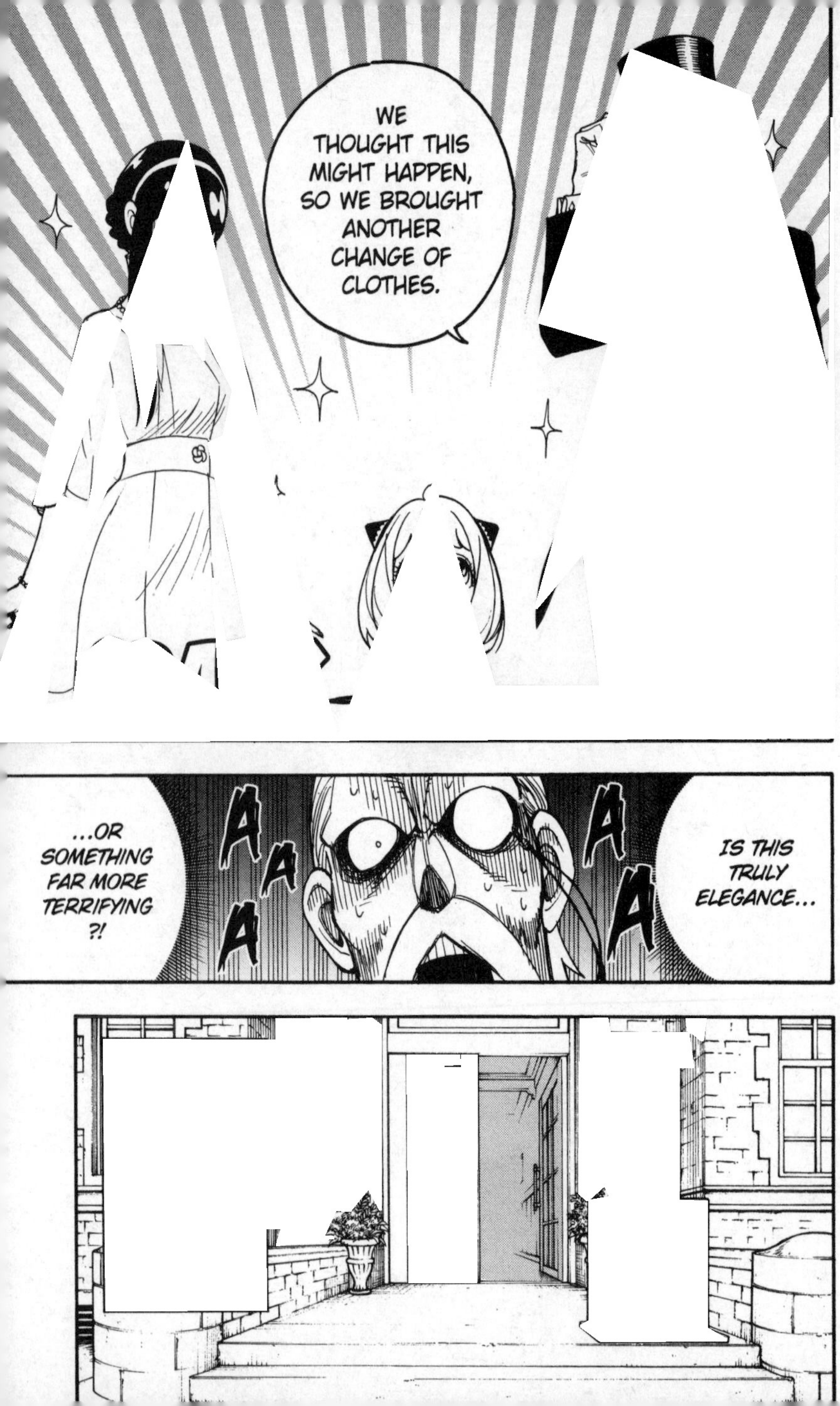
WE THOUGHT THIS MIGHT HAPPEN, SO WE BROUGHT ANOTHER CHANGE OF CLOTHES.
AAA
IS THIS TRULY ELEGANCE...
AAA
...OR SOMETHING FAR MORE TERRIFYING?!

SPY×FAMILY

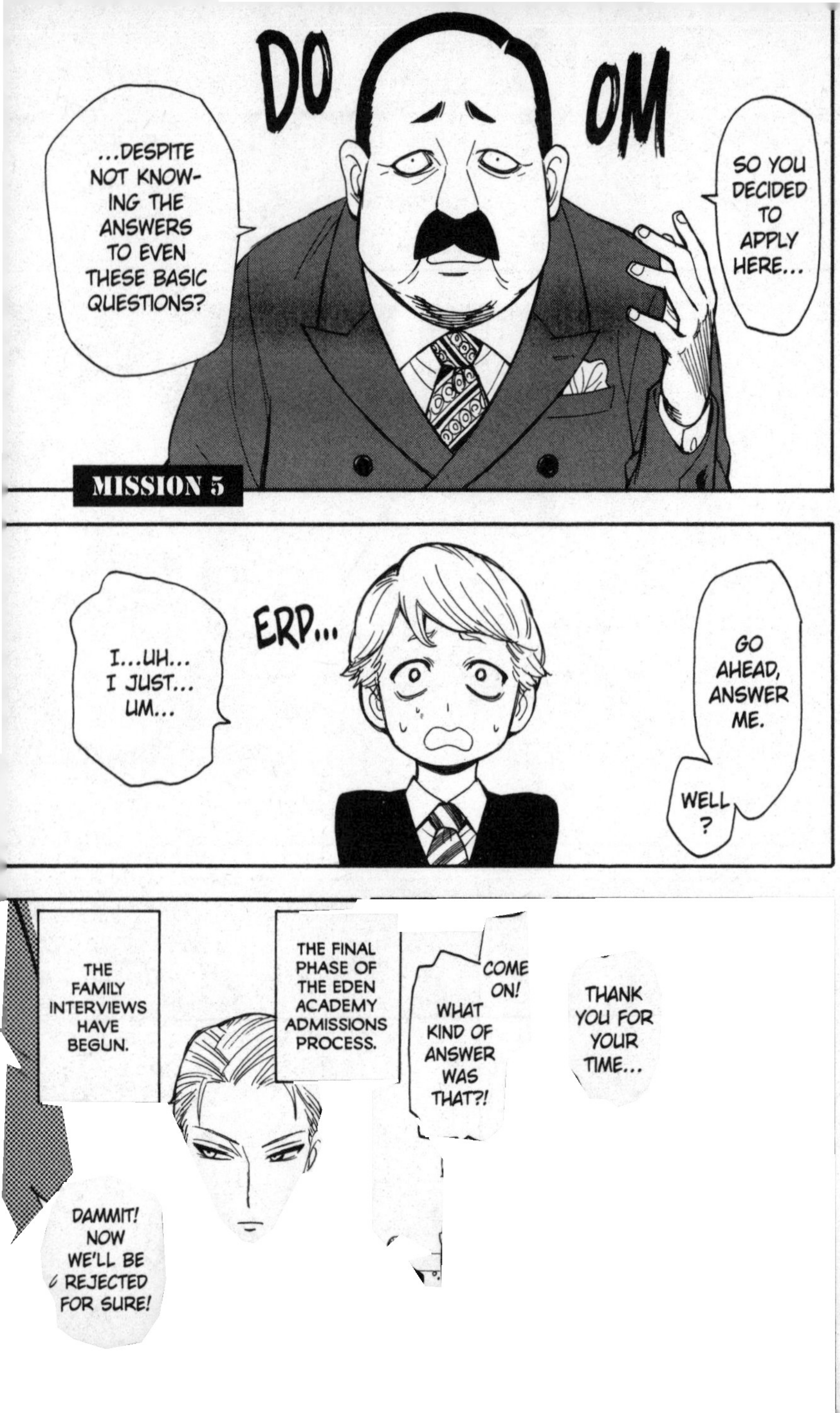
SO YOU DECIDED TO APPLY HERE...
DOOM
...DESPITE NOT KNOWING THE ANSWERS TO EVEN THESE BASIC QUESTIONS?
MISSION 5
GO AHEAD, ANSWER ME.
WELL?
ERP...
I...UH... I JUST... UM...
THANK YOU FOR YOUR TIME...
COME ON!
WHAT KIND OF ANSWER WAS THAT?!
THE FINAL PHASE OF THE EDEN ACADEMY ADMISSIONS PROCESS.
THE FAMILY INTERVIEWS HAVE BEGUN.
DAMMIT! NOW WE'LL BE REJECTED FOR SURE!

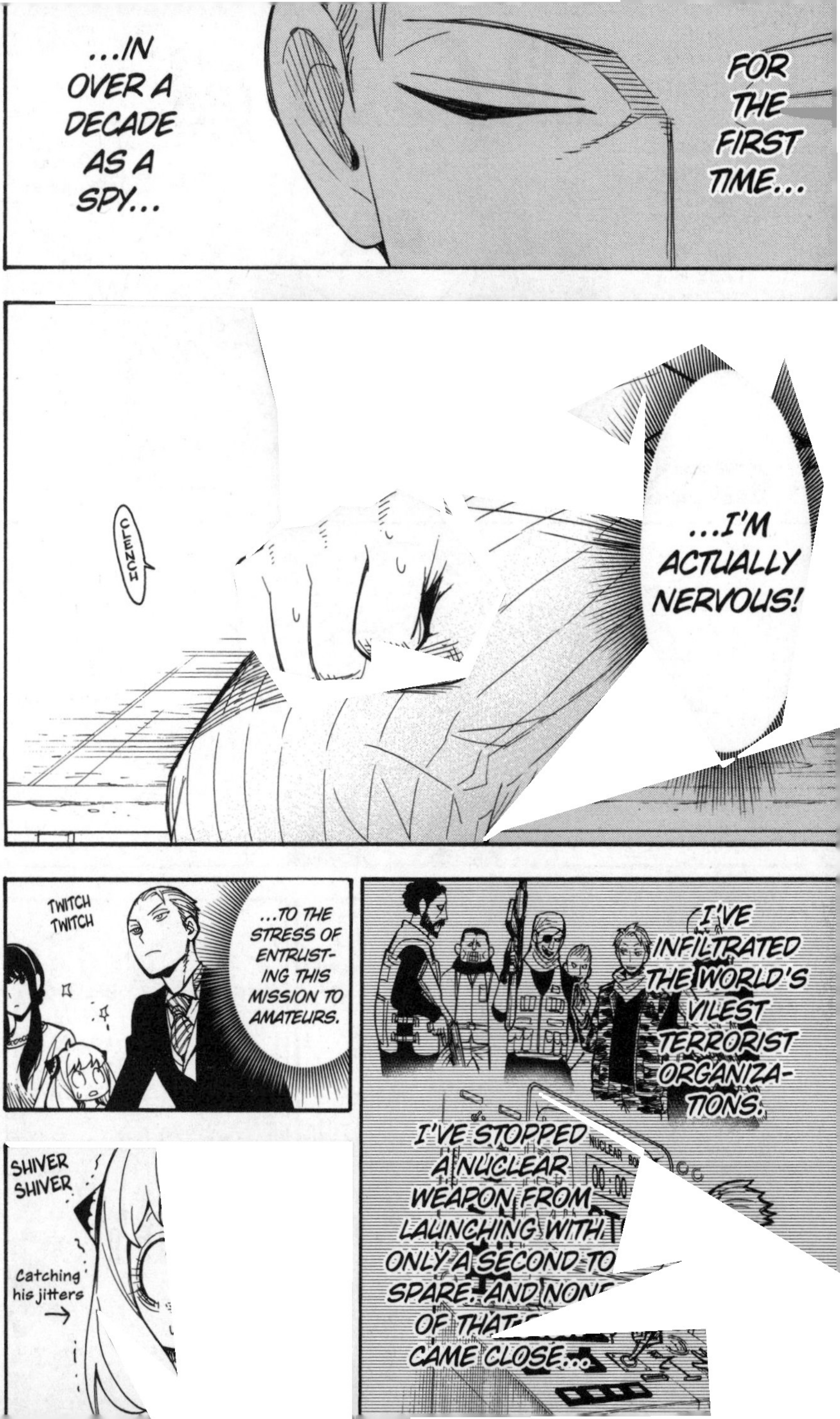
FOR THE FIRST TIME...
...IN OVER A DECADE AS A SPY...
...I'M ACTUALLY NERVOUS!
CLENCH
I'VE INFILTRATED THE WORLD'S VILEST TERRORIST ORGANIZATIONS.
I'VE STOPPED A NUCLEAR WEAPON FROM LAUNCHING WITH ONLY A SECOND TO SPARE, AND NON
OF THAT
CAME CLOSE...
...TO THE STRESS OF ENTRUSTING THIS MISSION TO AMATEURS.
TWITCH TWITCH
SHIVER SHIVER
Catching his jitters →

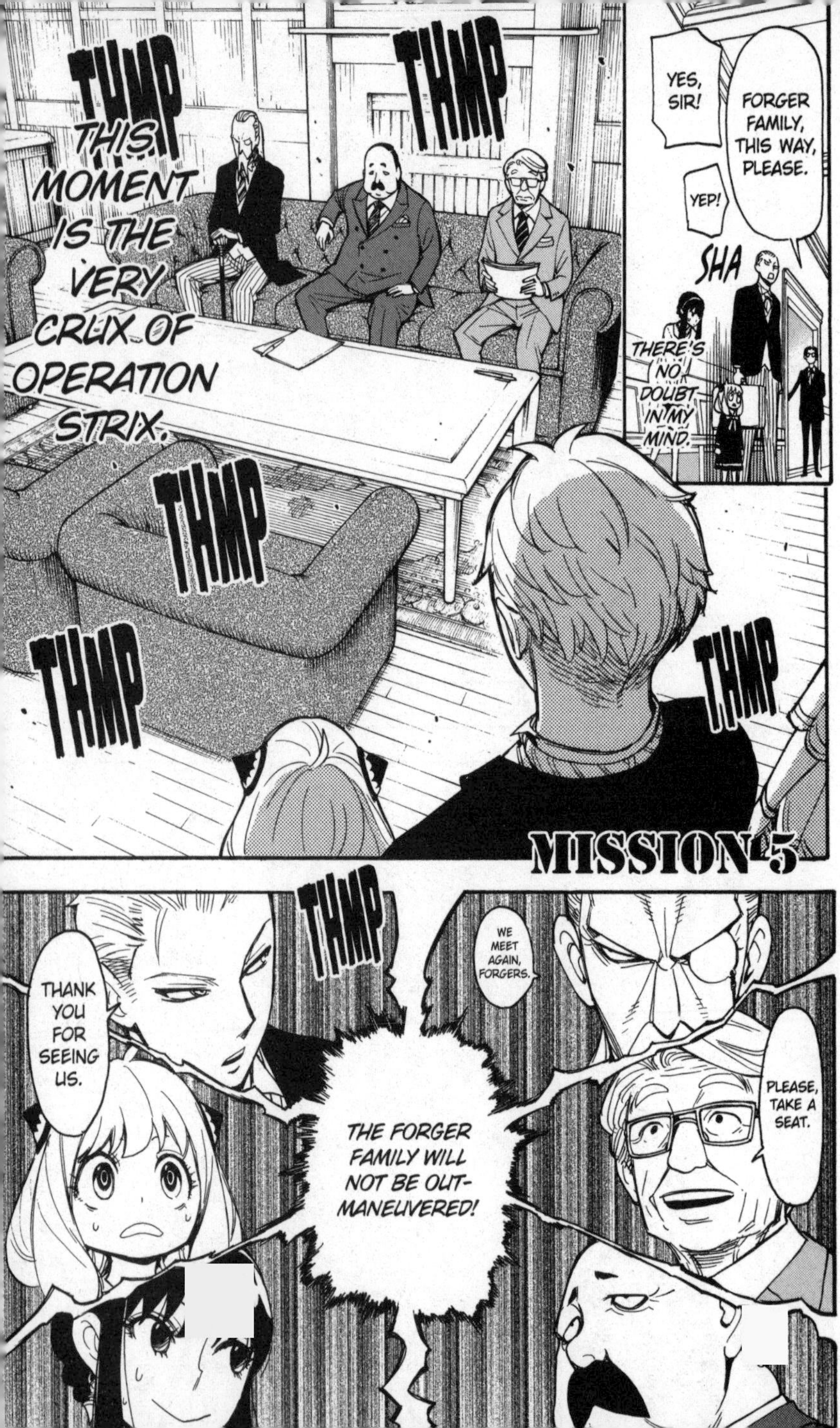
FORGER FAMILY, THIS WAY, PLEASE.
YES, SIR!
YEP!
SHA
THERE'S NO DOUBT IN MY MIND.
THMP
THMP
THIS MOMENT IS THE VERY CRUX OF OPERATION STRIX.
THMP
THMP
THMP
MISSION 5
THMP
WE MEET AGAIN, FORGERS.
PLEASE, TAKE A SEAT.
THANK YOU FOR SEEING US.
THE FORGER FAMILY WILL NOT BE OUT-MANEUVERED!

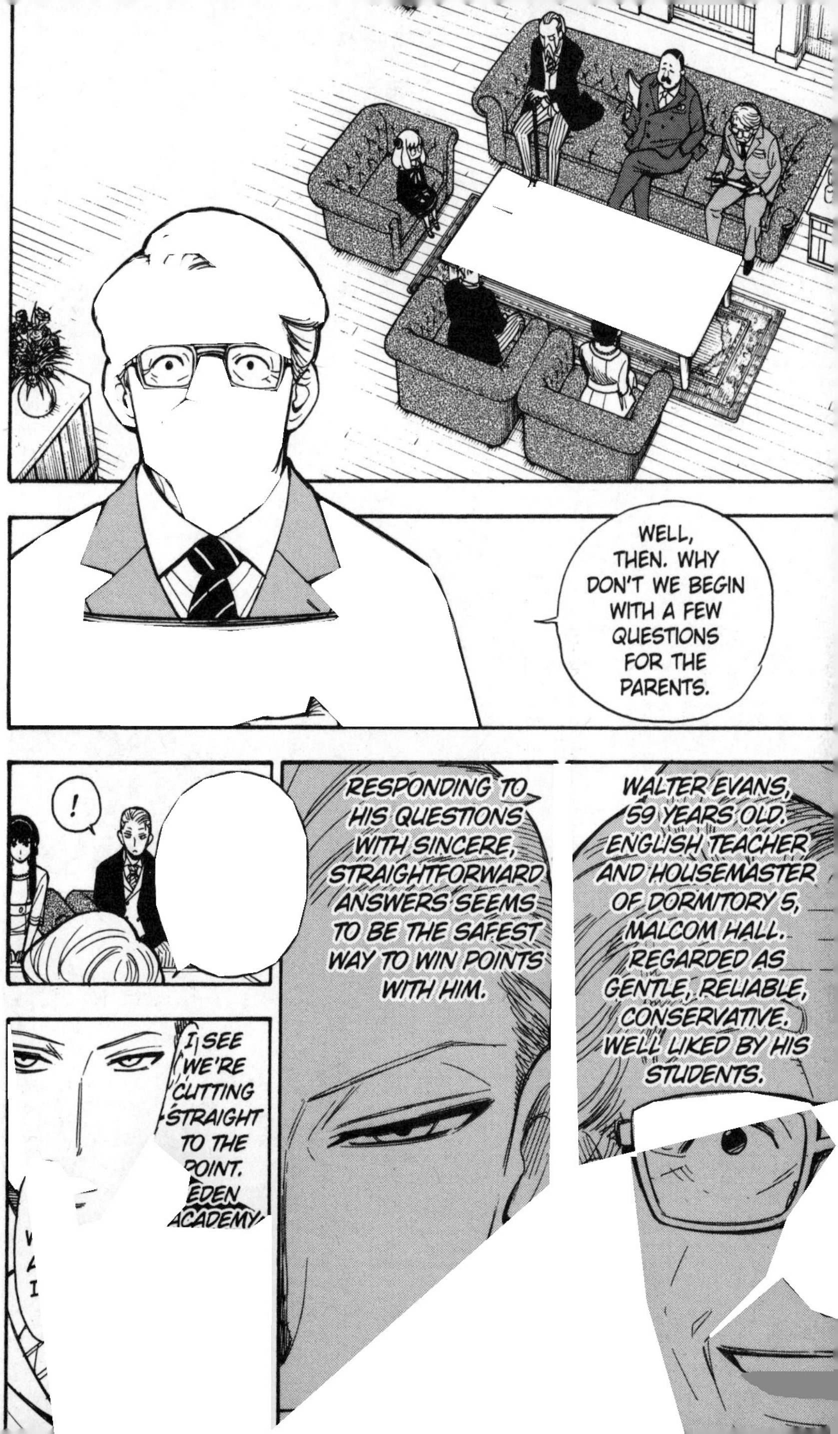
WELL, THEN. WHY DON'T WE BEGIN WITH A FEW QUESTIONS FOR THE PARENTS.
WALTER EVANS, 59 YEARS OLD. ENGLISH TEACHER AND HOUSEMASTER OF DORMITORY 5, MALCOM HALL. REGARDED AS GENTLE, RELIABLE, CONSERVATIVE. WELL LIKED BY HIS STUDENTS.
RESPONDING TO HIS QUESTIONS WITH SINCERE, STRAIGHTFORWARD ANSWERS SEEMS TO BE THE SAFEST WAY TO WIN POINTS WITH HIM.
!
I SEE WE'RE CUTTING STRAIGHT TO THE POINT. EDEN ACADEMY

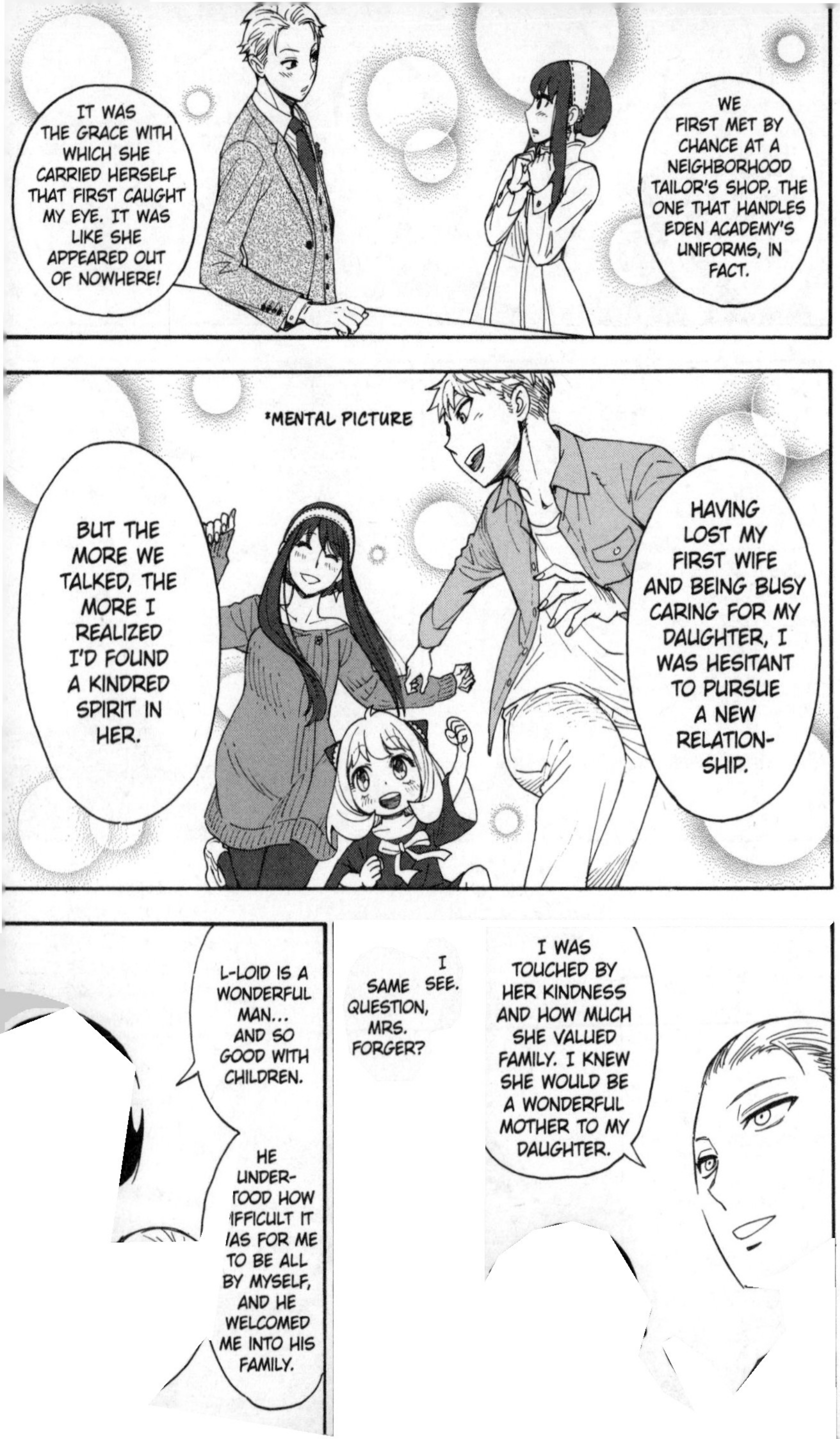
WE FIRST MET BY CHANCE AT A NEIGHBORHOOD TAILOR'S SHOP. THE ONE THAT HANDLES EDEN ACADEMY'S UNIFORMS, IN FACT.
IT WAS THE GRACE WITH WHICH SHE CARRIED HERSELF THAT FIRST CAUGHT MY EYE. IT WAS LIKE SHE APPEARED OUT OF NOWHERE!
*MENTAL PICTURE
HAVING LOST MY FIRST WIFE AND BEING BUSY CARING FOR MY DAUGHTER, I WAS HESITANT TO PURSUE A NEW RELATION-SHIP.
BUT THE MORE WE TALKED, THE MORE I REALIZED I'D FOUND A KINDRED SPIRIT IN HER.
I WAS TOUCHED BY HER KINDNESS AND HOW MUCH SHE VALUED FAMILY. I KNEW SHE WOULD BE A WONDERFUL MOTHER TO MY DAUGHTER.
I SEE.
SAME QUESTION, MRS. FORGER?
L-LOID IS A WONDERFUL MAN... AND SO GOOD WITH CHILDREN.
HE UNDER- TOOD HOW IFFICULT IT IAS FOR ME TO BE ALL BY MYSELF, AND HE WELCOMED ME INTO HIS FAMILY.

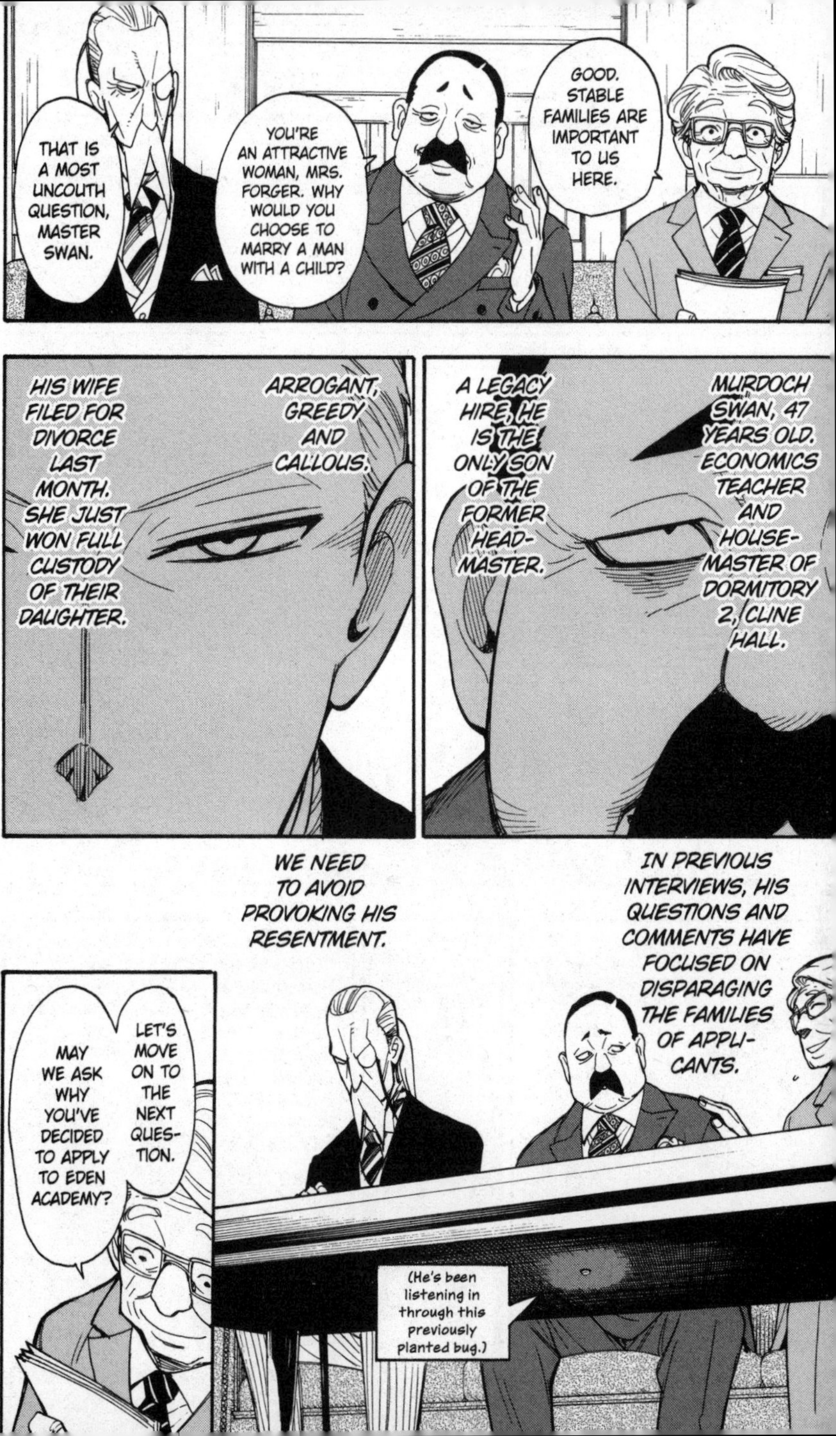
GOOD. STABLE FAMILIES ARE IMPORTANT TO US HERE.
YOU'RE AN ATTRACTIVE WOMAN, MRS. FORGER. WHY WOULD YOU CHOOSE TO MARRY A MAN WITH A CHILD?
THAT IS A MOST UNCOUTH QUESTION, MASTER SWAN.
MURDOCH SWAN, 47 YEARS OLD. ECONOMICS TEACHER AND HOUSE-MASTER OF DORMITORY 2, CLINE HALL.
A LEGACY HIRE, HE IS THE ONLY SON OF THE FORMER HEAD-MASTER.
ARROGANT, GREEDY AND CALLOUS.
HIS WIFE FILED FOR DIVORCE LAST MONTH. SHE JUST WON FULL CUSTODY OF THEIR DAUGHTER.
IN PREVIOUS INTERVIEWS, HIS QUESTIONS AND COMMENTS HAVE FOCUSED ON DISPARAGING THE FAMILIES OF APPLI-CANTS.
WE NEED TO AVOID PROVOKING HIS RESENTMENT.
LET'S MOVE ON TO THE NEXT QUES-TION.
MAY WE ASK WHY YOU'VE DECIDED TO APPLY TO EDEN ACADEMY?
(He's been listening in through this previously planted bug.)

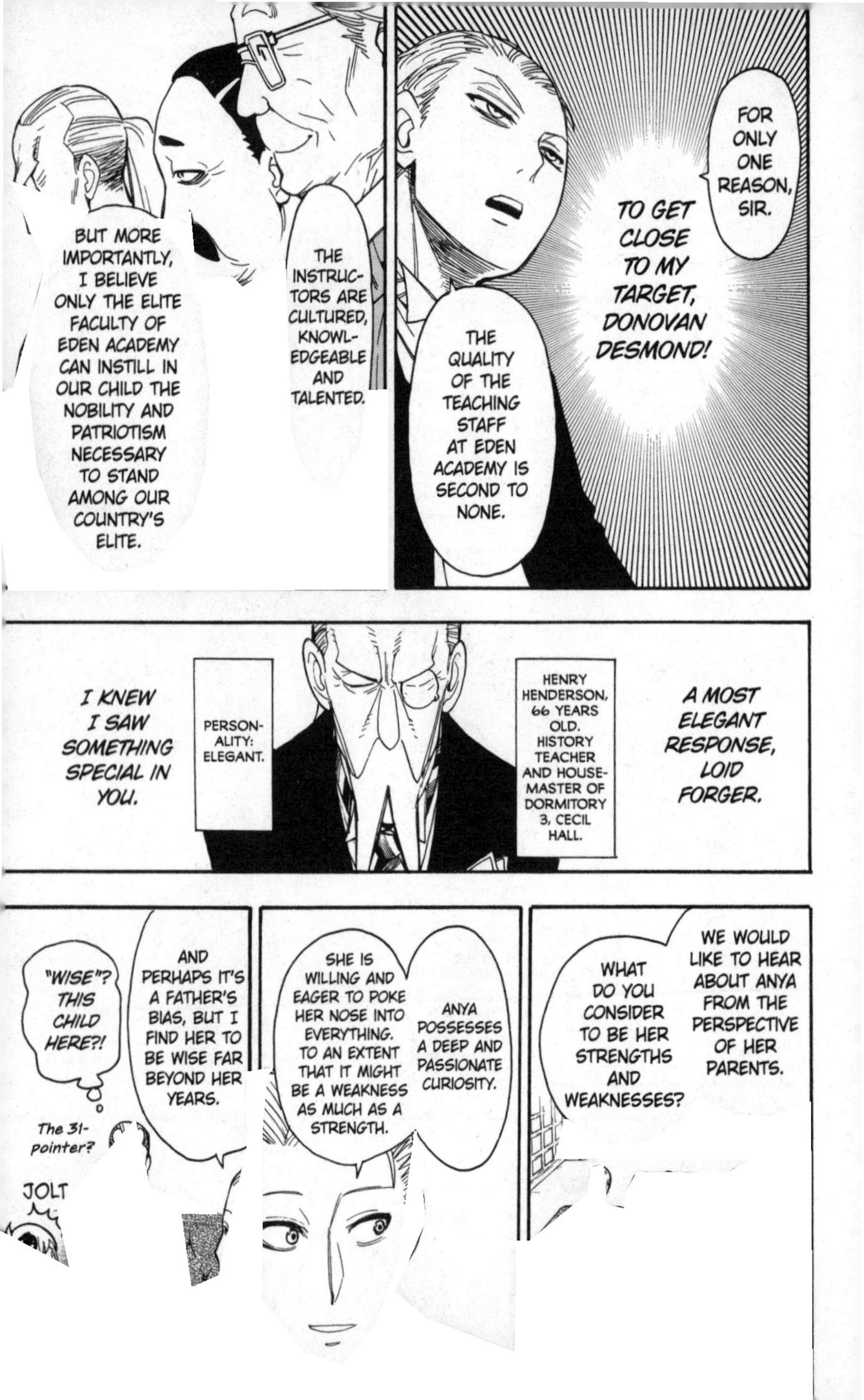
FOR ONLY ONE REASON, SIR.
TO GET CLOSE TO MY TARGET, DONOVAN DESMOND!
THE QUALITY OF THE TEACHING STAFF AT EDEN ACADEMY IS SECOND TO NONE.
THE INSTRUCTORS ARE CULTURED, KNOWLEDGEABLE AND TALENTED.
BUT MORE IMPORTANTLY, I BELIEVE ONLY THE ELITE FACULTY OF EDEN ACADEMY CAN INSTILL IN OUR CHILD THE NOBILITY AND PATRIOTISM NECESSARY TO STAND AMONG OUR COUNTRY'S ELITE.
A MOST ELEGANT RESPONSE, LOID FORGER.
HENRY HENDERSON, 66 YEARS OLD. HISTORY TEACHER AND HOUSEMASTER OF DORMITORY 3, CECIL HALL.
PERSONALITY: ELEGANT.
I KNEW I SAW SOMETHING SPECIAL IN YOU.
WE WOULD LIKE TO HEAR ABOUT ANYA FROM THE PERSPECTIVE OF HER PARENTS.
WHAT DO YOU CONSIDER TO BE HER STRENGTHS AND WEAKNESSES?
ANYA POSSESSES A DEEP AND PASSIONATE CURIOSITY.
SHE IS WILLING AND EAGER TO POKE HER NOSE INTO EVERYTHING. TO AN EXTENT THAT IT MIGHT BE A WEAKNESS AS MUCH AS A STRENGTH.
AND PERHAPS IT'S A FATHER'S BIAS, BUT I FIND HER TO BE WISE FAR BEYOND HER YEARS.
"WISE"? THIS CHILD HERE?!
The 31-pointer?
JOLT

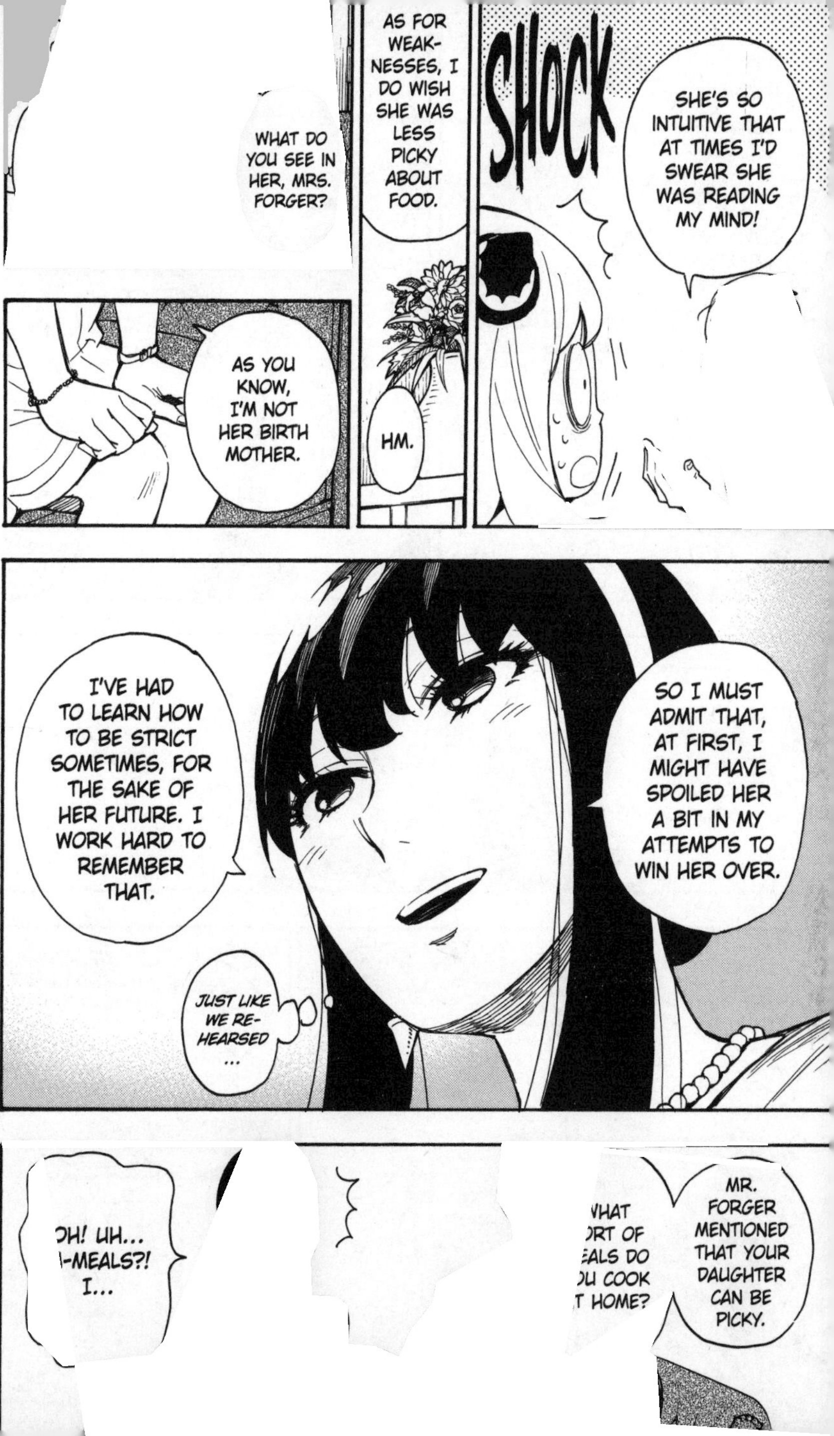
SHE'S SO INTUITIVE THAT AT TIMES I'D SWEAR SHE WAS READING MY MIND!
SHOCK
AS FOR WEAKNESSES, I DO WISH SHE WAS LESS PICKY ABOUT FOOD.
HM.
WHAT DO YOU SEE IN HER, MRS. FORGER?
AS YOU KNOW, I'M NOT HER BIRTH MOTHER.
SO I MUST ADMIT THAT, AT FIRST, I MIGHT HAVE SPOILED HER A BIT IN MY ATTEMPTS TO WIN HER OVER.
I'VE HAD TO LEARN HOW TO BE STRICT SOMETIMES, FOR THE SAKE OF HER FUTURE. I WORK HARD TO REMEMBER THAT.
JUST LIKE WE REHEARSED...
MR. FORGER MENTIONED THAT YOUR DAUGHTER CAN BE PICKY.
WHAT ORT OF EALS DO OU COOK T HOME?
OH! UH... -MEALS?! I...

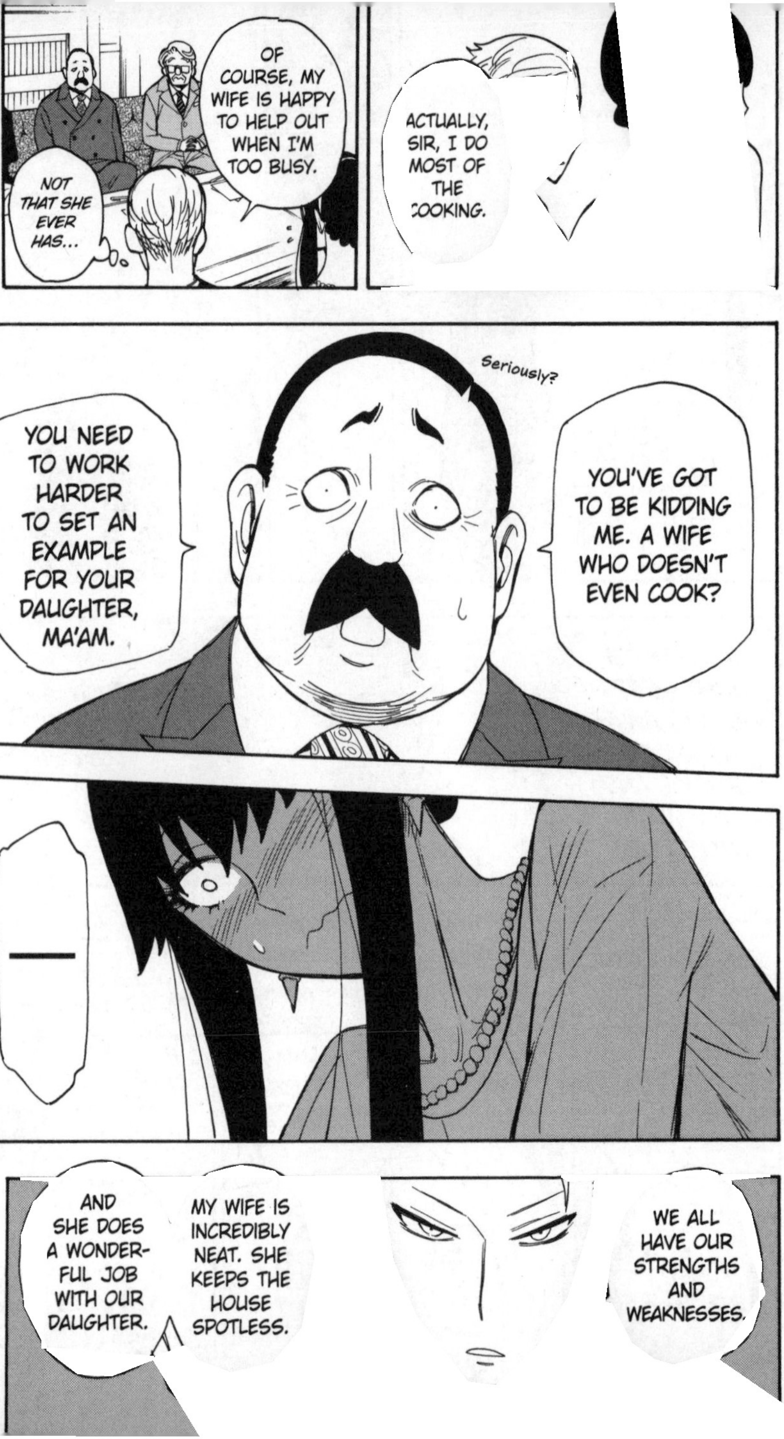
ACTUALLY, SIR, I DO MOST OF THE COOKING.
OF COURSE, MY WIFE IS HAPPY TO HELP OUT WHEN I'M TOO BUSY.
NOT THAT SHE EVER HAS...
Seriously?
YOU'VE GOT TO BE KIDDING ME. A WIFE WHO DOESN'T EVEN COOK?
YOU NEED TO WORK HARDER TO SET AN EXAMPLE FOR YOUR DAUGHTER, MA'AM.
—
WE ALL HAVE OUR STRENGTHS AND WEAKNESSES.
MY WIFE IS INCREDIBLY NEAT. SHE KEEPS THE HOUSE SPOTLESS.
AND SHE DOES A WONDER-FUL JOB WITH OUR DAUGHTER.

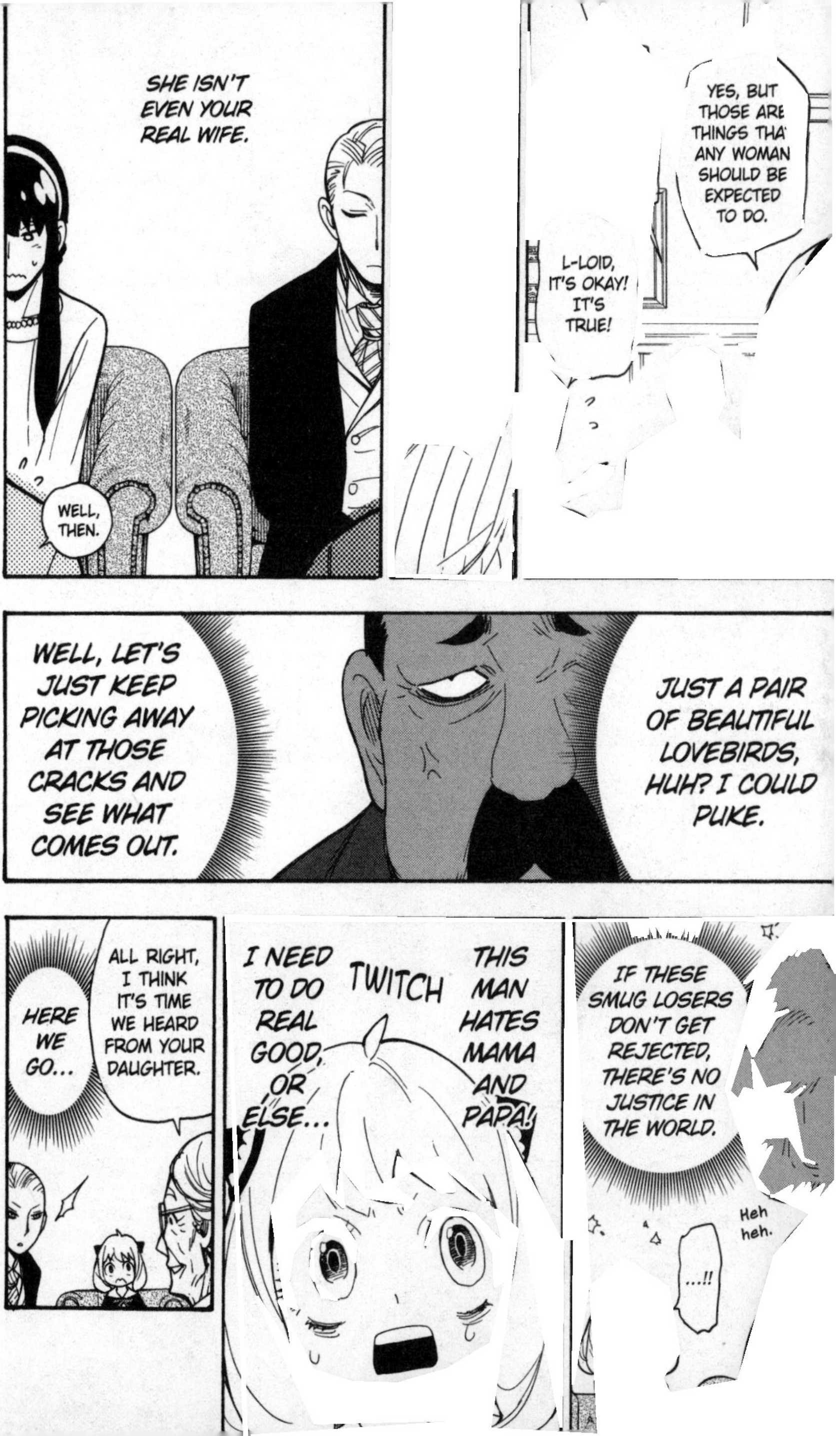
YES, BUT THOSE ARE THINGS THAT ANY WOMAN SHOULD BE EXPECTED TO DO.
L-LOID, IT'S OKAY! IT'S TRUE!
SHE ISN'T EVEN YOUR REAL WIFE.
WELL, THEN.
JUST A PAIR OF BEAUTIFUL LOVEBIRDS, HUH? I COULD PUKE.
WELL, LET'S JUST KEEP PICKING AWAY AT THOSE CRACKS AND SEE WHAT COMES OUT.
IF THESE SMUG LOSERS DON'T GET REJECTED, THERE'S NO JUSTICE IN THE WORLD.
Heh heh.
...!!
THIS MAN HATES MAMA AND PAPA!
TWITCH
I NEED TO DO REAL GOOD, OR ELSE...
ALL RIGHT, I THINK IT'S TIME WE HEARD FROM YOUR DAUGHTER.
HERE WE GO...

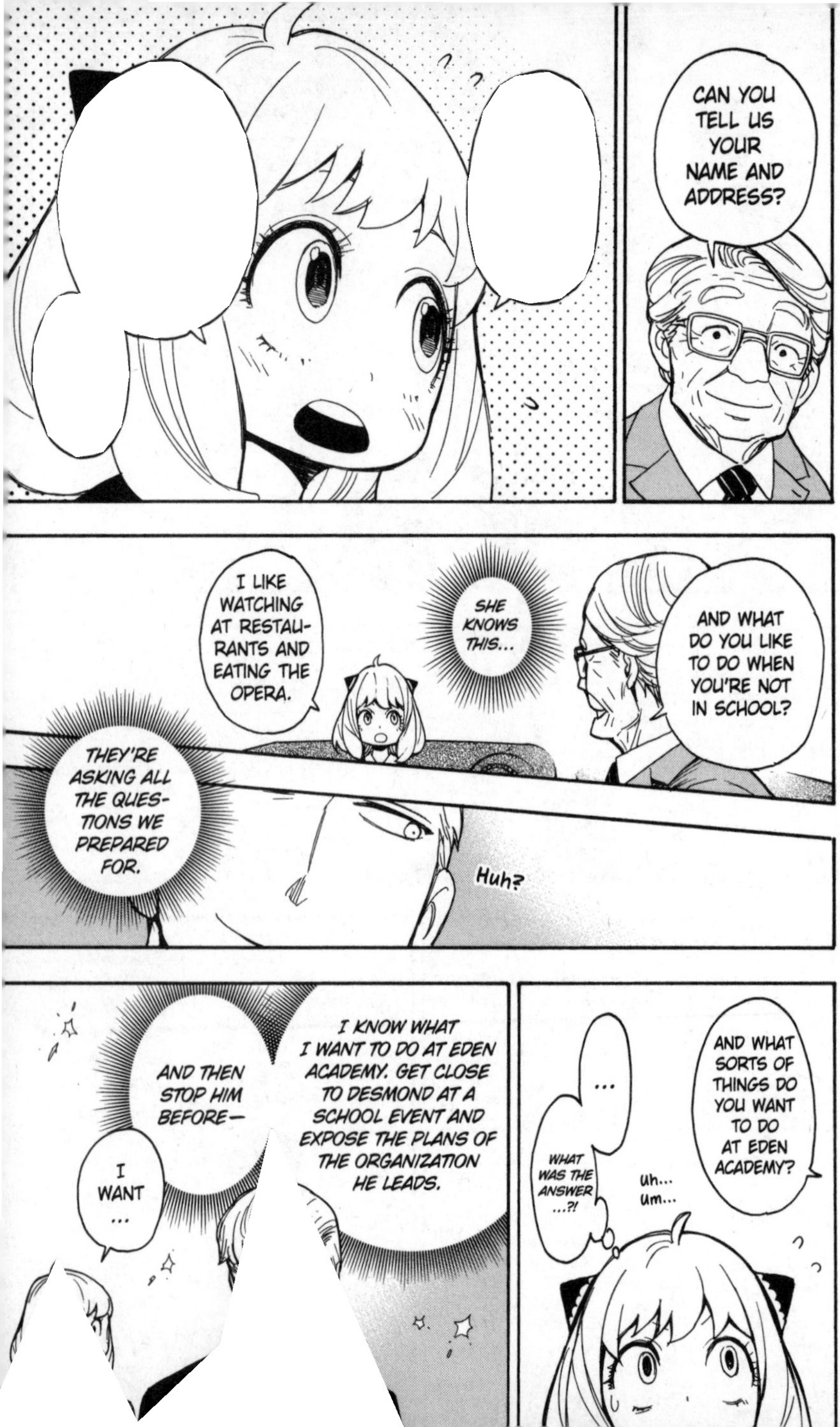
CAN YOU TELL US YOUR NAME AND ADDRESS?
AND WHAT DO YOU LIKE TO DO WHEN YOU'RE NOT IN SCHOOL?
SHE KNOWS THIS...
I LIKE WATCHING AT RESTAURANTS AND EATING THE OPERA.
Huh?
THEY'RE ASKING ALL THE QUESTIONS WE PREPARED FOR.
AND WHAT SORTS OF THINGS DO YOU WANT TO DO AT EDEN ACADEMY?
...
Uh... Um...
WHAT WAS THE ANSWER ...?!
I KNOW WHAT I WANT TO DO AT EDEN ACADEMY. GET CLOSE TO DESMOND AT A SCHOOL EVENT AND EXPOSE THE PLANS OF THE ORGANIZATION HE LEADS.
AND THEN STOP HIM BEFORE—
I WANT ...

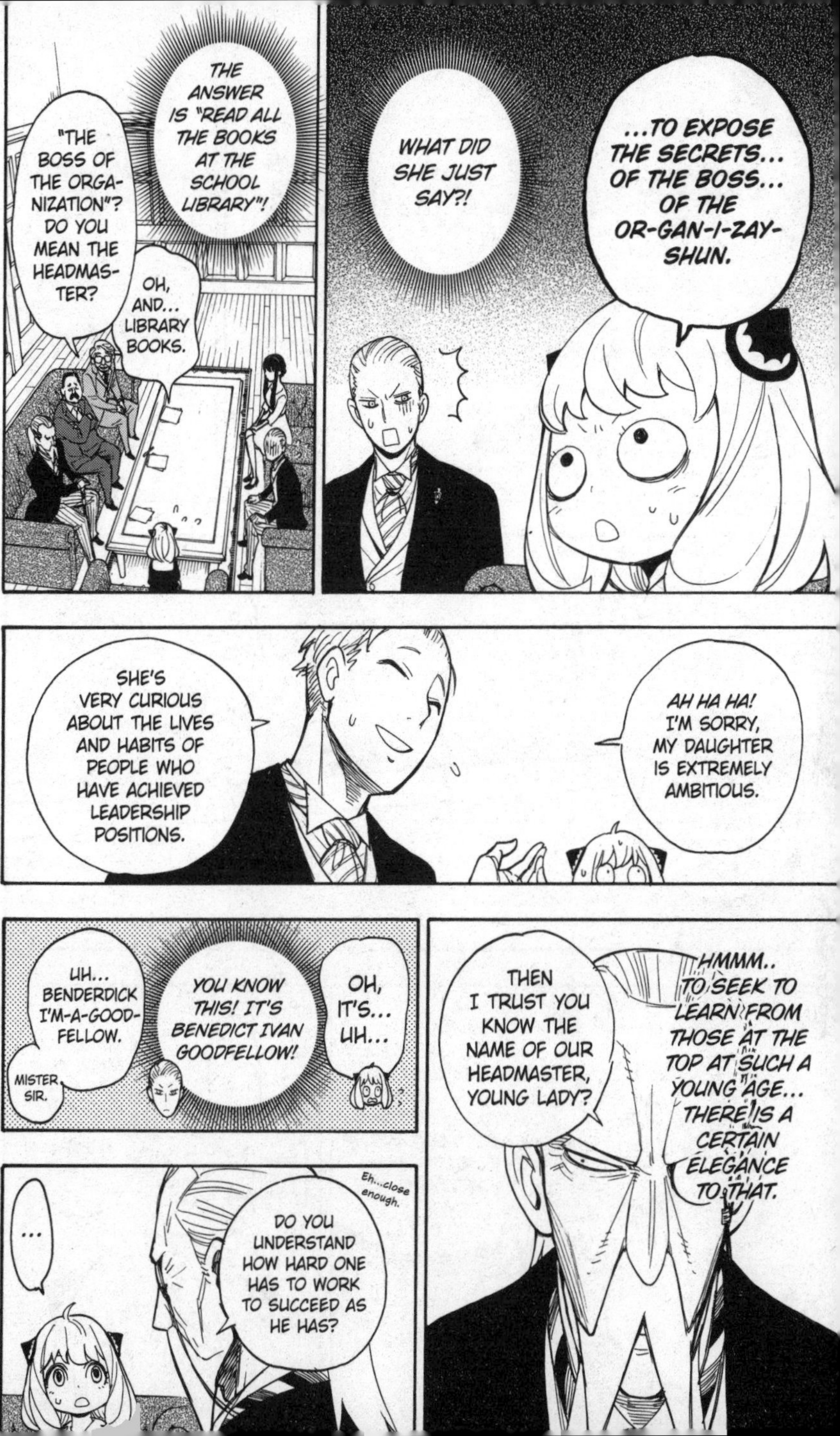
...TO EXPOSE THE SECRETS... OF THE BOSS... OF THE OR-GAN-I-ZAY-SHUN.
WHAT DID SHE JUST SAY?!
THE ANSWER IS "READ ALL THE BOOKS AT THE SCHOOL LIBRARY"!
"THE BOSS OF THE ORGA-NIZATION"? DO YOU MEAN THE HEADMAS-TER?
OH, AND... LIBRARY BOOKS.
AH HA HA! I'M SORRY, MY DAUGHTER IS EXTREMELY AMBITIOUS.
SHE'S VERY CURIOUS ABOUT THE LIVES AND HABITS OF PEOPLE WHO HAVE ACHIEVED LEADERSHIP POSITIONS.
HMMM.. TO SEEK TO LEARN FROM THOSE AT THE TOP AT SUCH A YOUNG AGE... THERE IS A CERTAIN ELEGANCE TO THAT.
THEN I TRUST YOU KNOW THE NAME OF OUR HEADMASTER, YOUNG LADY?
OH, IT'S... UH...
YOU KNOW THIS! IT'S BENEDICT IVAN GOODFELLOW!
UH... BENDERDICK I'M-A-GOOD-FELLOW.
MISTER SIR.
Eh...close enough.
DO YOU UNDERSTAND HOW HARD ONE HAS TO WORK TO SUCCEED AS HE HAS?
...

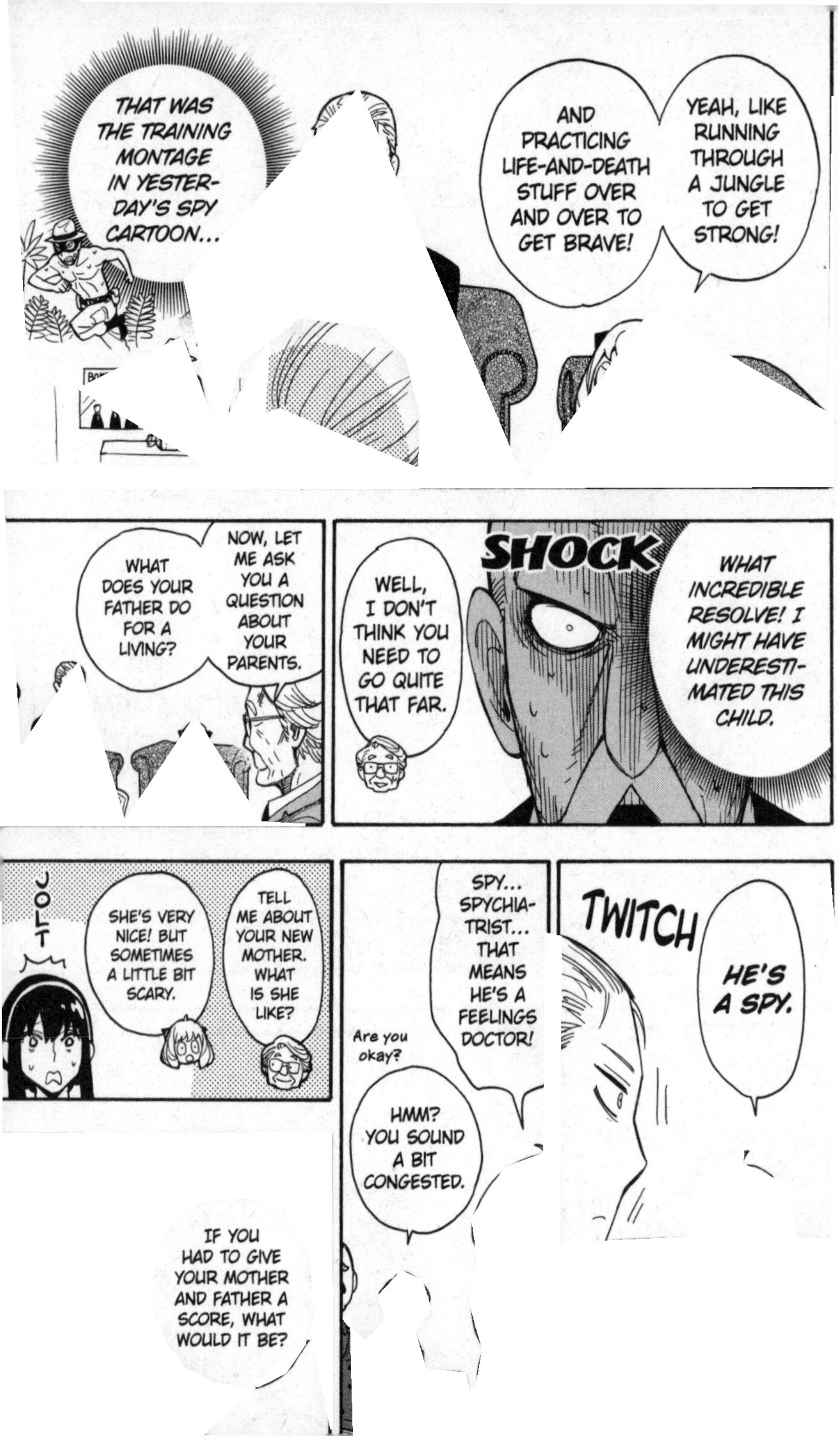
YEAH, LIKE RUNNING THROUGH A JUNGLE TO GET STRONG!
AND PRACTICING LIFE-AND-DEATH STUFF OVER AND OVER TO GET BRAVE!
THAT WAS THE TRAINING MONTAGE IN YESTER-DAY'S SPY CARTOON...
SHOCK
WHAT INCREDIBLE RESOLVE! I MIGHT HAVE UNDERESTI-MATED THIS CHILD.
WELL, I DON'T THINK YOU NEED TO GO QUITE THAT FAR.
NOW, LET ME ASK YOU A QUESTION ABOUT YOUR PARENTS.
WHAT DOES YOUR FATHER DO FOR A LIVING?
TWITCH
HE'S A SPY.
SPY... SPYCHIA-TRIST... THAT MEANS HE'S A FEELINGS DOCTOR!
Are you okay?
HMM? YOU SOUND A BIT CONGESTED.
TELL ME ABOUT YOUR NEW MOTHER. WHAT IS SHE LIKE?
SHE'S VERY NICE! BUT SOMETIMES A LITTLE BIT SCARY.
JOLT
IF YOU HAD TO GIVE YOUR MOTHER AND FATHER A SCORE, WHAT WOULD IT BE?

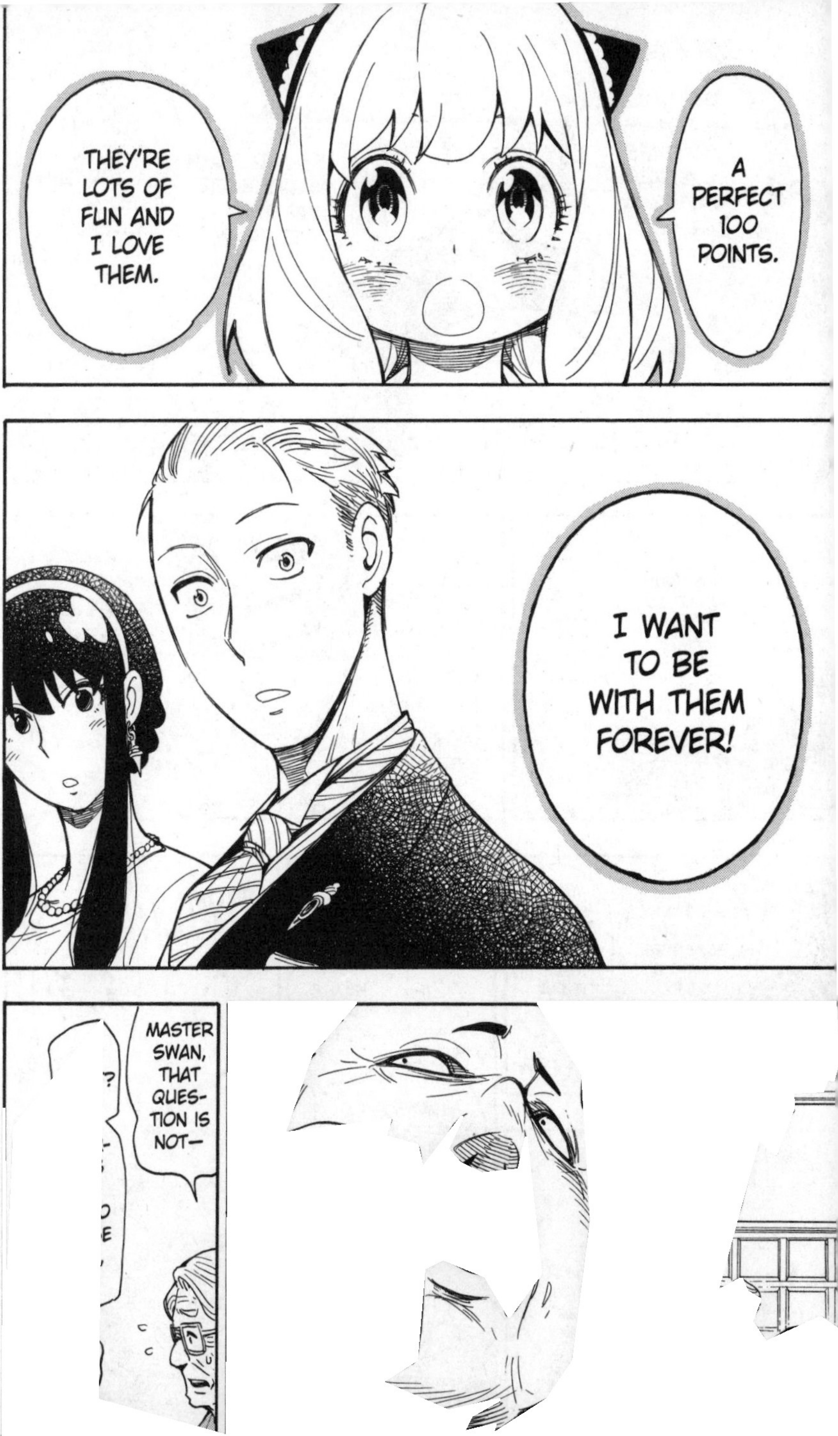
A PERFECT 100 POINTS.
THEY'RE LOTS OF FUN AND I LOVE THEM.
I WANT TO BE WITH THEM FOREVER!
MASTER SWAN, THAT QUES-TION IS NOT—

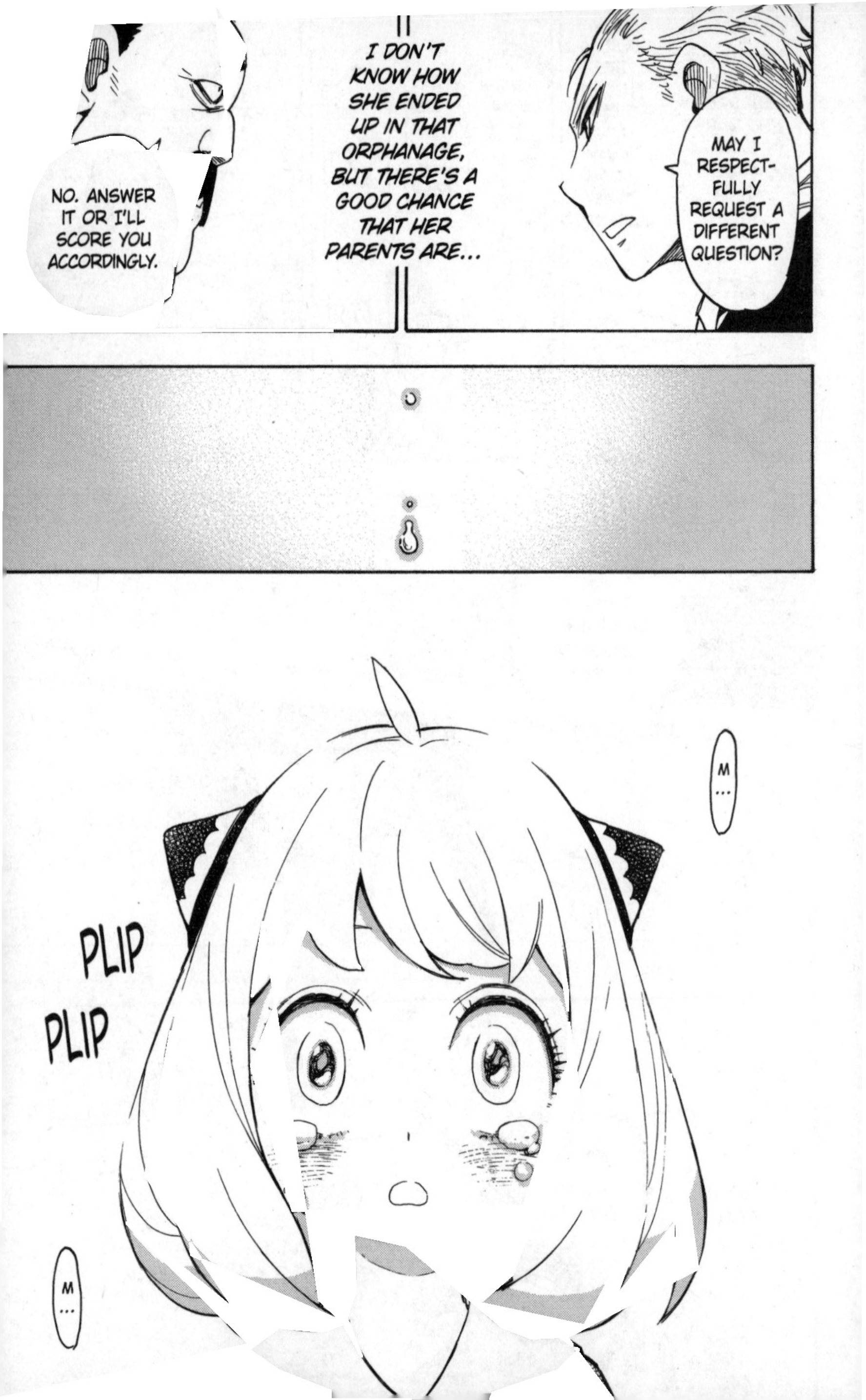
MAY I RESPECT-FULLY REQUEST A DIFFERENT QUESTION?
I DON'T KNOW HOW SHE ENDED UP IN THAT ORPHANAGE, BUT THERE'S A GOOD CHANCE THAT HER PARENTS ARE...
NO. ANSWER IT OR I'LL SCORE YOU ACCORDINGLY.
M...
PLIP PLIP
M...

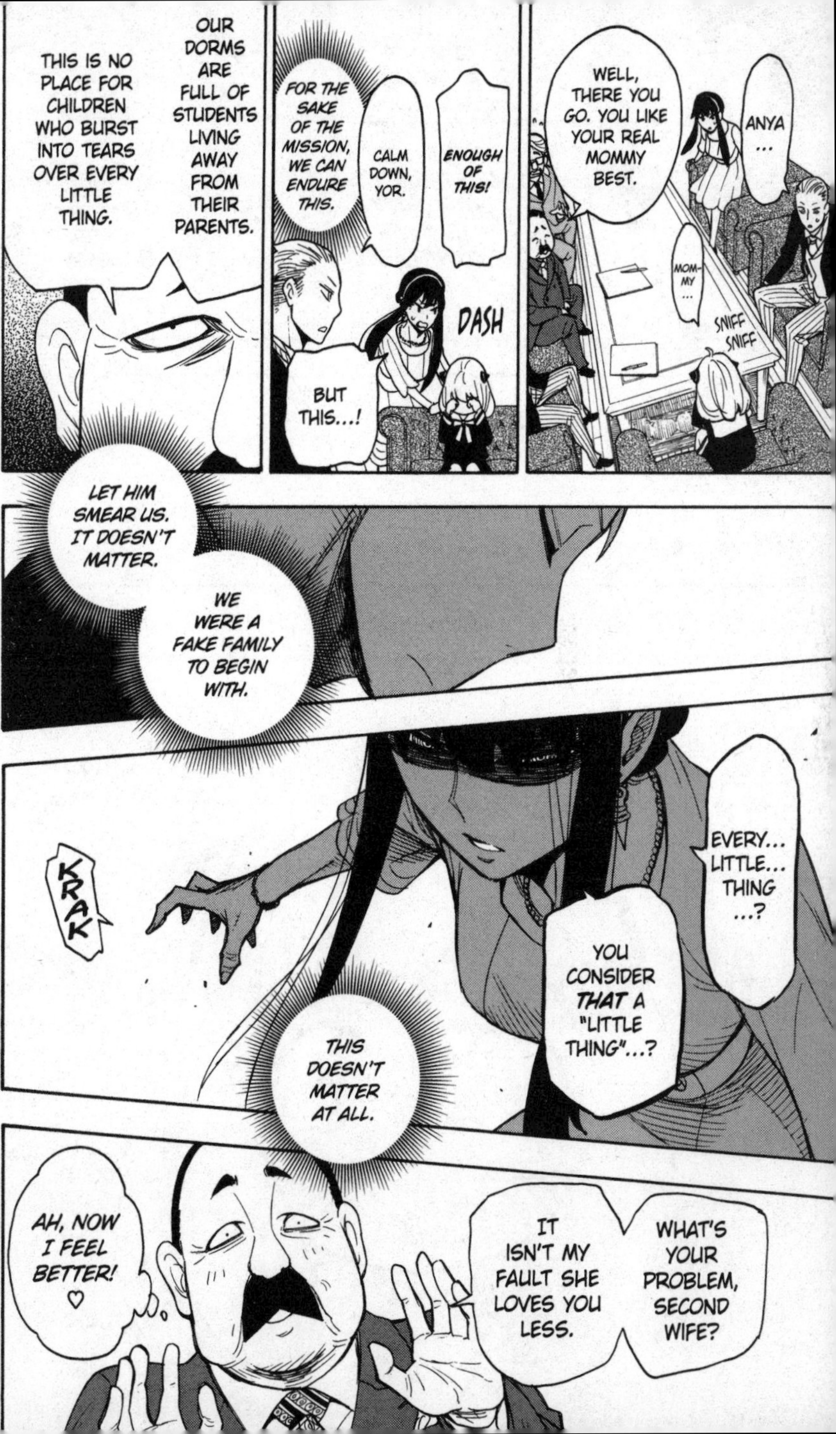
ANYA...
WELL, THERE YOU GO. YOU LIKE YOUR REAL MOMMY BEST.
MOM-MY...
SNIFF SNIFF
ENOUGH OF THIS!
CALM DOWN, YOR.
FOR THE SAKE OF THE MISSION, WE CAN ENDURE THIS.
DASH
BUT THIS...!
OUR DORMS ARE FULL OF STUDENTS LIVING AWAY FROM THEIR PARENTS.
THIS IS NO PLACE FOR CHILDREN WHO BURST INTO TEARS OVER EVERY LITTLE THING.
LET HIM SMEAR US. IT DOESN'T MATTER.
WE WERE A FAKE FAMILY TO BEGIN WITH.
EVERY... LITTLE... THING...?
YOU CONSIDER THAT A "LITTLE THING"...?
KRAK
THIS DOESN'T MATTER AT ALL.
WHAT'S YOUR PROBLEM, SECOND WIFE?
IT ISN'T MY FAULT SHE LOVES YOU LESS.
AH, NOW I FEEL BETTER! ♡

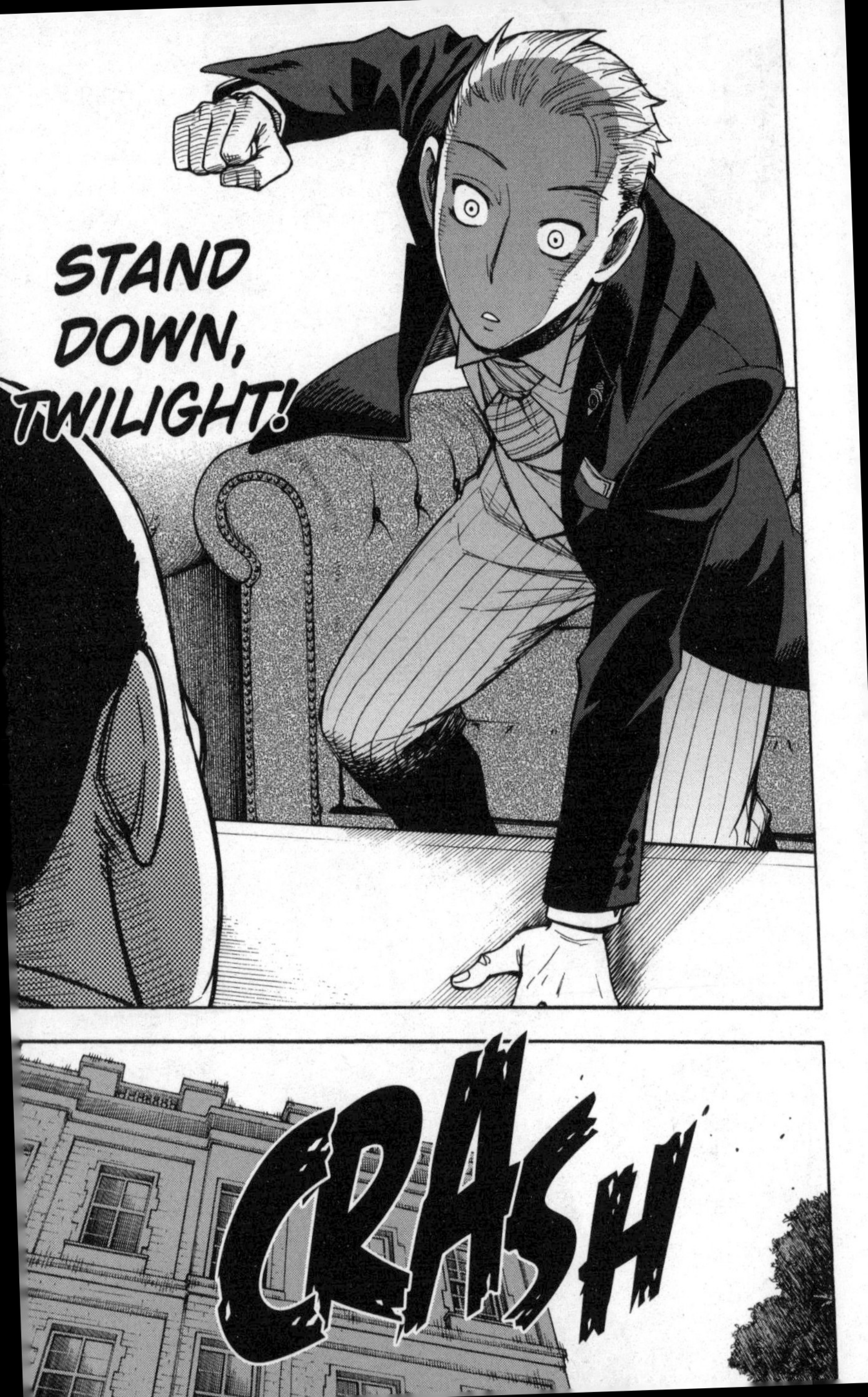
STAND DOWN, TWILIGHT!
CRASH

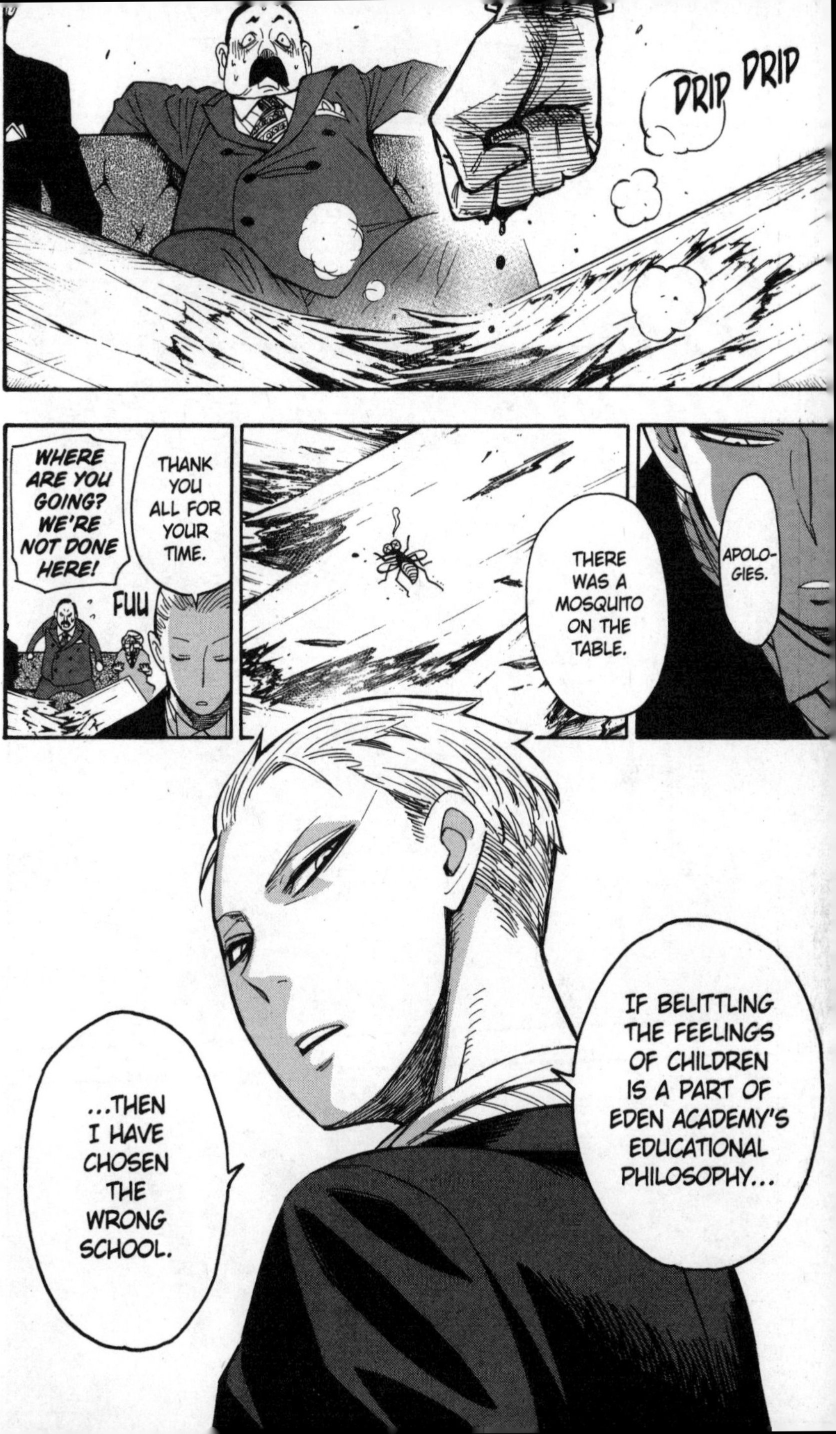
DRIP DRIP
APOLO-GIES.
THERE WAS A MOSQUITO ON THE TABLE.
THANK YOU ALL FOR YOUR TIME.
WHERE ARE YOU GOING? WE'RE NOT DONE HERE!
FUU
IF BELITTLING THE FEELINGS OF CHILDREN IS A PART OF EDEN ACADEMY'S EDUCATIONAL PHILOSOPHY...
...THEN I HAVE CHOSEN THE WRONG SCHOOL.

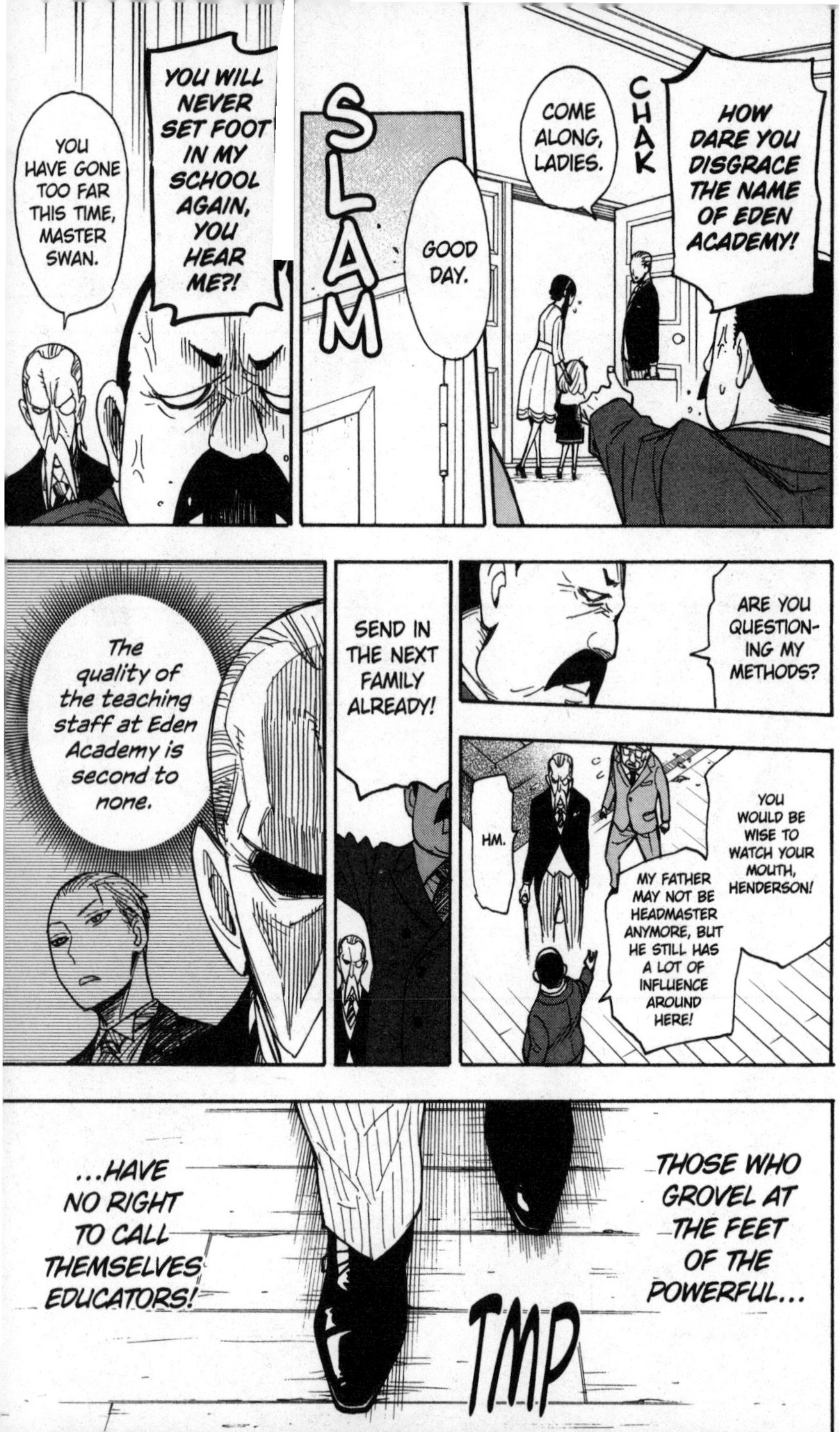
HOW DARE YOU DISGRACE THE NAME OF EDEN ACADEMY!
CHAK
COME ALONG, LADIES.
GOOD DAY.
SLAM
YOU WILL NEVER SET FOOT IN MY SCHOOL AGAIN, YOU HEAR ME?!
YOU HAVE GONE TOO FAR THIS TIME, MASTER SWAN.
ARE YOU QUESTIONING MY METHODS?
YOU WOULD BE WISE TO WATCH YOUR MOUTH, HENDERSON!
MY FATHER MAY NOT BE HEADMASTER ANYMORE, BUT HE STILL HAS A LOT OF INFLUENCE AROUND HERE!
HM.
SEND IN THE NEXT FAMILY ALREADY!
The quality of the teaching staff at Eden Academy is second to none.
THOSE WHO GROVEL AT THE FEET OF THE POWERFUL...
TMP
...HAVE NO RIGHT TO CALL THEMSELVES EDUCATORS!

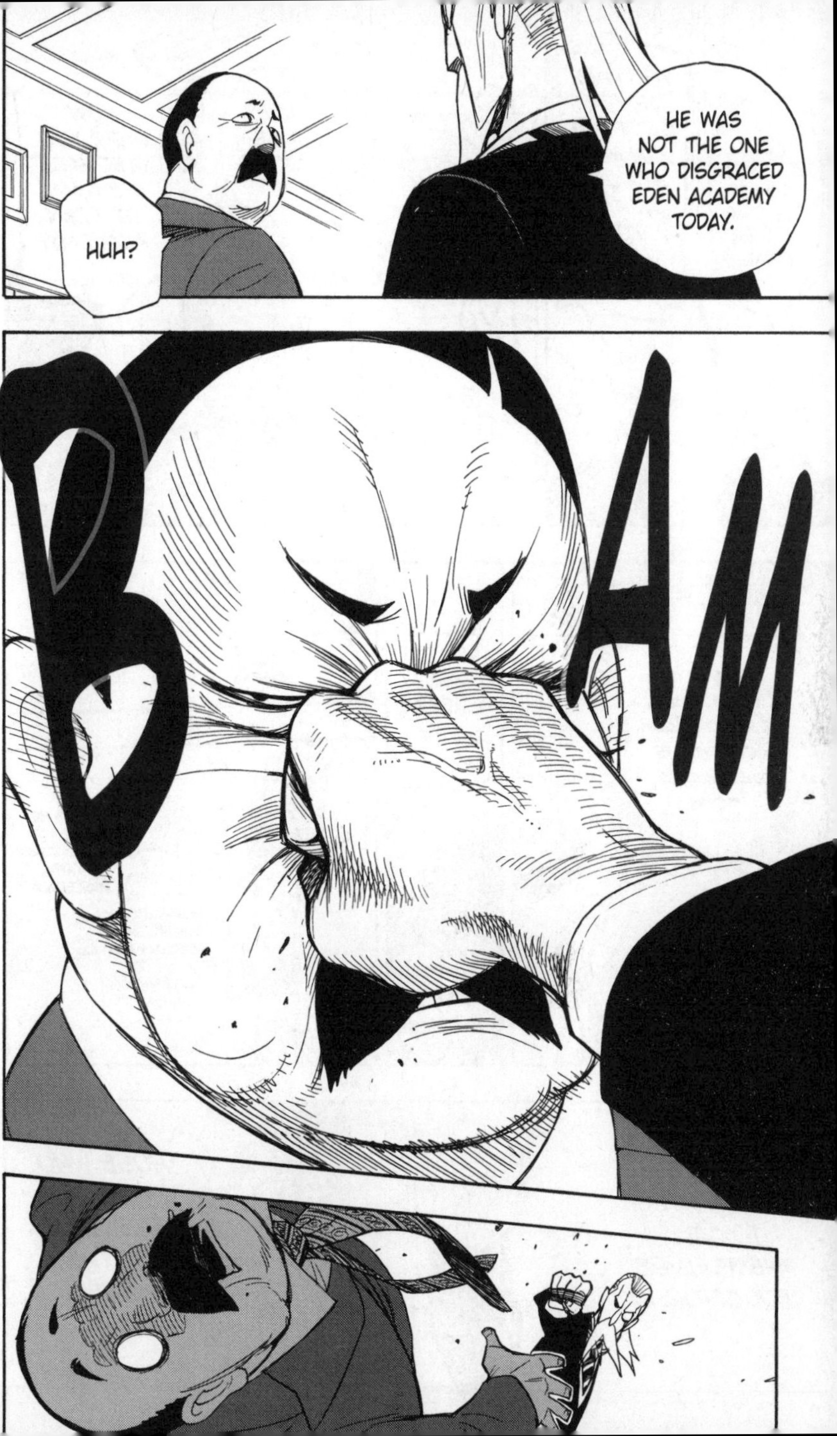
HE WAS NOT THE ONE WHO DISGRACED EDEN ACADEMY TODAY.
HUH?
BAM

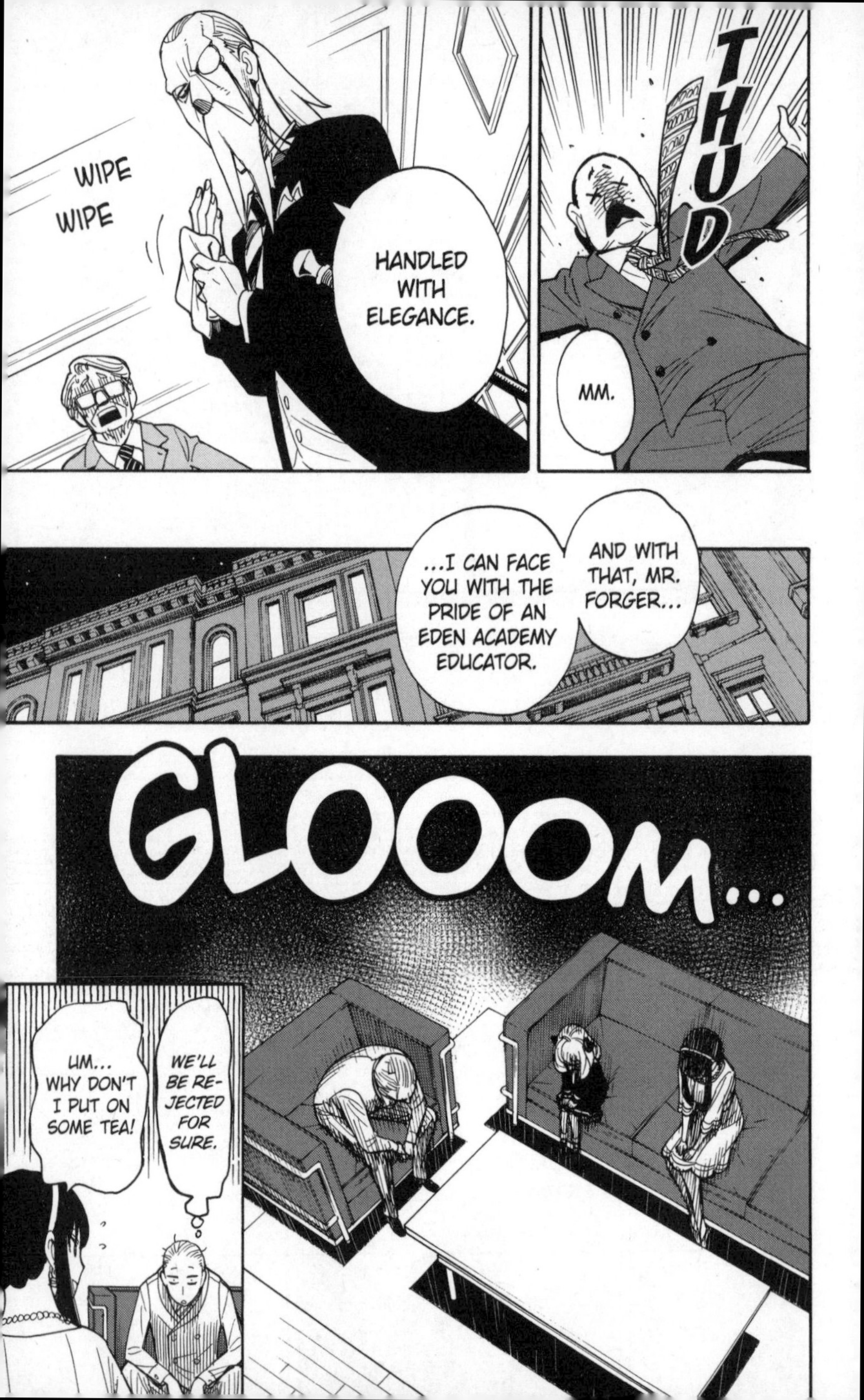
THUD
MM.
HANDLED WITH ELEGANCE.
WIPE WIPE
AND WITH THAT, MR. FORGER...
...I CAN FACE YOU WITH THE PRIDE OF AN EDEN ACADEMY EDUCATOR.
GLOOOM...
WE'LL BE RE-JECTED FOR SURE.
UM... WHY DON'T I PUT ON SOME TEA!

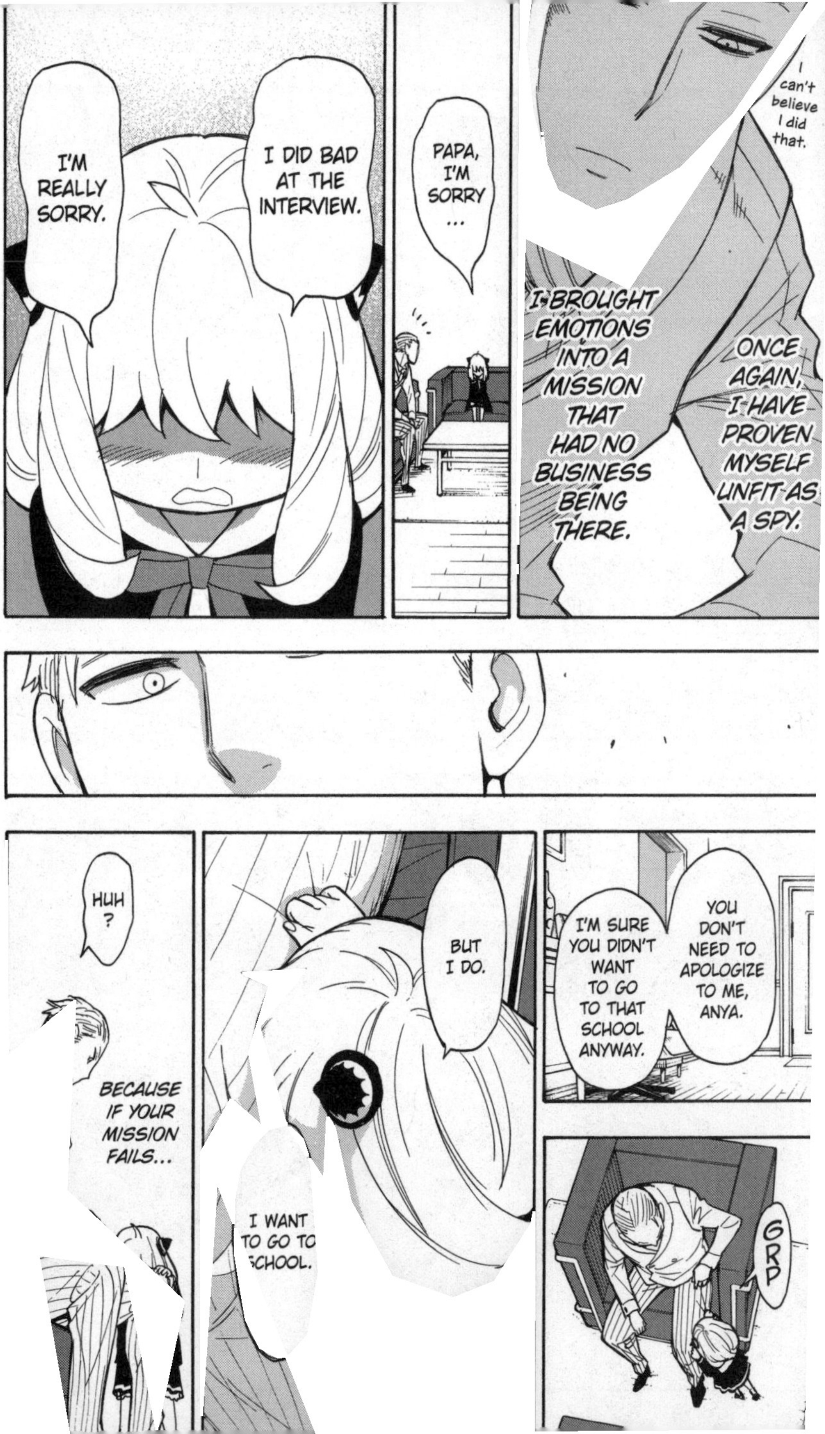
I can't believe I did that.
ONCE AGAIN, I HAVE PROVEN MYSELF UNFIT AS A SPY.
I BROUGHT EMOTIONS INTO A MISSION THAT HAD NO BUSINESS BEING THERE.
PAPA, I'M SORRY...
I DID BAD AT THE INTERVIEW.
I'M REALLY SORRY.
YOU DON'T NEED TO APOLOGIZE TO ME, ANYA.
I'M SURE YOU DIDN'T WANT TO GO TO THAT SCHOOL ANYWAY.
GRP
BUT I DO.
I WANT TO GO TO SCHOOL.
HUH?
BECAUSE IF YOUR MISSION FAILS...

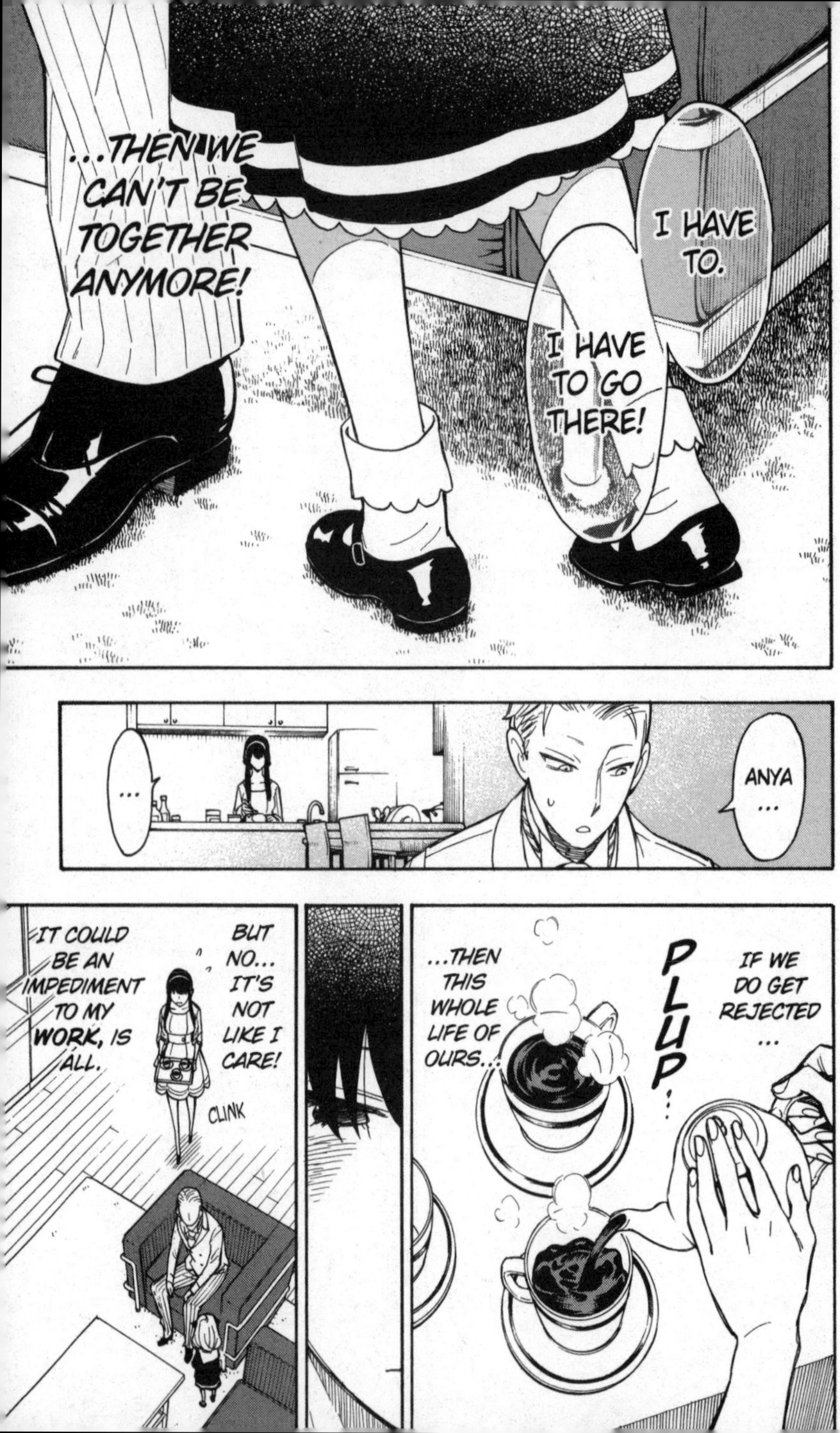
I HAVE TO.
I HAVE TO GO THERE!
...THEN WE CAN'T BE TOGETHER ANYMORE!
ANYA ...
...
IF WE DO GET REJECTED ...
PLUP...
...THEN THIS WHOLE LIFE OF OURS...
BUT NO... IT'S NOT LIKE I CARE!
IT COULD BE AN IMPEDIMENT TO MY WORK, IS ALL.
CLINK

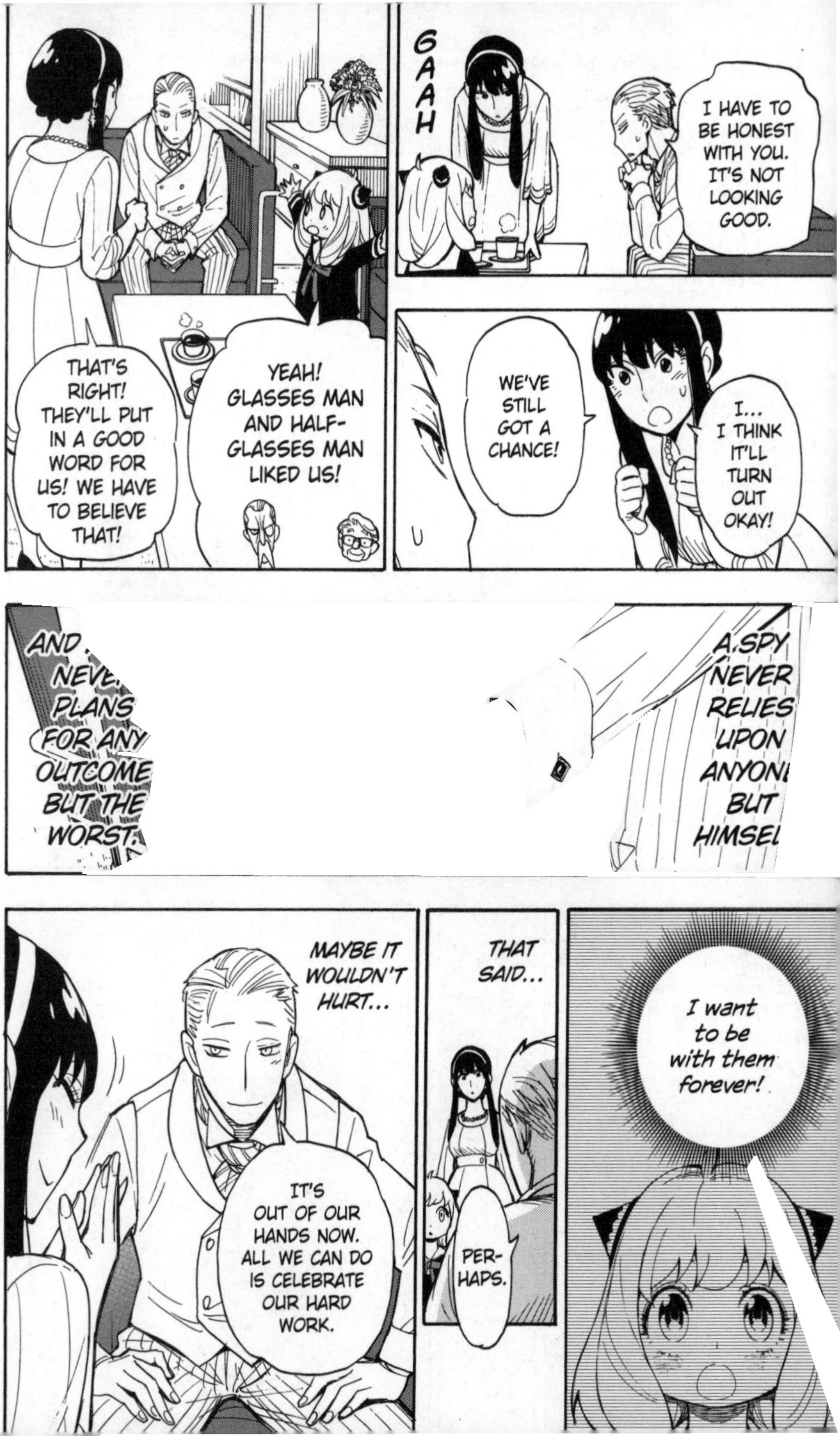
I HAVE TO BE HONEST WITH YOU. IT'S NOT LOOKING GOOD.
GAAH
I... I THINK IT'LL TURN OUT OKAY!
WE'VE STILL GOT A CHANCE!
YEAH! GLASSES MAN AND HALF-GLASSES MAN LIKED US!
THAT'S RIGHT! THEY'LL PUT IN A GOOD WORD FOR US! WE HAVE TO BELIEVE THAT!
A SPY NEVER RELIES UPON ANYON BUT HIMSEL
AND NEVE PLANS FOR ANY OUTCOME BUT THE WORST.
I want to be with them forever!
THAT SAID...
PERHAPS.
MAYBE IT WOULDN'T HURT...
IT'S OUT OF OUR HANDS NOW. ALL WE CAN DO IS CELEBRATE OUR HARD WORK.

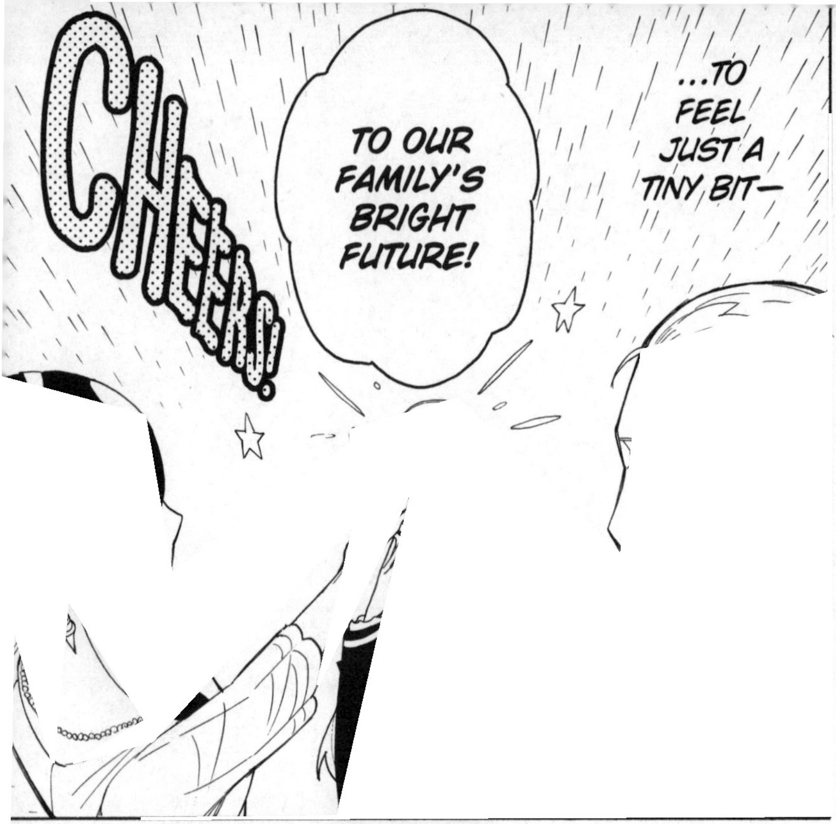
...TO FEEL JUST A TINY BIT—
TO OUR FAMILY'S BRIGHT FUTURE!
CHEERS!

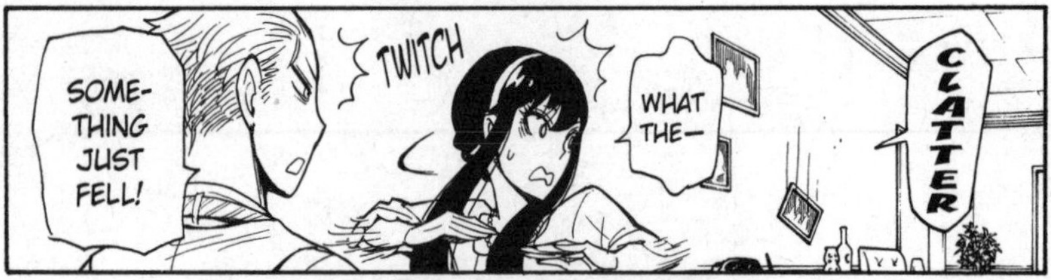
CLATTER
WHAT THE—
TWITCH
SOME-THING JUST FELL!

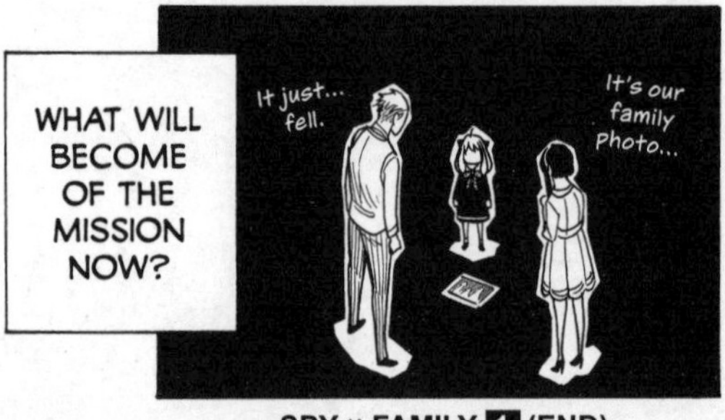
It's our family Photo...
It just... fell.
WHAT WILL BECOME OF THE MISSION NOW?

SPY × FAMILY 1 (END)

SPY×FAMILY

SPYxFAMILY CONFIDENTIAL FILES (BONUS)

TOP SECRET
EYES ONLY

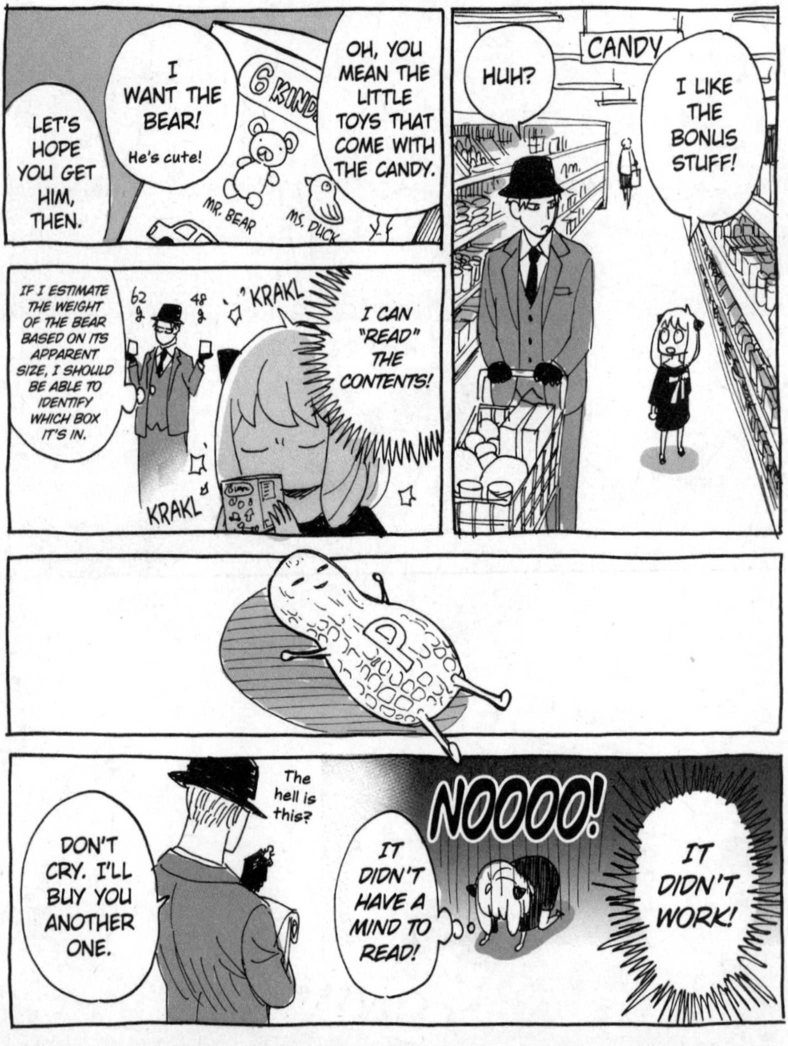
CANDY
I LIKE THE BONUS STUFF!
HUH?
OH, YOU MEAN THE LITTLE TOYS THAT COME WITH THE CANDY.
6 KIND
MR. BEAR
MS. DUCK
I WANT THE BEAR!
He's cute!
LET'S HOPE YOU GET HIM, THEN.
I CAN "READ" THE CONTENTS!
KRAKL
62 g
48 g
IF I ESTIMATE THE WEIGHT OF THE BEAR BASED ON ITS APPARENT SIZE, I SHOULD BE ABLE TO IDENTIFY WHICH BOX IT'S IN.
KRAKL
IT DIDN'T WORK!
NOOOO!
IT DIDN'T HAVE A MIND TO READ!
The hell is this?
DON'T CRY. I'LL BUY YOU ANOTHER ONE.

FRANKY'S SECRET FILES

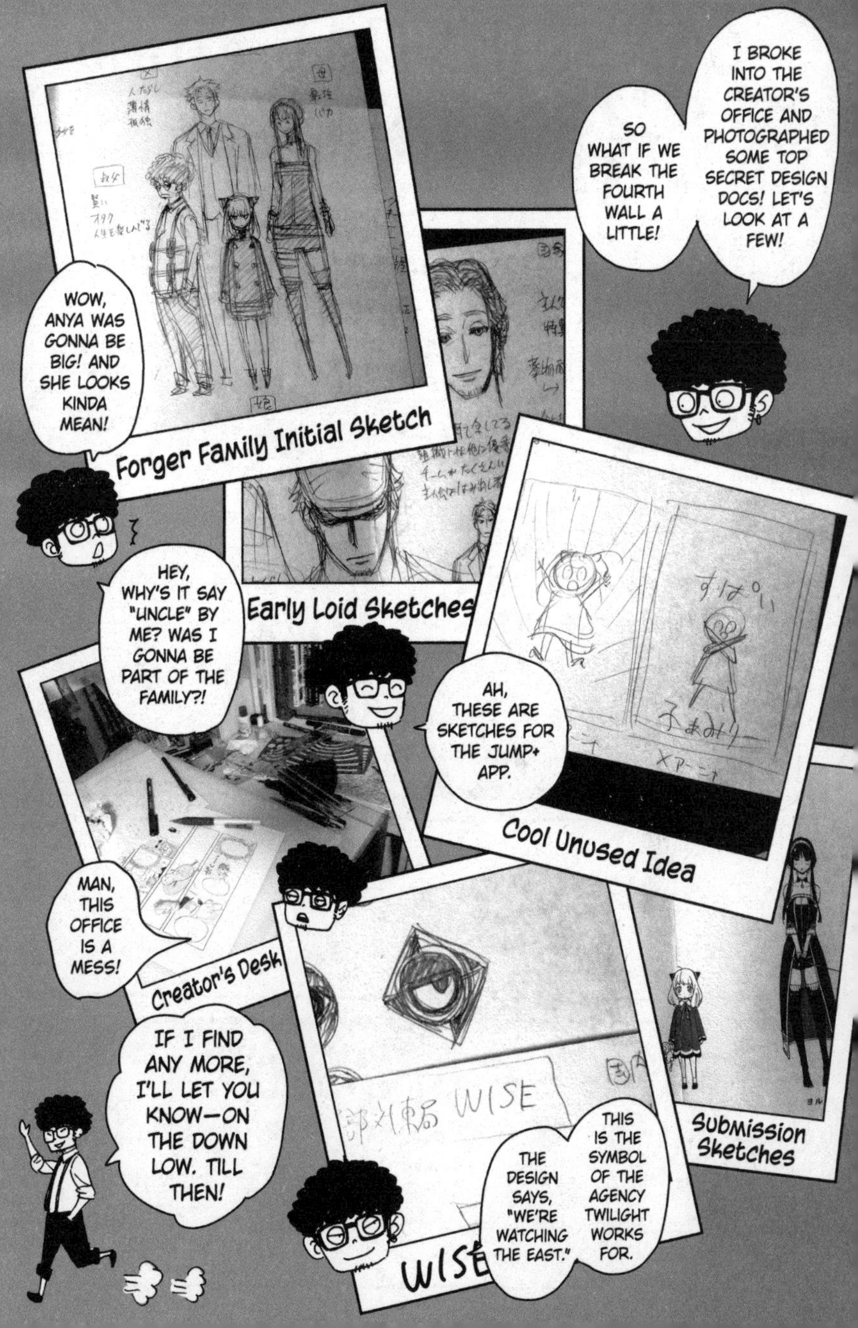
I BROKE INTO THE CREATOR'S OFFICE AND PHOTOGRAPHED SOME TOP SECRET DESIGN DOCS! LET'S LOOK AT A FEW!
SO WHAT IF WE BREAK THE FOURTH WALL A LITTLE!
Forger Family Initial Sketch
WOW, ANYA WAS GONNA BE BIG! AND SHE LOOKS KINDA MEAN!
Early Loid Sketches
HEY, WHY'S IT SAY "UNCLE" BY ME? WAS I GONNA BE PART OF THE FAMILY?!
Cool Unused Idea
AH, THESE ARE SKETCHES FOR THE JUMP+ APP.
Creator's Desk
MAN, THIS OFFICE IS A MESS!
Submission Sketches
WISE
THIS IS THE SYMBOL OF THE AGENCY TWILIGHT WORKS FOR.
THE DESIGN SAYS, "WE'RE WATCHING THE EAST."
WISE
IF I FIND ANY MORE, I'LL LET YOU KNOW—ON THE DOWN LOW. TILL THEN!

SPYxFAMILY VOL.1
SPECIAL THANKS LIST

·CLASSIFIED·

ART ASSISTANCE	
MAEHATA	YUICHI OZAKI
MAFUYU KONISHI	AMASHIMA
MASAHITO SASAKI	KEISUKE HOSHINOYA
KAZUKI NONAKA	YASUKO EMI
HIKARI SUEHIRO	NAO EMOTO

GRAPHIC NOVEL DESIGN
HIDEAKI SHIMADA

GRAPHIC NOVEL EDITOR
KANAKO YANAGIDA

MANAGING EDITOR
SHIHEI LIN

THANK YOU SO MUCH FOR BUYING VOLUME 1 OF *SPY X FAMILY*.
I HOPE TO SEE YOU AGAIN IN VOLUME 2!

—TATSUYA ENDO

EYES ONLY   READ & ~~DESTROY~~   EYES ONLY

TWILIGHT'S PROFILE: REVEALED!

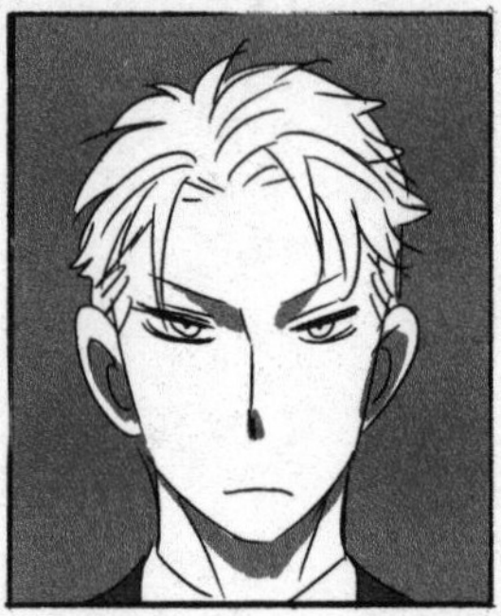

Name: [redacted]

Agent Name: Twilight

Known Aliases: Loid, Robert

Age: [redacted]

Sex: M

Blood Type: [redacted]

Height: 187 cm   Weight: 70–90 kg

Hair: Blond   Eyes: Blue   Underpants: Black

Birth Date: [redacted]   Birthplace: [redacted]

Father: [redacted]   Mother: [redacted]

Address: 128 Park Ave, West Berlint

Occupation: Intelligence Agent

Work Experience: [redacted]

Military Career: [redacted]

Education: [redacted]

Specialty: Disguise

Hobby: Nothing

Wanted For [redacted]

Remarks

[redacted]

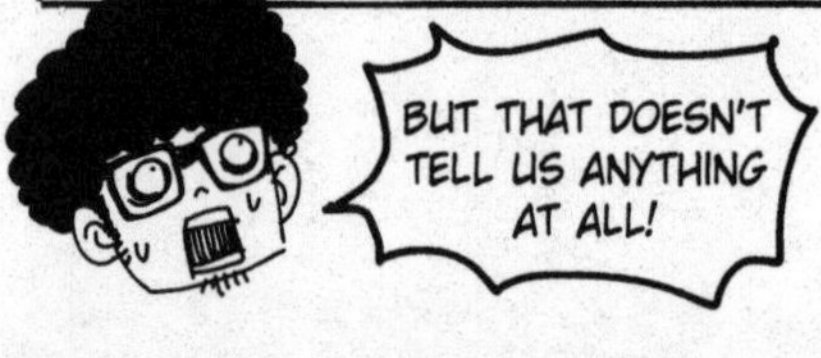
BUT THAT DOESN'T TELL US ANYTHING AT ALL!

I'm a big fan of movies and anime where the characters are hiding who they really are. I love the tension of "Will they be discovered?" and the anguish of them wanting to reveal their secrets and not being able to.

There isn't any of that in this manga, but I hope you'll enjoy it anyway.

—TATSUYA ENDO

Tatsuya Endo was born in Ibaraki Prefecture, Japan, on July 23, 1980. He debuted as a manga artist with the one-shot "Seibu Yugi" (Western Game), which ran in the Spring 2000 issue of *Akamaru Jump*. He is the author of *TISTA* and *Gekka Bijin* (Moon Flower Beauty). *Spy x Family* is his first work published in English.